Evald Ilyenkov's
Philosophy Revisited

Edited by Vesa Oittinen

KIKIMORA PUBLICATIONS

Series B : 13 Helsinki 2000

Evald Ilyenkov's Philosophy Revisited

ISBN 951-45-9263-8
ISSN 1455-4828

Aleksanteri-instituutti
Graphic design: Vesa Tuukkanen

Gummerus Kirjapaino Oy
Saarijärvi 2000

Contents Содержание Inhalt

Contributors

David Bakhurst, Professor
Department of Philosophy, Queen's University
Kingston, Ontario, CANADA

Andrew Chitty, Dr.
University of Sussex
UNITED KINGDOM

Jan Derry, Dr.
School of Education, University of Birmingham
UNITED KINGDOM

Janette Friedrich, Dr.
Faculté de Psychologie, Université de Genève
SWITZERLAND

Judith Gregory, Dr.
Department of Informatics, Systamarbeid
University of Oslo, NORWAY

Wladislaw Hedeler, Dr.
Berlin, GERMANY

Pertti Honkanen, MA, journalist
Helsinki, FINLAND

Jantzen, Wolfgang, Professor
Osterholz-Scharmbeck, GERMANY

Peter E. Jones, Dr.
Communication Studies, Sheffield Hallam University
UNITED KINGDOM

Tarja Knuuttila, Dr.
Institute of Activity Theory and Developmental Work Research
University of Helsinki, FINLAND

Reijo Miettinen, Professor
Institute of Activity Theory and Developmental Work Research
University of Helsinki, FINLAND

Feliks T. Mikhailov, Academician, Professor
Institute of Philosophy, Russian Academy of Science
Moscow, RUSSIA

Ilkka Niiniluoto, Professor, Vice Rector
Institute of Philosophy
University of Helsinki, FINLAND

Aleksei G. Novokhatko, Dr.
Ilyenkov Archive
Moscow, RUSSIA

Vesa Oittinen, Docent, Dr.
Institute of Philosophy,
University of Helsinki, FINLAND/
Institute of Historical Studies
University of Umeå, SWEDEN

Jussi Silvonen, Dr.
Finnish Institute of Occupational Health
Helsinki, FINLAND

Matti Vartiainen, Docent, Dr.
Institute of Psychology
University of Helsinki, FINLAND

Nikolai Veresov, Dr.
University of Oulu
Kajaani Educational Research Unit, FINLAND

Evert van der Zweerde, Dr.
Department of Philosophy
University of Nijmegen, THE NETHERLANDS

OPENING WORDS

ILKKA NIINILUOTO

On behalf of the Department of Philosophy, University of Helsinki, it is a great honour for me to open the Symposium on Evald Ilyenkov. The Symposium is a joint project of the Department of Philosophy (Faculty of Arts), the Center for Activity Theory and Developmental Work Research (Faculty of Education), and the Alexander Institute. It is thus a multidisciplinary enterprise in a positive sense. The main effort in planing and organizing the Symposium has been made by Dr. Vesa Oittinen to whom we are all most grateful.

Evald Ilyenkov was born in Smolensk in 1924. He started his studies at the Institute of History, Philosophy and Literature in the University of Moscow. After the World War he continued his studies and defended in 1953 his candidate thesis on the questions of dialectical logic in Marx's economic works. From 1953 to his untimely death in 1979 he worked at the Institute of Philosophy in the Academy of Science of the Soviet Union.

Ilyenkov's study of the dialectics of abstract and concrete in Marx's *Capital* appeared in 1960. Combining his interest in the history of philosophy with contemporary debates, he published in 1968 his doctoral dissertation on "the question of the nature of thought".

Ilyenkov's book on Dialectical Logic appeared in Russian in 1974, and as an English translation in 1977. In this work, he tried to combine the Marxist-Leninist theory of knowledge with methodological questions about special scientific disciplines. In his posthumous work, he discussed Lenin's conception of materialist dialectics.

Ilyenkov's works had a profound impact on Soviet philosophy and his studies influenced also a generation of Western Marxism. Today Ilyenkov would be 75 years old. His voluntary death already for twenty years ago prevented him from seeing the decline of Soviet Union, followed in the Western Marxism by the flight back to historical studies in Hegel and eventually to disappointed postmodernism. I will not make any guess at the judgment that Ilyenkov might have given about the present state of the world. But during this conference we shall hear several assessments of the significance of his work and its continuing relevance. I am very impressed by the programme which includes papers both by Ilyenkov's close friends, his followers in the study of human actions, and his admirers in contemporary theories of language, semiotics, and aesthetics.

Coming myself from the Anglo-Saxon tradition of analytic philosophy, I should like to make a personal remark. In the late 1970s I read an English translation of Ilyenkov's article *The Concept of the Ideal,* which I found strikingly similar to Karl Popper's conception of the World 3 of human social constructions. In 1981 I read a Finnish translation of Ilyenkov's essay on the genesis of human personality through concrete action and interaction with the material and social environments. Both articles defend very interesting views which are materialistic in an enlightened way but at the same time critical of vulgar interpretations of materialism. Ilyenkov's views on the development of human personality continued the great tradition of cognitive psychology in the Soviet Union. One can understand that his independent views gave emphasis and a voice to ideas that were not very fashionable in the Soviet philosophy in the 1970s but make him a most interesting object of study among contemporary philosophers and psychologists.

More generally, when the new Millennium is starting, it will be worthwhile and rewarding to assess and re-evaluate the achievements of philosophers and psychologists who worked in the tradition of Marxist dialectics both in the Soviet Union and other countries. It is no doubt that their publications contain parts that strike us as dogmatic errors. But just like in the study of medieval philosophy, we are now able to distinguish the genuine philosophical ideas from the particular theologically or politically correct form 'n which they were dressed in the historical context. The symposium on Evald Ilyenkov is an example of such efforts of reconsidering the history of contemporary philosophy.

INTRODUCTION:
PARADOXES OF ILYENKOV
AND THE SOVIET PHILOSOPHY

VESA OITTINEN

The Helsinki symposium on 7th–8th of September 1999 was held just 20 years after the death of Evald Vasilyevitch Ilyenkov (1924–1979), demonstrating that the legacy of this perhaps most original of the Soviet philosophers is still relevant. However, it is noteworthy that in many contributions to this symposium Ilyenkov's relation to Marxism was altogether ignored. Even where his work was seen in continuity with the tradition of Marx's thought, the focus was on the most unorthodox aspects of Marxist philosophy, despite the fact that Ilyenkov regarded himself not only as a Marxist, but as a Marxist-Leninist who was writing such texts as *The Leninist Dialectics and Metaphysics of Positivism* (1980, English edition 1982) from a very "orthodox" perspective. There are, in fact, many paradoxes, not only in the way Ilyenkov's philosophy was and is received, but in that philosophy itself. As an introduction to this symposium volume, I would like to address some "neuralgic points" of Ilyenkov's thought and Soviet philosophy in general.

Paradoxes and Unexpected Connections

In his foreword to a collection of Ilyenkov's texts on aesthetics that was
published posthumously in 1984, his older friend and mentor Mikhail Lifshits wrote as follows in an often cited passage:

> I read his early manuscript on the dialectics of Marx's *Capital* and realized that the
> war years and the post-war occurrences had not altogether wiped out the best of the
> heritage of the previous decades. By some miracle the seeds that were then sown on
> a favourable ground began to grow – although in a different, not immediately recog-
> nizable form. Evald Ilyenkov, with his living interest in Hegel and the young Marx
> (who was discovered in the 20s and 30s here at home, not abroad, as is often claimed
> due to lack of information or other causes), with his deep understanding of the
> dialectics in the *Capital* of Marx and in the *Philosophical Notebooks* of Lenin, stood
> out as an heir of our thoughts [...] When I read the works of Evald Ilyenkov today, I
> see his delicate and at the same time restless nature in every line he wrote. I see his
> passionate striving to make explicit that the earthly, non-religious revival of life was
> approaching (Lifshits 1984, 6–7).

Lifshits' reference to the "heritage of the previous decades" remains somewhat cryptic and is open to interpretations. It may refer to the "Dialectician" current of early Soviet Marxism embodied in the Deborin school which
was repressed by the emerging Stalinism in the beginning of the 1930s. This
approach would define Ilyenkov as an advocate of the Deborinist cause. James Scanlan has, indeed, tried to fix the originality of Ilyenkov's philosophy
with the help of such classifications as "neo-Deborinism" and "neo-Hege-
lianism" (cf. Scanlan 1985, 120–121). In some respect this corresponds rather well to Ilyenkov's undoubtedly "Hegelian" and humanistic opposition
to the technocratic tendencies of the Khrushchev era and would in this manner take into account at least some features of the dispute between the Debo-
rinites and the Machists in the 20s.[1] But there are other possible interpretations, too. One which, it seems to me, has hitherto largely escaped the attention of the historians of Soviet philosophy,[2] would be in linking Ilyenkov's
thought with the version of Marxism proposed by Georg Lukács – not the
early, messianic Lukács of *History and Class Consciousness,* but the already
established philosopher who lived during the 1930s and the war years in
Soviet exile, where he wrote *The Young Hegel* and then, in at an advanced
age in Budapest, the *Ontology.* In fact, as early as in 1956, while still only a
student, Ilyenkov, who knew German, was planning to translate Lukács's
Young Hegel into Russian. In this connection he addressed some terminological questions in a letter to the author, who had by then already returned to
Hungary. Lukács answered, saying that owing to the geographical distance

between them it would be better to address his old friend Lifshits in Moscow. Although Lifshits lived in the same town as Ilyenkov, the young philosophy student had never before heard of him (cf. Vanslov 1997, 94). The first contact led to a friendship between Ilyenkov and Lifshits, which ended only with Ilyenkov's tragic death in 1979.

Although I do not believe that the direct influence of Lukács on Ilyenkov was decisive for the development of his thought, there are undoubtedly some parallel strands in their philosophical views. Space does not allow me go make a thorough comparison here, however it is obvious that both share the same concept of the ideal (the ideality). According to this view, the ideal is not a purely mental entity, but does exist outside individual minds in social activity and in social institutions. This interpretation of the ideal resembles Hegel's concept of "spirit" (and especially of "objective spirit"),[3] in that the ideal is not seen – as the Kantians do – as something merely subjective and that – on the contrary – the ideal is always imbued with a socially mediated materiality which gives ideas an objectivity of their own.

Thus, arguing that logical categories are in reality not purely logical, Lukács cites Marx's famous introduction to the *Grundrisse,* where Marx writes that the categories (for Lukács, all categories, although it seems that Marx himself is here speaking of categories of political economy only) must be understood as "forms of presence and determinations of existence" (*Daseinsformen und Existenzbestimmungen*) of society and mankind (cf. for example Lukács 1951, 133 or Lukács 1972, 25). Consequently the categories are, according to Lukács, not merely subjective forms, not only gnoseological categories, but have an ontological basis or, more precisely: they exist outside the individual subjects in society and in social forms of human activity.

The formulation that categories are forms of human existence and society recurs in many texts of the mature Lukács, and in his *Ontology* it forms the unquestioned point of departure for the construction of his system. It is strange, however, that Lukács repeatedly cites Marx incorrectly. In the *Grundrisse,* where the formulation occurs, Marx says that economic categories are expressions of forms and determinations of the existence of the society and the subjects.[4] So then, Marx does not say – contrary to what Lukács would have us know – that the categories *are* forms of existence of society, but only that they *express* those forms. The difference is quite essential. It reveals that Lukács is in fact "Hegelianizing" Marx even when reading the *Grundrisse,* which, however, is already the most Hegelian work of the mature Marx himself on economics.

Fundamentally, Ilyenkov says the same thing when he writes in his *Dialectical Logic* that "the materialistic concept of thought" developed by

Marx and Engels will significantly alter the interpretation of the nature of the logical categories:

> The forms of thinking, the categories, were not understood as mere abstractions from sensibility conceived of in an unhistorical way, but primarily as conscious reflection of the general forms of the sensible-objective activity of social man. The real, material *[predmetnyi]* equivalent of the logical forms was not seen only in the abstract and general contours of the object the individual is intuiting, but in the forms of actual human activity, changing the forms of nature in accordance to his ends (Ilyenkov 1984a, 185).

This point of view, which both Lukács and Ilyenkov share, I would call a "social ontology" (the German equivalent would be a *Gesellschaftsontologie*), and I would define it as a philosophical position in Marxism according to which the categories and ideas have a kind of existence of their own in intra-individual social relations and in culture.

No matter how very Marxist this viewpoint may appear at a first glance – after all, did not Marx always stress the dependance of ideas on the material basis of the society? – it leads to grave problems for the materialistic ambitions of the very same Marxist philosophy. If the ideas have an existence in society outside the mind, this seems to imply that they are not only subjective, but at the same time in some way objective and self-sufficient entities which "exist" in society in a like manner as the Platonic ideas in their "heavenly place". Moreover, this seems to cause the differences between subjective and objective, ideal and material, to disappear. The unexpected result of these philosophical circumlocutions appears to be that both Lukács and Ilyenkov are actually preaching a kind of "philosophy of identity" not altogether unlike the systems of the German idealists Schelling and Hegel.

I would stress the paradoxical nature of the consequences. The tree of Soviet philosophy, fertilized with the wisdom of Lenin, Marx and a long line of pre-Marxist materialists, seems to bear fruits which come as surprise for everyone. The allegedly orthodox Leninist Marxism of Ilyenkov not only turns out to be something altogether different – one is actually justified in wondering whether it is materialism at all. Soviet supporters of Ilyenkov's views have usually avoided considering all the consequences this paradox. Instead they have tried to play down the baffling results. So, for example, V. A. Lektorski has recently described how Ilyenkov's views were received:

> [T]he author of the original conception of the ideal was immediately held accountable for all mortal sins: guilty of objective idealism (how else! Evald Vasilyevitch thinks that the ideal may exist outside the individual consciousness!), of deviating from the truths of Marxism-Leninism, etc. The naive psychologism which was prevailing in the philosophy of those times was unable to digest the unusual ideas of this thinker (Lektorski 1999, 10).

I think, however, that it would be sad if we whisked away the difficulties of Ilyenkov's concept of the ideal by merely branding all his critics as dogmatists who were unable to digest new insights. That would mean resorting to an *ad hominem* argument, which has never been very convincing. In fact, the question of the "social existence" of ideas is certainly not a trivial philosophical problem which, as such, is wholly independent of the possible motives of Ilyenkov's adversaries.

Immediately after the above cited words Lektorski continues, saying that Ilyenkov in fact was only following "a renowned philosophical tradition": both Sir Karl Popper and the late Wittgenstein had defended the opinion that "the content of the ideas" should not be sought in the individual consciousness (ibid., 10).[5] But if this is the case – and Ilyenkov's concept of the idea is, indeed like not only Hegel's, but equally Popper's well-known theory of the "third world" (the world between subjective and objective worlds, where, in his view, ideas reside) – then we must add on Ilyenkov's account yet a new paradox – for Popper is the arch-enemy of Hegel and of all such Hegelian stuff which Ilyenkov and the Ilyenkovians would regard as sacred.

Ambiguities in Soviet Philosophy

The non-trivial ambiguities in Ilyenkov's work lead naturally to the question whether there might be, besides the "open" tension between philosophy and ideology, some hidden and deeply rooted conflicts in the Soviet tradition itself, of which Ilyenkov's paradoxes are but the most manifest expression. Indeed, it seems that at the very root of the philosophical programme of Soviet Marxism there is an unsolved conflict which can best be studied in the oeuvre of its founding father, Lenin.

Many researchers have already pointed out that Lenin's theoretical heritage is not as coherent the official Soviet ideology tried to depict it. It is rather obvious that there are many points of divergence between Lenin's *Materialism and Empirio-Criticism,* written in 1909 against the Machist subjective idealist current which at this time was widespread among the Bolshevik intellectuals, on the one hand, and the *Philosophical Notebooks,* which is essentially a conspect of Hegel's Logic with Lenin's own commentaries which Lenin wrote down in the library of the canton of Bern (Switzerland) in 1914–1915, on the other. Some think that when writing the former work, Lenin still shared the traditional philosophical viewpoint of the Marxism of the Second International, and consequently was a materialist in the manner of Kautsky and Plekhanov and an adherent of the "theory of reflection" (i.e. the view that our knowledge is but a reflection, a mirroring of the external world), whereas five years later he had transformed into a Hegelian dialectical thinker and abandoned the vulgar theory of reflection.

Recently this interpretation has been emphatically advanced by Kevin Anderson, who has claimed in *Lenin, Hegel and Western Marxism,* that in 1914, sitting at the Bern canton library desk and studying Hegel, Lenin had "already in his notes on the introduction to the *Science of Logic* [...] begun to break with the simplistic categories of idealism versus materialism that had been the philosophical foundation of the Marxism of the Second International" (Anderson 1995, 34). And a little later, citing a passage from the *Philosophical Notebooks,* whereLenin discusses "the idea of the transformation of the ideal into the real", Anderson concludes: "In a certain sense, this is the turning point of the entire Hegel Notebooks, the point where Lenin begins to identify himself fairly openly with Hegel's idealism" (ibid.,40).

In such a extreme form, Anderson's thesis of the "two Lenins", the crude materialist and the refined dialectician, is rather problematic. To begin with, one should not forget that the *Philosophical Notebooks* were, after all, only notes meant for personal use and not for publication. It is, in fact, often difficult to decide whether, in a certain *Notebook* passage, Lenin is expounding his own thoughts or merely paraphrasing Hegel. This circumstance alone calls for a cautious approach.

But on the other side, there is an unmistakable shift in Lenin's philosophical interests between 1909 and 1914–1915. In *Materialism and Empirio-Criticism* Lenin sets out to defend the materialism as it was understood by the "orthodox" theoreticians of the Second International such as Kautsky and Plekhanov. Here Lenin's target was the subjectivistic and "activist" philosophy of the Machists, which was embraced by such important figures of the Bolshevik intelligentsia as Alexander Bogdanov, and which was already about to be regarded as the proper philosophy of the Bolshevik left. In 1914, the situation was changed. In Lenin's analysis, it had now become clear that a new epoch had begun – "the epoch of imperialism and proletarian revolutions". Consequently, Lenin broke with the Second International, which according to him was entangled in a deterministic view of history and man and was unable to seize the opportunities of the new era. While the Second International Marxists thought that the future socialist society would come with a necessity like that which was working in the processes of the natural history, the quest for Lenin was now to find an expression for the active role of the subjective factor in history. (That this was a demand at that time in leftist circles worldwide can be seen from the fact that Antonio Gramsci began to develop in Mussolini's prisons his own interpretation of Marxism as the philosophy of praxis, relying here not accidentally on Italian Hegelian tradition, notably on the "activist" philosophy of Giovanni Gentile.)

In short, Lenin's *Philosophical Notebooks* can be seen as an attempt to find an adequate formulation for a Marxist philosophy that would avoid the deterministic and objectivistic world-view of the Second International. But not only the Scylla of objectivism had to be shunned, the Charybdis of subjectivism lurked here on the other side, as Lenin's experience from the polemics against Bogdanov and the Empiriocriticists had shown. I think that precisely this situation explained Lenin's initial interest in the dialectics of Hegel. Far from suddenly turning into a full-blooded Hegelian, Lenin merely tried to find in Hegel conceptual tools to master the problem of the new epoch: to ground the role of the subjective factor in the development of the society and history of humanity in general.

How well did Lenin succeed in reformulating Marxist philosophy? It seems to me that his work was but half-done. Lenin never definitively left the positions he had defended in 1909 in *Materialism and Empirio-Criticism,* stressing always that the "lecture of Hegel" demanded by a renewed Marxist philosophy would be a materialistic interpretation. However, the history of the Soviet philosophy demonstrates clearly that the nature of this "materialistic turning upside-down" of Hegel remained controversial to the last days of the USSR. The remaining impression is, thus, that of ambivalence, and I think that David Bakhurst has in a pertinent manner described the content of the philosophical testament of Lenin:

> I want to suggest that Lenin's position is ambiguous […] The first, "conservative" option is to try to reinstate the external world with the terms of subject–object dualism. The conservative realist insists that "behind" or "beyond" our ideas exists a material world that provides the content on which our minds go to work […] The second possible response to Empiriocriticism […] proposes that we reject outright the "two-worlds epistemology" in which the debate has so far been posed. On this "radical" realism, there are not two worlds that must somehow be shown to be connected by the ingenuity of the philosophers, but one: The subject is located in objective reality […] The radical holds that we need to overcome the idea that the contents of our mind somehow come between us and reality […] If the conservative response is in the spirit of eighteenth-century, or "classical", empiricism, the radical expresses an antagonism to subject–object-dualism reminiscent of Hegel (Bakhurst 1991, 114–116).

Thus, the *fundamentum inconcussum* of Soviet philosophy was much more labile than generally assumed. The philosophical heritage of Lenin was not only open to interpretations in the usual way the works of the thinkers of the past are, but in itself deeply ambiguous. Indeed, one of the sympathetic traits of the now extinguished Soviet philosophy was that it at least made efforts to

overcome the dualism of the "two cultures" (as C. P. Snow once formulated
the problem), that is, the splitting of the modern culture into scientific-technical
and humanistic spheres, by striving towards a higher synthesis not altogether
unlike that of Hegel a century earlier. But the synthesis did not come about:
instead, in subsequent discussions of the Soviet philosophers, both the
"Machists" and"Dialecticians" of the 20s as well as the "scientists" and
"Hegelians" of the 60s could with equal right make claims on Lenin as the
guarantee of their ideas. For the case of Ilyenkov this means, as Bakhurst
puts it:

> While the germ of radical realism [i.e. "Hegelianism" – V.O.] in Lenin's philosophy
> exercised a formative influence on Ilyenkov's philosophical concerns, Lenin also
> inspired the very school of scientific empiricism that Ilyenkov came to see as his
> principal opponent (Bakhurst 1991, 123).

Ilyenkov and Soviet Culture

We could interpret the unsolved ambiguity of Soviet philosophy as proof of
the fact that splitting and segmenting into autonomous areas of culture is an
essential characteristic of every modern society. Hence, it would be but a
utopian endeavour to try to create a higher synthesis or a "unifying" philosophy. If we look at Soviet philosophy as a mirror and quintessence of Soviet
culture (or, more accurately, as the Soviet project of modernity), then it is
obvious that the paradoxes of Ilyenkov's philosophy are not mere idiosync-
rasies of its author. Ilyenkov's situation in the field of the Soviet society and
culture in general was also paradoxical, and by his life and work he ultimately expressed the goals and flaws of the Leninist experiment of constructing
an alternative form of modernity.

Ilyenkov was not a dissident. He suffered of course from ideological
mobbing, but in the Soviet Union this was rather inevitable for everybody
who happened to be a creative person. It has been said that especially the
harassing by some "cyberneticians" in the Institute of Philosophy of USSR
Academy of Sciences, accompanied by subsequent publication bans so
depressed Ilyenkov in his last years that he was driven to suicide (for details
and further references, see Richter 1994, 9–10). It should be noted, however,
that Ilyenkov was not completely marginalized in Soviet philosophical culture:
he had some influential friends, for example L. K. Naumenko, who saw to
that the Party publishing house Politizdat printed his books in large editions
(for example the second, posthumous 1984 impression of *Dialekticheskaia
logika* was 40,000 copies). And with good reason, for despite many adversities

Ilyenkov took the pronounced goals of the Party seriously: to build a socialist society of civilized and culturally educated citizens.

The philosophy Ilyenkov proposed was thus not an end in itself, but rather a tool for promoting the coming of the New Man, or as the promoter of the philosopher Lev Naumenko put it, for "preparation of people for the greatest of all historical achievements – the creation of communism" (Naumenko 1982, vi). He criticized indefatigably the technocratic tendencies in Soviet society and all those who saw the building of socialism only as an "engineer's task", without deeper humanistic or cultural aspirations. Indeed, it is no wonder that Ilyenkov's most fierce adversaries were people with a "scientific" world outlook, people who in the Soviet Union naturally presented themselves as Marxists but in reality were nearer to a Skinnerian behaviorism or positivism. Felix Mikhailov, even he a close friend of Ilyenkov, has pinpointed the deeper socio-cultural meaning of this dispute between the "Scientists" and the "Hegelians":

> How wonderful were the passionate works that appeared after the war, devoted to excavating from the mummified texts of Marx ideas from the culture of European rationalism. The Hegelian logic they found in Marx – the logic of the self-development of the organic system of human social being – was sharply opposed to the ruling ideology, which had subordinated itself to the empirical logic of scientific discourse. One need only remember the administration's devotion at this time to Pavlov. In that context, all one could discuss were the conditional and unconditional reflexes which supposedly underlay and determined all functions of the organism, including those of the so-called "second signal system" (speech, language). These empty Pavlovian ideas formed the basis of vulgar, mechanistic theories of personhood, consciousness and cognition, which were ideal for representing human beings as malleable, wholly subordinate to social influences that ultimately could be controlled by the state (Mikhailov 1995, 78).

From this, it should be clear that the viewpoint Ilyenkov expounded was far from that of a solitary thinker only. He belonged to the generation of the 60s, or, more precisely, to the so-called *shestidesiatniki,* whose ideals and goals took form in the "thaw" period of Khrushchev's reign, which began after the 20th Congress of the Soviet Communist Party in 1956.[6] The *shestidesiatnik* intellectuals still believed that it would be possible to reform the socialist system, and consequently the disappointment was great when it became clear that the development of the Soviet society in Brezhnev's times did not progress towards a more humane and cultural socialism, but instead regressed towards stagnation and ultimately entered a cul-de-sac.

Maybe one could say that Ilyenkov was not only the man who gave the philosophical formulation to the feelings of the Soviet *shestidesiatniki,* but who resembled a certain type of critical intellectual in the so-called "real socialism" of the 60s and 70s in general. As a further example I would mention the GDR philosopher and aesthetician Lothar Kühne, who to my mind belongs to the same category of intellectuals than the "Ilyenkovians": not dissidents, they aimed at a reform of the everyday socialism by reviving the critical potential of Marxism which had petrified in clichés in the hands of Party ideologists. The "real socialism" was for them acceptable only insofar as it could be seen as a preparatory stage for a the more developed communism. Even Kühne criticized the realities of the German Democratic Republic not from a liberal or anti-communist point of view, but seen from the perspective of a future communist society which was set by the system itself as its more or less obligatory goal.

In a very "Ilyenkovian" manner he saw, in contrast to the economism of the planning bureaucrats, the "fundamental trait of the communist notion of wealth" in the human personality, in dependency here on certain relevant passages from Marx's *Grundrisse*. With good reason, the German sociologist Michael Brie calls Kühne's position that of an "orthodoxically thinking heretic".

The tragedy of this position – which Ilyenkov, as far as I can see, shares – lies in the fact that despite critical opposition one remains true to the system and is thus imprisoned in an illusion (cf. Brie 1993, 40, 42-43, 48). Kühne committed suicide in the 70s, and so did Ilyenkov. It would be interesting to speculate how their views might have developed if they had experienced perestroika and then the crash of the system of the "real socialism". In every case it seems certain that the excesses of post-socialist liberalization would not have been to their taste.

Be this as it may, Ilyenkov was convinced that philosophy would have an eminent formative role in the culture; especially dialectics was seen him as the "hypostasis of culture". Dialectics, as Vadim Mezhuev sums up, was for him "the logical form, the way of existence of Man in the culture, as contrasted to the formal way of existence connected with the understanding only (formal-rational as Weber would say) in the contemporary capitalist civilization. He who thinks dialectically, lives according to the laws of culture, has a developed and free individuality, in short, is a personality" (Mezhuev 1997, 52).[7] This is surely true, but then we must say that at least in his conviction that philosophy can change the world better Ilyenkov is eminently un-Hegelian. For Hegel, philosophy plays not an active constructive role in the history, but, as the famous bon mot about the Owl of Minerva makes clear, only comments *post festum* what happened.

On the Present Volume

I am sure that the present volume on Ilyenkov's philosophy and his influence will hardly remain the only one of its kind, even in near future. Although each of the about 20 contributions here analyzes Ilyenkov's thought and activity from a different viewpoint, the subject matter is in no way exhausted yet. My conviction is that it is precisely Ilyenkov's paradoxes that make him constantly up-to-date and relevant – if he had succeeded in constructing a coherent philosophical position within the Diamat tradition, it would hardly be noticed today any more. After all, most of the Diamat constituted "boring stuff" *(skuchnoi predmet)*, as the Russians themselves like to say: a more or less finished system, where it was not possible to add anything substantially new. However, genuine philosophical positions resemble medieval cathedrals in that they are never finished. What Descartes, Spinoza, Kant, Hegel or Marx wrote, are only projects that have not been carried fully out in the sense that central issues of philosophy have been formally and definitively settled. Ilyenkov, with his unfinished undertaking, is thus in a good society.

The Helsinki symposium would not have succeeded without the assistance of a great many of persons. It was arranged by three institutes of the University of Helsinki, viz. the Institute of Philosophy, the Institute of Developmental Work Research and the Aleksanteri (Alexander) Institute, whose staff I would like to thank. Markku Kivinen, Päivi Paloposki and Elina Kahla of the Aleksanteri Institute were especially helpful in organizing the symposium, as were also Professors Yrjö Engeström and Ilkka Niiniluoto. In addition, I benefitted from valuable hints from Gudrun Richter (Berlin), Nikolai Veresov (Oulu/Kajaani) and David Bakhurst (Kingston/Ontario). My special thanks belong to the curator of the Ilyenkov archive in Moscow, Dr. Alexei Novokhatko, and the daughter of the philosopher, E. E. Illesh, who kindly gave permission to publish a hitherto unknown manuscript of Ilyenkov in an appendix to this volume.

Notes

[1] Ilyenkov even explicitly criticized the Machists of the 20s in an article written about 1977 and entitled *Dialektika i mirovozzrenie*. Here, Ilyenkov first repudiated the positivist reduction of the role of philosophy only to the "scientific world outlook" and then continued: "This is exactly how our notorious 'Machists' were thinking in the 20s: Skvortsov-Stepanov, Sarabianov, A. Timiriazev and others, who attempted to 'throw overboard' all other manners of understanding philosophy and its role in the development of the materialistic world outlook. They thought that every othe way of seeing the problem was 'Hegelianism'..." (Ilyenkov 1991, 348).

[2] Ilyenkov's affinities to Lukács (via Lifshits) are mentioned – but only incidentally – in two contributions to the volume *Drama sovetskoi filosofii. Evald Vasilyevitch Ilyenkov (Kniga-dialog)*, published by the Institute of Philosophy of the Russian Academy of Sciences, Moscow 1997 (articles by V. G. Arslanov and V. V. Vanslov). From Arslanov's contribution it appears that there are many as yet unpublished and undoubtedly very interesting materials in the Lifshits archives.

[3] For Hegel, the Spirit *(der Geist)* is, as Vittorio Hösle remarks, the realphilosophical pendant of the "highest logical category", viz. the category of the Absolute (see Hösle 1988, 340). As such, it is not merely formal, but has a "real" content. The Hegelian concept of spirit is thus tacitly polemical against the Kantian view, according to which human thinking, as distinguished from the senses, is a purely subjective and formal activity devoid of any real content. Hegel's spirit, on the contrary, presupposes that subjectivity will be mediated by objectivity (cf. *Enzyklopädie*, e. g. §§ 388, 389, 440 sqq., 482 sqq.)

[4] "...dass die Kategorien daher Daseinsformen, Existenzbestimmungen, oft nur einzelne Seiten dieser bestimmten Gesellschaft, dieses Subjekts *ausdrücken*" (Marx 1974, 26–27, my emphasis – V. O.)

[5] To be exact, it need not be a problem that the content of the idea has its origin outside the idea which the subject has, if we take the "content" simply as the intentional object of the idea. Even Kant admitted that the content of our ideas is derived from the outer world (from the "things-in-themselves", which, affecting our sensibility, give the material of the knowledge). The real problem is that Ilyenkov very clearly emphasizes that not only the content, but even the form of the idea exists outside the subjects (see, e.g. Ilyenkov 1984a, 168: "The ideal exists immediately only as a form (manner, figure) of the activity of the social man..."). Speaking in Kantian terms, this would amount to saying that the origin of the synthesis of the manifold, which first makes ideas and concepts possible, is not situated in our mind, but in the outer world. But this Kantian formulation is not the only possible one. We could even paraphrase the old poser of the Schoolmen in an "Ilyenkovian" disguise: do the *ideae* exist *ante societatem, in societate* or possibly *post societatem*? That the question can be formulated in such seemingly very different traditions shows its universality.

6 As Vadim Mezhuev remarks, with his first lectures and published articles in the 50s Ilyenkov had already become the "commonly acknowledged leader of the 'philosophical thaw' [...] It is precisely to him that my generation owes the conscious departure from the dogmatism and scholasticism of the official philosophy which flourished in education and propaganda and was formed already in the period of the Stalinism" (Mezhuev 1997, 47).

7 As one can easily see, this is the old dispute of "culture" vs. "civilization" in a new, Soviet form – a further antinomy, whose explication would doubtless be an interesting task for future research.

Literature

Anderson, Kevin (1995), *Hegel, Marx and the Western Marxism,* Urbana and Chicago: Univ. of Illinois Press

Brie, Michael (1993), *Die Tragödie eines kommunistischen Intellektuellen zwischen Mauer und Menschheitsutopie,* in: Brie, M. and Hirdina, K. (eds.), *In memoriam Lothar Kühne,* Berlin: GSFP

Drama sovetskoi filosofii. Eval'd Vasil'evitch Il'enkov (Kniga-dialog), Moscow 1997 [published by the Institute of Philosophy of the Russian Academy of Sciences]

Hegel, G. W. F.(1959), *Enzyklopädie der philosophischen Wissenschaften im Grundrisse [1830],* Hamburg: Felix Meiner Vlg.

Hösle, Vittorio (1988), *Hegels System,* 1 – 2, Hamburg: Felix Meiner Vlg

Ilyenkov, E. V. (1982), *Leninist Dialectics and the Metaphysics of Positivism,* London: New Park Publications

Ilyenkov, E. V. (1984) (= 1984a), *Dialekticheskaia logika,* izd. 2-oe,Moskva: Politizdat

Ilyenkov, E. V. 1984 (= 1984b), *Iskusstvo i kommunisticheskii ideal,* M: Iskusstvo

Ilyenkov, E. V. (1991), *Dialektika i mirovozzrenie,* in: E. V. Ilyenkov, *Filosofiia i kultura,* Moskva: Politizdat

Iljenkow, E. W. (1994), *Dialektik des Ideellen. Ausgewählte Aufsätze,* Münster/ Hamburg: LIT Verlag

Lektorski, V. A. (1999), *Ob Eval'de Vasil'evitche Il'enkove,* in: Lektorski, V. A. (ed.), *E. V. Il'enkov: lichnost' i tvorchestvo,* Moskva: "Iazyki russkoi kul'tury"

Lifshits, M., *Pamiati Eval'da Il'enkova,* in: Ilyenkov 1984b

Lukács, Georg (1951), *Existentialismus oder Marxismus?,* Berlin

Lukács, Georg (1972), *Zur Ontologie des gesellschaftlichen Seins. Die ontologischen Grundprinzipien von Marx,* Darmstadt/Neuwied: Luchterhand

Marx , Karl (1974), *Grundrisse der Kritik der politischen Ökonomie [Rohentwurf],* Berlin: Dietz Verlag

Mezhuev, V. M. (1997), *Eval'd Il'enkov i konets klassicheskoi marksistskoi filosofii,* in: *Drama sovetskoi filosofii*

Mikhailov, Felix (1995), *The Soviet Self: A Personal Reminiscence,* in: Bakhurst, D. and Sypnowich, Chr. (ed.), *The Social Self,* London etc.: SAGE Publications

Naumenko, L. (1982), *To the Reader,* in: Ilyenkov 1982

Richter, Gudrun (1994), *Einführung,* in: Iljenkow 1994

Scanlan, J. P. (1985), *Marxism in the USSR. A Critical Survey of Current Soviet Thought,* Ithaca/London

Vanslov, V. V. (1997), *Il'enkov: estetika i zhizn,* in: *Drama sovetskoi filosofii*

Vodolazov, G. G. (1997), *Il'enkov kak problema,* in: *Drama sovetskoi filosofii*

3

THE LIVING AND THE DEAD IN ILYENKOV'S PHILOSOPHY

DAVID BAKHURST

Introduction

The focus of my paper is Ilyenkov's aesthetics. My choice of topic might surprise you; indeed, I am rather surprised myself! When I proposed a talk with this title, I intended to examine the degree to which Ilyenkov's philosophy is of lasting relevance. Which aspects of his thought speak to us today and which are now of merely historical interest? Yet, when I began work on my argument, I started to have reservations. After all, the enduring significance of Ilyenkov's thought – especially his work on the problem of the ideal – is a prominent theme in my book, *Consciousness and Revolution* (Bakhurst 1991a), and in a string of articles I have written subsequently (Bakhurst 1990, 1991b, 1995a, 1995b, 1996, 1997a, 1997b, Bakhurst & Padden 1991). I decided it was time for something fresh.

It is not just that I wanted to avoid repeating myself. Rather, I was concerned that my successive attempts to represent and refine Ilyenkov's ideas were taking me farther and farther from Ilyenkov himself. Let me explain.

I never knew Ilyenkov as a living philosopher. My interest in Russian philosophy began in 1980, the year after his death. At that time, I had the good fortune to meet Felix Mikhailov in Moscow. Inspired by discussion with Mikhailov – from which it was evident that philosophy in the USSR could not be as moribund as the Western literature made out – I returned to spend the academic year 1982–83 in Moscow, where, thanks to Mikhailov, I was privileged to be able to discuss philosophy with the likes of Vladimir Bibler, Vladislav Lektorsky, and the late Vasili Davydov.[1] In such company the name of Ilyenkov was often mentioned and I came to see his work as a suitable focus for a reconstruction of the history of Soviet philosophy, and as a source philosophical insight that would reward serious study.

Studying Ilyenkov, however, was not easy. While my mentor Mikhailov was the embodiment of living philosophical ingenuity – playful, lightning-quick, and ready to discourse on any subject at the drop of a hat – I knew the dead Ilyenkov's ideas only from their objectification in print. And, as you are aware, Ilyenkov's published legacy presents significant problems of interpretation. What were the effects of censorship and self-censorship? How should one characterise the tortuous context, intellectual and political, in which his works were written? To what degree did the Soviet academic world limit the means Ilyenkov had, not just to express his ideas, but to frame them even to himself? Were Ilyenkov's protestations of orthodoxy "true belief", or were they meant as a kind of indictment of the establishment, or even as irony? Of course, I had a lot of help in struggling with these questions from Ilyenkov's friends and colleagues (and some of his enemies), though their readings in turn presented fascinating hermeneutical problems.

Thus the picture of Ilyenkov that emerges in my writings is the product of a great deal of interpretation and speculation. And my reading was further complicated by the fact that my background and philosophical sensibilities are very different from Ilyenkov's own. This no doubt lent my perspective a desirable critical distance, but my efforts to bring Ilyenkov's ideas to bear on what I considered "live issues" may also have been a source of distortion. I do not apologise for this: it is hardly unusual for philosophers to acquire in death an identity that would have surprised them when they were alive. But I did feel that at this special conference, I should not simply return to my portrait of Ilyenkov and, as it were, add a few refining brush-strokes, but try, so far as possible, to go back to the subject himself in search of a new perspective on his thought. For this reason, I chose to consider texts that I have not dwelt on before: Ilyenkov's writings on the philosophy of art.

Through the Looking Glass

Between 1960 and 1972, Ilyenkov wrote a series of papers on art (Ilyenkov 1960, 1964, 1969, 196?/1984, 1972). They discuss such questions as the nature of beauty, the concepts of aesthetic sensibility and imagination, and the relation of artistic and scientific understanding. They focus mainly on the visual arts, though reference is made to literature and music. I shall begin by concentrating on one in particular, *Chto tam, v Zazerkal'e?* ("What's there, through the looking glass?"), published in 1969. This is a curious article, which displays some of the best of Ilyenkov's philosophical style, and some of the worst. It shows his talent for combining abstract philosophical speculation with anecdotal material of a highly popular and accessible kind. It is typically passionate, witty, and forceful. But as I shall show, the position Ilyenkov advances is extremely problematic. Indeed, it seems to cast his entire philosophy in an unfavourable light.

Chto tam, v Zazerkal'e? begins by posing the question of the relation of beauty, goodness, and truth. Ilyenkov immediately endorses what he describes as the "ancient" solution that the three somehow represent a "unity in diversity". On this account, the good, the beautiful, and the true all spring from the same source; they represent three different expressions of one and the same thing. Ilyenkov admits that this solution sounds counterintuitive to contemporary ears. We feel today that there are no internal relations between these concepts. In so far as science is governed by the regulative ideal of truth it is a morally neutral endeavour. And the facts science discovers can as easily be put in the service of evil as of good, as Hiroshima stands witness. Likewise, we do not feel there need be anything morally edifying about the beautiful, or aesthetically pleasing about the good. The beautiful is morally relevant only in so far as it is one among the things we care about. A painting is not more beautiful for its being morally uplifting, nor is it morally edifying merely in virtue of its beauty. And, of course, the pursuit of beauty need not coincide with the pursuit of truth. In fact, the simple yet high ideal of the classical solution seems wholly at odds with the modern temperament, habituated as it is to the ideas that evil is unavoidable, that violence and cruelty can be objects of aesthetic appreciation, that the progress of science might lead us to the abyss. In such a climate, we might expect to see a loss of confidence in art – with the artworld oscillating between the reduction of art to amusement and varieties of "anti-art" – but not an affirmation of the coincidence of the beautiful with the true and the good.

Ilyenkov does not so much argue for the classical position, as attempt to articulate a form of humanism that locates the coincidence of truth, beauty, and goodness in the ideal of properly human relations among human beings and between human beings and nature. He reminds us that we should not portray the relation of beauty, truth, and goodness as if it were one between platonic forms. Rather, we should see their relation as disclosed by the relation between art, science, and morality, the practices that have beauty, truth, and goodness as their respective objects. Ilyenkov argues that art, science, and morality are three different expressions of human self-consciousness, and as such they represent three distinct mirrors in which we see ourselves. Pursuing this metaphor, he argues that when the images these three disciplines reflect are somehow incommensurate with one another, we are tempted to conclude that each reflects a distinct realm. There is, however, an alternative conclusion: that the human relations they reflect are somehow out of kilter or "abnormal" (Ilyenkov 1969, 312). Where our relations to each other and to nature are harmonious, Ilyenkov maintains, the images cast by science, art, and morality will coincide, and truth, beauty, and goodness will be seen to be one. "Hence", Ilyenkov writes, "the harmonious unity of truth, goodness, and beauty is a criterion of the maturity of genuine human relations" (Ilyenkov 1969, 311).

In light of this, Ilyenkov argues, it is urgent that we define a criterion to determine what is "real" or "proper" (*podlinnoe*) art. We must not avoid this issue, in the style of Pontius Pilate, by feigning a commitment to relativism, aesthetic or epistemological. No such views carry real conviction. They are just an excuse to remain silent on the hard questions, and silence, Ilyenkov tells us, "is a nightmarish thing" (309).

Yet despite these words, Ilyenkov fails to make explicit what he takes the "true criterion" to be. He answers the question largely in the negative. For example, he asserts that real art cannot be in the service of evil:

> Genuine art cannot be immoral by its very nature and, by the same token, immoral art is always false art – not art but a talentless surrogate, formally adroit perhaps, but an essentially contentless falsification of aesthetic values (Ilyenkov 1969, 311).

Nor can real art further the aims of pseudo-science. Genuine art cannot perpetuate images of beauty that in some or other way reinforce the bogus conceptions of "pseudo-" or "half-scientific" theories "empty of humanistic values" (313).

The result seems to be the view that genuine art is distinguished by the contribution it makes to human flourishing, to the furtherance of free and fulfilled humanity. And there is a suggestion that Ilyenkov thinks that the same criterion can be applied to genuine science or morality. The measure of these forms of self-consciousness is their contribution to the self-realisation of humanity.

In case his humanism appear too "abstract", Ilyenkov illustrates his position with a story. He describes visiting an exhibition of Pop art in Vienna in 1964, when he was part of a Soviet delegation to a philosophy congress. Ilyenkov tells how, since he was already acquainted with Pop art though reproductions, he entered the exhibition in suitably ironic mood. But

> after ten minutes my ironic-sarcastic apperception – being "a priori", though certainly not "transcendental" – had been completely swept away and destroyed by the avalanche of direct perceptions pounding my senses (314).

In its place, Ilyenkov found himself overcome with a mixture of disgust, dismay, and abhorrence.

Ilyenkov discusses some of the works that provoked this reaction and, though he cannot bring himself to mention the artists by name, it is clear that the exhibition contained works by Warhol, Rauschenberg, and possibly a number of earlier pieces deemed precursors of Pop art, such as Duchamps's *Fountain*. Ilyenkov discusses his soul-searching attempt to explain to himself his antipathy. He considers the view that Pop art expresses, not frivolity but agony; that it embodies the death, or perhaps the suicide, of art. (He puts this view into the mouth of the director of the museum trying to placate the bemused Soviet delegation.) Might Ilyenkov's reaction be one of grief? No, for he counters the death-of-art thesis with an alternative interpretation: Pop art is rather a mirror which shows us an image of people in an alienated world. It displays

> what human beings are turned into by this mindless, upside-down and inside-out world. A world of things, mechanisms, instruments, a standardised, formulaic world of dead schemata, a world made by human beings but flying beyond the control of their conscious wills. An incomprehensible and uncontrollable world of things made by man in his own image. A world where dead labour has become a despot ruling over the labour of the living (320).

Thus Ilyenkov explains his gut-reaction to Pop art: it is depressing because it is a true reflection of a distorted world, and since it cannot see itself for what it is, it simply serves to affirm and perpetuate that mindless world.

Ilyenkov in the Mirror of Pop Art

Ilyenkov's dismissal of Pop art is undeniably rather crude. Indeed, such is his exasperation that one wonders whether he simply lacked the cultural resources to form a suitably nuanced understanding of the art he derides. For example, there is a moment of pathos in the article when Ilyenkov describes his horror at confronting a Warhol canvass consisting in numerous reproductions of the *Mona Lisa*.[2] Ilyenkov is outraged at this act of defamation and laments that if he were now ever to see the real *Mona Lisa*, his experience would be ruined by the memory of this parody in which all the enigmatic individuality of the original is lost through the repetition of the image.

How sad, one feels, that during Ilyenkov's precious trip to the West, Vienna should have been staging an exhibition of Warhol rather than da Vinci. But the real pathos is that, had Ilyenkov's conference taken him to Paris rather than to Vienna, his sighting of the *Mona Lisa* in the Louvre would no doubt have been as disappointing as Warhol's pastiche. For, of course, the relatively small canvass hangs under glass and must be viewed at some distance, since one must fight with the hoards of visitors, mainly tourists who are "doing" the Louvre. The canvass cannot be studied, it must rather be glimpsed, and one's glimpses serve merely to remind one of the hackneyed image one knows so well from reproductions. This is what the mystique of the *Mona Lisa* has become. And it is this that is targeted by Warhol. But this seems lost on Ilyenkov.

Yet despite this, it might be argued that Ilyenkov's unease with Pop art is defensible. After all, Pop art existed in an air of permanent paradox. While at its beginning the movement was undoubtedly subversive – exposing the vacuity of mass-imagery and fleeting images of television and advertising, and parodying consumerism and celebrity – it so revelled in what it exposed that it only served to affirm the culture it pastiched. Nor can Pop be redeemed by casting it as intellectual, rather than socio-political art, designed to pose the great question "What is art?" For although it certainly posed this question, it has absolutely nothing meaningful to say in response to it. The result of this supremely knowing, but ultimately inarticulate, reflexivity was that art was reduced to consumption. An object is art insofar as it is something art collectors will buy, a position that Warhol happily embraced. With this, the apparently democratic elements of Pop became eclipsed, for not anyone can turn junk into art: only celebrated artists have the Midas touch. Hence Pop's cult of celebrity and Warhol's corresponding vision of equality: fifteen minutes of fame for everyone.

It would thus not be difficult to gloss over the infelicities of Ilyenkov's argument, and grant him at least that the phenomenon of Pop art does reflect something about the confusions of Western culture in the 1960s. I think, however, that there are two reasons why it would be unduly sympathetic to Ilyenkov to leave the matter there.

First, Ilyenkov's scorn is not directed at Pop art alone; rather, he sees Pop as the inevitable culmination of the whole modernist tradition, which "from beginning to end, from cubism to pop" represents "a form of aesthetic adaptation of human beings to the conditions of an 'alienated world'" (323).[3] While it is at least possible to present Pop art as a reflection of the bankruptcy of capitalist culture, it is hardly plausible to portray, say, cubism in such a light. Ilyenkov comes across as a narrow-minded socialist realist. Moreover, Ilyenkov's realism seems to be more than a moral injunction that "progressive" art should further the revolution. It appears to rest on the idea that the function of all art is ultimately to reflect or represent reality: to show what is, what might be, what should be. Thus he can tolerate modernist art only where it is plausible to see the artist as striving to represent reality. Ilyenkov seems to approve, therefore, of Picasso's *Guernica*, which he can portray as a depiction of the horror of the bombing of the Basque town, but a cubist still-life makes no sense to him. For Ilyenkov, cubist art could only be a mirror of a twisted reality. It seems not to occur to him that representation may not be the only legitimate purpose of art. As he sees it, if art does not reflect reality then its purpose can only be to amuse or entertain, and the latter role is far too frivolous to be the essence of art.

Second, while the idea that the measure of art is its contribution to human flourishing is a defensible, if contentious, position, it invites abuse in familiar ways. Combined with a dogmatic conception of where our flourishing lies, and a teleological conception of history, such a position, for all its "humanistic" ideals, can be invoked to license the criticism of art of political grounds, a distinction between "progressive" and "reactionary" art, and so on – in short, all the well-known techniques of Soviet criticism. Ilyenkov makes no attempt to acknowledge how arbitrary such criticism can be and how much damage it can do to the entire intellectual culture. What, one wonders, did Ilyenkov make of those Russian avant garde artists, many of whom saw their work as an expression of the ethos of revolution and a contribution to the new order? And what was his view of the Stalinist cultural revolution that swept them aside?

Moreover, Ilyenkov's position seems equally to license the critique of *scientific* theories on political grounds. To maintain that science without humanistic ends is pseudo-science is to suggest that it is legitimate to dismiss a scientific theory because it fails to serve humanity. And in *Chto tam, v Zazerkal'e?* (313), Ilyenkov seems to criticise his bête noire, cybernetics, on just these grounds. But this is to deny that science should be governed by the regulative ideal of truth, unless of course Ilyenkov is prepared to identify true conceptions of the world with those that promote human well being. But this would put him perilously close to endorsing a conception of "proletarian science".

Thus it appears that Ilyenkov's humanism contains a sinister element that seems to affirm the very Stalinist orthodoxy that he is so often represented as opposing.

A Second Look

My efforts to take a fresh look at Ilyenkov's philosophy have led us to uncomfortable conclusions. You will be relieved, however, that I think such conclusions premature. This will become evident once we look carefully at some of Ilyenkov's other writings on aesthetics.

In 1960, at the height of his creative powers, Ilyenkov wrote a short paper *O "spetsifike" iskusstva* and he followed this in 1964 with the lengthy *Ob esteticheskoi prirode fantazii*. These writings cast Ilyenkov's philosophy of art in a rather different light. They too advance a radical form of humanism, but insofar as they accord art a "purpose" it is simply to "develop the productive forces of humanity", where the latter are understood "in the broadest possible sense" as the "capacity creatively to transform nature" (Ilyenkov 1960, 217). Moreover, art's contribution is not principally to provide appropriate representations of reality, but to cultivate in us a form of aesthetic sensibility that enables certain higher forms of perception. Ilyenkov argues that while the fundamental forms of human perception are formed spontaneously as the child assimilates the basic patterns of life activity of the community, the higher forms must be actively developed. The history of art, Ilyenkov maintains, is a key resource in this process. Art teaches us to see things differently (Ilyenkov 1960, 215; 1964: 231–236).

Ilyenkov argues that aesthetic sensibility, as he understands it, essentially involves the exercise of creative imagination. By "imagination", he means not just the capacity to envisage "what is not", but the ability to see particular facts in a way that at once captures their uniqueness and reveals how certain general schema are applicable to them. As Ilyenkov puts it, imagination enables us to see the "universal individuality" of the facts. This is illustrated by the kind of creative "recasting" of an object in certain acts of discovery. Suddenly, a way of solving a hitherto intractable problem emerges by, as it were, "reorganising" the facts. The facts acquire a new "shape" – a new "profile" – in which what was formally salient has receded, throwing new features into relief. In like manner, imagination is also at work when we grasp how various features, hitherto perceived as distinct and isolated, in fact constitute parts of an organised whole. In short, imagination enables us to see significance in things, significance we grasp in an act of perceptual apprehension rather than through ratiocination. The history of art, Ilyenkov asserts, is a "treasure trove" of examples of the creative exercise of imagination so conceived, and it presents for us a gallery of problems we may solve only through the acquisition of imagination.

It is important that, for Ilyenkov, aesthetic sensibility is a capacity that has application in all dimensions of cognition and not just the appreciation of art:

> Art develops a universal sensibility, by means of which human beings enter into active contact *[deistvennyi kontakt]* not only with each other but also with nature (1960, 215).

Ilyenkov thus repeatedly stresses that the exercise of imagination is as crucial for scientific and philosophical cognition as it is for art. In this, he explicitly departs from Hegel's vision of art (which he admires), according to which art, though it represents an essential stage in spirit's path to self-understanding, is superseded by philosophy. In contrast, Ilyenkov argues that art and science (which, for Ilyenkov, includes philosophy) are necessary partners: science cannot live without art, as it demands the cultivation of imagination; art cannot despise science insofar as its object is the very world which science discloses to us (Ilyenkov 196?/1984, esp. 332).

Ilyenkov insists on universality of aesthetic sensibility in part to defend art against positivistic attacks inspired by the "scientific-technological revolution" of the 1960s, attacks that celebrated the objectivity of natural science and relegated art to a vehicle for the expression of emotion and attitude. There is, however, a further and deeper reason for Ilyenkov's insistence. At the root of his Marxism lies a disdain for the division of labour, where human beings are able to reproduce their existence only by the partial or "one-sided" development of their capacities. Ilyenkov is not just concerned about the specific effects of the division of labour under industrial capitalism. Rather, he attacks any form of specialisation that forces us to cultivate some of our capacities at the expense of others, and urges the creation of conditions that facilitate the individual's "all-round" development.

It is important to understand Ilyenkov's talk of "all-round" development properly. It is not, for example, intended to evoke a utopia in which everyone is somehow capable of anything. For Ilyenkov, the hallmark of distinctively human activity is that it is informed by reason, and the hallmark of reason is universality. Ilyenkov sometimes explains this by saying that human beings have the power to adapt their activity in light of novel and peculiar circumstances, and he loves to invoke Spinoza's example of how the human hand is not antecedently determined by its structure to manipulate objects of any particular shape but is able to adapt its form to accommodate the object before it (Ilyenkov 1974, 34). The activity of a rational animal is not simply called forth by the interplay of its internal structure and causal forces impinging upon it. Rather, rational animals conform their activity to the objective requirements of the circumstances in which they find themselves. Their activity is guided by reasons rather than produced by causes. The key thought here is that our activity is rational – and thus evinces our humanity – to the degree that it is, not (or not merely) causally determined, but an expression of the recognition of objective reasons. Thus rationality demands that our psychological powers are supremely plastic, able to accommodate the form of any circumstance reality presents us with.

Ilyenkov sees the division of labour as a hindrance to this plasticity and for this reason he resists views that drive a wedge between scientific cognition and aesthetic appreciation and privilege science over art. It is not that he aspires somehow to incorporate the scientific and the aesthetic into a single mode of cognition. Rather, he endorses what we might call the unity of the cognitive virtues: no particular cognitive capacity can be properly attuned to reality unless it is part of a whole in which all the other psychological capacities are equally so attuned.

Ilyenkov's vision of rational action is intimately connected with his conception of freedom. Freedom is manifest in human actions that are guided by reasons – that issue from an appreciation of what ought to be – and a being is free to the degree to which it possesses the capacity to act in appropriate recognition of reasons as they present themselves. Thus, Ilyenkov endorses the famous adage of German classical philosophy that freedom involves the recognition of necessity. This does not mean, of course, that we are free to the extent that we knowingly acquiesce before causal forces, but that free acts are those which are dictated by rational necessity, by an appreciation of objective reasons. A being manifests freedom insofar as it charts an appropriate course through the world of reasons, a course for the most part dictated by the geography of that world. On this view, free acts are contrasted with behaviour that is the outcome of causal forces beyond our control, but they are also contrasted with acts that are merely "arbitrary" (*proizvol'no*) expressions of the will and hence cannot be explained as issuing from an appreciation of objective reasons. The existentialist idea that a truly free choice is one utterly unencumbered by constraint rests on a mistake: free acts must chart a course between the Scylla of causal determination and the Charybdis of arbitrary volition.

We have made a brief tour of certain important ideas that figure in Ilyenkov's writings on the philosophy of art in the early 1960s (and which, it goes without saying, have their origins in the German classical tradition): his notion that art serves to cultivate certain "higher" forms of perception and the attendant concepts of aesthetic sensibility and the creative imagination; his view of the unity of the cognitive virtues; his hostility to the division of labour; and his ideal of essentially human activity, rational and free. We might add that Ilyenkov sees the activity of the artist, engaged in the production of "real" art as a paradigm of free, creative activity. With these ideas in place, we may better understand Ilyenkov's hostility to modern art.

Modernism represents a rupture, a self-conscious breaking of tradition, a search for a new conception of the role of art, which was often cast in terms of an explicit opposition to everything that had gone before. The "negativity" of modernism, provoked of course by the emergence of technologies that threatened to make representational art obsolete, affronts Ilyenkov's vision of the history of art as a coherent, ever expanding and developing repository of resources for the education of the senses. Much modernism (though not all) scorns such a conception and embodies that scorn in its works.

As we have seen, Ilyenkov looks to art above all to cultivate the development of creative imagination. In much modern art, however, Ilyenkov can only see imagination in league with arbitrariness. Where art celebrates the unconstrained and the non-sensical, or where it is simply an expression of the arbitrary will of the artist, we see the "free play" of the imagination, but not imagination in the service of genuine freedom, which is always constrained by reason. We thus cannot represent these works as expressions of the genuine exercise of creative imagination, but merely as objectifications of arbitrary will. They do not, therefore, cultivate the imagination as a cognitive resource. Moreover, Ilyenkov takes the irrationalism of modernism to affirm the division of labour, by dramatically opposing art to genuine cognitive inquiry. Thus, he sees modernism as a natural partner of early-twentieth century positivism, with its strict opposition between the factual and the normative, belief and desire, description and expression (196?/1984, 329). To embrace these dichotomies is to relegate aesthetic sensibility and thereby to advance an impoverished conception of cognition.

My purpose here is not to defend Ilyenkov's position. He is, I believe, wrong to suppose that modern art (if we can talk as if "modern art" were a single phenomenon) does not cultivate the exercise of creative imagination, as he understands it. Good modern art certainly encourages new ways of seeing, indeed, it shows us how much more there is to see than can be captured by traditional representation. Nevertheless, once cast in its proper context, Ilyenkov's position is certainly defensible and far from a crude, unreflective reduction of the aesthetic to the political.

This conclusion does not, however, excuse the way Ilyenkov makes his case in *Chto tam, v Zazerkal'e?*, which appears to endorse a form of socialist realism that invites us seriously to misunderstand Ilyenkov's purpose.

Art and the Affirmation of Life

I want to conclude with some remarks about themes deep within Ilyenkov's humanism, and that return us, perhaps surprisingly, to the theme of the living and the dead in Ilyenkov's philosophy.

Ilyenkov's notion of free, creative activity lies at the heart of his concept of "genuinely human relations" among human beings and between us and nature. Our relation to nature is not merely a relation to a local environment that impinges upon us and causes us to act in various ways; rather, we see ourselves as inhabitants of a "world", which our concepts disclose to us and in which we find significance. We see this world at once as infinite in its ever-receding horizons, and as the setting, the home, of our life activity. To relate to another person in a "genuinely human" way is to recognise her as a source of rational subjectivity like oneself, to see her as the subject of a life charted though the world. In relating to another, our activity expresses rationality in responding to the expression of rationality manifest in the activity of the other. Intersubjectivity is premised upon such reciprocal attunement to the meaning in each other's movement.

I want to suggest that, for Ilyenkov, free creative activity is a kind of life principle. Such activity represents life in its fullest expression. And his famous response to the problem of the ideal can be seen as an attempt to explain the origin of this principle, one that explores how free, creative activity develops through a kind of "bootstrapping": As a result of collective human action, significance is objectified in the natural world making possible a "normative" relation to nature in which agents respond to their surroundings in light of their meaning, moulding their activity to ideal, rather than merely physical forms. So a world of reasons is created which calls forth rational activity, and which thereby issues in the objectification of further modes of significance, facilitating further activity, and so on. Crucially, Ilyenkov sees this process as the enlivening of the brutely physical environment, the breathing of life into "dead" nature. Human beings express their rational powers in so far as they assimilate the capacities to inhabit the world so animated by the life activity of humanity.

This humanistic vision informs all of Ilyenkov's thought, including his thinking about art. It is present explicitly in *Ob esteticheskoi prirode fantasii*, where he advances the anthropocentric (indeed anthropomorphic) view that in cognition we are always in touch primarily with nature "humanized" by activity, and then invokes this to argue that judgements of beauty, even "natural" beauty, are always derived from our conceptions of the fittingness of artefacts to human purposes and ends (see Ilyenkov 1964, 257–275). For present purposes, however, the key idea is the notion that free creative activity is the highest expression of life, and such activity is possible only in a world laden with significance through the very objectification of human agency, the process which, as it were, gives life to reason. Throughout Ilyenkov's writings, this concept of life is contrasted with mechanism, with the workings of "dead" physicality, with production of "behaviour" through the causal efficacy of structures blindly interacting in accord with physical law. For Ilyenkov, the mechanical, the standardised, the formulaic represent death in contrast to the life-affirming character of free, creative activity. He rails against the social circumstances that make human beings behave like machines and against those theories which portray human behaviour in mechanistic terms. Hence his horror of cybernetics, with its celebration of the machine, and of all forms of reductive, deterministic materialism.

The metaphors of the living and the dead are found throughout Ilyenkov's writings, and his humanistic affirmation of life against forces of mortification might be deemed the overarching theme of his philosophy. This certainly helps us understand Ilyenkov's celebration of what he called "genuine" art, an expression of our rational power to animate nature through free, creative activity, as well as his antipathy to Pop, with its celebration of mass production and mechanical reproduction. "I want to be a machine", Warhol declared (cited in Hughes 1980, 348). This, for Ilyenkov, could only mean the suicide of the artist. To attack the whole of modernism on these grounds must be misguided, though we can see now why Ilyenkov, with his historicist conception of art, was horrified at the idea that art's history might culminate in this. For Ilyenkov, Pop represented not just the death of art, but the art of death.

Conclusion

In this paper, I have tried to take a fresh look at prominent themes in Ilyenkov's philosophy by approaching them from the perspective of his writings on aesthetics. My argument has, I hope, cast new light on the humanism which seems to infuse his whole work. It remains to ask, then, what is living and what is dead in Ilyenkov's humanistic vision?

The concept of activity, as it figures in Ilyenkov's writing on the ideal, is usually taken to be the most significant part of his legacy. Its importance lies, I think, in particular insights which it forces upon psychology and the philosophy of mind; namely, to take account of the extent to which our capacity to transform our environment influences dramatically the scope and limits of human minds. In the grand philosophical scheme – as a kind of derivation of the very possibility of the relation of subject and object – the position presents epistemological problems that threaten to be insuperable. These are problems of the kind that haunted Kant about our knowledge of "things in themselves", and of the kind that haunted Hegel about "bootstrapping" explanations. Moreover, Ilyenkov's secular historicism, within which philosophical anthropology tells the story of humanity's self-creation, surely no longer carries conviction. It is simply too anthropocentric; it accords human beings too great a place in the order of things, a sentiment that invites ethical as well as metaphysical objections.

For all that, however, I believe that Ilyenkov's essentially Kantian conception of free creative activity as responsiveness to rational necessity, is extremely powerful. The claim that our very humanity is expressed in a manner in which we navigate the world of reasons and in the way in which we respond to others as bearers of rational subjectivity is an insight of deep significance. It is an idea that is regaining some currency in Western thought, notably in John McDowell's recent work (1994), and I believe there is potential here for Ilyenkovian ideas to prosper in a fruitful dialogue.

Ilyenkov's affirmation of reason, freedom, and life gives his philosophy an optimistic and inspiring character. Yet his philosophy is also haunted by darker themes, one of which is the morbid image of humanity overtaken by mechanistic forces. Sometimes I wonder whether Ilyenkov, as he grew older, feared that in his own imagination was becoming ever less creative, that his writing was becoming formulaic, and that the intellectual life force so evident in his very early writings was weakening. And I wonder whether his way of responding to this was to become more aggressive and dogmatic, while at the same time trying to mask his failure of imagination with a kind of desperate wit. Perhaps writings like *Chto tam, v Zazerkal'e?* were the result. Ilyenkov must have known that his strategy could only fail, and perhaps it was the recognition of that failure that cost him so dear in the end.

These are just speculations. No doubt there are others better placed to comment of the forces that weighed upon Ilyenkov in the last decade of his life. I want simply to stress how important it is that now, twenty years since Ilyenkov's death, we aspire to an honest assessment of his legacy, one which appreciates the brilliance of his achievements, but does not shy from his shortcomings, one which recognises both the depth of Ilyenkov's humanism, and the humanity of his tragedy.

Notes

[1] Bakhurst 1995c provides a record of one of the seminars we held at the Institute of General and Pedagogical Psychology.

[2] Presumably Warhol's *Thirty are Better than One* (1963).

[3] Ilyenkov expresses his hostility to modernism in other writings; see e.g. 1964, 244 (where surrealism is the target) and 196?/1984, 32–30.

Bibliography

Bakhurst, David (1991a), *Consciousness and Revolution in Soviet Philosophy: From the Bolsheviks to Evald Ilyenkov*. Cambridge: Cambridge University Press.

Bakhurst, David (1990), *Social Memory in Soviet Thought*. In: David Middleton and Derek Edwards (eds.), *Collective Remembering*. London: Sage, 203–226.

Bakhurst, David (1991b), *Political Emancipation and the Domination of Nature: the rise and fall of Soviet Prometheanism*. In: *International Studies in the Philosophy of Science*, 1 (3), 215–226.

Bakhurst, David (1995a), *Lessons from Ilyenkov*. In: *Communication Review*, 1 (2), 155–178.

Bakhurst, David (1995b), *On the Social Constitution of Mind: Bruner, Ilyenkov and the Defence of Cultural Psychology*. In: *Mind, Culture and Activity*, 2 (3), 158–171.

Bakhurst, David (1995c), *Social Being and the Human Essence: An Unresolved Issue in Soviet Philosophy*. In: *Studies in East European Thought*, 47, 3–60.

Bakhurst, David (1996), *Filosofiia deiatel'nosti*. In: *Voprosy filosofii*, no.5, 72–79. [Translated as *The Philosophy of Activity*, in: *Russian Studies in Philosophy. A Journal of Translations*, 36 (1) (Summer 1997), 47–56.]

Bakhurst, David (1997a), *Meaning, Normativity and the Life of the Mind*. In: *Language and Communication*, 17 (1), 33–51.

Bakhurst, David (1997b), *Activity, Consciousness and Communication*. In: M. Cole, Y. Engeström and O. Vasquez (eds), *Mind, Culture and Activity. Seminal Papers from the Laboratory of Comparative Human Cognition*. Cambridge: Cambridge University Press, 147–163.

Bakhurst, David and Carol Padden (1991), *The Meshcheryakov Experiment: Soviet Work on the Education of Blind-Deaf Children*. In: *Learning and Instruction*, 1, 201–215.

Hughes, Robert (1980), *The Shock of the New*. London: BBC.

Ilyenkov, E.V. (1960), *O "spetzifike" iskusstva* ["On the 'specifics' of art"]. In: Ilyenkov 1984, 213–224.

Ilyenkov, E.V. (1964), *Ob esteticheskoi prirode fantasii* ["On the aesthetic nature of the imagination"]. In: Ilyenkov 1984, 224–277.

Ilyenkov, E.V. (1969), *Chto tam, v Zazerkal'e?* ["What's there, through the looking glass?"]. In: Ilyenkov 1984, 300–324.

Ilyenkov, E.V. (196?/1984), *Gegelevskaya kontseptsiia krasoty i istiny* ["The Hegelian conception of beauty and truth"]. In: Ilyenkov 1984, 324–332.

Ilyenkov, E.V. (1972), *Proidena li tablitsa umnozheniia?* ["Have we done our multiplication tables?"]. In: Ilyenkov 1984, 206–212.

Ilyenkov, E.V. (1974), *Dialekticheskaia logika*. Moscow: Politizdat.

Ilyenkov, E.V. (1984) *Iskusstvo i kommunisticheskii ideal* ["Art and the Communist Ideal"]. Moscow: Iskusstvo.

McDowell, John (1994), *Mind and World*. Cambridge, MA: Harvard.

4

Диалектика как логика рефлексивного мышления

Ф.Т. Михайлов

Вместо эпиграфа приведу памятный мне отрывок из разговора профессора-экономиста со своим коллегой. Их беседу я поневоле подслушал в очереди за зарплатой ещё в старом здании МГИМО[1] у Крымского моста. Монолог профессора в то время был для меня ошеломляющей «радостью нечаянной». Не мог я тогда ожидать от экономиста (сейчас – тем более) *логической рефлексии* на тексты, открывающие *исторический смысл* проблем социально-хозяйственной деятельности людей. Потому и воспроизвожу его здесь за давностью лет хотя и не дословно, но по смыслу абсолютно точно:

    – Если хотите понять самую суть «Капитала» Маркса, – читайте Ильенкова. Он – единственный, кто понял эту книгу в соответствие с её подзаголовком: «Критика политической экономии». Критика её логики. Нашей с Вами науке, прежде всего стремящейся к строгости изложения фактов и выводов, издавна присуща логика взаимоопределения понятий по их всеми принятому смыслу. И Маркс не против строгости и последовательности, но его понятия – это категории самой истории. Это реальные общности людей, прописанные в историческом времени. Смысл таких категорий возникает в сознании читателя по мере углубления мысли автора в историю образования этих общностей. Возникает как живой образ реальных

способов и средств разрешения противоречий между группами людей, участвующих в жизненно для них важном обмене общественной и хозяйственной деятельностью и тем самым объединяющим их в ту или иную общность. Именно поэтому Ильенков называет логику Маркса диалектической логикой…

Memento…

Не будет большим преувеличением назвать проблему логики научного знания – центральной проблемой философии XX столетия. (Но и до сих пор за ней скрывается более общая проблема – проблема логики преображающего мир мышления как такового). Сразу же после Канта, философы-классики XIX века становились классиками в упорном поиске разумного основания для явного соответствия логики познающего мышления порядку необъяснимой целесо-образности объективного мира. Или же слава их осеняла тогда, когда, отчаявшись от неизбежных на этом пути неудач, противопоставляли они логике рациональности иррациональность воли… Воли к власти, к бунту, к смерти, словом – к жизни.

Ну а XX век – это век находки ТЕКСТА в качестве посредника между логикой мышления индивида (уже тем самым *психологически* субъективной) и объективным порядком осмысливаемой онтологии бытийных процессов. Казалось бы, найден единственно возможный вариант решения проблемы, названной выше: текст культуры – реальность интерсубъективная. Это значит, что, с одной стороны, она субъективна как сама мысль, с другой – это реальность, впитавшая в себя опыт дел и мысли сотен поколений, столь же *надындивидуальна* и потому объективна, как и вся воспринимаемая природа.

Тем самым, в отличие от непредсказуемости аффективных проявлений мышления индивида, довлеющая себе логика любого текста, сохраняя аподиктичность его всеобщих (общих для всех индивидов) интерсубъективных смыслов, превращает любой текст в единственно ответственного за им же и устанавливаемую гармонию между *душой* – индивидуальностью самосознания человека, и *духом* – вносящим в душу каждого из нас сверхызбыточную для актуальности мышления эстетическую смыслоёмкость Бытия.

Однако, в любом случае оставалась всё же не решённой *рационально логически* проблема *онтологических* предпосылок (истока, начала) интерсубъективной логики текстов. Вроде бы этот исток как некое начало мирского порядка (отсюда и все хронотопы реального для мира движения, все инварианты объективно текущих процессов) как раз в *феномене* текста культуры слился со всегда субъективной «логикой» восприятия, с формами аффекта и мышления, но это была просто новая, не скрою: более удачная, версия *неизбежности* такого слияния. *Возможность* же его оставалась без обоснования, а, тем самым, и без понимания. Текст, раскрыв свою функцию носителя смысла и чувства, заменив собою цхуйт античных мыслителей, Единое неоплатоников, средневекового Творца, да и Бога Спинозы, заметался между миром вещей и миром идей, но так и не стал обоснованным смыслообразом их тождества. Что и сохраняло противопоставление *психологизма* мышления и его же… *логизма*.

Но так было, так пока есть… в «благоустроенных странах». О чём – чуть позже. У нас же «общее дело» философии принимало чуть ли не с начала века совсем иной оборот…

…В то время, когда Эвальд Васильевич Ильенков ещё только начинал свою действительно фундаментальную критику эмпиристского мышления вообще и научного в особенности, вопрос о том, что такое логика, решался у нас в самых зубодробительных традициях борьбы с инакомыслием. Ведь тогда именно *борьба* была Логикой отечественного философствования. И начиналась она всегда с жадного поиска ещё *не ведомых* врагов.

Врагов искали и «находили» не только в биологии и кибернетике, но и в физике. Но прежде полагалось обнаружить их в *недрах* марксистско-ленинской философии. Правда весьма и весьма неглубоких. Видимо поэтому долго искать не пришлось. Очень скоро нашли «механицистов» и «меньшивиствующих идеалистов». Столь же быстро объектом *партийной философской* критики стала формальная логика, объявленная логикой антидиалектической метафизики, согласно предписаниям Сталина, враждебной идеологии пролетариата. Как всегда, на помощь ищущим приходили цитаты из текстов *классиков марксизма-ленинизма*. Слова Ф.Энгельса о том, что от философии остались лишь формальная логика и диалектика, повторялись столь же часто как «Отче наш» среди молитв. Понималось это как призыв добить формальную логику. А замечание В.И. Ленина на полях конспекта «Логики» Гегеля: *гносеология, логика, диалектика… не надо трёх слов – это одно и то же*, можно было смело считать эпиграфом ко всем публиковавшимся инвективам *против* всё той же формальной логики. Ясно ведь: если логика и диалектика одно, то никакой другой логики и быть не может! *Не* диалектика, антидиалектика (метафизика со *своей* чисто формальной логикой) – есть не что иное, как тот же «механицизм», неизбежно приводящий к «меньшивиствующему идеализму», а то и к чему-нибудь похуже…

Кстати, вне пафоса всеобщей яростной *борьбы на уничтожение*, сами эти тексты ничего воинственного в себе не несли. Они были рождены, обретая философский смысл в контексте гегелевского полагания логики категорий как логики становления исторических форм духовно-практического бытия людей, «снятой» мышлением. Потому и Э.В. Ильенков не редко их цитировал, пытаясь передать их рациональный смысл. Но у группы так называемых «диалектических логиков», выделившейся из массы *диалектических и исторических материалистов* и по партийному воинствующей, эти высказывания «классиков» оказались именно оружием и именно в борьбе против формальной логики. И не только против Аристотелевой, но и против современной, символической. Дело борьбы дошло до курьёза: «диалектики», кроме Аристотелевой логики другой не знавшие, стали сочинять формы *диалектических* суждений, умозаключений и доказательств, типа: «S есть = не есть P» (есть и не есть в то же время и в том же отношении), призванные заменить классическое «S есть/не есть P». Правда, длилось это не долго: нелепость подобных потуг была слишком уж явной. Но ещё большей нелепостью было бы принять первые работы Э.В. Ильенкова по *диалектической логике* за нечто подобное описанному только что и по интенции, и по смыслу. В предисловиях к двум их изданиям в книге «Диалектическая логика» об этом сказано верно и достаточно. Своим воспоминанием о былом я преследовал иную цель: всего лишь напомнить о том, в какой атмосфере они рождались. Но вернёмся к заботам философов в XX веке.

Проблема онтологических предпосылок логики: психологизм и логизм

В.Виндельбанд и Г.Риккерт убедительно обосновали своё смущение по поводу обращения Канта к классической философской дихотомии: трансцендентальности и трансцендентности, как к проблеме принципиально онтологической. Но в таком случае изначальная способность продуктивного воображения, трансцендентальное единство апперцепции, а, тем самым, и синтетические суждения a priori, должные были получить и получали у Канта атрибуцию *онтологических предпосылок* логической креативности. Отсюда с неизбежностью следует, что онтологией креативных возможностей логики вновь оказывается вся сфера психического. Для Риккерта в этом проявилась Кантова приверженность «остаткам рационализма». На самом же деле, как считал Риккерт, формы *рациональности* в логике любого дискурса и формы *эмоциональности* в аффективно-эстетическом проживании *ценностей* жизни равно трансцендентны уже потому, что не принадлежат *эмпирии* аффективно осмысленного Бытия. Ведь нельзя же путать предмет мысли (тем более теоретической!) с эмпирическим предметом.[2] Знание как задача мышления (и оно же – его предмет) не отражение, не сколок с эмпирически данной реальности, но продукт понимания. Но не копирующего, а *преображающего* …nicht Abbild, aber *umbildende.*[3] (Кстати, *umbildende* – гениальная находка Риккерта!).

Но отсюда с неизбежностью следовало, что, с одной стороны, любая попытка обосновать логические формы, логическое следование допущениями эмпирического характера, нацело исключена. *Тем более психологию следует исключить из логики, логику из психологии, так как в настоящем их бытии психология не может обосновать ни один из логических законов, как и ни один логический закон не может обосновать мышление как феномен.*[4] Но при всей эпистемологической продуктивности прозрений неокантианцев, ими была сохранена дихотомия субъективности и интерсубъективности, а вместе с ней и проблема онтологических предпосылок логики познающего мышления и её способности к *преображающему пониманию* своего предмета так и осталась тайной за семью печатями.

В это же самое время именно логика, но уже *изнутри*, подверглась своему самому коренному преображающему пониманию: Джон Стюарт Милль был ниспровергнут освоением в качестве аксиомы исходной априорности её форм и законов следования. Вместе с тем была отброшена за ненадобностью предпосылка эмпиристского их обоснования. Такая свобода от «привязки» к психологически осмысляемому опыту породнила логику с математикой, изначально пользовавшейся такой свободой. Благодаря этому и началась эпоха бурного развития логики новой – математической.[5] Почти одновременно тот же процесс освободил физику от иллюзий ползучего эмпиризма (аксиоматизация и математизация физики!), в биологии с открытием гена возникла возможность аксиоматизации: как писал К.Х. Уоддингтон, постулаты Ф. Крика (субмолекулярная биология) открыли путь к формированию начал теоретической (фундаментальной) биологии: «Генотип можно сравнить с системой аксиом Евклида, а фенотип с трёхтомным учебником евклидовой геометрии…».[6] Так стоит ли нам, через сотню лет стоящим на пороге третьего тысячелетия, напоминать друг другу социальные, экономические и технические следствия этого процесса? Стоит потому, что подавляющее большинство учёных и философов-*эпистемологов* и сегодня воспринимает все эти впечатляющие следствия как *подтверждение практикой* полной победы логики дискурса над логикой, претендовавшей на разрешение не текстуальных, а бытийных *противоречий*, да ещё с помощью пресловутого *диалектического* мышления.

Тут, видимо, следует обратиться к Францу Брентано. Мне кажется, нельзя не согласиться с львовским философом и логиком Янушем Саноцкиим[7] в том, что Брентано не был понят даже последователями, в частности – Э.Гуссерлем, как и другими *неоклассиками* XX века. На мой взгляд, смелая попытка Брентано найти *интенциональное* обоснование логики в исходном тождестве субъективной мотивации всех актов человеческой жизнедеятельности с надындивидуально-индивидуальной реальностью смысла понятий, с реальностью инвариантов логического следования из суждений (высказываний) была, как ни покажется сие странным, ближе к не менее смело постулированию Спинозой субстанциального тождества атрибутов протяженности и мышления и к немецким классикам – к исторически ищущему себя тождеству мышления и бытия, чем к банальному психологизму.

Но именно психологизм увидели логики начала века в стремлении Брентано преодолеть и в логике картезианское располюсование субъективности и объективности. То есть, ничего кроме попытки обосновать логические формы и приёмы мысли (явно надындивидуально «объективные»)… *неупорядоченностью психической жизни индивидов!* Первую отповедь Брентано получил от Фреге. Это была жёсткая защита логики, её аподиктической атрибутивности, от… *ветряных мельниц.* Ибо Брентано и сам понимал формы логики как единую, строгую и не зависимую от произвола случайных эмоций… *субъективную* реальность; и именно потому она для него ниоткуда не могла возникнуть, кроме как из сплава *объективно-внешнего* содержания психических актов (процессов) с их импульсной интенцией… на других *нацеленного* переживания. Но это как раз и значит, что одно здесь не может определять другое. Это значит, что одно не может быть без другого, ибо *психологическая интенция всегда адресована.* То есть, реализуется (становится реальной и для субъекта) овнешняясь, объективируясь, опредмечиваясь. Развить мысль Брентано стоило бы так: онтологию логики не ищите в бесчувственном мире простирающих и длящих себя вещей; не ищите её и в мире индивидуальных переживаний человеком состояния его собственных нервов (в чём вы видите онтологию психики), а ищите её в исходной, изначальной и неизбывной адрессованности актов пространственно-временного овнешнения для себя и других своих субъективных интенций.

Похоже ли это на попытку психологического обоснования логических форм мысли? Да, если заранее интенциональность каждого акта жизнедеятельности человека считать психологически и только психологически определённой бессознательным, предсознанием и, вообще, чем-то из непознаваемых глубин устремлённым наружу. Нет, не похоже, если понять, что внутренний мир человека – мир смысла, мир аффектов – это перманентное проживание своего тождества с со смыслами и аффектами единственного доступного нам внешнего мира – мира живой культуры общения людей, вовлекшей в себя Вселенную.

Но и до сих пор логики ищут *онтологические предпосылки* логики в чём-то подобном «предустановленной гармонии» разных миров – психических актов и реалий объективного мира… Наш выдающийся логик В.А.Смирнов не раз писал о том, что этот поиск – дело философии.[8] Убеждён, что именно Э.В.Ильенков (его друг между прочим), занимаясь этим делом всю жизнь, нашёл и реально обосновал эти предпосылки. Но остался не понятым так же, как и Брентано.

Так что же такое – диалектическая логика?

Вне истории культуры духовной жизни поколений нельзя понять ни одной психологической интенции индивида. Как нельзя понять ни одного акта, формирующего и воспроизводящего духовную культуру поколений, вне истории их духовно-практической деятельности – общественной, социальной, политической, с необходимостью включающей в себя и деятельность, расширенно воспроизводящую средства и способы самой их физической жизни.[9] Нерасчленимый атом духовно-практического бытия людей – это не что иное, как сохраняющее и изменяющее их жизнь *обращение* друг к другу и к себе самим. Субъективно целеустремлённое обращение к субъективности друг друга.

Его принципиально нельзя отождествлять с текстом, как посредником между душой и миром: хотя обращение, как и текст, изначально *субъект-объектно*, однако лишь потому и текст обладает столь реальной *идеальностью*, что в нём овнешненно и воплощено (от слова *плоть*) *обращение*. Обращение интенционально по определению; его невозможно отделить как от субъективной целевой мотивации (с любым текстом такая операция отделения производится постоянно), так и от внешне предметных *всеобщих* способов и средств живой триединой речи: вербальной, музыкальной, изобразительной. Это следует пояснить.

Обращение – это речь, речь вербальная, музыкальная, изобразительная. Это акт креативного преобразования образов смыслочувствия. Текст – его результат, его продукт, представленный языковыми знаками, упакованный в смысловую или эмоциональную форму грамматическими и логическими правилами, эстетическими канонами, математическими законами временных и пространственных мер мира. Процесс творения жив в обращении, в тексте он погашен. Правда, до тех пор, пока текст поверяется как таковой на предмет его соответствия «требованиям его же жанра». Как только текст заговорит голосом читающего (слышащего, видящего его пластическую форму), то он тут же приобретает свою исходную ипостась, становясь живым эмоционально смысловым обращением автора к воспринимающему его субъекту. Недаром М.М.Бахтин (и не только он) видел во втором соавтора первого.[10]

Только приобретая внешнюю свою ипостась – становясь звучащим или написанным словом, звучащей музыкальной фразой, зримым или слышимым символом и знаком, изображением, скульптурой, архитектурной формой строений, селений и городов, математической или логической формулой... словом, вещью, объективно внешней для всех и для всех тут же внутренне субъективно переживаемой, эта самая *субъективность* интенции обращения *находит себя*... в себе и тем «удваивается»: становится для субъекта обращения актом переживания своего «Я». Она не существует даже для него, не быв овнешнённой в виде образа на Кантовом априорном пространстве ожидаемого восприятия или в форме «про себя» пропеваемого звука, проговариваемого текста и т.п. Без чего не существует у субъекта даже позыва к той или иной интенции, не существует и самого его внутреннего мира – самой его психики. И, напротив, вне перманентно рождаемой в переживании противоречий смыслообразов внешнего мира, а, тем самым, и сугубо интимной психической интенции (мотива, цели, воли и т.п.), не возможно обращение urbi et orbi как её, интенции, овнешнение, не возможно её превращение в «вещь-для-всех». Это даже не слитность субъективного и объективного, как в тексте. Это – акт рождения в человеке осознаваемого объективного мира, а главное – это акт рождения реально-идеальной сути его тождества со своим родом – с человечеством.

К этому и шёл всю свою творческую жизнь Эвальд Ильенков. Действительно, если мышление как *преображающее понимание* мира оперирует эмоциональными смыслообразами этого мира, овнешнённо запечатлёнными в *творениях триединой речи*, обращённой людьми друг к другу и к себе самим, создающей, сохраняющей и вновь преображающей их изначальную общность, то всеобщие (общие для всех) способы, какими достигается сия цель, приобретают в мышлении функцию уже его, мышления, фундаментальных категорий.[11] Поэтому *понять* мышление *в развитии его содержания* (а только так его и можно *принять* как понятие самого себя) возможно лишь реконструкцией истории возникновения и укоренения в духовно-практической деятельности людей *всеобщих, духовно преображённых способов* их отношения друг к другу, к менталитету и форме своих общностей, а через них – и к объективным условиям, средствам и формам их физического существования, к преображаемой их трудом природе.[12] Это работа непосредственно в материале и с материалом.

Обращение Э.В.Ильенкова к категориям абстрактного и конкретного в «Капитале» Маркса – первый продуктивный его шаг в том же направлении. Столь же трудно переоценить значение целого ряда его блестящих работ эстетического цикла, в которых он писал о категории *воображение*. Но я об этом уже не раз писал.[13] Серия его фундаментальных статей об *идеальном* как категории отождествляющего себя с миром мышления и по сей день служит обоснованием *онтологических предпосылок* символической логики прежде всего потому, что проясненной реальностью *идеального* она снимает не только картезианское располюсование *протяжённости* (и дления) тел вещного мира и *душевной духовности* человеческого бытия, но и неоклассическое противопоставление объективно строгой логике текста её же субъективной (мыслительной) природе.

Нет, у Э.В.Ильенкова не психологией готовилось онтологическое обоснование логики! Он, как и Ф.Брентано, не намеревался найти его в душе одинокого *внемирного* человека. Но и не искал его в «тварном» и «товарном» мире злых, завистливых и трусливых страстей людских, разрушающих людскую общность как само основание человеческого бытия. Напротив, он всё творческое время своё посвятил исследованию противоречивого процесса становления и восстановления тождества человека со своим родом – с тем, что в каждом из нас оживает, гаснет и снова живёт всеобщим смыслом, всеобщими аффектами добра, истины и красоты. Тождество противоположностей – всеобщий принцип этого смысла, творящий каждую категорию преображающего и тем самым понимающего мир мышления. Потому и логика его – логика диалектическая, логика мысленного и творческого разрешения противоречий, но не речи, а бытия.

Так понятая логика – логика противоречия в смыслах бытия, не имеет другой претензии, кроме той, которую как свою функцию она осуществляет исторически: быть способом и формой предметно-содеражательного, *воображающего* (творческого!) мышления, способного... нет, не в противо-*речениях* исключающих друг друга «высказываниях о...», а в выявляемых формах реальной, бытийной саморазорванности и самоотрицании жизни человека в равнодушном к нему мире. И, тем самым, она была и остаётся отнюдь не логикой математического *упорядочивания текста*, даже в том случае, когда таковое обеспечивает смысловые прорывы в неведомое.[14] Здесь – царство логики математической, хотя между двумя этими «логиками» нет стены: мысль, открывшая в *процессе* самопреобразования своих смыслов новый (!) способ постижения тождества противоположностей, «работая» с со смыслообразами как *заготовками* текста, только тогда и становится ясной самому мыслящему, когда выливается в связный и упорядоченный текст, давая работу так называемой формальной логике.

Ссылки

[1] Московский государственный институт международных отношений.

[2] Риккерт 1998, 106–108. Здесь берёт начало (или получает второе дыхание) определение предмета *строгого* мышления как «идеализированного» предмета или «объекта», утвердившееся в философском осмыслении основания современной логики. Той самой, формальной, сиречь – математической.

[3] Там же, 184.

[4] Там же, 109.

[5] Правда, новой её можно считать лишь благодаря продуктивности и эвристичности мощных средств и методов её саморазвития. Предмет и задачи остались прежними. В связи с этим стоит напомнить, что именно на пути её саморазвития рождались те рефлексивные способы алгоритмизации логических средств мышления, которые обернулись в том числе и глобальной компьютеризацией *всех видов* рутинной и творческой деятельности человечества.

[6] Уоддингтон 1970, 17.

[7] Я. Саноцкий перевёл и опубликовал со своими комментариями в журнале «Вопросы философии» ряд неизвестных у нас работ Брентано. Блестяще защищённая им в июне этого года в Институте философии РАН диссертация детально и убедительно обосновывает нетривиальные выводы его исследования творчества Ф.Брентано.

[8] Более подробно см. мою статью (Михайлов 1998 б).

[9] Так же и с той же необходимостью включающей в себя общественную, социальную и политическую их жизнь.

[10] Беда всех ступеней школы, унаследовавшей чуть ли не средневековую интенцию к забиванию памяти учащихся именно текстами, как раз и прежде всего в том, что ни дети в средней школе, ни студенты в большинстве высших не овладевают способностью к живой речи, обращённой к ним, а потому и требующей живого, здесь и теперь рождаемого ответа. Это равно относится и к словесному творчеству, и к математике, и к физике и ко всем учебным предметам, не столько задаваемым, сколько даваемым в виде готовых чужих текстов. Потому и получают все учащиеся готовые ответы, на вопросы, которые у них самих не возникали.

[11] Начиная от Аристотелевых: качество, количество, причинение, претерпевания и т.д., через гегелевские категории бытия, рефлексивные категории сущности и т.д., и кончая категориями рода, семьи, народа, производства, войны, мира, бунта, культуры, творчества и т.д.

[12] Независимо от философской ориентации в XX веке такая работа была весьма плодотворной: структуралисты, постструктуралисты, герменевтики,

историки культуры… У нас – А.Ф.Лосев, М.М.Бахтин, А.Я.Гуревич, М.М.Лотман, А.А.Аверинцев, Л.М.Баткин и мн. др.

[13] См. Михайлов 1997, 115–138, Михайлов 1999, 28–73.

[14] Причины таких прорывов в *кентаврической* природе предмета теории, в этих текстах запечатлённой. О ней я писал и в книгах Михайлов 1990 и Михайлов 1998 а (часть 1), и ряде других работ.

Литература

Михайлов, Ф. Т. (1990), *Самосознание индивида и общественное сознание.* М., «Наука»

Михайлов Ф.Т. (1997), *Он сам – целая школа.* В кн.: *Драма советской философии. Эвальд Васильевич Ильенков.* М., ИФРАН, 115–138.

Михайлов, Ф. Т. (1998)(=1998 а), *Самосознание: моё и наше,* М., ИФРАН.

Михайлов, Ф. Т. (1998 б), *Почти полвека длился спор...* В ж. *Вопросы философии* № 2, 1998.

Михайлов, Ф. Т. (1999), *Воображение – главная сила души человека.* В кн. *Э.В.Ильенков: личность и творчество.* М., «Языки русской культуры», 28–73.

Риккерт, Генрих (1998), *Философия жизни.* Киев: «Ника-Центр», «Вист-С».

Уоддингтон К.Х. (1970), *Основные биологические концепции.* В кн. *На пути к теоретической биологии.* М.

5

EVALD ILYENKOV AND SOVIET PHILOSOPHICALCULTURE

EVERT VAN DER ZWEERDE

Introductory Remarks

In this paper[1], I want to return to a topic that may seem to have lost its relevance: Soviet philosophy. A thing of the past, a thing, moreover, that nobody really liked anyway. I am not returning to it because I liked it, but because likes and dislikes, though certainly to be be taken seriously, should not guide our scholarly work, and also because a discussion of Soviet philosophical culture adds an important complementary perspective to a discussion of Evald Ilyenkov.

In fact, three different, but not mutually exclusive perspectives on a historical figure like Ilyenkov can be adopted. First of all, on the level of philosophical ideas and theories proper, one can be interested in Ilyenkov as a possible source of inspiration and of valuable insights, accessible through any of his texts; on this level, the question whether one is addressing "the real Ilyenkov" or "the whole Ilyenkov" is irrelevant, if only because we know that many philosophical positions have originated from a questionable interpretation of an earlier position. On a second level, one can be interested in Ilyenkov in his entirety, as a thinker or theoretician, accessible to us through the aggregate of his published, written, spoken, and reported texts; here we are indeed interested in the question about "the real Ilyenkov", despite the many difficulties of textual and hermeneutic nature that may confront us, if only because we know that tracking down the complexities and inconsistencies of a philosopher's thought can improve our insight in philosophy as such, and throw light even on questions and problems that were hidden to Ilyenkov himself. On a third level, finally, one can be interested in the historical development of philosophy, and here one has to concentrate not only on the text, but also on the context of his philosophical activity, on the historical background, the cultural, political, social, and economic circumstances. It is on this third level that I shall, for the present purpose, concentrate.

My contribution to this symposium, therefore, is an attempt to reconstruct the context within which Ilyenkov's philosophical endeavour can be situated. My aim is to *neither* reduce his philosophical importance to his "being part of Soviet philosophy", *nor* disregard this fact as irrelevant, but to move between the Scylla of reductionism and the Charybdis of "philosophism", and to do justice both to the "nature" of philosophy and to the way in which philosophy exists in historical time, in social, political, and economic reality. Generally speaking, my claim is that the context in which philosophers think, work, and write, is not something external to their intellectual activity, but intrinsically bound up with it, whether or not they themselves address this bond, or are even aware of it.

Two aspects of the current situation urge me to bring this topic to the fore. One is that the end of Soviet philosophy and of its confrontation with Western philosophy means a liberation of the philosophical thought, theories, and ideas developed by philosophers in the USSR. Ilyenkov is certainly among those who deserve the renewed attention of the globalizing philosophical culture that we live in. Through the works of those few people in the West who seriously studied his philosophical heritage, as well as through translations into Western languages of a number of his works, Ilyenkov is in principle accessible.[2] Further, one may expect contemporary Russian philosophers to investigate as well as to revive and develop the philosophical "school" or "schools" founded by Ilyenkov.[3] Conferences like the present one, finally, will resuscitate interest and, possibly, reopen discussions that may seem closed.

On the other hand, the end of Soviet philosophy also means a liberation of historical study and comparative analysis of Soviet philosophical culture as it actually existed. This topic, too, deserves our serious attention. After all, whether we regard Soviet philosophy as a degeneration of Marxism, as a case of philosophy under totalitarian control, as mere ideology, as a modern form of scholasticism in the pejorative sense of that term, or, as I would suggest, a highly complex phenomenon to which these definitions and others apply, it remains, one way or another, an important episode in the historical development of philosophy, comparable to other episodes in many of its features, but unique in their combination.[4] To study and to understand it, however, means not simply to read Central Committee resolutions or to find out who was a KGB-officer at the *Filosofskii fakultet* of Moscow State University. Rather it means to study Soviet philosophical culture as a whole and in its concrete complexity, which includes such questions as what kind of difference it makes for the activity of professional philosophers that there is a latest statement on philosophy by the Central Committee or that there is a KGB-informer present at every department meeting.

With respect to both aspects just indicated, there is a tendency to disconnect them. This tendency, which can be summarized in the slogan "Let's finally do philosophy and forget about politics and ideology!" is natural, understandable, and to a certain degree justified. However, it fails to understand not only Soviet philosophy, but philosophy in general, if it boils down to an abstract distinction between the philosophical work done by, in the case at hand: Ilyenkov, and the philosophical culture in which this work was done: Soviet philosophical culture. This distinction corresponds, to an extent, to the nature of philosophical thought itself, but it also matches interests and desires that can be gathered under the heading of "depolitization". It is both easier and more pleasant to create a dichotomy between good philosophers and bad *apparatchiki*, and do away with the latter, along with everything Soviet, as "unfavorable circumstances for philosophy". In my opinion, however, this is a limited and mistaken perception, and we should perform a double move of both contextualization and decontextualization, as well as, in a third move, realize that in the case of living philosophical thought, i.e. in the case of a philosophical life like Ilyenkov's, the distinction of text and context is highly abstract. Every philosopher is part of a concrete situation which she or he not only experiences, endures, and reflects upon, but also creates, reproduces, and criticizes. This applies no less to Soviet philosophers than to their non-Soviet colleagues.

In this paper, I want first to discuss the notion of philosophical culture as the place of philosophy, focussing on its relation to the political. In the second part, I shall give a concise analysis of Soviet philosophical culture. In the third part I will use this analysis to situate the figure of Ilyenkov, as well as illustrate my analysis with the example offered by his case.

The Political in Philosophical Culture[5]

The question "What is philosophy?" has been a fundamental question in
philosophy since its very beginning, but only the 20th century has seen the
development of a separate discipline called meta-philosophy, simultaneously in Western philosophy, with the journal *Metaphilosophy* appearing since
1970, and in Soviet philosophy, with the beginning of meta-philosophical
reflection in 1969.[6]

"What is...?"-questions are typically philosophical questions: the
question "What is archaeology?" is a philosophical question, not an
archaeological question, whereas the question "What is philosophy?" is a
philosophical question, too, and arguably the first philosophical question.
Meta-archaeology is part of philosophy, in fact of philosophy of science, but
meta-philosophy is part of philosophy, too. The question "What is
archaeology?" has an empirical, descriptive, as well as a normative,
prescriptive aspect to it. The question "What is philosophy?" also has an
empirical and a normative aspect to it, but in addition it has a third, reflexive
aspect.[7]

Strangely enough, however, meta-philosophical reflection is very often
limited to this third aspect. The *philosophie spontanée des philosophes*, to
make a variation on Althusser's *philosophie spontanée des savants*, can be
qualified as "philosophism," i.e. a tendency to deny everything non-
philosophical, to draw a clear line between the philosophical properly speaking
on the one hand, and everything ideological, economic, and political on the
other, expelling in fact the second category from the domain of philosophy.[8]

The world that we live and think in, however, does not correspond to
these divisions. Althusser's once famous thesis that philosophy is, in the
final analysis, "class-struggle on the level of theory" now appears as an
outdated formula, since few philosophers think in terms of class-struggle.[9]
But the reference to class-struggle should not be confused with an element of
the thesis that remains important, viz. that philosophy always is related, in a
philosophically relevant way, to "the political". With "the political" I refer
not to "politics," but to a basic fact of human society, namely the existence of
asymmetric relations of power that are not facts of nature, but stem from
decisions by human beings – "politics," by contrast, is the variety of ways
and forms in which human beings try to organize and "deal with" this
fundamental fact.[10] Rather than claiming that the political is what philosophy
"in the final analysis" is about, I want to stress that, whatever else it is,
philosophy is never politically neutral, i.e. that it is always related to
asymmetric relations of power and conflict, *and* that this fact should be part

of meta-philosophical reflexion. "The political" is related to the general feature of reality that whenever something is posited, manifests itself, or is stated, something else is excluded, and that to the extent to which this is the result of human action, this exclusion can be questioned. Consequently, every (meta-)philosophical statement or thesis is not (only) a description of a state of affairs, but also a decision which excludes other realities or possibilities.

Everything is political, but nothing is merely political. Philosophy is political because it is an activity of finite human individuals that takes place in society, and that is subject to practical decisions, asymmetrical relations of power, and mechanisms of inclusion and exclusion. Philosophy takes place within the world philosophers live in, even though they may think it does not, and this world is, among others, the result of decisions of a political nature.

Further, philosophy is political in the sense that philosophical theories, esp. when they are inclined to universal statements, are suitable elements of ideology, which I define as a possible function of any theory to motivate the commitment and action of social groups, and to legitimize a specific status quo, a purpose which this theory can serve, irrespective of whether the theoretical claims are true, false, or indeterminate in truth-value.[11]

Finally, philosophy is "political" in another, more fundamental sense. Every philosophical position is, in the end, founded in a decision to adopt or not to adopt a principle, an a priori, an axiom as fundamental, to regard or not to regard a fact, an event, a personal experience as crucial, to treat or not to treat an opposition, a transition, a dichotomy as decisive. These decision are "political" since they have to do with primordial non-self-evident choices that presuppose and exclude an opposite possibility. If we agree that truth, with the possible exception of purely formal truths, is not manifest, we should also acknowledge that every alleged truth presupposes a decision which is not self-evident philosophically, however self-evident it may be on a personal level or within a scientific paradigm. Stress on this aspect is justified as it tends to be underestimated and understated. (At other times it has been overstated, e.g. in Soviet *kritika sovremennoi burzhuaznoi filosofii*, the highly politicized "critique" of non-Soviet philosophy.)

This embedding of philosophical thought in concrete reality contrasts with another, no less important, aspect of philosophical thought, namely the fact that, unlike scientific thought, it is radically free. Philosophy is free with respect both to its form and to its content, which further implies that it is indeterminate with respect to its function.

a) Concerning *form*, philosophy differs from other types of intellectual human activity in that it is not a priori bound to any particular form: philosophy can take both a literal and a verbal form, it can choose any literary genre, and it can also be performative, the most well-known examples being the *kunikoi* of Greek Antiquity and the Russian *iurodivye* [Fools in God]. The fact that certain forms, esp. relatively strict forms such as *summa*, treatise, or "system", have dominated historically, may give reason to think that these forms are particularly appropriate, but this is countered by the nostalgic desire for more directly appealing forms such as the dialogue, the "meditation", or the polemical essay. *Which* forms philosophy actually takes and how this changes, synchronically, from one philosophical culture to another (including different positions within that culture), and, diachronically, from one historical period to another, is an important subject for metaphilosophical reflexion, but can never provide an argument for any particular choice. As a result, the "temptation" to use other forms is a permanent element of every philosophical culture.

Thus the sudden transition from Soviet to post-Soviet philosophical culture, i.e. the instability of philosophical culture in Russia in the late 1980s, manifested itself among others in a shift from the impersonal, dry style that was typical of the "planned production" of philosophical texts in the Soviet period, to a much more free and personal essay-like genre, in which the standards of not only Soviet, but also Western academic philosophical text-production were transgressed.[12] In fact, forms that were widespread in philosophical counter-culture emerged as the dominant forms, exemplified by such authors as Merab K. Mamardashvili, Vladimir S. Bibler, or Grigorii S. Pomerants.[13] Of course, one can argue that the only criterium is that philosophy is the expression of thought, but expression can range from explicit formulation to implicit suggestion, the constant element being thought, not the way it is expressed.

b) With respect to its *content*, i.e. to the "what" of philosophy, freedom is even greater. Any philosophical statement can be confronted with questions and doubts concerning its implications and presuppositions, and these questions and doubts can in turn give rise to new statements, to which the same applies. With respect to any philosophical statement, the number of alternatives is larger than one, which implies the existence of an infinite field of possibilities. For example, if one philosopher holds that reality is made up of two different substances, this opens the possibility of claiming any other number of substances, from one to infinite, as well as the possibility of questioning the very notion of substance. Which on purely logical grounds means that with respect to the notion of substance alone, the number of possible philosophical positions is infinite.

Surely, philosophers will usually employ a selection criterion which says that only those positions are to be taken seriously which "make sense." But the fact that other cultures and other periods have seen the development of positions that clearly no longer make sense to us, e.g. the development in Neo-Platonism of positions that gave different numbers of emanations from the World-Soul, shows that this cannot be an a priori criterion. Nor can the exclusion of certain claims and positions because they are thought to belong to another realm, such as science, art, or religion. The claim that certain types of statement are *not* to be regarded as philosophical because they fall within the competence of science is either a statement of fact or itself a philosophical claim, and in neither case a priori given. Paul Feyerabend's "Anything goes!" may or may not apply to science, but it certainly applies to philosophy.

c) The *function* of philosophy, finally, is indeterminate and unpredictable, and fundamentally beyond the control of philosophers. Could Karl Marx have foreseen the role that his notion of a specifically "asiatic mode of production" would play in disputes between Soviet and Chinese communists after 1949, or could Karl Popper have predicted the function of his concept of "open society" in the current economic support of Russian academics by George Soros? If meaning is use, then the actual function of philosophical theories and concepts does not depend on the significance ascribed to them by their originators, i.e. they have an independent existence. If meaning is not reducible to use, then we should at least distinguish between different functions, uses and abuses. There is nothing "wrong" with this, but to fail to recognize these aspects of philosophical culture is to idealize philosophy and to introduce an abstract distinction between the proper and the improper, the pure and the impure.

Philosophical thought, because it is radically free in both its form and its content, is potentially subversive in its function, and hence presents a danger to any established order. This point, the exemplary demonstration of which remains the case of Socrates, cannot be taken too seriously, not so much because all philosophers should think of themselves as potential anarchist revolutionaries, but because not to see this point is to fail to understand an important aspect of philosophical culture, namely the *control* of this potential danger. This control can come from the outside, in the form of censorship or permanent surveillance, it can also come from within, and as a rule these two directions will coexist and cooperate. If these mechanisms are in place, and working "properly", they protect philosophical culture from external intervention while disciplining it internally: Soviet philosophical culture – and the Soviet *kollektiv* in general – offers a clear example of this "disciplinary effect" of philosophical culture, but similar mechanisms are at work in Western academic philosophical culture.[14]

In fact, philosophy as a discipline, a subject, a profession only exists to the extent to which disciplining mechanisms are in place. If a student enters a philosophical faculty (any philosophical faculty, from Plato's Academy to

MGU's *filosofskii fakultet*), she or he faces a series of decisions: to accept and adopt, or not to accept and adopt certain rules of the game and tricks of the trade, to accept and adore, or not to accept and adore, certain professors as exemplary "genuine philosophers", to accept and admire, or not to accept and admire, certain philosophical texts as paradigmatic or classical. If this student does not identify with these instruments of discipline, she or he is forced to either quit the discipline altogether, or to join the sub- and counterculture which accompanies most philosophical establishments (and where changes in dominant culture as a rule are prepared).

At the same time, philosophical cultures can differ greatly in the extent to which they allow for variety and change. Professional philosophers in Western philosophical culture are generally too much accustomed to their situation of "academic freedom" to realize how strongly the free development of philosophy, i.e. its development according to, on the one hand, the inner logic of its problems and questions and, on the other hand, the ways in which philosophers relate to topics and events occurring in society and culture at large, depends upon the stability and freedom that characterizes the situation in which they work. Such a relatively stable situation in which philosophical thought can exist and develop, be taught and learned, and be studied from a historical perspective, is precisely "philosophical culture".

Philosophical culture thus is where philosophy takes place. A place is a particular part of space, distinct from other parts. Like any place, philosophical culture has borders, size, and a number of qualities that make it a good or bad place for philosophy. But unlike physical places – a room, a building, a country – these borders, sizes, and qualities are themselves of a discursive nature. They have to be stated, defined, confirmed, and they can be questioned, redefined, and violated in meta-philosophical discourse.

A central notion in this respect is the notion of "normality". Very often, the "normal" is identified with an actual state of affairs, which means to raise a fact into a norm. When, however, we use "normal" in a stronger sense, i.e. that of corresponding to a norm, it becomes a critical notion, allowing us to say that philosophical culture is "normal" to the extent to which it corresponds to the *nature* of philosophy. And if that nature is to be free in the sense of self-determining with respect to form and content, as well as in the sense of being indeterminate with respect to its function, a philosophical culture can be said to be normal to the extent to which it allows for philosophers to develop their thought in unlimited freedom as regards content and form, and without any possible function being beforehand prescribed or excluded.

From this definition of normality, it is immediately clear that no empirically existing philosophical culture will ever be fully "normal". In other words: we are necessarily speaking in terms of level, extent, and attempt, and of critique, adaptation, and normalization. To employ a notion of "normality" means to locate the norm of philosophical culture in the "nature" of philosophy itself, and neither in any actually existing philosophical culture, nor in the subjective preferences of philosophers.

Freedom of thought is important for philosophy and part of its normative conditions, not because philosophers like to say what they want and are entitled to that liberty, but because they can only do their job properly under such conditions. It is important to continue to ask the question about the quality or level of philosophical culture, not only, but also with respect to Soviet philosophical culture, and to ask about right and wrong, normal and abnormal not only from a moral, but also from a professionalist point of view: the perspective of what is "good for philosophy." To say that Soviet philosophical culture was not "good for philosophy" is a true statement, but it does not tell us very much, unless we specify in which ways and to which extent it was "bad for philosophy."

2. Ideology and Philosophy: Soviet Philosophical Culture

Soviet philosophical culture was *unique* in being explicitly related to an ideology which functioned as the legitimatization of a "totalitarian" social and political system. In this sense, one can say that the subordination of philosophy to its ideological function – in principle and in general, not in every detail – is what defined Soviet philosophy, and what made it an integral part of the "system".

In 1998, a two-volume book appeared with the title *Filosofiia ne konchaetsia...*, largely a collection of articles published earlier in *Voprosy filosofii*. As the editor-in-chief, Vladislav Lektorskii, states in the introduction to the first volume, it is difficult to understand "how philosophy was possible under conditions of total repression of creative freedom."[15] Three solutions to this puzzle suggest themselves: a) philosophy is not possible under such conditions and hence there was no philosophy in the Soviet Union; b) "total repression of creative freedom" was not the actual situation in the USSR; c) contrary to a widespread meta-philosophical conviction, philosophy does not require creative freedom in order to exist. In my view, each of these three possibilities contains some truth.

a) There still exists a widespread view, among professional philosophers in the West and in the ex-USSR, that there was no genuine philosophical thought at all in the USSR. The fact that this opinion is mistaken is not what is interesting about it. What is important is that the "story" that Soviet philosophy told and displayed about itself, the "image" it generated of a large collective of philosophical *apparatchiki* steadily elaborating and improving, under the guidance of such figures as F.V. Konstantinov, M.B. Mitin, and P.N. Fedoseev, a once and for all true system of dialectical and historical materialism, was so effective that it can rightly be called an ideology of Soviet philosophy which inwardly served to discipline philosophers who, in one way or another, were not willing to suit the role-model, and outwardly to discredit Soviet philosophy in the eyes of most of their colleagues.[16]

Soviet philosophical culture was dominated by an official philosophy that left little room for alternative positions or schools. Instead of priding itself with a figure like Ilyenkov, the *filosofskii fakultet* of MGU chased him away – imagine the university of Helsinki ostracizing Jaakko Hintikka for not being an orthodox Wittgensteinian-Russellian! At the same time, Ilyenkov continued to work, as did so many others, within the institutional framework of Soviet philosophical culture, many of his works were published, and he did exert considerable influence on philosophers, psychologists, and pedagogues.

b) Total repression of creative freedom indeed was not the situation in the USSR: as in many other fields, the "system" was much more oriented towards the prevention of phenomena and developments that would have to be repressed, than towards repression itself. The freedom of creative work in philosophy was limited but real, restricted but sometimes considerable. Total freedom would have undermined the Soviet system, as it would gnaw at its ideological legitimization, but total repression of freedom would have rendered impossible the development, refinement, and adaptation to new circumstances of a "progressively more coherent and consistent, more believable and teachable" ideology.[17]

The period of the "thaw", the *ottepel* had demonstrated the unstable balance of dogma and development. The philosophical establishment explicitly took the decision "to do philosophy", but as Bernard Jeu rightly stated: "...si on a pris la décision de philosopher, il faut aller jusqu'au bout. On ne peut pas prévoir toutes les conséquences qui en résulteront dans le développement du contenu de la pensée. Problèmes et réponses vont inéluctablement s'enchaîner."[18] But to go "jusqu'au bout" of philosophical argument was the last thing the Soviet system would allow for, relying as it did ideologically on the dogmatic solution of a number of philosophical problems at the core of Marxism.

c) Finally, in order to exist philosophical culture does not necessarily presuppose total freedom of thought, discussion, publication. As several people have shown, philosophical culture was preserved to a considerable extent through intensive teaching of and research into the history of philosophy: so-called *istoriko-filosofskaia nauka* served as a niche for creative work in philosophy: "…in times that were hard for our philosophy, some of my colleagues still managed to survive as philosophers. They were forced to find themselves some 'ecological niches' (for example, in history of philosophy, in logic, etc.) and to continue their work staying within them."[19] At the same time, it must be recognized that this solution was second best only, and that in order to deploy its potential, a philosophical culture needs more freedom of expression, discussion, and development than was granted to it by Soviet reality.

The best way to understand Soviet philosophy is in terms of its function, being the aspect which, in the end, determined its development and "fate". The latter can be aptly caught with the word stagnation: apart from social, economic and political factors which made the system stop working, there were two factors within Soviet philosophical culture which account for its stagnation. On the one hand, there was a requirement of permanent development of philosophical theory, i.e. of the *content* of philosophical culture, but on the other hand there was the requirement that this developing theory should remain a development of Marxist-Leninist philosophy, i.e. of a dogmatic system performing, first and foremost, an ideological *function*. The tension between these two requirements is reflected in the *form* of most Soviet philosophical production: quasi-endless repetition of the same definitions and quotes, minute changes in position, ritual incantation of the *klassiki marksizma-leninizma*, or playing off one *klassik* against the other in order to back slight changes in philosophical position; to study Soviet philosophical texts indeed required the "infinite capacity for dulness and the ability to sustain one's attention in the face of repetition, nonsense, distortion, prosaic style, and banality after banality" that Richard T. De George pointed to.[20]

So, Soviet philosophical culture was "bad for philosophy" and "abnormal" in the sense of not corresponding to the nature of philosophical thought in several ways:

i) The subordination of philosophy to its ideological function of providing the theoretical foundation of an official ideology both made necessary and justified direct political intervention as well as the more indirect control through "party-philosophers," the prototype of which was provided by the "bolshevizators" Mark B. Mitin and Pavel F. Iudin, who resolved philosophical controversy in the name of orthodox Marxism-Leninism in 1931.[21]

ii) The dogmatic resolution of the "basic question" of philosophy as inherited from Engels, and the creation, on this foundation, of a "system" of dialectical and historical materialism which, despite its intellectual poverty and its philosophical contradictoriness, effectively occupied the place of the central philosophical disciplines of epistemology and metaphysics, and seriously hampered development of these fields.

iii) The creation of an ideology of Soviet philosophy, which, by representing Soviet philosophy as a collective attempt at a simultaneously scientific and partisan [*partiinaia*] system of philosophical disciplines, served to discipline Soviet philosophical culture inwardly as well as to defend it against bourgeois or revisionist influences, thus limiting the development of philosophical thought according to its inner logic.

iv) The separation of philosophical "doctrine" [*uchenie*] as taught at institutions of higher education, so-called *vuzovskaia filosofiia*, from the research conducted within the realm of *akademicheskaia filosofiia*, i.e., most of all, at the Institute of Philosophy of the Academy of Sciences, which both contributed to a public image of philosophy as something utterly dogmatic and "boring" – *skuchnyi predmet* – and to the tendential isolation of philosophical research from education and society.

v) The effective isolation of Soviet philosophical culture from the international philosophical scene, even, to a large extent, from non-Soviet Marxist philosophical circles through delegation and publication policies based on loyalty and privilege rather than on intellectual qualifications.

The case of Evald Ilyenkov

What can the case of Ilyenkov tell us about Soviet philosophical culture, and which light can the reality of that culture throw on Ilyenkov's position and influence? At least four elements deserve to be mentioned:

a) To begin with, one of the remarkable, though unsurprising, features of Soviet philosophical culture was the absence of *critical* social and political philosophy. There was development in related fields such as philosophy of culture and philosophy of history, but not in social and political philosophy proper. The "wedding of centralized political control to a system of philosophy with claims to universality," to quote Loren Graham, resulted, among many other things, in a radical pseudo-politization of philosophy, namely in the eradication of the political from philosophy, and thus in its effective depolitization.[22]

The so-called "critical Marxists", of which Ilyenkov was one, disposed of a powerful instrument for the analysis of social and political reality, namely Marxism itself, especially after they got acquainted with "the whole Marx."[23]

Even if his own interest clearly was more in the field of logic, methodology, and philosophy of science, language, and mind, the possibility of an extension in the direction of social and political philosophy was, to say the least, obvious, and it is unlikely that he failed to see this possibility. The fact that the did not, at least not in publications, turn Marx directly against the reality legitimized by "Marxism-Leninism" in ways similar to those of "intellectual Marxists" in Poland or Yugoslavia, remains a remarkable fact, explicable not only, it seems to me, as a result of censorship or control, but also as a result from Ilyenkov's loyalty to the Soviet system or, perhaps more adequately, to the idea of a society that "real existing socialism" was the imperfect realization of.

The "convinced Marxist and communist" Ilyenkov set out to apply historical materialism to Soviet reality, but in a constructive rather than critical manner.[24] As Aleksandr F. Zamaleev writes in his *Kurs istorii russkoi filosofii*: "In a whole series of works, such as *Gegel' i 'otchuzhdenie'* [Hegel and Alienation], *Chto zhe takoe lichnost?* [What is the Person?], *Kosmologiia dukha* [Cosmology of Spirit] and others, he consistently defended the thesis that alienation is in no way a 'local', i.e. specifically capitalist problem, 'it is, he wrote, a world-historical problem, which world history has not yet practically resolved'."[25] His *Marks i zapadnyi mir* [Marx and the Western World] was published in English in 1967, but could not appear in the USSR until 1988, due to its "anti-Marxist nature".[26]

By stressing the Western background and the internationalism of Marxism and by calling Lenin a "son of the West", Ilyenkov opposed official Soviet patriotism, which more often than not was Great-Russian nationalism in disguise, and used Marxist theory as an *autonomous means* to criticize not only capitalism but also the "negative phenomena" of Soviet society.[27] By restating classical Marxist tenets like the gradual disappearance of the state, money and formal justice, Ilyenkov showed that Soviet society still has a long way to go, and although he himself remained convinced of the historical inevitability of communist society, it is clear that a statement such as "these nightmares [reference is to Aldous Huxley's *Brave New World*, and George Orwell's *1984*, EvdZ] [...] do not scare us. We understand these tendencies as our yesterday, although not yet completely outlived," *could* only be condemned as "anti-Soviet".[28]

b) A second feature that makes Ilyenkov stand out against the background of Soviet philosophical culture has to do with the form and style of his work. As David Bakhurst rightly stated: "Ilyenkov writes not as a Soviet delegate presenting an official line, but as an autonomous scholar addressing the specific concerns of the symposium in his own voice."[29] The first two words of his *Marks i zapadnyi mir* are: "I think...," to which he might well have added: "…therefore I am a potential enemy of the people."[30] Being a Soviet philosopher meant to accent limitations other than those resulting from one's intellectual capacities, since "the danger that free thought, even within the Marxist framework, poses to entrenched political parties is too great to be tolerated."[31] He also stated that he *personally* preferred communism," and gave his *"own* answer to the four questions that were formulated in the brochure of this symposium [italics mine, EvdZ]."[32]

Further, when Ilyenkov claimed that "the school must teach to think" and that "to think" meant "to think on the level of contemporary logic – dialectics, like the logic and theory of knowledge of the materialism of Marx – Engels – Lenin," he was illustrating the basic contradiction of Soviet philosophy, for it is not self-evident that when pupils learn to think, they will do so along Marxist-Leninist lines. At the same time, this was a *sine qua non* of Soviet philosophy until the days of Gorbachev.[33]

Finally, omnipresent *langue de bois* made such clear voices as that of Ilyenkov stand out even more: his *Idoly i idealy*, for example, is not only a book in which, as the publisher states, "not everything is indisputable" (the underlying assumption that a Soviet reader would normally expect philosophical literature to contain nothing but indisputable statements is quite telling in its own right), it also is a book which, with its lively style, its mildly anti-semitic cartoon to illustrate the dialogue with "Adam Adamych", and its direct discussion with "a certain book" in which it is said that "God created man to his own image and likeness," stands in stark contrast with the bulk of Soviet philosophical production.[34]

c) A third element has to do with the separation of *akademicheskaia filosofiia* and *vuzovskaia filosofiia*. In 1955, Ilyenkov was deprived of the right to teach at MGU, but, as his former colleague Korovikov argues, "fortunately for our genuine philosophy, E.V. Ilyenkov [...] at that time was already a collaborator of the Institute of Philosophy of the Academy of Sciences of the USSR, and [...] could continue his devoted creative work."[35] Fortunate as this indeed was, the separation of teaching and research, of which Ilyenkov is not the only example, had strong effects on philosophical culture.

In the first place, his philosophical views could not influence larger numbers of students as "one out of several positions," but their influence was limited to colleagues and *aspiranty*. Secondly, the isolated activity of researchers led to the creation of "schools" of Soviet philosophers, groups of likeminded persons who, despite the differences of opinion among them, were bound up with each other in ways that resemble more the traditional half-legal, half-conspirational *kruzhok* than a philosophical "school" in the sense of a discipline, a research program, a division of labor, et cetera.[36] And thirdly, the isolation of philosophers in research institutions excluded or at least limited the putting to the test of philosophical positions in public debate, rather than in the protected atmosphere of the *zhëltyi dom* or the heat of discussions *na kukhne*.

d) Finally, a fourth element is related to the content of Ilyenkov's philosophical thought. One of the topics that occupied him was the relationship between the philosophical systems of Hegel and Spinoza, and the related question of the feasability of a materialist dialectic. This topic is, in a way, central to the whole tradition of modern rationalism (in a wide sense, including both Spinoza and Hegel), and it was a hot topic in Western Marxist philosophy for some time, too. Ilyenkov's *Dialekticheskaia logika*, first published in Russian in 1974, appeared in 1977 in English translation in Moscow, but it apparently was not known to Pierre Macherey when he published his *Hegel ou Spinoza* in 1979.[37]

So, the Soviet work done in this field by Ilyenkov not only failed to "work" within non-Soviet philosophical culture, due to the enforced isolation of Soviet academic philosophy from the international philosophical scene, but the actual presence of a translation of a recent major Soviet work did not make a difference either: Ilyenkov was not even "discovered" in Marxist circles of the "Leninist school" founded by Louis Althusser. (I remember from my own student years, when students and staff were often sympathetic to Marxist thought, that "Soviet Marxism" had a very bad reputation – the standard image of Soviet philosophy was certainly not limited to "anti-Marxist bourgeois circles").

This was not accidental: Ilyenkov, like most of his Soviet colleagues, was doing philosophy in what Scanlan has called "the grand manner, advancing a general theory of reality in all its guises, from subatomic particles to international politics," and although this approach is not absent in Western philosophical culture, it certainly is not dominant. The fact that this "grand manner" dominated Soviet philosophical culture is due to the fact that the Soviet system based itself on the idea of a scientific-philosophical theory (the famous *nauchno-filosofskoe mirovozzrenie marksizma*), and depended on this idea for its ideological legitimatization.[38] It is beyond doubt that Ilyenkov was critical of many elements of the dogmatic version of this *mirovozzrenie*, but it is also beyond doubt that his energy was directed towards an improvement of this "grand unified theory" rather than towards a critique of the very idea of such a theory. The nostalgic dream of doing philosophy in the grand manner is not absent in Western philosophical culture, nor is ideological legitimatization through reference to scientific expertise, but in contemporary philosophical culture the idea of plurality of positions as belonging to the nature of philosophical itself dominates, and that this hinders an appreciation of Ilyenkov as a philosopher. When there was a potential audience, his thought did not reach it, and now that it can reach it, there is no audience left. Such a "rupture" is not necessarily irreparable, but a substantial Ilyenkov-reception is very unlikely to happen today, or will require enormous efforts.

On the whole, Ilyenkov can be regarded as a truly tragic figure, whose career and fate demonstrate that it was impossible to be at the same time a fully respectable and accepted member of Soviet philosophical culture *and* an independently thinking philosopher *and* someone loyal to the Soviet *opyt* in the double sense of experiment and experience.[39] Irrespective of Soviet reality in the post-Stalin era, irrespective of the sincere, yet vain attempts of those who attempted to reform the system from within, Ilyenkov remained, I think, true to the *idea* of Soviet society, i.e. to the idea of the possibility of the construction of a social, political, economic, cultural, and human reality on the basis of a philosophically arguable and scientifically justifiable grand theory. Compared to, for example, Merab Mamardashvili, Ilyenkov's tragedy was that he remained a serious – as Leszek Kolakowski called it – "intellectual Marxist".[40] Quite obviously, he was not a philosophical *apparatchik*, but just as obviously he was not a dissident either. He tried to be a Soviet Marxist-Leninist philosopher, and fully demonstrated the contradictions contained in that expression.

Conclusion: Accomodating the Soviet *opyt* in Philosophy

In the late 1980s and early 1990s, there were lively discussions in Russia about whether or not there had existed anything worthy of the label "philosophy" in Russia during the Soviet period.[41] In the second half of the 1990s, more "distanced" investigations have begun to appear, and this process is likely to continue.[42] However, it is one thing to restore a *national* philosophical heritage, but it is quite another to make this "Fatherland Philosophy" [*otechestvennaia filosofiia*] part of the common heritage of "World Philosophy" – these very categories should become the objects of critical investigation to begin with.

This goal seems rather remote today. For example, a recent Dutch publication presents 60 figures who have shaped the intellectual climate of the 20th century, and who "in any case are going to stand the test of time."[43] Six of these are of Dutch origin, the others foreign, but are there any Soviet or Russian philosophers, scientists, or intellectuals among them? The answer is: no. No Lev Vygotskii, no Aleksandr Luriia, no Mikhail Bakhtin, no Evald Ilyenkov, no Merab Mamardashvili, no Pavel Florenskii. The two figures that come closest of all are Emmanuel Levinas and Ilya Prigogine.

Of course, any work of this kind is marked with a degree of arbitrariness. For example, Thomas Kuhn is included while Paul Feyerabend is not, and some figures that should have been included immediately come to mind: Willard V.O. Quine, John Austin. Still, works like the one mentioned reflect received views, they reflect the spontaneous self-awareness of a philosophical culture, if only because the book has to appeal to buyers. So, apparently, neither Russian nor Soviet philosophers have made their way into the gallery of philosophers of the 20th century. This, I believe, has to do more with the phenomenon of Soviet philosophical culture that dominated Russian thought in this century, than with the real significance of those thinkers: Vygockii, Luriia, and Bakhtin have found their way into psychology, physiology, and literary theory respectively, but Ilyenkov, Mamardashvili, and Florenskii did not reach their potential audience among philosophers.

When in 1993 the lexicon *Filosofy Rossii XIX–XX stoletii (biografii, idei, trudy)* appeared, my first reaction, like presumably that of most other scholars, was one of enthusiasm. During many years of studying Soviet philosophical culture, I had gathered as much information of a biographical and bibliographical nature on Soviet philosophers as I could, often from very remote sources. And here it was: a full collection of the "Who is who in Russian philosophy?" type, made possible, surely, by *perestroika* and the end of the Soviet system. Informative, objective, reliable information, marking the end of Volkhonka-watching and of "philosophical sovietology".

It was shortly after the publication of the first edition of *Filosofy Rossii* that a young Russian philosopher – not mentioned in the book, and rather proud of this – gave his verdict: it was, according to him, a means for post-Soviet philosophers to rehabilitate themselves collectively. By treating "neutrally" and "objectively" all Russian philosophers, from Karsavin to Konstantinov and from Mamardashvili to Mitin, he argued, the authors "normalized" and "desovietized" their own history and made themselves the legitimate participants of a philosophical culture that has not changed that much, after all: the same people largely occupy the main posts in philosophical establishment. I think that he undeniably had a point.

Since 1993, *Filosofy Rossii* has been enlarged and republished, and this year the third edition has appeared, enlarged to 944 pages, where the first counted 222 pages, and the second edition 752 pages. Apparently, it serves a purpose, and the value of factual information is beyond dispute. At the same time, publications of this kind have a neutralizing effect, which makes it more difficult to pose the question what was and what was not 'normal' in

Soviet philosophical culture. They thus testify to the difficulty of dealing with the Soviet phenomenon in the field of philosophy.

In the beginning of this paper, I have suggested three complementary perspectives on a figure like Ilyenkov. Having attempted to situate Ilyenkov in Soviet philosophical culture, I want to come back to these perspectives. I think that, in order to "normalize" the inclusion of the Russian and Soviet philosophical heritage in historically developing and presently globalizing philosophical culture, and in order to give the phenomenon of Soviet philosophical culture a place, three things are required:

– the increased actual use, by Russian and non-Russian philosophers, of the ideas and theories of Russian philosophers, including those of the Soviet period, in their own work;

– monographs and intellectual biographies, both by ex-participants of Soviet philosophical culture and by "outsiders," on the more important philosophers of the Soviet period;

– renewed studies of Sovet philosophical culture, both as a whole, and of its parts.

A part from this, the Soviet *opyt* shows the need for permanent reflexion, by philosophers, upon the philosophical cultures that they participate in and which they reproduce. The end of Soviet philosophical culture means the end of a culture that in historically unique ways was bound up with a social and political system that had one particular, artificially unified philosophical theory as its ideological basis. The disappearance of this historical phenomenon does not mean, however, the end of the political relevance of philosophy, let alone lessen the desirability of philosophical reflexion upon it.

Notes

[1] This paper is based on investigations, supported by the Foundation for Research in the field of Philosophy and Theology, which is subsidized by the Netherlands Organization for Scientific Research (NWO).

[2] Bakhurst 1991, Friedrich 1993; for translations, see the bibliographies in these two books, as well as in Ilyenkov 1994.

[3] See Lektorskii et al. 1998, vol. ii, 4f.

[4] See van der Zweerde 1997 (a), esp. ch. 2, and 1997 (b); see also the classical studies by Bochenski, Wetter, Blakeley, Scanlan, and Jeu.

[5] For a more elaborate discussion of 'philosophical culture', see van der Zweerde 1997 (c), pp.31–54.

[6] Also in 1970, K.A. Mikhailov welcomed T.I. Oizerman's *Problemy istoriko–filosofskoi nauki* (Moskva: Mysl', (1969) 1982^2) as 'the first attempt at a systematic exposition of a Marxist [...] "meta-philosophy"' (Mikhailov 1970, p.160).

[7] I disagree strongly, at this point, with Konstantin Pigrov, who argued that metaphilosophy is a 'view from the outside' (Pigrov 1977, p. 7); the relationship between philosophy and metaphilosophy is more like that between a language and its meta-language, than like that between physics and metaphysics.

[8] Althusser 1974.

[9] L. Althusser, *Eléments d'autocritique* (Paris 1974), quoted from Manschot, 1980,160.

[10] See Freund 1986, 44f.

[11] This definition I derive, with some adaptations, from Kline 1964, 174.

[12] On planning in philosophy, see e.g. Mikhailov 1991.

[13] See Swiderski 1993 and van der Zweerde 1996.

[14] See, for an illuminating analysis of the Soviet *kollektiv*, Kharkhordin 1999, esp. chapter 7, 279–328).

[15] Lektorskii et al. 1998, vol. i, 4.

[16] A classical illustration remains Kline 1963.

[17] De George 1967,47.

[18] Jeu 1969, 23, and 66, where he refers to soon-to-be *akademik* F.V. Konstantinov's call for 'creative and independent thought.'

[19] Mamardashvili 1990, 27; cf. van der Zweerde 1990.

[20] De George 1984, 10f.

[21] See Iakhot 1981 for a detailed rendering.

[22] Graham 1987, 6.

[23] See Mikhailov 1993.

[24] Gudrun Richter, in: Ilyenkov 1994, 10.

[25] Zamaleev, 1996, 328.

[26] Ilyenkov 1967 and 1988; Ilyenkov was invited, but he could not go since "he was in hospital" (Lobkowicz et al. 1967, xii), but as the editor of the first publication in a Soviet journal has it: "To put it plainly, 'they didn't let him go'" (Novokhat'ko 1988, 98); cf. Chernyak 1987, 83, and Bakhurst 1991, 7f.

[27] Ilyenkov 1988, 101.

[28] Ilyenkov 1988, 107-111.

[29] Bakhurst 1991, 8.

[30] Ilyenkov 1991, 156.

[31] De George 1984, 17; cf. Goerdt 1984, 100.

[32] Ibid., 168.

[33] Ilyenkov 1968, 211.

[34] Ilyenkov 1968, 4, 5, and 44; on *langue de bois* cf. Françoise Thom, *La langue de bois* (Paris: Juillard, 1987).

[35] Korovikov 1998, 477.

[36] Cf. Lektorskii et al. 1998, vol. ii, 3ff.

[37] Pierre Macherey, *Hegel ou Spinoza* (Paris: François Maspero, 1979; 2nd edition Paris: La Découverte, 1990).

[38] See, e.g., T.I. Oizerman, *Nauchno-filosofskoe mirovozzrenie marksizma* (Moskva: Nauka, 1989), and Scanlan 1985, 21.

[39] Cf. Kharkhordin 1999, 350.

[40] Cf. Kolakowski 1977.

[41] E.g., Rozov 1988, or Volodin et al. 1991.

[42] See, for example, *Kruglyi stol* 1997, Gethmann & Plotnikov 1998, and Lektorskii et al., 1998.

[43] Achterhuis 1999,7.

Literature

Achterhuis, H., et al. (eds.) (1999), *De Denkers; een intellectuele biografie van de 20e eeuw*. Amsterdam & Antwerpen.

Althusser, L. (1974), *Philosophie et philosophie spontanée des savants*. Paris.

Bakhurst, B. (1991), *Consciousness and Revolution in Soviet Philosophy; From the Bolsheviks to Evald Ilyenkov*. Cambridge.

Blakeley, T.J, Rapp, F..J. (eds.), (1984), *Contemporary Marxism; Essays in Honor of J.M. Bochenski* (Dordrecht), 9–18.

Chernyak, L., [*review of Scanlan 1985*]. In: *Studies in Soviet Thought*, 1987, 33, 80–90.

De George, R.T., *Philosophy*, in: G. Fischer (ed.) (1967), *Science & Ideology in Soviet Society* (New York), 47–81.

De George, R.T., *The Critique of Marxist Philosophy: (1956–1981)*, in: J.J. O'Rourke, Th.J.

Freund, J. (1986) (1965), *L'essence du politique*. Paris.

Friedrich, J. (1993), *Der Gehalt der Sprachform; Paradigmen von Bachtin bis Vygotskij*. Berlin.

Gethmann, C.F., N. Plotnikov (1998), *Philosophie in Russland; Tendenzen und Perspektiven*. Bad Neuenahr – Ahrweiler.

Goerdt, W. (1984), *Russische Philosophie; Zugänge und Durchblicke*. Freiburg & München.

Graham, L.R., (1987) (1966), *Science, Philosophy, and Human Behaviour in the Soviet Union*. New York.

Iakhot, I. (1981), *Podavlenie filosofii v SSSR (20-30 gody)*. New York.

Ilyenkov, E.V., *From the Marxist-Leninist point of view*, in: Lobkowicz et al. 1967, 391–407.

Ilyenkov, E.V. (1968), *Ob idolakh i idealakh*. Moskva.

Ilyenkov, E.V., *Marks i zapadnyi mir*, in: *Voprosy filosofii*, 1988, 10, 99–112.

Ilyenkov, E.V. (1991), *Filosofiia i kultura*. Moskva.

Ilyenkov, E.V. (1994), *Dialektik des Ideellen; Ausgewählte Aufsätze*. Münster & Hamburg.

Jeu, B. (1969), *La philosophie soviétique et l'Occident; Essai sur les tendances et sur la signification de la philosophie soviétique contemporaine (1959–1969)*. Paris.

Kharkhordin, O. (1999), *The Collective and the Individual in Russia; A Study of Practices*. Berkeley.

Kline, G.L., *Soviet Philosophers at the Thirteenth International Philosophy Congress*. In: *The Journal of Philosophy*, 1963, 60, 738–743.

Kline, G.L., *Philosophy, Ideology, and Policy in the Soviet Union.* In: *The Review of Politics* 1964, 26, 2, 174–190.

Kolakowski, L., *Aktuelle und nichtaktuelle Begriffe des Marxismus,* in: Oelmüller, W. (ed.), 1977, *Weiterentwicklungen des Marxismus.* Darmstadt. 13–29.

Korovikov, V.I., *Nachalo i pervyi pogrom,* in Lektorskii et al. 1998, vol.ii, 477.

Kruglyi stol "Filosofiia v SSSR: versii i realii (materialy diskussii)". In: *Voprosy filosofii* 1997, 11, 3–38.

Lektorskii, V.A. (ed.) et al. (1998), *Filosofiia ne konchaetsia...; iz istorii otechestvennoi filosofii: XX vek,* vol. i *[1920-50-e gody],* vol. ii *[1960-80-e gody].* Moskva.

Lobkowicz, N. (ed*.) et al* (1967), *Marx and the Western World.* Notre Dame.

Mamardashvili, M.K., *Byt' filosofom – eto sud'ba,* in: idem 1990, 27–40 (orig. in *Filosofskaia i sotsiologicheskaia mysl'* 1989, 2, 29–36)

Mamardashvili, M.K. (1990), *Kak ia ponimaiu filosofiiu.* Moskva.

Manchot, H. (1980), *Althusser ovet het marxisme.* Nijmegen.

Mikhailov, F.T., *Umer li Marks v Rossii?* In: *Filosofskie issledovaniia,* 1993, 1, 79–89.

Mikhailov, F.T., *Kak delaiutsia knigi pri diktate plana (pokaiannoe pis'mo v redaktsiiu zhurnala 'Voprosy filosofii').* In: *Voprosy filosofii,* 1991, 3, 183–184.

Mikhailov, K.A., *Analiz stanovleniia nauchno–filosofskogo znaniia.* In: *Filosofskie nauki,* 1970, 5, 160.

Novokhat'ko, A.G., *Predislovie k publikatsii.* In: *Voprosy filosofii,* 1988, 10, 98.

Pigrov, K., *Pozitivnaia nauka kak metafilosofiia: sotsiologiia mudrosti,* in: Moreva, L. (ed.) (1997), *Metafilosofiia.* St.Petersburg. 7–18.

Rozov, M.A., Filosofiia bez soobshchestva. Voprosy filosofii, 1988, 8, 23–37.

Scanlan, J.P. (1985), *Marxism in the USSR; A Critical Survey of Current Soviet Thought.* Ithaca & London.

Swiderski, E.M., *The Crisis of Continuity in Post–Soviet Russian Philosophy,* in Smith, B. (ed.), 1993, *Philosophy and Political Change in Eastern Europe.* LaSalle. 135–164.

Volodin, A.I. (ed.), *et al.,* 1991, *Otechestvennaia filosofiia: opyt, problemy, orientiry issledovaniia,* vyp. 6: *Izzhivaia 'zhdanovshchinu'.* Moskva.

Zamaleev, A.F. (1996), *Kurs istorii russkoi filosofii.* Moskva.

Zweerde, E. van der, *Recent Developments in Soviet Historiography of Philosophy.* In: *Studies in Soviet Thought* 1990, 39, 1–53.

Zweerde, E. van der, *Der Ausgang der sowjetischen philosophischen Kultur (1986–1993),* in Eimermacher, K. et al. (eds.), 1996, *Russland, wohin eilst du? Perestrojka und Kultur,* 2 vols. Dortmund. Vol. ii, 699–744.

Zweerde, E. van der (1997) (a), *Soviet Historiography of Philosophy; Istoriko-filosofskaja nauka.* Dordrecht.

Zweerde, E. van der, (1997) (b), *Soviet Scholasticism Revisited.* In: Symposium 2, 1997, 1–14.

Zweerde, E. van der, (1997) (c), *Reflections on Philosophical Culture,* in: Moreva L. (ed.), 1997, *Metafilosofiia.* St.Petersburg. 31–54.

6

Leontjew, Iljenkow und die Meschtscherjakow-Debatte - Methodologische Bemerkungen

Wolfgang Jantzen

Vorbemerkung

1975 zog der Wissenschaftliche Rat der psychologischen Fakultät der Moskauer Lomonossow-Universität Bilanz über das erfolgreiche Studium von vier taubblinden Studenten. Der Bericht über dieses "beispiellose Experiment", so die Überschrift einer Veröffentlichung in der Zeitschrift *Gesellschaftswissenschaften* (Gurgenidze und Iljenkow 1976), eröffnete die sogenannte Meschtscherjakow-Debatte. Sie wird fortgesetzt durch einen Artikel von Iljenkow (1977) in der Zeitschrift *Kommunist.* 1989 organisieren Iljenkows Opponenten um Dubrowski und Narski eine Tagung zur Kritik und Verurteilung von Iljenkow (Dubrowski et al. 1989). Bakhurst (1991) sowie Bakhurst und Padden (1991) nehmen kritisch hierzu Stellung. 1993 äussert sich Friedrich zur Debatte, 1997 Keiler. Dabei wird aus der Meschtscherjakow-Debatte sehr bald eine Iljenkow-Debatte, welche sich zu Teilen in eine Leontjew-Debatte, durch Kozulin (1984, 1986, 1996) initiiert und fortgeführt, einreiht (insbesondere bei Keiler 1997).

Was diese Debatten über das normale Mass wissenschaftlicher Diskussion und Kritik hinaus kennzeichnet, sind immer wieder auftretende Versuche, den Gegner moralisch zu diskreditieren, häufig verbunden mit mangelnder Rekonstruktion von dessen Argumenten. Zieht man Hannah Arendt (1986) heran, so könnte man als Kern einer solchen Vorgehensweise jeweils die Konstruktion eines objektiven Gegners betrachten, von dem der jeweilige gegnerische Debattant lediglich ein zu identifizierendes, zu isolierendes und manchmal auch zu vernichtendes Exemplar darstellt. Anders lassen sich die Prädikate, Iljenkow sei der Lyssenko der Breschnew-Ära (Dubrowski et al. 1989), oder Leontjews Aneignungs-Vergegenständlichungs-Konzept, in enge Verbindung zur Meschtscherjakows Vorgehen und Iljenkows Philosophie gesetzt, sei eine "Nachgeburt des Stalinismus" (Keiler 1997, 242), nicht erklären. Und auch Iljenkows Rede ist an manchen Stellen durchaus von herabsetzender Polemik durchsetzt, ohne die Argumente der Gegner ernsthaft zu prüfen.

Obwohl es reizen würde, gerade in der Situation der Postmoderne und des heraufbeschworenen "Endes der Geschichte" eine Soziologie derartiger Diskurse[1] zu versuchen, verzichte ich hierauf völlig und versuche statt dessen, den inneren Kern der Kritik freizulegen. Daran anschliessend möchte ich die Auseinandersetzung vom Standpunkt der Forschung ausgehend (vgl. Wygotski 1985) in den Kontext der Entwicklung einer nicht-klassischen Psychologie (Sokolowa 1999) einordnen, oder mit Wygotski (ebenda) gesprochen, in die Entwicklung einer allgemeinen Philosophie der Psychologie als Herausbildung eines psychologischen Materialismus (vgl. auch Jantzen 1991).

In inhaltlicher Hinsicht kreist die Diskussion vor allem um das Problem der "menschlichen Natur" als "gesellschaftliche Natur": In welchem Verhältnis stehen biologische und soziale Determiniertheit beim Aufbau der psychischen Prozesse?

Stationen der Debatte

1. In der Diskussion an der Lomonossow-Universität (Gurgenidze und Iljenkow 1976) bemerkt Leontjew (der im wesentlichen Darstellung und theoretische Auswertung vorträgt), dass die Befunde der Taubblindenpädagogik reichhaltiges Material "zur weiteren argumentierenden Erarbeitung der marxistisch-leninistischen Erkenntnistheorie" liefern (207), da sich hier der Prozess der Umgestaltung der Natur durch den gesellschaftlichen Menschen äussert, "der allein jene höchste und spezifische Form der Psyche schafft

und formt (und nicht etwa 'erweckt'), die als menschliches Bewusstsein oder kurz 'Seele' bezeichnet wird" (207). Unter Bedingungen sehr früher Taub-blindheit sei die Psyche jedoch "– wenn in diesem Fall von einer Psyche überhaupt die Rede sein kann – etwas völlig Amorphes, Unorganisiertes, Chaotisches, und das sowohl objektiv als auch subjektiv gesehen. Keine ei-nigermassen stabilen Abbilder können sich in diesem Strom von Empfin-dungen herauskristallisieren" (212).

2.   Diese These von der sozialen Erschaffung der Seele wiederholt Iljenkow (1978) grob popularisiert in seinem Artikel im *Kommunist*. Aber nicht das behindertenpädagogische Skandalon, das früh taubblinde Kind werde zu einer Art "menschenähnlicher Pflanze [...] und das bei völlig normalem Gehirn" (411), wird zum Ansatz von Kritik,[2] sondern die Behauptung: "Es gab überhaupt keine Psyche, und von selbst konnte sie nicht entstehen" (412). Weder Orientierungsreflex noch Kommunikation seien in diesem Stadium festzustellen. Vielmehr erfolge die ursprüngliche Menschwerdung durch die gemeinsam geteilte Tätigkeit als elementarste Form des sozialen Verkehrs, im Rahmen derer – um die wichtigsten Erörterungen aus Meschtscherjakows Buch (1999) nachzutragen – zunächst durch die Führung des Erwachsenen die Selbstversorgung möglich wird, dann der Aufbau von aus dieser Tätigkeit gewonnenen, natürlichen Gesten, und dann der Übergang in den Raum der Sprache als eigentlicher Ort des sozialen Erbes der Menschheit, Form des Ideellen. Insofern erbringt Meschtscherjakows Arbeit eine erste und systematische Grundlegung der Taubblindenpädagogik auch im vorsprachlichen Bereich, die in dieser Hinsicht mit modernen blindenpädagogischen Konzepten in weitgehendem Einklang steht (vgl. Jantzen 1999).

3.   Die inhaltliche Kritik von Dubrowski et al. (1989) zentriert sich einerseits auf empirische Fragen: Die vier Studenten seien nicht von Geburt an taubblind gewesen; derartige Kinder hätten im Meschtscherjakow-Experiment wegen Organpathologie nicht die höheren Stufen erreicht, und, da total Taubblinde in der Regel über angeborene Hirnschädigungen verfügten, sei dies auch nicht möglich. Auf dem Hintergrund seiner Auffassung des Ideellen als Gehirnfunktion (1983) erklärt Dubrowski andererseits die These von der Herausbildung der Psyche von Null aus zum Mythos.

4.   Bakhurst (1991) sowie Bakhurst und Padden (1991) identifizieren diese Debatte als Wiederholung einer Debatte der 20er Jahre zwischen Mechanisten und Deborinisten; ich vermute jedoch, dass dahinter eine Debatte zwischen Cartesianern und Spinozanern steht.

5.   Keiler (1997) führt gegen Leontjews Begriff der gegenständlichen Tätigkeit, den er nicht systematisch vom Tätigkeitsbegriff trennt (hier argumentiert er vergleichbar Kozulin), einen von Feuerbach kommenden

"humanistischen Materialismus" an, welchen er wohl bei Wygotski, nicht aber bei Meschtscherjakow, Iljenkow und Leontjew auszumachen vermag. Er führt hierzu aus den Selbstberichten der taubblinden Studenten eine Reihe von Passagen an, nach denen persönliche Anerkennung und emotionale Beziehung seiner Ansicht nach zu kurz gekommen seien. Der Schlüssel hierzu liege darin, dass in Leontjews Konzept der andere Mensch nicht wie bei Feuerbach oder Wygotski "der erste Gegenstand des Menschen" sei (335). Sicherlich lässt sich Meschtscherjakows Buch in dieser Richtung lesen, aber was ist mit dem nicht mehr geschriebenen Buch über "Kommunikation", das er ankündigte,[3] bzw. mit den Auswertungen von Obuchowa (1999), die gerade den emotionalen Kontakt als wesentlichste Voraussetzung hervorhebt? Im Zentrum von Keilers Kritik steht darüber hinaus Leontjews und Iljenkows Theorie des Ideellen, die als "Theorie des objektiven Geistes" aus einem von beiden nicht zitierten bürgerlichen Erbe übernommen sei.

6. Weitaus differenzierter ist Friedrichs (1993) Kritik an der Theorie des Ideellen in Verbindung mit der Theorie der gegenständlichen Tätigkeit. Im Verhältnis von Sprechen und Denken lasse diese der Sprache lediglich eine zeichentheoretische Interpretation zukommen. Friedrich rekonstruiert bezogen auf Megrelidze, Wygotski und insbesondere den Bachtin-Kreis eine Theorie der Sprachform, welche die Bedeutung als Einheit von Form und Inhalt in historisch bedingten und historisch wirkenden Sprachformen ausmacht und nicht in einem Reich reiner Bedeutungen in Form des Ideellen. Der von ihr herausgearbeitete Begriff der Sprachform weist eine deutliche Nähe zu Bourdieus Begriff des Habitus[4] auf.

Fasse ich diese Debatte zusammen, so kreist sie neben spezifisch behindertenpädagogischen Fragen sowie Problemen der Empirie vor allem um drei Aspekte:

- das Verhältnis von Biotischem und Sozialem in der Entwicklung des Psychischen,
- das Verhältnis von gegenständlicher und sozialer Tätigkeit,
- das Verhältnis von Denken und Sprechen.

Dabei hat es den Anschein, dass die Debattanten häufiger dem Gegner vorwerfen, ihre eigenen Fragen nicht zu bearbeiten, anstatt sich ein Bild zu verschaffen, was dessen Ansatz leistet.

Wir sehen eine spezifische Krisendebatte vor uns, ähnlich jener, welche Wygotski bezogen auf die Krise der Psychologie für die zwanziger Jahre wiedergibt. Vielleicht können Wygotskis (1985) wissenschaftstheoretische Erörterungen angesichts dieses Problems von Nutzen sein, um die vorliegende Debatte zu ordnen.

Die Krise der Psychologie als Hintergrund der Meschtscherjakow-Debatte

Krisen dieser Art sind paradigmatische Krisen, die beim Übergang von Beschreibungswissen zu Erklärungswissen auftreten, zumal dann, wenn, wie Toulmin (1981, 51) dies vermerkt, ein neues "Ideal der Naturordnung" ins Spiel kommt. Das Problem derartiger Übergänge liegt, so Wygotski (1985), in der notwendigen Justierung von Bedeutungen, die bei Ausweitung über einen bestimmten Grad hinaus ihren Erklärungsgehalt verlieren. Daher ist es erforderlich, jenseits der Krisensymptome von Empirismus, Eklektizismus und ungenauer Sprache eine allgemeine Philosophie des Faches auf der Basis einer strikt induktiv-analytischen Methode zu entwickeln. Die naturwissenschaftliche *Induktion* auf der Basis des realen oder des Gedankenexperiments, mit dessen theoretisch steuernden Begriffen jede Empirie untrennbar verbunden ist, verlangt ihre Aufhebung in der *Analyse*, welche der Induktion wesensgleich ist, da sie deren Vielfalt negiert, d.h. sich aufhebt.

Gleichzeitig geht es darum, Begriffe gleicher Abstraktionshöhe nicht nur hinsichtlich ihres Gegenstandsbereichs zu justieren, der durch Empirie und Induktion, also durch die Auswertung des Beschreibungswissens, vorgegeben ist, sondern auch zu einer Justierung von erklärenden Begriffen unterschiedlicher Abstraktionshöhe zu gelangen. In dieser systematischen Justierung der Begriffe vom Standpunkt eines psychologischen Materialismus sieht Wygotski die Möglichkeit, einen Massstab für die je spezifischen Ebenen der Analyse zu entwickeln. Seitens der Philosophie ist der Massstab zu gross, seitens der Einzelwissenschaft zu klein. Die jeweils nötigen Veränderungen des Massstabes und die Konkretisierung der Leitsätze führen von beiden Seiten her zur Methodologie, zur allgemeinen Wissenschaft. Für deren Konstruktion misst Wygotski sowohl Karl Marx für den dialektischen Materialismus allgemein, als auch Spinoza für einen psychologischen Materialismus fundamentale Bedeutung zu (249 ff.). Dies rührt daher, dass Spinoza eine nicht cartesianische, d.h. monistische Theorie des Leib-Seele-Problems liefert und damit die Überwindung einer Teilung in zwei Psychologien, einer geistes- und einer naturwissenschaftlichen, ermöglicht.

Den Grundgedanken der Justierung von Begriffen greift Wygotski (1972) erneut in *Denken und Sprechen* auf. Unter dem Aspekt der Beziehungen der Allgemeinheit diskutiert er die Justierung von Begriffen am Beispiel der Längen- und Breitengrade der Erdkugel. Er bezeichnet als "Länge" eines Begriffs seine jeweilige Justierung auf einem Längengrad zwischen dem extrem abstrakten und dem extrem anschaulichen Pol und als "Breite" eines Begriffs seine Position, welche er unter anderen Begriffen gleicher "Länge" einnimmt, also seine Ausdehnung auf einem gegebenen Breitengrad bei gesetzter Abstraktionshöhe. "Diese Stellung eines Begriffs im System aller Begriffe, die durch seine Länge und Breite bestimmt wird, nennen wir das *Mass der Allgemeinheit* eines gegebenen Begriffs" (1972, 267; Hervorh. W.J.). Jede individuell aufgebaute Bedeutung drückt daher eine *Struktur der Verallgemeinerung* aus, welche "die in ihrem Bereich mögliche Äquivalenz der Begriffe bestimmt" (267). Dabei denkt Wygotski die hinter den unterschiedlichen Strukturen der Verallgemeinerung existierenden Masse der Allgemeinheit selbst als Resultate eines historischen Prozesses (vgl. Wygotski 1985, 97ff.), hier mit striktem Bezug auf Spinozas Methodenlehre im *Traktat über die Verbesserung des Verstandes* (Spinoza 1977).

Wenn Spinoza nun von der philosophischen Ebene aus die bisher weitestgehende begriffliche Ordnung des psychologischen Materialismus geleistet hat (insbesondere in der *Ethik*), wenn auch in sehr abstrakter Form, von der aus nicht ohne Verletzungen des Massstabs zur Psychologie übergegangen werden kann, so bietet es sich andererseits für die Psychologie an, in Ausweitung ihrer Massstäbe, also bei der Herausbildung neuer Strukturen der Verallgemeinerung, sich dieses philosophischen Begriffssystems als methodologischen Spiegels zu bedienen. Exemplarisch hat dies Wygotski (1996) in seinem Manuskript *Die Lehre von den Emotionen* realisiert, in welchem er die bestehenden neuropsychologischen Emotionstheorien mit dem von Spinoza aufgezeigten und aufgehobenen Grundmuster des cartesianischen Dualismus konfrontiert (vgl. Jantzen 1996).

Da Iljenkow sich explizit auf Spinoza bezieht, da Leontjews Theorie in strikt spinozanischer Weise argumentiert, gerade in dem in der Debatte nicht wahrgenommenen Aspekt, dass hinter der *gegenständlichen Tätigkeit* nicht nur die *Tätigkeit* als Fähigkeit, einen Gegenstand im Psychischen zu setzen, existiert, sondern dahinter die *engagierte Tätigkeit* des Subjekts,[5] da schliesslich auch Galperins Ausarbeitung der Interiorisationstheorie, die in mancherlei Hinsicht für das Denken in der sowjetischen Taubblinden-pädagogik Pate gestanden hat, nur zu deutlich spinozanisch beeinflusst ist,[6] werde ich im folgenden Spinozas Ethik als allgemeinen Rahmen eines möglichen psychologischen Materialismus benutzen und die Beiträge in der Debatte selbst als Explikationen unterschiedlicher Kapitel in Spinozas Ethik lesen.

Iljenkow und das zweite Buch der "Ethik"

Der erste Teil der *Ethik* handelt von "Gott", also von der unendlichen Natur, d.h. von der Ontologie. Der zweite Teil der *Ethik* handelt von der "Natur und dem Ursprung der Seele", insbesondere auch von der Erkenntnistheorie, und damit exakt vom Kern der Meschtscherjakow-Debatte. Welche Vorstellung hat Iljenkow (1994) von diesem Prozess?

Einerseits ist Seele für ihn die "Gesamtheit beweglicher funktionaler Organe" (103), andererseits wird die menschliche Persönlichkeit von alters her Seele genannt (225), Persönlichkeit selbst aber ist wieder die "Gesamtheit menschlich-funktionaler Organe" (241). Bewusstsein und Willen als wesentlicher Inhalt der Persönlichkeit sind daher biologisch nicht kodiert, sondern nach Ursprung und Wesen rein sozial (211). "Die Bedeutungen brechen die Welt im Bewusstsein des Menschen" (214), d.h. im Unterschied zum Tier besteht beim Menschen eine ideelle Ebene.

Nun ist sich Iljenkow andererseits jedoch sehr bewusst, dass ein Verbleiben in dieser Bestimmung von Seele ihn zurück in den Cartesianismus führen würde:

> Denn der kardinale Unterschied eines denkenden Körpers von der Bewegungsweise eines beliebigen anderen Körpers, der von Descartes und den Cartesianern ziemlich klar gesehen, aber nicht verstanden worden ist, besteht darin, dass der denkende Körper die Form (Trajektorie) seiner Bewegung im Raum aktiv aufbaut (konstruiert) entsprechend der Form (Konfiguration und Lage) eines anderen Körpers (Iljenkow 1994, 71).

Zwar kann der Unterschied vom Mensch zum Tier nach wie vor im cartesianischen Kriterium der Sprache wahrgenommen werden (vgl. Chomsky 1971), nicht aber in der Differenz von mechanischer Konstruktion des Tieres und Beseeltheit des Menschen, dies verbietet Spinozas Erkenntnistheorie ebenso wie seine Theorie der Affekte. "Die Handlungen der Tiere, besonders der höchstentwickelten, fallen gleichfalls, wenn auch in beschränktem Masse, unter Spinozas Bestimmung des Denkens" (72). Dies ist sowohl unter dem Aspekt des Erwerbs von Selbstempfindung (96) als auch in Form sensomotorischer Schemata anzunehmen, denen eine Trajektorie als Abbild des äusseren Dings im Raum zugrunde liegt (105), also ein Prozess, "der die Form eines Dinges reproduziert" (291). Tiere haben folglich wie Menschen als denkende Körper "gleichsam eine eigentümliche geographische Karte vor Augen, die den Gesamt 'Lageplan' aller anderen Körper darstellt" (26).

So taucht die Frage auf: "Was unterscheidet denn nun das menschliche Selbstgefühl (das Selbstgefühl eines menschlichen Organismus) von seiner biologischen Voraussetzung, vom 'Selbstgefühl überhaupt'"(248)? Aus dieser

Klemme, dass einerseits sensomotorische Fähigkeiten vorausgesetzt werden
müssen, um die Verknüpfung von Sprache und Denken zu erklären, dass
andererseits aber auch Tiere über vergleichbare sensomotorische Muster
verfügen, befreien sich Iljenkow und Leontjew mit der These der von Anfang
an qualitativen Unterschiede der Menschen durch die Entwicklung höherer
menschlicher Bedürfnisse gegenüber den bloss organischen Bedürfnissen
bei den Tieren. Während jedoch bei Leontjew (vgl. 1998, 11) diese
Abgrenzung relativ bleibt, wird sie bei Iljenkow absolut. Dies ist der
Hintergrund, auf dem er jede, nicht durch gemeinsam geteilte Tätigkeit,
vermittelte Aktivität der taubblinden Kinder der Sphäre des bloss organischen
Selbstbewusstseins bzw. der bloss organischen Bedürfnisse zuordnet, obgleich
er theoretisch in der Lage sein sollte, das Verhalten taubblinder Kinder als
Kompensation sensorischer Deprivation zu lesen. Denn "eine Individualität,
der die Möglichkeit versperrt ist, sich in einer wirklich wichtigen [...]
bedeutsamen Handlung auszudrücken [...] sucht den Ausweg für sich selbst
unwillkürlich in Nichtigkeiten" (266), in "Stereotypen des Lebens" (267).

Dieser naturalistische Fehlschluss ist meines Erachtens ein Resultat
einer spezifischen Spinozalektüre, die bei Iljenkow im wesentlichen auf Teil
II der *Ethik* beschränkt bleibt. Er erkennt nicht, dass Körper und Geist im
Körper an der Grenze zwischen Affekten des Körpers und Affekten der Seele
eines vermittelnden Dritten bedürfen, das bei Spinoza die Affekte selbst
sind.

Während Cartesius in der Frage des vermittelnden Charakters der
Emotionen in seiner bekannten Lösung mit der Zirbeldrüse scheitert, legt
Spinoza diese Thematik anders an. Zwar ist die erste Idee des Denkens, das
ist die Idee des eigenen Körpers, möglich ohne einen anderen Modus des
Denkens (*Ethik* II, Grundsatz 3), doch kommen die weiteren Modi wie Liebe,
Begierde und andere Gemütsaffekte dadurch ins Spiel (ebenda), dass jedes
Ding im Sein zu beharren strebt und dieses Streben (*conatus*) nichts anders
als die wirkliche Wesenheit des Dinges selbst ist (*Ethik* II, Lehrsatz 6 u. 7).
Das Ding ist aber durch die Bestimmtheit seines Körpers (vgl. Spinozas
Theorie des Körpers; *Ethik* II, Lehrsatz 13 einschliesslich der Lehnsätze und
der Folgerungen) im Falle des taubblinden Menschen bereits menschliches
Ding, das aufgrund der Organisation seines Gehirns umfassende funktionale
Organe bilden kann. Daher ist seine Begierde (*cupiditas*) als seine Wesenheit
(*Ethik* III, Definitionen der Affekte 1) vor allem auf dem Umgang mit anderen
Menschen gerichtet. Dies folgt aus Spinozas Lehre der Gemeinbegriffe in
Teil II der *Ethik* (Lehrsatz 39 und 40) sowie der insbesondere in Teil IV
entwickelten Theorie der Gemeinschaft (vgl. Jantzen 1995). Darüber hinaus
erfolgt die weitere Ausarbeitung dieser Dimension bei Feuerbach, worauf
Keiler (a.a.O.) zu Recht verweist.

Indem die Rückübersetzung der spinozanischen Erkenntnistheorie in eine Theorie des Körpers ebenso wie in eine Theorie der Affekte im Unterschied zu Spinoza nicht unternommen wird, bleibt Iljenkow vor allem Erkenntnistheoretiker und daher in der Frage der Selbstbewegung des Subjekts weitgehend begrifflos.

Bei Obuchowa, die zu dieser Zeit wöchentlich mit Iljenkow bei Leontjew zum Gedankenaustausch zu Gast war (persönliche Mitteilung, Januar 1999), liest sich die Sicht der taubblinden Kinder völlig anders:

> Beide Kategorien von Kindern [normale und taubblinde; W.J.] beginnen ihre psychische Entwicklung unter Bedingungen der integralen Einheit des Kindes und des Erwachsenen in ihrer gemeinsam geteilten Tätigkeit (joint activity), gerichtet auf die Befriedigung elementarer organischer Bedürfnisse. Die bedeutendsten Bedingungen sind hier die emotional positiven Beziehungen zwischen dem Kind und dem Erwachsenen. Es folgt der explizite Hinweis auf den Umgang von Meschtscherjakow mit Nina Ch. (Obuchowa 1999).

Die begrenzte Lektüre Spinozas unter dem Aspekt der Erkenntnistheorie hat m.E. weitere Folgen, die ich hier nur andeute, ohne näher auf sie einzugehen:

1. Die mangelnde Berücksichtigung des Attributs der Ausdehnung und seiner Realisierung im Modus des Körpers führt zur spezifisch cartesianischen Trennung von Amodalität und Funktionalität des Abbilds bei Iljenkow (1994) und Leontjew (1981) sowie von zeichentheoretisch bestimmter Sprachform und Bedeutung tragendem Sprachinhalt (vgl. Chomsky 1971). Insoweit ist Friedrichs Kritik in vollem Umfang berechtigt, ohne dass damit Iljenkows herausragende erkenntnistheoretische Leistung (Bestimmung des Abbilds als Trajektorie;[7] Theorie des Ideellen) herabgewürdigt würde.

2. Spinozas Wahrheitstheorie wird von Iljenkow nur teilweise genutzt. Denn die Gewissheit der wahren Erkenntnis wird über die adäquate Idee der eigenen Erkenntnis (*Ethik* II, Lehrsatz 43, Beweis) hinausgehend auch affektlogisch begründet und mit einer Theorie ethischer Erkenntnis verknüpft. Die wahre Erkenntnis kann einen Affekt nicht hemmen, sofern sie wahr ist, sondern nur sofern sie selbst Affekt ist (IV, Lehrsatz 14). Und das gesamte Teil V der *Ethik* handelt von der Hemmung der Affekte selbst durch Affekte, die *sub specie aeternitatis,* also durch Verbindung mit der Idee "Gottes", d.h. der Wirkweise der unendlichen Natur, welche den Menschen einschliesst, entstehen. Und erst damit ist der Prozess des Begreifens der (konstruktiven und konstitutiven) Genesis der Vernunft abgeschlossen, welche das Reich des Ideellen ausmacht: Die Ideen in der Form menschlicher Ideen, die Bedeutungen eingeschlossen in die Affekte.

Was aber ist mit Leontjew? Die gesamte bisher wiedergegebene Debatte verfehlt es, die von ihm erarbeitete Bedeutung von Tätigkeit als engagierter Tätigkeit herauszuarbeiten. Und gerade in dieser Dimension erweist er sich als würdiger Nachfolger Wygotskis.[8]

Leontjew und der dritte Teil der *Ethik*

Leontjews *Tätigkeit, Bewusstsein, Persönlichkeit* (1979) lässt sich in den Kapiteln 2 und 3, "Die psychische Widerspiegelung" bzw. "Das Problem der Tätigkeit in der Psychologie", sowie in der ersten Hälfte des Kapitels 4 "Tätigkeit und Bewusstsein" weitgehend parallel zu Iljenkows Erkenntnistheorie bzw. zum Teil II der *Ethik* lesen. Allerdings erfolgt im Kapitel 2 schon der Hinweis, dass der Begriff des Abbilds "den Begriff der *Engagiertheit*, das Subjektsein" einschliesse (58; Hervorh. i.O.). Im Kapitel 3 wird nach der Behandlung der doppelten Existenz der Tätigkeit – als äussere gegenständliche Tätigkeit und innere Tätigkeit, welche den Gegenstand setzt – auf das Zusammenfallen von Bedürfnis und Gegenstand im Prozess der gegenstandssetzenden Tätigkeit verwiesen. Dies führe zur Entstehung der Einstellung im Sinne von Uznadze (89).[9]

Zur "Allgemeinen Struktur der Tätigkeit" (3.5.) heisst es, dass hinter dem (subjektiv gesetzten) Gegenstand der Tätigkeit immer ein Bedürfnis stehe und insofern dieser Gegenstand das eigentliche Motiv sei (101).

Aber erst in Kapitel 4 wird systematisch eine dem Teil III der *Ethik*, "Vom Ursprung und der Natur der Affekte", entsprechende Argumentation entwickelt. Gefragt wird nach dem gemeinsamen Dritten, das bei Spinoza die Vermittlung von Körper und Seele im körperlichen Ding darstellt, nach dem Streben des menschlichen Dings, in seinem Sein zu verharren. Sofern wir von Affektionen des Körpers, die durch etwas entstehen, das in oder ausserhalb von uns geschieht, die adäquate Ursache sind, wir also handeln, entstehen Affekte, die auf Freude und Begierde beruhen (Def. 2, Lehrsatz 59). Sind wir hingegen nicht die adäquate Ursache der Affektionen, so leiden wir, es entstehen Affekte der Leidenschaft. Teil III der *Ethik* zeigt die Genesis der unterschiedlichen Affekte als Form der Genesis der Ideen.

Man kann nun, wie Piaget (1995) dies in "Intelligenz und Affektivität in der Entwicklung des Kindes" tut, Form und Inhalt, Energetik und Struktur strikt parallelistisch trennen und gerät damit in ein ähnliches Dilemma, wie es Friedrich (1993) für Leontjews und Iljenkows zeichentheoretische Trennung der Sprachform vom Sprachinhalt aufgezeigt hat.

Leontjew hingegen geht einen anderen Weg, indem er die psychologische Kategorie des persönlichen Sinns entwickelt. Dieser Begriff ermöglicht im Verhältnis zum Begriff der Bedeutung eine Theorie der untrennbaren Einheit beider Aspekte. Wie von Friedrich (1993) für Bachtin aufgezeigt, bestimmt "die Interaktion von innen her und nicht als von aussen interiorisierte die Struktur der Äusserung" (156), in diesem Falle die Struktur des Sich-Setzens der Tätigkeit im Gegenstand. Auf jeder Ebene der Entwicklung des Bewusstseins stellt der Sinn "von etwas" (148) eine latente Bewusstseinsebene dar. Er entspricht als persönlicher Sinn in dieser Hinsicht Bourdieus (1987) Kategorie des im Habitus niedergeschlagenen sozialen Sinns ebenso wie Bachtins Begriff der Sprachform, insofern in ihm "soziale Werte als Formgebilde existieren" (Friedrich 1993, 161).

Nach Leontjew trennen und vereinigen sich in den angeeigneten Bedeutungen die Sinneseindrücke der äusseren Welt und die Formen des sinnlichen Erlebens der eigenen Bedürfnisse. (1979, 147). Ebenso wie die äussere Sinnlichkeit das Abbild, d.h. die Bedeutung, mit der Welt verbindet, so verbindet die Engagiertheit des Subjekts, sein persönlicher Sinn, die Bedeutungen mit ihm selbst als körperlichem Subjekt (143). Schon bei den Tieren bedeutet die Untrennbarkeit der dort gegebenen Wahrnehmung des Objekts von den Bedürfnissen nicht deren Übereinstimmung. Aber erst auf der Ebene des Menschen dringt, tritt bzw. taucht das System der verbalen Bedeutungen in diese inneren Zusammenhänge ein.

Was Leontjew unter persönlichem Sinn versteht, wird nur verständlich, wenn dieser im *System psychischer Zusammenhänge* näher bestimmt wird. Dieses System hat Vergangenheit in Form der Bedürfnisse, welche in die Gegenwart hineinragen. Die Bedürfnisse wirken im Psychischen ebensowenig unmittelbar, wie es die sozialen Bedeutungen tun. Das von Leontjew kritisierte *Unmittelbarkeitspostulat* ist auch bei den Übergängen zwischen Körper und Idee des Körpers zu reflektieren. Das Bedürfnis ist aber nichts anderes als eine Idee vom Bedarf des Körpers, die noch nicht mit einer adäquaten Idee des Handelns in der äusseren Welt verknüpft ist. Erst diese Verknüpfung im durch die Tätigkeit gesetzten Gegenstand, der zugleich ihr Motiv bildet, gewährleistet den Übergang von der Leidenschaft zum Handeln. Das Bedürfnis ist im antizipierten Produkt unter dem Aspekt der Tätigkeit repräsentiert, es ist Motiv geworden, kann sich jedoch in seinem Inhalt nur in der Form der Handlung realisieren.

Bedürfnisse beziehen sich im Raum des Psychischen auf die Vermittlung der Vergangenheit des denkenden Körpers in die Gegenwart, *Motive* hingegen auf Vermittlung des denkenden Körpers in der Gegenwart mit einer möglichen Zukunft im adäquaten Handeln, also in der gegenständlichen Tätigkeit. Dies geschieht über die Setzung des Gegenstands in der Tätigkeit im psychischen Prozess, und damit als Konstruktion möglicher Zukunft. In dieser Hinsicht befindet sich die Leontjewsche Tätigkeits- und Handlungstheorie in strikter Übereinstimmung mit der von Spinoza im dritten Buch der Ethik.

Die *Emotionen* selbst begreift Leontjew als tätigkeitsrelevant, nicht aber als handlungs- oder operationsrelevant (189). Sie "ordnen sich nicht die Tätigkeit unter, sondern sind ihr Ergebnis und der Mechanismus ihrer Bewegung" (188). Sie zeigen in der Vorwegnahme der Adäquatheit der Handlung bereits deren Möglichkeit im Unterschied zur nicht adäquaten Handlung an. Folglich sind sie untrennbar mit der Genesis der Ideen verbunden. In deren Entwicklung bilden sie andere Strukturen und differenzieren sich durch die Vermittlung der Ideen in ihren Formen (Freude, Trauer, Bewunderung, Furcht, Hoffnung usw.), wie dies die Entwicklung der Emotionen in Spinozas Affektenlehre aufzeigt. Auch wenn Leontjew keine Entwicklungstheorie differentieller Emotionen vorgelegt hat, so ist doch deutlich, dass er dem parallelistischen Cartesianismus Piagets in dieser Frage auf keinen Fall zustimmen könnte.

Was aber ist der persönliche Sinn? Nach Leontjew stimmen Emotion und Sinn ursprünglich überein, also am Anfang ontogenetischer (und phylogenetischer; vgl. Leontjew 1973) Entwicklung, "denn offensichtlich werden auf den niederen Stufen die Bedürfnisgegenstände durch die Emotion gleichsam direkt angezielt" (Leontjew 1979, 192). Erst durch die den Körper affizierenden und von im durch Handlungen transformierten Gegebenheiten der äusseren Welt, aus denen durch diese Transformation adäquate Ideen entstehen, verbinden sich die Bedürfnisse in Form unterschiedlicher Motive mit der Gegenständlichkeit der Welt. Und erst in diesem Prozess trennt sich der Sinn von den Emotionen, entsteht persönlicher Sinn "infolge der sich im Laufe der Entwicklung vollziehenden *Aufspaltung der Motivfunktionen*" (ebd.). Er bildet in dieser Hinsicht die subjektive Einheit der Affekte des Subjekts mit seinen Ideen, jene "latente" Bewusstseinsebene, von der Leontjew (a.a.O., 147) mit Bezug auf Wygotski spricht (vgl. zur Kategorie Sinn auch Jantzen 1987, 1994).

Die Ideen Wygotskis, Iljenkows, Galperins, Meschtscherjakows können somit als verschiedene theoretische Explikationen des spinozanischen Projektes einer nicht-klassischen Philosophie und Psychologie begriffen werden. Dieses Projekt hat über Spinoza hinaus seine Entwicklung im "Philosophischen Diskurs der Moderne" erfahren, in welchem Habermas verschiedene Strömungen ausmacht.

Schlussbemerkungen: Der philosophische Diskurs der Moderne und das spinozanische Projekt

In seinem gleichnamigen Buch unterscheidet Habermas (1989) mit dem Produktionsparadigma von Hegel und Marx sowie dem auf Nietzsche aufbauenden Subjektivitätsparadigma zwei seiner Ansicht nach zentrale Paradigmen im philosophischen Diskurs der Moderne, denen er ein eigenes, drittes als "Kommunikationsparadigma" entgegenstellt. Friedrichs (1993) Arbeit zur Sprachform zeigt, dass es umfangreiche, nicht cartesianische Quellen gibt, die sich in dieses Paradigma einfügen. Aber damit nicht genug: Was Habermas gänzlich übersieht, ist ein auf Spinoza gründendes, erstmals von Feuerbach expliziertes, von Keiler für die Kritische Psychologie eingefordertes, aber unterdessen über Buber (vgl. Wolf 1992) und Lévinas (vgl. Taureck 1991) längst philosophisch ausgeführtes Dialogparadigma, das für die Psychologie vergleichbar u.a. in den Konzeptionen von Wallon (vgl. Voyat 1984) und Spitz (z.B. 1988) seinen Niederschlag gefunden hat.

Man könnte diese Paradigmen im wesentlichen als Explikationen zu Spinozas viertem Teil der *Ethik* lesen, aber dies darzustellen wäre schon ein anders Thema. Alle vier Paradigmen im philosophischen Diskurs der Moderne berühren noch nicht Wygotskis Forderung nach einem psychologischen Materialismus, der sich keineswegs wie das von Habermas skizzierte Subjektparadigma mit der subjektiven Verweigerung eines "Ja" zur Entfremdung begnügen kann, sondern angemessene Vorstellungen von einem humanen Leben in der Immanenz zu entwickeln hätte. Hier finden sich für die Ausarbeitung eines psychologischen Materialismus nicht nur die genannten Vorarbeiten, auch weitere Versuche einer nicht-klassischen Psychologie wie z.B. die von Freud, Piaget, Wallon bilden für die Herausarbeitung einer spinozanischen Psychologie eine wahren Schatz an Erklärungs- und Beschreibungswissen, dessen begriffliche Justierung auf der Tagesordnung steht.

Bemerkungen

[1] Vgl. zur ähnlich gelagerten Bettelheim-Debatte Kaufhold 1999.

[2] Mit Bezug auf die Singer-Debatte muss eine derartige Klassifikation – eine vergleichbare liefert bei Singer (1984) den Ansatz zu Euthanasie-Forderungen – aus behindertenpädagogischer und ethischer Perspektive scharf zurückgewiesen werden; vgl. Jantzen 1993, 1998a, 1998b.

[3] Laut persönlicher Mitteilung von F. Michailow und A.G. Nowochatko steht die Veröffentlichung dieser Arbeit unmittelbar bevor.

[4] Vgl. z.B. Schwingel 1998

[5] Leontjew hat sich allerdings erst durch Iljenkows Einfluss direkt mit Spinoza auseinandergesetzt (pers. Mitteilung von Felix Michailow), andererseits drücken bereits die *Materialien über das Bewusstsein* aus den 30er Jahren (Leontyev 1989/90) den gleichen spinozanischen Denktypus aus wie die Ausführungen in *Tätigkeit, Bewusstsein, Persönlichkeit* (Leontjew 1979).

[6] Vgl. Haenen (1996) zum Einlass von Iljenkow auf Galperin. Leider geht Haenen einem Einfluss Spinozas nicht nach, obgleich ein solcher durch die drei Arten der Orientierunsgrundlage, die Spinozas drei Arten der Erkenntnis nur allzusehr ähneln, naheliegt. Wenn auch Philosophie und psychologische Ausarbeitung für Galperin zwei deutlich unterschiedene Aspekte darstellten, so war er doch laut persönlicher Mitteilung seiner langjährigen Mitarbeiterin N.F. Talysina (Jan. 1999) ein hervorragender Spinoza-Kenner.

[7] Der Verweis auf die zeitliche, konstruktive Dimension des Abbilds als Trajektorie entspricht dem bewegungsphysiologischen Denken von N.A. Bernstein (1988). Durch die Aufnahme der Dimension der Zeit hat dies weitreichende Folgen für Psychologie und Erkenntnistheorie; vgl. auch Jantzen 1994.

Literatur

Arendt, H. (1986), *Elemente und Ursprünge totaler Herrschaft*. München.

Bakhurst, D. (1991), *Consciousness and Revolution in Soviet Philosophy. From the Bolsheviks to Evald Ilyenkov*. Cambridge.

Bakhurst, D; Padden, C. (1991), *The Meshcheryakov Experiment: Soviet Work on the Education of Blind-Deaf Children*. In: *Learning and Instruction*, 1991, 1, 201–215.

Bernstein, N.A. (1988), *Bewegungsphysiologie*. Leipzig.

Chomsky, N. (1971), *Cartesianische Linguistik*. Tübingen.

Dubrovsky, D.I. (1988), *The Problem of the Ideal*. Moscow.

Dubrowski, D. et.al. (1989), *Slepogluchonemota: Istoritscheskie i metodologitscheskie aspekty. Mify i realnost*. Moskwa.

Friedrich, Janette (1993), *Der Gehalt der Sprachform. Paradigmen von Bachtin bis Vygotskij*. Berlin.

Gurgenidze, G.S.; Iljenkow, E.W. (1976), *Ein beispielloses Experiment sowjetischer Psychologen*. In: *Gesellschaftswissenschaften*, 1976, 6, 2, 206–235.

Habermas, J. (1989), *Der philosophische Diskurs der Moderne*. Frankfurt/M.

Haenen, J. (1996), *Piotr Gal'perin - Psychologist in Vygotsky's Footsteps*. New York.

Iljenkow, E.W. (1977), *Die Herausbildung der Psyche und der Persönlichkeit: Ergebnisse eines Experiments*. In: *Demokratische Erziehung*, 1977, 3, 4, 410–419.

Iljenkow, E.W. (1994), *Dialektik des Ideellen*. Münster.

Jantzen, W. (1987), *Allgemeine Behindertenpädagogik* Bd.1. *Sozialwissenschaftliche und psychologische Grundlagen*. Weinheim.

Jantzen, W. (1991), *Psychologischer Materialismus, Tätigkeitstheorie, marxistische Anthropologie*. Berlin.

Jantzen, W. (1993), *Das Ganze muss verändert werden... Zum Verhältnis von Behinderung, Ethik und Gewalt*. Berlin.

Jantzen, W. (1994), *Am Anfang war der Sinn. Zur Naturgeschichte, Psychologie und Philosophie von Tätigkeit, Sinn und Dialog*. Marburg.

Jantzen, W. (1995), *Gemeinschaft und Gesellschaft im Lichte von Spinozas Philosophie*. In: *Jahrbuch für systematische Philosophie*, 1995, 6, 152–159.

Jantzen, W. (1996), *Das spinozanische Programm der Psychologie: Versuch einer Rekonstruktion von Vygotskijs Methodologie des psychologischen Materialismus*. In: Lompscher, J. (Hrsg.), *Entwicklung und Lernen aus kulturhistorischer Sicht*, Bd., Marburg, 51-65.

Jantzen, W. (1998), *Die Zeit ist aus den Fugen ... – Behinderung und postmoderne Ethik. Aspekte einer Philosophie der Praxis*. Marburg.

Jantzen, W. (1998), *Singerdebatte und postmoderne Ethik.* In: *Marxistische Blätter*, 1998, 36, 2, 50–61.

Jantzen, W. (1999), *Einführung.* In: Meschtscherjakow, A.I., *Helen Keller war nicht allein – Taubblindheit und die soziale Entwicklung der menschlichen Psyche.* Berlin.

Kaufhold, R. (1999), *Falsche Fabeln vom Guru? Der "Spiegel" und sein Märchen vom bösen Juden Bettelheim.* In: *Behindertenpädagogik*, 1999, 38, 2, 160–186.

Keiler, P. (1997), *Feuerbach, Wygotski & Co. Studien zur Grundlegung einer Psychologie des gesellschaftlichen Menschen.* Berlin.

Kozulin, A. (1984), *Psychology in Utopia.* Cambridge/Mass..

Kozulin, A. (1986), *The Concept of Activity in Soviet Psychology. Vygotsky, His Disciples and Critics.* In: *American Psychologist*, 1986, 41, 3, 264–274.

Kozulin, A. (1996), *Commentary.* In: *Human Development*, 1996, 39, 328–329.

Leontjew, A.N. (1973), *Probleme der Entwicklung des Psychischen.* Frankfurt/M.

Leontjew, A.N. (1979), *Tätigkeit, Bewusstsein, Persönlichkeit.* Berlin.

Leontjew, A.N. 1981, *Psychologie des Abbilds.* In: *Forum Kritische Psychologie*, 1981, 9, 5–19.

Leontyev, A.N. (1989), *Notes on Consciousness.* Part I. In: *Activity Theory*, 1989, 3/4, I–VIII.

Leontyev, A.N. (1990), *Notes on Consciousness.* Part II. In: *Activity Theory*, 1990, 5/6, I–VIII.

Leontjew, A.N. (1998), *Bedürfnisse, Motive, Emotionen.* In: *Mitteilungen der Luria-Gesellschaft*, 1998, 5, 1, 4–32.

Meschtscherjakow, A.I. (1999), *Helen Keller war nicht allein – Taubblindheit und die soziale Entwicklung der menschlichen Psyche.* Berlin.

Obuchova, L. F. (1999), *The Problem of General and Specific Regularities of the Psychic Development of Deaf-Blind Children.* Moscow, unpublished.

Piaget, J. (1995), *Intelligenz und Affektivität in der Entwicklung des Kindes.* Frankfurt/M..

Schwingel, M. (1995), *Pierre Bourdieu zur Einführung.* Hamburg.

Singer, P. (1984), *Praktische Ethik.* Stuttgart.

Sokolowa, E. E. (2000), *Leontjews frühe Arbeiten und ihre Rolle in der Entwicklung seiner Psychologie (Einleitung).* In: Leontjew, A.N., *Frühschriften 1926–1936.* Münster.

Spinoza, B. (1977), *Die Ethik nach geometrischer Methode dargestellt.* Hamburg.

Spitz, R.A. (1988), *Vom Dialog.* München.

Taureck, B. (1991), *Lévinas zur Einführung.* Hamburg.

Toulmin, S. (1981), *Voraussicht und Verstehen. Ein Versuch über die Ziele der Wissenschaft*. Frankfurt/M..

Uznadze, D.N. (1966), *The Psychology of Set*. New York.

Voyat, G. (Ed.) (1984), *The World of Henri Wallon*. London.

Wygotski, L.S. (1972), *Denken und Sprechen*. Frankfurt/M..

Wygotski, L.S. (1985), *Die Krise der Psychologie in ihrer historischen Bedeutung*. In: Wygotski, L.S., *Ausgewählte Schriften*. Bd. 1. Köln, 57–278.

Wygotski, L.S. (1996), *Die Lehre von den Emotionen. Eine psychologie-historische Untersuchung*. Münster.

Wolf, S. (1992), *Martin Buber zur Einführung*. Hamburg.

7

Ilyenkov and Foucault - Paradoxes and Impossible Connections

Jussi Silvonen

1. Impossible Connection?

At the first sight, it might be difficult to see any rational similarities or connections between Ilyenkov and Foucault. On the contrary, it would be easy to state that their philosophical programmes are as different as possible. The former is a Marxist philosopher from the Russian socio-historical school, the latter a French post-modern critic of Marxism and modern science in general. I will argue, however, that there is at least some interesting conceptual similarity in their work. I will concentrate on the concept of the Ideal which was in the very heart of Ilyenkov's philosophical programme (Ilyenkov 1977a), and on the idea of Truth Games (Foucault 1991a) which was so fundamental to Foucault. Common in both concepts is an attempt to articulate one essential aspect of human activity, or maybe even better, human activity systems.

2. Ilyenkov: The Philosopher of the Incorporeal

The concept of the Ideal or Ideality is one of the core categories of Ilyenkov's work. According to Rahmani (Rahmani 1973, 78–79), Ilyenkov took with this conception an extreme socio-genetic position inside Soviet philosophy. His famous article *The Concept of the Ideal* (Ilyenkov 1977a), as well as his book *Dialectical logic* (Ilyenkov 1977b) were disputed, and Ilyenkov was strongly criticised for deviating from the materialist point of view (see also Kozulin 1984). What is so special in his concept of "the Ideal"?

In the following, I will take a closer look at both mentioned texts. My aim is to highlight some essential – at least from my point of view – aspects of the Ideal by Ilyenkov.

2.1. The Problem of Ideal

Ilyenkov gives the following definition of the Ideal in his essay:

> "Ideality" in general is [...] a characteristic of the materially established (objecti-vised, materialised, reified) images of human social culture, that is, the historically formed modes of human social life, which confront the individual possessing cons-ciousness and will as a serial "supernatural" objective reality, as a special object comparable with material reality and situated on one and the same spatial plane (and hence often identified with it). (Ilyenkov 1977a, 79)

What is essential here is that Ilyenkov does not deny the importance of the idealistic tradition in philosophy while analysing the problem of ideal. "The objectivity of the 'ideal form' is no fantasy of Plato's or Hegel's, but an indisputable and stubborn fact" (Ilyenkov 1977a, 90). Nevertheless, he is not, of course, satisfied with the solution provided in the idealistic discourse. Instead, he is looking for a real, consistent materialist solution of the problem of the Ideal.

The traditional point of view of reflection theory, presented in every standard textbook of Marxist philosophy, is Ilyenkov's starting point. As we will see the reflection hypothesis is, in his opinion, not a sufficient solution of the problem of Ideal. Ilyenkov challenges the orthodox point of view by his conceptions of the Ideal as a special social form of existence, as a form of activity, and as a potential space for actions.

Reflection through labour?

Ilyenkov first defines the Ideal as "the subjective image of objective reality, i.e. reflection of the external world in the forms of man's activity, in the forms of his consciousness and will" (Ilyenkov 1977b, 252). The human capacity to reflect adequately the external world on the plane of ideality is a result of long history of the transformation of the world. The use of tools, i.e. labour, is an essential factor in this process.

> The ideal [is] the special function of man as the subject of social labour activity, accomplished in forms created by the preceding development." "The ideal, as the form of social man's activity, exists where the process of the transformation of the body of nature into the object of man's activity, into the object of labour, and then into the product of labour, takes place (Ilyenkov 1977b, 257 and 265).

The labour activity can be seen as a series of metamorphoses forming a cycle: thing-deed-word-deed-thing. The ideal image of the thing exists only in this cyclic movement. It "appears as the product and form of human labour, of the purposive transformation of natural material and social relations effected by social man. The ideal is present only where there is an individual performing his activity in forms given to him by the preceding development of humanity" (Ilyenkov 1977b, 266 and 277).

By defining the Ideal by the labour process, Ilyenkov gives us a universal definition of it. However, this definition is not an exhaustive one. Ilyenkov writes: "an individual is performing his activity *in forms given to him* […]". Consequently, the analysis of the Ideal needs a historical specification.

A form of existence (the case of the value form)?

In the next step, Ilyenkov looks at the specific historical form of the Ideal in a capitalist society. He's starting point is the famous analysis of the value form given by Marx in the first three chapters of *Das Kapital* (Marx 1983). Ilyenkov reads these chapters very carefully, and gives a bold interpretation of the text. In *Das Kapital*

> Marx defines the form of value in general as "purely ideal" not on the grounds that it exist only "in the consiousness", only in the head of commodity-owner, but on quite opposite grounds. The price or the money form of value, like any form of value in general, is ideal because it is totally distinct from the palpable, corporeal form of commodity in which it is presented […] In other words, the form of value is Ideal, although it exists outside human consciousness and independently of it (Ilyenkov 1977a, 72).

In *Das Kapital*,

> when analysing money – that familiar and yet mysterious category of social pheno-
> mena – Marx describes as "ideal" nothing more or less than the value-form of pro-
> ducts of labour in general *[die Wertform überhaupt]* (Ilyenkov 1977a, 85).

> "Ideality" is a kind of stamp impressed on the substance of nature by social human
> life activity, a form of the functioning of the physical thing in the process of this
> activity. So all the things involved in the social process acquire a new "form of
> existence" that is not included in their physical nature and differs from it completely
> – their ideal form (Ilyenkov 1977a, 86).

The result of this analysis is somewhat paradoxical. On the one hand, the
Ideal is the reflection of the external world in the consciousness, but on the
other hand, it is at the same time something existing outside of the human
consciousness and even independently of it. This needs obviously further
examination.

A form of activity

The paradoxical result of Marx's analysis can be understood, if we deconstruct
it in terms of relations and activity:

> Ideality […] is the form of a thing, but it is outside of this thing, and in the activity
> of man, as a form of this activity. Or conversely, it is the form of a person's activity
> but outside this person, as a form of the thing (Ilyenkov 1977a, 87).

> Materialism in this case does not consist at all in identifying the ideal with the mate-
> rial processes taking place in the head. Materialism is expressed here in understan-
> ding that the ideal, as a socially determined form of the activity of man creating an
> object in one form or another, is engendered and exists not in the head but with the
> help of the head in the real objective activity (activity on things) of man as the active
> agent of social production (Ilyenkov 1977b, 261).

> That is not surprising; the ideal as a form of human activity exists only in that activi-
> ty, and not in its results, because the activity is a constant, continuing negation of the
> existing, sensuously perceived forms of things, is their change and sublation into
> new forms, taking place in accordance with general patterns expressed in ideal forms.
> When an object has been created society's need for it is satisfied; the activity has
> petered out in its product, and the ideal itself has died (Ilyenkov 1977b, 275).

Ilyenkov's point of view is relational. He speaks about *forms* of activity. The
Ideal exists only in activity, but this activity has always specific forms, determined socially. Ilyenkov does not analyse, surprisingly, these forms of acti-

vity in detail. He only makes some short notes about alienation and social institutions as moderators of the forms of ideality in the seventh essay in *Dialectical Logic* (Ilyenkov 1977b).

A potential space between individuals

The last point I will add to the list of definitions of the Ideal given by Ilyenkov will concern the nature of the Ideal as a potential space for actions:

> The ideal exists there where there is a capacity to recreate the object in space, relying on the word, on language, in combination with a need for the object, plus material provision of the act of creation (Ilyenkov 1977b, p. 264).

> Without a constant re-idealising of the real objects of human life activity, without their transformation into the ideal, and so without symbolisation, man cannot in general be the active subject of social production (Ilyenkov 1977b, 276).

> A materialist philosopher, who understands the "corporeality" of personality not in a narrow sense, who sees it primarily in an aggregate (ensemble) of object-related tactile relations of a given individual to another individual (other individuals), mediated by the things created by their labour, will look for the resolution of the "personality structure" in space, outside the organic body, the individual, and precisely for this reason – paradoxical as it may seem – precisely for this reason in the personality's internal space (Ilyenkov, cited in Petrovsky 1990, 423–424).

Ilyenkov gives here important specifications of his concept of activity. First: Symbolisation, transformation into the Ideal is a necessary condition of all social production. Secondly, the Ideal exists where there is a capacity to recreate the object in space, with words. Thirdly, the personality's internal space is created outside the organic body, on the plane of the Ideal.

Ilyenkov defines the human agency in a reciprocal way: as determined and as determining. In this mutual relationship, the Ideal makes the subjectivity possible; it creates spaces and zones of development.

3. Foucault: The Philosopher of the Truth

The second axis of my paper is Foucault's philosophy of discursive praxis, his concept of Truth Games.

3.1. A nomad, escaping all definitions?

Foucault might be, and with reason, characterised as a philosophical nomad, always on the move, shifting surprisingly between different extreme positions. Foucault described these shifts with rhetorical tactics, making his work appear as series of provocative moves from one promising theme to another. In his rhetoric, Foucault liked to turn well-known aphorisms in their opposites; i. e. Plato's idea of the body as "prison of the soul" to "the soul as the prison of the body" (Foucault 1991b), Clausewitz's idea of the war "as a continuation of politics" to "politics as a continuation of war" (Foucault 1984), Bacon's "knowledge as power" to "power as knowledge" (Foucault 1991b), Freud's idea of "culture as repression of sexuality" to "a discursive explosion around sex" (Foucault 1984) etc.

Although the first impression received from reading Foucault may be the multitude of ideas escaping all consequent logic, I will emphasise the contrary: the coherence of his work. I will read it as a systematic whole consisting of the three basic themes of knowledge, subjectivity and power. Actually, I assume that the analytical power of Foucault's work comes precisely from bringing together these three themes, from seeing knowledge, power and subjectivity in their immanent relations.

I have called, with my colleagues Sakari Heikkinen and Hannu Simola (Heikkinen, Silvonen, and Simola 1999), the totality of these three dimensions *the technologies of truth* consisting of techniques of discourse, self and government.

In his work, Foucault attempted to "resituate the production of true and false at the heart of historical analysis and political critique" (Foucault 1991d, 79):

> Each society has its regime of truth, its "general politics" of truth: that is, the types of discourse which it accepts and make function as true; the mechanisms and instances which enable one to distinguish true and false statements, the means by which each is sanctioned; the techniques and procedures accorded value in the acquisition of truth; the status of those who are charged with saying what counts as true (Foucault 1991e, 73).

It is now possible to present the totality of Foucault's work in one simple picture, putting together the main themes and concepts of his thinking.

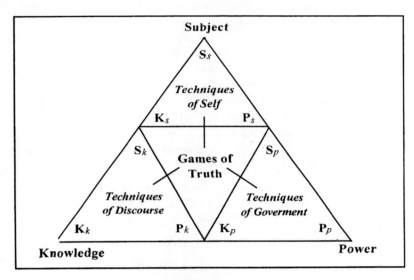

Figure 1: Foucauldian games of truth

This triangle of technologies of truth consists of three K–S–P -sub-triangles, each of which is further divided into three dimensions. Our Foucauldian triangle has the "magical" property that each of its elements, "angels", turns out to include the totality of three dimensions, too.

Technologies – or games – of truth are constructed of three kinds of techniques. The "rules" of the knowledge production can be termed *techniques of discourse*, how power works can be termed *techniques of government*, and the ways individuals construct their identities can be termed *techniques of self*. What is essential here is the mutual dependence of all these angels on each other. Power requires always acting subjects (reproducing power relations) as well as knowledge on which the operations of government are based.

Thus, for example, techniques of self is an element of technologies of truth, but at the same time it contains the three dimensions of knowledge (will to knowledge), power (art of governmentality) and subject (modes of subjectivation). But we may say as well that, e.g., the will to knowledge as a technique of self has its knowlege-axis (codification), subject-axis (self-examination) and power-axis (confession), and so forth.

The coherence implied in this triple formulation is, in my reading, an essential feature in Foucault's work. The continuity in Foucault's thinking, which he on several occasions emphasised (Foucault 1971; Foucault 1990), is also derived, besides from the links between his themes, from the analytical dimensions inherent in his work.

The K–S–P-triangle can be read as a diachronic model, too. If we gaze at the triangle hard enough, we may see Monsieur Foucault moving within it: starting from *the subject angle* (1) with *Madness and Civilization* (Foucault 1988), moving then to the *knowledge angle* (2) with *Order of Things* (Foucault 1973) and *Archaeology of Knowledge* (Foucault 1991a). He writes *Discipline and Punish* (Foucault 1991b) in the *power angle* (3), where he also starts his unfinished project of *The History of Sexuality* (Foucault 1984), the last two volumes of which (Foucault 1986; Foucault 1990) manifest the return to the subject angle (4).

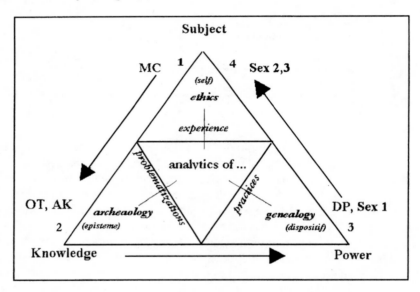

Figure 2: Development of Foucault's analytics

This triangle is, of course, our construction, not Foucault's. I am not saying it is a true Foucauldian one, but I am just playing my own theoretical games with him. The triangle makes some sense, anyway, I believe. It will place Foucault in the tradition of relational thinking in French social theory. In this sense, his theory is not so far from e.g. Bourdieu's sociology (Bourdieu and Wacquant 1992), as is usually thought. They both represents models of relational analysis of the social world.

3.2. Discourses as ideal forms of activity

Every technique of truth has its unique features. There is anyway something common in everyone of these techniques. Foucault understands these techniques as forms of action, as relations between acting individuals. These practices are ideal and material. "The great model of language (langue) and signs" (Foucault 1991e, 56) is not enough to describe the essence of these forms of activity. Instead, "the philosophy of event should advance in the direction, at first sight paradoxical, of an incorporeal materialism" (Foucault 1971, 23).

"<Truth>, (thought in original) understood in this way, is not, then, to be sought only in theoretical formulations such as those of philosophy or science; it can and must be analyzed in every manner of speaking, doing, or behaving, in which the individual appears and acts as subject of learning, as ethical or juridical subject, as subject conscious of himself and others. In this sense, <truth> is understood as the very form of action – as action insofar as it implies the play of true and false, the acceptance or refusal of rules, the relation to oneself and other" (Foucault 1991c, 334–335). "Doing is inherent in the discursive" as Wahl put it (Wahl 1992, 69).

Maybe these quotations are not enough to make clear the whole intention of Foucauldian analysis. They, however, illustrate well Foucault's attempt to express truth production in terms of activity, and in terms of social relations. Moreover, they make clear that Foucault is looking for a form of analytics, which could include in itself the tools, the techniques, the social artefacts used by individuals participating in the games of truth.

4. Discussion

I started my paper inquiring into the incompatibility of the ideas of Ilyenkov and Foucault. I have tried to demonstrate the deceptive simplicity of dualistic contradictions between different philosophical programmes. Although incompatible on some planes, the programmes of Ilyenkov and Foucault are complementary in some other respects.

What can we learn, then, from Ilyenkov's concept of the Ideal? The most important aspect deals with the intention to go beyond simple dichotomies of idealism and materialism or of the body and the soul. We can see that it is not possible – or sensible – to distinguish the Ideal from the practical activity. Even more, the ideal aspect of the practical activity is becoming increasingly important in our late-modern society.

Ilyenkov's analysis of the Ideal could even have a new actuality in the discussions about virtual realities created by new technologies. Ilyenkov reminds us about the fact that the Ideal has always been there – it is not something new established only now with cyber-space machines. Moreover, Ilyenkov reminds us that all virtual realities are, although ideal, objective ones. A materialist conception of the Ideal is needed to avoid the post-modern illusions of the virtual world.

If the concept of the Ideal in itself is in some way paradoxical, so is the fate of Ilyenkov's theory, too. He was looking for a theory of human activity, combining ideal and concrete object-oriented aspects of this activity in their special social forms. He failed however, as did many Russian scholars of the socio-historical school, to develop a concrete methodology for empirical research, for the analyses of concrete historical forms of the activity on the plane of the Ideal. What is lacking here is the mediation between theory and actual research activities.

If we compare the work of Foucault and the work of Ilyenkov, it is easier to get the point. Foucault analysed the concrete forms and ways in which the truth was constructed in different activities and discourses, e. g. in medical and school discourses. Foucault perhaps was more successful in the analysis of the ideal aspects of collective practices. His analysis of the discursive techniques is one possible complement to Ilyenkov's concept of Ideal.

Foucault was, however, a historian looking for the past (keeping the present in the mind). It is understandable that he also had no methodology for the research of actual activities and interactions in the present social world. Both Ilyenkov and Foucault failed to develop a methodology for empirical research corresponding to their own theoretical concepts. A more concrete methodology is needed for the analysis of the human activity in the social world. To be effective, this methodology has to overcome the dichotomy between ideal and material activity and combine theoretical and empirical levels of inquiry in concrete research acts.

It seems to be that the development of concrete research methods has been most successful where the research has been an open circle between theoretical concepts and empirical data. I have in mind ethnomethodology, grounded theory, and similar developments.

Growing up from these traditions, many theoretical innovations emerge, which can be seen as relevant developments in the problem field opened in the works of Ilyenkov – and Foucault, too. I have in my mind concepts like artefact in the sense used by Marx Wartofsky (Wartofsky 1979), or the theory of interaction developed by Anselm Strauss (Strauss 1993).

The socio-historical tradition itself has developed rapidly in the last twenty years. Paradoxically, this development has mostly not occurred in Russia but in western European countries and in the United States, e.g. such theories as the cultural psychology of Michael Cole (Cole 1996), or the developmental work research model of Yrjö Engeström (Engeström 1987). These and other current developments of cultural-historical studies (see Chaiklin, Hedegaard, and Jensen 1999; Moll 1990; Smith, Harré, and Van Langenhove 1995; Wertsch, Del Río, and Alvarez 1995) are showing that there is an ongoing shift "from the realm of general ideas and fragmentary empirical studies into the realm of massive empirical research." (Tulviste 1999, 76).

I believe that we should overcome not only the dichotomy of ideal and matter, but also the dichotomy of theoretical and empirical research. Moreover, this requires a bold dialogue – or as Engeström put it "a multivoiced formation" (Engeström 1999, 35) – between all theories, articulating some way the Ideal and the practical aspects of socio-cultural activities of human beings.

Literature

Bourdieu, P., Wacquant, L., J.D. (1992), *An Invitation to Reflexive Sociology.* Chicago: The University of Chicago Press

Chaiklin, S., Hedegaard, M., Jensen, U. J., eds. (1999), *Activity Theory and Social Practice.* Aarhus: Aarhus University Press

Cole, M. (1996), *Cultural Psychology: A Once and Future Discipline.* Cambridge: The Belknap Press of Harvard University Press

Engeström, Y. (1987), *Learning by Expanding.* Helsinki: Orienta-Konsultit

Engeström, Y. (1999), Activity theory and individual and social transformation. In *Perspectives on Activity Theory*, ed. Y. Engeström, R. Miettinen, R.-L. Punamäki, pp. 19–52. Cambrigde: Cambridge University Press

Foucault, M. (1971), Orders of discourse. *Social science information,* 10:7–30

Foucault, M. (1973), *The Order of Things. An Arhaeology of the Human Sciences (Les Mots et les choses 1966).* New York: Vintage Books

Foucault, M. (1984), *The History of Sexuality. Volume I: An Introduction (La Volonté de savoir 1976).* Trans. Hurley, Robert. Harmondsworth: Penguin Books

Foucault, M. (1986), *The Care of the Self. The History of Sexuality, vol. 3 (Le Souci de Soi 1984).* London: Penguin

Foucault, M. (1988), *Madness and Civilization. A History of Insanity in the Age of Reason (Histoire de la Folie 1961).* Trans. Howard, Richard. New York: Vintage

Foucault, M. (1990), *The Use of Pleasure. Volume 2 of the History of Sexuality (L'Usage des plaisirs 1984).* Trans. Hurley, Robert. New York: Wintage Books

Foucault, M. (1991a), *The archaeology of knowledge (L'Arhéologie du savoir 1969).* Trans. A.M. Sheridan Smith. London: Routledge

Foucault, M. (1991b), *Discipline and Punish. The Birth of the Prison (Surveiller et punir 1975).* Trans. Sheridan, Alan. London: Penguin Books

Foucault, M. (1991c), Preface to "The History of Sexuality", Volume II. (Original work 1984). In *The Foucault Reader*, ed. P. Rabinow, pp. 333–339. London: Penguin Books

Foucault, M. (1991d), Questions of method (original work 1980). In *The Foucault Effect. Studies in Governmentality*, ed. G. Burchell, C. Gordon, P. Miller, pp. 73–86. London: Harvester Wheatsheaf

Foucault, M. (1991e), Truth and Power. In *The Foucault Reader*, ed. P. Rabinow, pp. 51–75. London: Penguin Books

Heikkinen, S., Silvonen, J., Simola, H. (1999), Technologies of Truth: Peeling Foucault's Triangular Onion. *Discourse,* 28:141–157

Ilyenkov, E. V. (1977a), The Concept of the Ideal. Trans. Robert Daglish. In *Philosophy in the USSR. Problems of Dialectical Materialism*, ed. Anonym, pp. 71–99. Moscow: Progress

Ilyenkov, E. V. (1977b), *Dialectical Logic. Essays on Its History and Theory (Dialektizeskaja logika 1974)*. Trans. H. Campbell Creighton. Moscow: Progress

Kozulin, A. (1984), *Psychology in Utopia. Toward a Social History of Soviet Psychology*. Cambridge, Massachusetts: The MIT Press

Marx, K. (1983), *Capital. A Critique of Political Economy. Volume 1. (Das Kapital1867/Capital 1887)*. Trans. Moore, Samuel & Aveling, Edward., ed. F. Engels Moscow: Progress

Moll, L. C., ed. (1990), *Vygotsky and Education*. Cambridge: Cambridge University Press

Petrovsky, A. (1990), *Psychology in the Soviet Union. A Historical Outline*. Trans. Lilia Nakhapetyan. Moscow: Progress

Rahmani, L. (1973), *Soviet Psychology. Philosophical, Theoretical and Experimental Issues*. New York: International Universities Press

Smith, J. A., Harré, R., Van Langenhove, L., eds. (1995), *Rethinking Psychology*. London: Sage

Strauss, A. (1993), *Continual Permutations of Actions*. New York: Aldine de Gruyter

Tulviste, P. (1999), Activity as Explanatory Principle in Cultural Psychology. In *Activity Theory and Social Practice*, ed. S. Chaiklin, M. Hedegaard, U. J. Jensen, pp. 66–78. Aarhus: Aarhus University Press

Wahl, F. (1992), Inside or outside philosophy? In *Michel Foucault. Philosopher*, ed. T. J. Armstrong, pp. 65–79. New York: Harvester Wheatsheaf

Wartofsky, M. W. (1979), *Models. Representations and the Scientific Understanding*. Boston Studien in the Philosophy of Science, eds. R. S. Cohen, M. W. Wartofsky, XLVIII Dordrecht: D. Reidel Publishing Company

Wertsch, J. V., Del Río, P., Alvarez, A., eds. (1995), *Sociocultural Studies of Mind*. Cambridge: Cambridge University Press

8

Ascending from the Abstract to the Concrete and Constructing a Working Hypothesis for New Practices

Reijo Miettinen

Introduction

In his book *Dialectics of the Abstract and the Concrete in Marx's Capital* (1982), E.V. Ilyenkov analyzed the Method of Ascent from the Abstract to the Concrete (MAAC) as a method of investigation of historically developing phenomena. The method aims at understanding the development of the object-phenomenon as it evolves from an original contradictory relationship, "cell", or initial abstraction into its present, mature and complex forms. Marx outlined this method in *Grundrisse*, in a passage on the method of political economy (1973, 100–108). In it, he introduces the concept of a "method of rising from the abstract to concrete" which has three basic steps. The study starts from the concrete "chaotic whole". It descends, then, to the abstraction of the basic determining categories. Thirdly, it "rises" again –

using the abstraction – to the concrete whole, this time as "a rich totality of determinations and relations" (ibid., 100).

Even in cases where a historical approach has been used in social sciences, the MAAC has not, to my knowledge, been applied or developed. The reasons are, no doubt, partly political, but they are also related to the content of Marx's analysis of capitalism. In his political economy, Marx traced the germ cell of a capitalist society (commodity and value), and then drew the whole system of concepts and determinations to uncover the developmental dynamics of capitalism. The unit of analysis is the capitalist society as a whole. This analysis, that took decades of work, seems too overwhelming a yardstick for the empirical social research of this day. On the other hand, one can ask: how did this project succeed in constructing the conceptual tools of analysing the diverse concrete developmental contradictions of local activities in society? In this paper, I shall focus on one important aspect of this problem: the relationship between the MAAC and the experimental activity.

Ilyenkov's Two Versions of the Relationship Between Theoretical Work and Practice

Ilyenkov does not deal much with the relationship between theoretical concepts and practice. In *Dialectics of the Abstract and the Concrete in Marx's Capital* there is a short passage on "Scientific abstraction (concept) and practice" (1982, 126–134). In it, Ilyenkov raises practice as an ultimate criterion of the objectivity of the concepts. He says that the truth of a concept is proved "[…] in complicated and mediated manner including the practical transformation of empirical reality." He further states that: "Practice is the highest instance in verifying a concept. The correspondence of a concept to an object is fully proved only when man succeeds in finding, reproducing or creating an object corresponding to the concept which he has formed" (ibid., 129).

This aspect, however, remains marginal in Ilyenkov's work on Marx's method in the study of capitalism. The example Ilyenkov uses in the afore mentioned passage consists of Lenin's criticism of Kautsky's view of the development of capitalism. Kautsky thought that capitalism will develop towards one single supertrust. This supertrust can then be nationalized by legal sanctions. No revolutionary practice is needed. Against this abstraction, Ilyenkov suggests Lenin's concept – based on Marx's analysis in *Capital* – of practice as a revolutionary political struggle of the working class. This conception seems, however, equally abstract. The concrete emancipatory contradictions of work, still strongly in the agenda of Marx's *Economic and Philosophic Manuscripts of 1844* and *Theses on Feurbach*, remained mostly uncovered in *Capital*. Here developed the conception of the allmighty oppressive force of the capital to the point, that only a "grand solution", the revolutionary practice through the party remained an option.

Ilyenkov does refer to experimental practice in dealing with one of the key issues in his philosophical work: the problem of human consciousness. He followed closely the experimental education work done by Alexander Meshcheryakov in the school for deaf, dumb and blind children in Zagorsk, set up in 1963. Meshcheryakov applied the basic ideas of cultural-historical activity theory to the development of those handicapped children (see Meshcheryakov 1979, 84–94). His basic conception was *joint activity* between the child and adult. It was first realized in the child's appropriation of simple basic skills of life (such as eating with a spoon), which both satisfy the biological needs of children and engender the need for communication and advance the development of intellect.

Ilyenkov wrote a paper on the methodological and theoretical significance of Meshcheryakov's work, *The genesis in personhood* (1977). In this paper, he argued that these experiments confirmed the conception that human psyche is not a gift of nature, but a socially-constituted phenomenon. Ilyenkov and the representatives of activity theory among them, A.N. Leontjev, P.J. Galperin, V.V. Davydov and A. Zaporozhets reflected on the significance of Meshcheryakov's experimental education (see Levitin 1982). The reflection comprised at least three ideas. First, they saw these experiments as experimental confirmation (*experimentum crucis*) of the socio-historical view of human psyche. Second, they underlined the theory as an invaluable tool in constructing a new kind of educational practice. Meshcheryakov's simple unit of analysis, joint action, starting from the elementary acts of self care, can be regarded as a kind of "cell" realized and enriched in the educational practice and its development. Third, in Meshcheryakov's experimental method, the theoretical study and the practical measures to enchance the development of the children formed a unity.

> The most important of all, that work can only be pursued if one has a clear accurate model of thought, of the human psyche in general [....] This is really an experimentum crusis for the theories of thought, intelligent creatures and the essence of human psyche in general (Ilyenkov in Levitin 1982, 227).

> In a deaf, dumb, and blind child, everything must be formed at a predetermined level – the construction of psychological processes is simultaneously a means of shaping the personality and a means of studying it. In the language of today, it can be called

unity of experimental training and instruction and the study of nature of psychological processes. (Davydov, in Levitin 1982, 232).

The status of *experimentum crucis* of Meshcheryakov's experimental activity has been questioned by several authors (see Bakhurst & Padden 1991).
Ilyenkov's argumentation was partly rhetoric, and he did not elaborate on the
case methodologically in any way comparable to that of *the Dialectics of the
Abstract and the Concrete in Marx's "Capital"*. It, however, shows that
Ilyenkov regarded the "ascending to the concrete" as taking place also through
the process of experimental activity, through directly observing how an evolving phenomenon takes shape in societal practice. This permits us to think
that the analysis of the method of *Capital* is not, necessarily, the only source
available in our endeavour to understand and develop the idea of the method
of ascending from the abstract to the concrete. The society and the individual, as systems, have different time spans in their developmental dynamics.
Correspondingly, the idea and possibility of experimental practice differs in
the case of these two systems.[1] Since I am focusing in this paper on the
studies of the development of local communities of practitioners, which find
their position between the history of society and the life histories of individuals, there is all the reason to take into account the methodological reflections
on both levels.[2]

Developmental Work Research and MAAC

An approach called developmental work research was developed during the
1980s and 1990s to study the change and development of work and other
activities (see Engeström 1987). The approach has derived its theoretical
background historically from activity theory, especially the work of A.N.
Leontjev. (Vygotsky 1978; Leontyev 1981). The idea of the MAAC influenced the approach, first of all. through the work of V.V. Davydov, who applied
it to create a didactic method for fostering the learning of theoretical thought
(Davydov 1990).

    In developmental work research, the unit of analysis is a concrete work
activity, understood as an object oriented, collective activity system
(Engeström 1987). The system evolves by solving its constantly emerging
internal contradictions. Since the approach focuses on change in the local
work activities, the problem of the relationship of thought to the practice is
focal. In the methodological cycle of developmental work research, the
historical-analytical study of work is connected to the practical-experimental
approach, that is, to the practical transformation of work (Figure 1). I will

suggest, that this cycle can be regarded as an application and transformation of the idea of the MAAC in studying the development of local activities or communities of practice and thought.

In the research cycle, the first phase is ethnography. It is comprised of the delineation of the activity to be studied, description of the key work procedures and tools, as well as the first characterization of the problems visible in the work. Also, the multiple perspectives of the various people in the community are depicted. This phase corresponds with the first step in MAAC, the "chaotic conception of the whole".

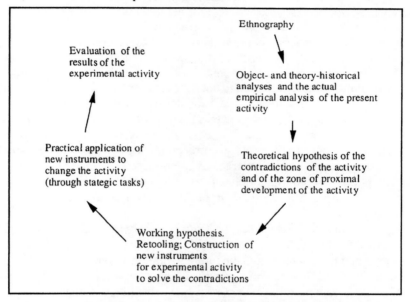

Figure 1. The methodological cycle of developmental work research (see Engeström   1987, 323).

Ethnography is followed by historical analyses of the development of the activity (object-historical analysis) and the development of its theoretical tools (theory historical analysis). These are complemented by the analysis of the problems of the present activity, the actual empirical analysis. This phase corresponds with the second step in MAAC, the formation of the theoretical abstraction, transition from the "chaotic conception of whole" to the concrete, historically and empirically grounded abstraction. It is oriented to the understanding of the contradictions of the activity. The disturbances and problems found in the actual empirical analysis are interpreted in the light of the historical analyses. The result of this phase is the theoretical abstraction, definition of the contradictions of the activity.

The historical analyses trace the origin of the activity and the central contradictory relationships within it. The results of the historical analyses are used for gaining understanding and interpreting the daily disturbances and problems of the actual work activity. In it, the present is understood both within the context of the global history of corresponding activities and in the context of the local, particular history of the activity.

The third phase of the methodological cycle is comprised of defining a hypothesis for [4] the reconstruction of the activity trough experimental activity in which the hypothesis with the corresponding new tools will be tested, evaluated and further elaborated. This hypothesis can be characterized as a practical form of the theoretical initial abstraction. It is based on the results of the historical and the actual empirical analyses of the present activity, being simultaneously oriented to the future, to the transformation of activity and to the solution of the contradiction defined by the previous analysis.

The fourth phase of the cycle is the experimental activity, the practical application and testing of the hypothesis and corresponding new instruments to change the activity. This phase corresponds with the third step in MAAC, the ascending from the abstract to the concrete. It leads to a concrete conception of the contradictions of the system which can be characterized in terms of dialectically concrete, in terms of "the rich totality of definitions and relations".

The relationship between the historical-analytical and the experimental-practical in the cycle is related to the interconnectedness of the past, the present and the orientation to the future in human activities. In the attempt at finding the initial abstraction, a genetically essential contradictory relationship takes place from the point of view orienting to the future, to the transformative practice. The concrete understanding of the contradictions constitutes a starting point for finding measures to change the activity for the resolution of these contradictions. This will serve as a working hypothesis for experimental practice. The working hypothesis can also be understood as a future-oriented form of a germ cell. Its development and growth into more complex forms and concrete manifestations starts with experimentation. The experimentation may then lead to transformation, expansion and stabilization of the practice as suggested by the germ cell hypothesis. This may lead to a qualitative change in the activity.

What is particularly challenging in the method, is the transition from analytical-theoretical work (of defining the contradictions) into experimental activity. Both of the these parts of the methodological cycle are essential. Without the historical grounding and the definition of the contradictions, the formulation of the hypothesis of change tends to remain voluntaristic, wishful or based on external ethical norms only, such as democracy or self-actualization. John Dewey, in his study on conditions of reflective and transformative activity, underlined this danger (Dewey 1938,474): "Purpose is vain and utopian unless based upon knowledge of existing conditions, which constitute both obstacles to overcome and the means by which the end must be executed."

Any working hypothesis is only an abstraction in relation to the forthcoming practice. One of the key arguments for the interventionist research strategy has been, that only trough experimental, practical activity the "real conditions" of change become visible, and the value and reality of a new alternative form of activity become tested. The new form is not testable theoretically only, but also through experiments which make visible those conditions and resistances that the traditional, non-interventionist study research would not uncover. In the experiments with, and implementation of, the new means and form of activity, new contradictions and relationships keep emerging between the humans, artifacts and rules.

In the methodological cycle of developmental work research, the tree steps of MAAC are accomplished through the analysis of the contradictions of the present activity, and in the experimental testing of the working hypothesis formulated and accepted by a local community of practitioners. The transition from the historical-analytical (definition of the contradiction) to the experimental-practical (testing the working hypothesis) is mediated by the hypothesis formation, which then, is the particularly demanding and decisive task in the method.

Working Hypothesis Between the Past and the Future

The Chicago pragmatists, John Dewey and George Herbert Mead developed a methodology of transformative social action through the formulation and experimental testing of a working hypothesis. Their concept can be used for conceptualizing the relationships between historical analyses and practice. The working hypothesis was the central concept in the method of the Chicago pragmatists to solve social problems intelligently and to reconstruct the society. They recognized, that the future is open ended and that all conceptions are by their nature hypotheses that must be tested in practice (see e.g. Strauss 1991). George Herbert Mead argued for the necessity of a working hypothesis in his paper *The working hypothesis in social reform* (1899). In the working hypothesis, the irrefutable interpenetratedness of the past, present and future in an activity is realized (Mead 1938, 347–348):

> The present is the combination of the future and the past in the process that is going on. The future is the control of the process, and the past is which is there as an irrevocable condition of the ongoing of the process [...]. The future comes in terms of the act, the past in terms of the field of the act. Where they merge in the process, we have the present.

Dewey used the terms "operative idea" and "possible relevant solution" as synonymous for the working hypothesis (1991, 133). In his description of the pattern of inquiry in *Logic, the Theory of Inquiry* (ibid., 105–129), the starting point for inquiry is an indeterminate situation (typically a habit, an established way of doing things, does not work). This indeterminate situation or "shock" of not being able to act on a routine basis leads to the process of reflection. It is composed of the definition of the problem, study of the conditions of action, and a suggestion for the problem-solution, that is, the working hypothesis. In characterizing these phases, Dewey underlines "observation of the conditions "that must be reckoned with or taken into account in any relevant solution that is proposed" (ibid., 113).

Dewey's characterization, however, lacks the idea of cultural mediation: he does not focus on the meaning of artifacts as part of the conditions. Correspondingly, he does not deal systematically with the significance of the construction of new instruments for the experimentation and transformation of the activity.

In the pragmatist method of solving social problems, the working hypothesis is formed by studying the conditions behind the problem and those enabling its solution. Even if the prior experience is thought to contribute to this analysis and to the formation of the working hypothesis, historical analysis is not explicitly included in the method. The whole process leading to the construction of the working hypothesis remains fairly unarticulated. In the methodological cycle of developmental work research, historical analyses constitute an essential part of finding basis for the working hypothesis and experimental action.

In the context of studying change and development of work, the process of the MAAC can be divided into two parts: analytical-theoretical and experimental-practical mediated by a hypothesis. This hypothesis seems to constitute a duality. First, there is the result of the analytical-theoretical work in the form of the hypothesis of contradictions and of the direction and possibilities of the development of the work. This theoretical abstraction must be turned into a working hypothesis so limited and articulated that it can be implemented, tested and evaluated. This means that instruments for the experiments must be developed and articulated. In activity theory this process is called "retooling".

Several complementary concepts and tools have been used within developmental work research to conceptualize and actualize the transition from the historical-theoretical analysis to experimentation. They have been presented as aspects, "forms" or modalities of the hypothesis. The concept of the *contradictions between the basic elements of the activity system* (object, subject, means, division of labour, rules), has been used to define contradictions in a way that helps the community to orient itself in designing the working hypothesis for future activity. Second, several concepts have been used to characterize the transition to the future alternative activity. One of them is the concept of *zone of proximal* development. It was originally defined by Vygotsky to characterize the social nature of the development of a child. It was extended to apply to collective activity by Engeström (1987, 174). Also the term *construction of a new model of activity,* or "hypothetical picture of the next, more advanced developmental form of the activity system" (Engeström 1987, 327), has been used. It is a sketchy overall characterization of a forthcoming new activity. It has often been presented in the form of a picture of the future activity system, covering all the elements of the activity. These kind of overall characterizations risk becoming wishful constructions, not testable in experimental activity, unless complemented with adequate tools or methods.

In the attempts to make the hypothesis a "working hypothesis", operative enough for experimentation, one of the elements of the activity has been taken as its starting point. *Constructing a new object and motive* for the activity, has been defined as pivotal for the collective hypothesis construction. It is based on the object-orientedness of activity theory: the object, outcome and use-value to be achieved gives meaning and motive for the activity. On the other hand, the thesis of mediation leads to emphasizing the *construction of new instruments for the activity.* The idea of retooling as a condition of change was introduced by Vygotsky is his concept of double stimulation in studying and enhancing a child's development. Experimentation and the evaluation of its results without an articulated and defined tool or method, is hardly possible. However, because of the systemic nature of activity, this experimentation also requires changes in the division of labour and rules.

One way of approaching the above discussed problem has been the concept of a *strategic task*: a task or action that is a vehicle of change for the whole activity system, representing "the points of probable breakthroughts into a qualitatively more advanced form of activity "(Engeström 1987, 334). One and the same action comprises the "seeds" of a new object and outcome, tools and division of labor. A.N. Leontyev studied the dynamics between acts and collective activity that emerged as result of the social division of labour (Leontyev 1981). Using his terms, strategic task is an action (or bundle of actions) that will later turn into a new type of activity. To take an example: at school, if a new type of teaching/learning method, radically different from the prevailing lesson- and classroom practice, develops into a dominant work form there, the teaching and learning activity will change qualitatively. In the following section, an attempt to implement such a method is being analyzed.

A strategic task with the experimentation of a new kind of tool system or method could be called a hypothesis of *a practical germ cell*. It can be characterized as something simple that will later developed into complex, extended and varied forms and, finally, turn into a new activity. To gain this status through experimental activity, it must retain its connection to the analysis of the historical contradictions of the present activity. Sustaining this connection, is a means of avoiding voluntarism and orientation to short-sighted problem solving, often typical to action research.

An Example of a Historical Germ Cell in the Analysis of Teaching Work: School Learning and its Reproduction

I will illustrate the relationship between historical-analytical and experimental by presenting an example of both in the context of studying teaching work. The example is based on my study on teacher's work in a vocational school, Helsinki Business Polytechnics (HBP) which was also a teacher education institution (Miettinen 1990, 1993 and 1999). A forthcoming state reform on vocational education requested supervising teachers to plan several new courses on the theory of learning and teaching in vocational education. Most of them felt the traditional classroom-, lesson-, and teacher-dominated teaching methods utterly inadequate for accomplishing this task. In the discussions and interviews they told that they missed theoretical tools of conceptualizing learning and connecting teaching to the developments in working life.

The contradiction of the teaching work in HBP was defined, in 1986, in the following way (Miettinen 1994): The rationalized static curriculum system and the school's subject-, text- and lesson-centered teaching practice is in contradiction with the aim of learning to understand and master the changing working life. It is this changing working life, where the students of the polytechnic will be work in, solving problems and creating new practices. A series of historical analyses with different time span and an actual-empirical analysis contributed to the definition of this contradiction.

Bernd Fichtner's (1984) and Yrjö Engeström's (1987) analyses of the inner contradiction by identifying two interrelated historical processes, the emergence of written language – and along with it, school text – and the emergence of independent school activity that became isolated from other societal activities. As a result, the knowledge at school became detached from the context of its generation and use.

Although texts, as a new kind of secondary artifact, immensely extended the possibilities of transmitting knowledge related to human practices, a paradoxical phenomenon took place. Instead of being an instrument of creativity, the text became a given, inert artifact that was mechanically reproduced. This was connected to the conception of knowledge during the Middle Ages: "Knowledge is understanding text. Getting to know reality means to learn what the authorities wrote about it" (Fichtner 1984, 53).

Engeström further defines the nature of school learning with the help of the concept of human activity, developed by Leont'ev (1978), according to which the nature of an activity is determined by its object and motive. According to Engeström (1987, 101) the essence of school learning or school-going activity is "the strange reversal of object and instrument. In school-going activity text takes the role of the object. This object is molded by pupils in a curious manner: the outcome of their activity is above all the same text reproduced and modified orally or in a written form" (Engeström 1987, 101). The reason for this reversal is the historical isolation of school from the rest of societal activities and as a result, the text to be studied is also isolated from the life activity of the students. For John Dewey, the problem of school in the turn of century was a problem of "book school". Passive reception and memorization produces the paradox of the combination of slavish dependency upon books with a real inability to use them. Dewey saw *as* the causes of the situation the separation and isolation of school from other activities of society and the decontextualization of the school text.

The vast literature covering school practices and classroom interaction in this century seemed to confirm the hypothesis of the contradiction included in the school learning. The studies on classroom interaction, for instance, have persistently shown some permanent features of classroom interaction. The teacher speaks about 70 % of the time. The teacher makes questions, which request the students to repeat what is written in a book. The pupils do not ask questions. Their speech is composed of the short answers to the questions of the teacher.[5]

The analysis of the Anglo-American curriculum theory in this century uncovered the modern mechanisms of reproducing school learning. The school administration and the early curriculum theory in the United States adopted Taylor's scientific management as their basic approach (see, Haber

1964 and Kliebard 1986). The essense of this approach was the control of schoolwork by means of specified goals and a clear division between planning and execution. Specialists (curriculum planners and authorities) were to decide the goals and contents. Teachers were to execute the plans. This model was realized through a new artifact: the officially approved, grade-specific standard textbook package. The package is comprised of grade-level specific textbooks, workbooks, teacher manuals and standard tests. The production of the packages is directed by commercial interests of the publishers. The rationalized curriculum practice with standard text-book packages formed the mechanism that extensively reproduced and further transformed the school learning in the second half of the 20th century.

The local history of teaching work in HBP was connected to the history of the Finnish teacher education institution called the "normal school". HBP became a normal school in 1952. The forms of teacher education in a normal school were regulated in detail by an order given by Ministry of Education. Teacher rehearsal was composed of listening to 200 lessons in the normal school, giving eight demonstration lessons and, finally, an official teacher test in the form of a lesson given to a jury of six persons including the representatives of Ministry of Trade and Industry and business life. The grade of the "teaching skill" and teacher studies was given on the basis of the lesson, nick-named by the teachers as the "parade lesson". This was a specific mechanism that reproduced the traditional school learning in HBP.

The actual empirical study of the teaching practice in HBP was done by interviewing teachers and by collecting the sample artifacts they used in teaching. This showed that teaching – and its tools – were continually concentrated on the planning of the lessons. The teachers felt tied by the subject- and lesson centered system. There was very little collaboration between the teachers of different subjects. There were innovative attempts by the various teachers to connect the teaching to the activities outside the school. These attempts were not, however, submitted to join discussion and, therefore, remained as individual attempts without any continuity or future elaboration. The actual-empirical study showed the relevance of the theory of school learning and showed the specific and historically unique forms it was expressing in HPB.

The theory of school learning includes a program for action or operative orientation: the knowledge must somehow be connected to real life practices and, therefore, transcend the boundary between the school and other societal activities. What are the concrete conditions of such transcending, what kinds of solutions are needed to achieve this, remain, however, open.

Formulating a Hypothesis of a Germ Cell for New Teaching Activity

The "cell" or initial hypothesis, based on historical analysis, depicted the basic contradiction of learning at school: decontextualized text turned into the object of activity. As a result, a specific type of learning emerges, the outcomes of which are hardly usable in life activities outside the school context. This initial abstraction also opens a general perspective for an alternative: returning the knowledge into contact with its generation and use. This initial hypothesis for change is a powerful abstraction, but, at the same time, abstract. A testable working hypothesis for change experiments is needed.

In the summer 1985, in discussions with the supervising teachers of HPB, we formed a model for the development of teaching and teacher education in HBP. The collaborative planning of large thematic curriculum units was founded as a central means for breaking and overcoming the lesson-, teacher- and text-book-centered traditional teaching methods that had enjoyed such a dominating position in the school.

The idea of a thematic unit combined the following three ideas. First, a thematic unit was defined in terms of the central concepts to be learned. Modeling was used to define these concepts and the core content of the unit. Second, the thematic unit was supposed to be relevant from the point of view of the evolving problems and challenges of working life. The planning of the thematic unit was to realize the connection of the school with the society. Third, the thematic unit was planned as a learning process for pupils on the basis of the activity theoretical model of learning, the investigative model of learning (Engeström 1994; Davydov 1982). On the basis of the model, the unit was divided into a series of pupil tasks designed to avoid teacher domination, to ensure active student participation and independent theoretical mastery of the substance of the theme unit.

In two years, 1986–1988, the curriculum thematic unit planning was extended to all school subjects in HBP, and dozens of curriculum units were planned and implemented. The analysis of these experiments showed that there were several contradictory ways of implementing the thematic unit planning: fusing to the old ways of teaching, turning into administrative formal exercise and an expansive way. It included collaboration between the teachers of different subjects, high student involvement and collaboration with actors outside the school.

The design and implementation of the thematic units meant considerable change in teaching. However, it did not succeed in resolving the basic contradiction uncovered by the historical-theoretical analysis. The teachers repeatable reported that the students' thoughts and solutions in thematic-units remained formal without grounding to or validation in the various conditions of working life. The planning tended to remain within the confines of school institution. A central conclusion made of thematic-unit experiments was: if the object of learning is the changing work practices, it is necessary to include people from these activities in the of learning process (Miettinen 1993; 1997). The experiments showed that the collaboration with the representatives of working life increased student motivation and brought a new, practice-based standard to the learning process. Therefore, a new social organization, network of learning was called for.[6] It would comprise teachers, students as well as practitioners and specialists from work organizations outside the school.

A new hypothesis for experimental activity was formulated by the teachers at HBP and Merikoski College in 1994. At HBP it was called "Net", referring to the network organization of the unit (Miettinen 1997, Peisa & Miettinen 1999). The basic features of the Net-type of studying are presented in Figure 2. The Figure characterizes the object of learning and the social organization of the project work.

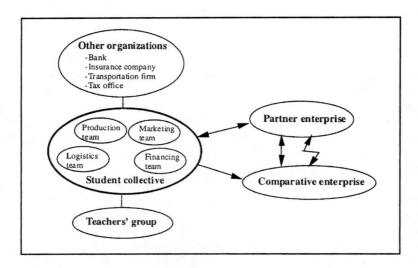

Figure 2. The object and social organization of learning in the alternative enterprise study project developed by HBP and other polytechnics

The object of learning in this project can be defined in two complementary ways. First, it is comprised of the conditions, means and actions
prerequisite for the foundation of a business firm. Secondly, the object
comprises the developmental possibilities and challenges of an existing
commercial firm, the partner firm. These challenges were made visible by
three steps in the project.

First, the student teams study the basic functions (production, marketing,
finance, logistics etc.) of the partner firm in its business environment. Second,
they form a conception of what is problematic and deserves to be reorganized
in the these business activities. Third, they make a business plan for an
alternative firm. That plan offers solutions to the problems they have been
able to recognize in the functions of the partner firm. Thus, the object of
learning includes the developmental possibilities and needs of an actual firm.
Since the students have no direct accountability to the partner firm, they can
freely develop alternative solutions in their plan. The suggestions emerging
from the plan are submitted to discussion with the firm, which is free to
chose whether to ignore, develop further, or implement them.

Figure 2 also displays the social organization of the project. The teachers
function as planners and initiators of the process, informants and sources of
knowledge for the students and also as evaluators of the solutions. Soon after
the start-off of the project, students take the initiative and become the main
subject in the process. The student collective independently organizes the
work of the project, produces the analyses and draws the alternative business
plan. The representatives of the partner firm provide information and access
to firm's activities for the student groups' analysis. They evaluate the quality
of the solutions proposed by the students and consider the usefulness of the
latter for themselves and proceed to study further or implement the suggestions.

The alternative enterprise method differs in many important respects
from the previous working hypothesis, the thematic-unit planning. The
students tested the knowledge and tools supplied by the courses of the
polytechnics in the analysis of the partner firm's situation and in planning the
alternative ways of realizing the firm's activities. The student teams also
looked for new tools outside the school to solve the problems they discovered.
The interactive analyses of the partner firm's problems, and search for relevant
tools for solution reflects one of the basic mechanisms of change in working
life. The students organize the planning work quite independently. They make
a project plan for their work and formulate the rules and norms for their
collaboration. The students also establish the network relationships necessary
for their project with actors outside the school context. In this sense, it can be
said that the new method meets, better than thematic-unit planning, the
perspective implied by the original theoretical hypothesis: bringing knowledge

into its context of use and transcending the boundary between the school an other societal activities.

The experimentation with network-based projects is now going on in several polytechnics in Finland: the ascending from the abstract to the concrete is still on its way. These experiments will show, whether this method can be further developed, implemented and established as an important form of learning. Its perfecting depends – among other things – on the possibility and skill of the polytechnics for constructing and maintaining mutually beneficial relationships between polytechnics, firms and other work organizations.

Conclusions

In this paper I have elaborated, how the idea of ascending from the abstract to the concrete, elaborated, among others, by Ilyenkov, can be applied and further advances in the study of the development of local work practices. It was suggested that the historical-theoretical work, which results in the definition of the initial abstraction, the contradiction of the activity, must be complemented with a working hypothesis for the experimentation and transformation of the work. This working hypothesis for experimentation is a practical germ cell, a strategic new action with new instruments that may later develop into a new activity. Testing and carrying further this hypothesis in the transformative practice, constitutes the ascending from the abstract to the concrete in the process. A methodological focal point in any developmental study on human activities, is the interconnection between and transition from the historical-theoretical form to the practical form of the hypothesis.

Notes

[1] In some sense, "real existing socialism" could be regarded as an experiment oriented to solving the contradictions of capitalism by applying the theory of the revolutionary party of the working class. This experiment, however, has failed.

[2] Silvia Scribner has analyzed the significance of the different levels of historical analysis in activity-theoretical tradition (1985). She concludes that between the general history of society and individual history, the level of individual societies or cultural groups is needed (Schribner 1985, 139). The analysis of the development of contradictions of a local activity system is an attempt to answer this challenge.

[3] A review of this research, see Cuban 1984. David Olson (1980) analyzed how text dominated the linguist interaction in a classroom. In normal interaction, questions are made for the purpose of asking for more information. In the classroom, the questions are for control: the teacher expects the pupils to reproduce what he already knows. Linguistic interaction in classroom constitutes a language game or speech genre particular to the school institutions (to the form of life at school, to the teacher- and text centered teaching practice).

[4] The concept of network of learning was first used by Philip Coombs (1985) in his analysis of the crisis of education

References

Bakhurst, D. & Padden, C. (1991), *The Meshcheryakov Experiment: Soviet Work on the Education of Blind–Deaf Children.* In: *Learning and Instruction* Vol. 1, 201–215.

Coombs, P.H. (1985), *The World Crisis of Education.* New York: Oxford University Press.

Cuban, L. (1984), *How Teachers Taught: Constancy and Change in American Classrooms 1890-1980.* New York : Longman.

Davydov, V. V: (1982), *The Psychological structure and Contents of Learning Activity*

In School Children. In: Glaser, R. & Lompcher, J. (eds.), *Cognitive and Motivational Aspects of Instruction.* Berlin: Deutscher Verlag der Wissenschaften, 37-44.

Davydov, V.V. (1990), *Types of Generalization in Instruction: Logical and Psychological Problems of Structuring School Curricula.* Reston, Virginia: National Council of Teachers of Mathematics.

Dewey, J. (1938), *The Determination of Ultimate Values or Aims trough Antecedent or Apriori Speculations or through Pragmatic or Empirical Inquiry.* In: Whipple, G. (ed.). *The 27ᵗʰ Yearbook of the National Society for the Study of Education.* Bloomington: Public Scholl Publishing Company, 463–477.

Dewey. J. (1991), Logic. *The Theory of Iinquiry.* In: *The Later Works of John Dewey,* Edited by Jo Ann Boydston. Volume 12. Carbondale & Edwardsville: Southern Illinois University Press.

Engeström, Y. (1987),. *Learning by Expanding. An Activity-theoretical Approach to Developmental Research.* Helsinki: Orienta-Konsultit.

Engeström, Y. (1995), *Kehittävä työntutkimus.* [Developmental work research]. Helsinki. Painatuskeskus.

Fichtner, B. (1984), *Learning and Learning Activity – Two Different Types of Learning in School and the Historical-societal Contexts of Their Development.* In: E. Bol, J. P. P. Haenen & M. A. Wolters (Eds.), *Education for Cognitive Development.* Den Haag: SVO, 47–61.

Haber, S. (1964), *Efficiency Uplift. Scientific Management in the Progressive Era 1890-1920.* Chicago: The University of Chicago Press.

Ilyenkov, E. V. (1981), *Psyyken ja persoonallisuuden synty: erään kokeen tuloksia.* [Original: The Genesis of Personhood 1977]. (trans. Airi Leppänen & Yrjö Engeström). In: *Tiede ja Edistys* 2/1981, 23-33.

Ilyenkov, E.V. (1982), *The Dialectics of the Abstract and the Concrete in Marx's Capital.* Moscow: Progress Publishers.

Kliebard, H. (1986), *The Struggle for the American Curriculum 1893-1958.* Thetford: Routledge.

Leont'ev, A.N. (1978), *Activity, Consciousness and Personality.* Englewood Cliffs: Prentice Hall.

Leontyev, A.N. (1981), *Problems of the Development of Mind.* Moscow: Progress.

Levitin, K. (1982), *One Is Not Born a Personality.* Moscow: Progress Publishers.

Marx, K. (1973), *Grundrisse. Foundations of the Critique of Political Economy.* London: Peguin Books.

Mead, J.H. (1899), *The Working Hypothesis in Social Reform.* In: *The American Journal of Sociology* V, 367–371.

Mead, J.H. (1938), *The Philosophy of Act.* Chicago, Illinois: The University of Chicago Press.

Meshcheryakov. A. (1979), *Awakening life. Forming Behavior and the Mind in Deaf-blind Children.* Moscow: Progress Publishers.

Miettinen, R. (1990), *Koulun muuttamisen mahdollisuudesta. Analyysi opetustyön kehityksestö ja ristiriidoista.* [On the Possibility of Changing the School – an Analysis of Development and Contradictions of Teaching Work]. Helsinki: Gaudeamus 1990.

Miettinen, R. (1994), *Oppitunnista oppimistoimintaan* [From Lesson to Learning Activity. A study on the Development of Commercial Teaching and Teacher Education in the Finnish Businessmen's' Commercial College in 1986-1991]. Helsinki: Gaudeamus.

Miettinen, R. (1997), *Networks of learning in Vocational Education. Life Long Learning.* in: *Europe* Vol 2(3), 147–153.

Miettinen, R. (1999), *Transcending Traditional School Learning. Teacher's Work and Networks of Learning.* In: Engeström, Y. & Miettinen, R. & Punamäki, R-L.(eds.) 1996. *Perspectives on Activity Theory.* Cambridge: Cambridge University Press, 325–344.

Olson. D.R. (1980), *On the language and authority of textbooks.* In: *Journal of Communication* 30(1),186-196.

Peisa, S. & Miettinen, R. (1999), *Integrating Learning and the Study of Change at Work: The Alternative Eneterprise method.* Paper presented in the The 8th European Conference for Research on Learning and Instruction. August 24.–28. 1999, Gothenburg.

Scribner, S. (1985), *Vygotsky's Uses of History.* In: Wetsch, J.V. (ed.) *Culture, Communication and Cogniton. Vygotskian perspectives.* Cambridge: Cambridge University Press, 119–145.

Strauss, A. (1991), *Mead's Multiple Conceptions of Time and Evolution: Their Contexts and Their Consequences for Theory.* In: *International Sociology* Vol. 6 (4), 411-426.

Vygotsky, L. (1978), *Mind in Society. The Development of Higher Psychological Processes.* Cambridge, Mass.: Harvard University Press.

9

VYGOTSKY, ILYENKOV AND MAMARDASHVILI: SEARCHING FOR THE MONISTIC THEORY OF MIND (METHODOLOGICAL NOTES)

NIKOLAI VERESOV

"A new [...] understanding of the facts can emerge only through the critical assimilation of the results of the previous development of thought..."
— *Evald Ilyenkov*

1. Introduction

The aim of my paper is to discuss some aspects of the monistic approach to the analysis of psychological problems. I will try to explore three variants of the philosophical monism, as presented in works of L. Vygotsky, E. Ilyenkov and M. Mamardashvili. I will first draw attention to certain interrelations between these approaches. Secondly, I will attempt to formulate some thoughts concerning to what could be defined as "monistic philosophy of psychology".

It seems that nowadays psychology does not always pay sufficient attention to its philosophical foundations. This is not surprising – the market of modern philosophies is so large (though not necessarily rich), that finding something appropriate is often just a matter of taste. In this respect resorting to "old names" (Descartes, Spinoza, Kant, Hegel, Marx) may appear somewhat archaic, an irrelevant old-fashioned philosophical design for building psychological theories. But the problems set out by those "old" philosophers (for example, the problem of *subject and object*, or of *substance*) surprisingly became essentially acute for the science in the end of the 20th century.

One such problem explored by the old philosophers was the problem of *monism* as an explanatory principle. This means (as I shall try to demonstrate below), that it is, for example, scarcely possible to understand correctly the *distinguishing features* of certain psychological theories unless we take into account the kind of monistic approach they were based on.

Hegel once stated that all serious philosophical theorising should start from Spinoza, i.e. from monism. What does this mean for a psychology that is basically constructed on the Cartesian idea of subjective (the internal) and objective (the external) realities as *two* interconnected but separated *worlds*? That radical dualism is rooted in the history of this discipline is very often considered as obvious and self-evident. But, as we can see from the history of science, even self-evident principles are matters that can change in a course of time.

For example, astronomy in the Middle Ages was evidently based on the idea of two types of mechanics, celestial and Earth-bound, each ruled by a different set of laws. Heliocentrical model which can be considered a monistic view, changed the situation radically. This "non-classical" model was not based on common sense, but nevertheless corresponded completely to the idea that the world is one.

But let us imagine that astronomers were still today continuing their search for connections and interrelations between heavenly and Earth-bound mechanics because such a picture corresponds to common sense and everyday experience. What results could we expect from such a search? The more data they will obtain the more complicated the overall picture of the interrelations of these two mechanics would be. And a more complicated overall picture would consequently require an increasing number of explanatory principles. Finally, a surfeit of principles would only lead to a flood of new "theories".

Isn't this, in fact, a rather accurate description of modern psychology? Almost all the experimental and empirical data are analysed from a dualistic "internal-external" initial explanatory premise. Are any other approaches possible? At any rate, the presupposition that the monistic approach (that is, "psychological heliocentrism") is possible (and even necessary) should perhaps be taken into account when discussing perspectives on the future development of this science. A hundred years ago John Dewey described the basic situation quite clearly when he wrote that "the older dualism between sensation and idea is repeated in the current dualism of peripheral and central structures and functions; the older dualism of body and soul finds a distinct echo in the current dualism of stimulus and response" (Dewey, 1896, 357–358). Has anything changed?

There are a number of names in the history of philosophy (especially Russian names, although not exclusively so), which show that we cannot say that nothing changed from the times of John Dewey. These include L. Vygotsky, E. Ilyenkov and M. Mamardashvili undoubtedly belong to them.

At first glance, these thinkers had differing backgrounds, theoretical and methodological orientations and perspectives. One could even say that they were opposite to each other in many respects. But there are at least two points around which we can find similarities within their approaches. I am referring to their impact on psychology, particularly with respect to the problem of the origins and nature of human consciousness and their *search for the monistic theory of mind*.

In this paper I will try to show which aspects of their thought speak to us today and could be applied to psychology. As for the differences, they do not always lie where the modern researchers commonly suppose.

2. Vygotsky and Non-Classical Philosophy of Psychology

Lev Vygotsky is well-known as a psychologist and methodologist in scien-ce.[1] We do not, however, know so much about his philosophical background. This leads to some difficulties in understanding his basic ideas and concepts, as I shall try to show.

D. Elkonin considered Vygotsky's theory a "the non-classical approach" in psychology (El'konin1989, 478). But what was the theoretical basis for such an approach? It seems that in the writings of Vygotsky we find what might be defined as a "non-classical philosophy" for "non-classical" psychology. This non-classical philosophy is very much connected with the ideas of a monistic explanation of human consciousness. The following will show better what I mean.

It is not only Marxism which can be considered as Vygotsky's philosophical orientation and basis. He was a son of the so-called "silver age or Russian culture". The language of that period of Russian culture, that is, the language of the theatre, of poetry and of art was the language which Vygotsky knew and understood. A. Potebnya and W. Humboldt, Descartes and Spinoza, Gustav Shpet and P. Blonsky, and many others were part of his social and cultural environment and thus "participated" in scientific "dialogues" with Vygotsky in ways in which the likes of Ivan Pavlov or Karl Marx did not. He was at no stage a solitary thinker, or a kind of messiah. The search for the possibility of a monistic approach to the problem of human consciousness was in the focus of his work (for more details see Veresov, 1999).

Having this in mind let us take a look on "non-classical psychology" of Vygotsky.

In *The Historical Sense of Psychological Crisis* (1926) Vygotsky claims that contemporary psychology is an empirical science. He treats empiricism as constituting a crisis in psychology and defines dualism as its epistemological source. Dualism is viewed as a sort of methodological disease.

What alternative to that disease did Vygotsky offer? What sort of monism did he bring to "classical psychology"?

In modern literature the "non-classical" Vygotskian psychology always associates with the idea of the social origins of mind and with the principle of mediation of higher psychological functions.

"All the higher functions originate as actual relations between human individuals" (Vygotsky 1978, 57). But looking from the philosophical perspective we hardly find anything new or "non-classical" here. Thus, Wilhelm Wundt propounded that higher psychological processes could only be investigated through the historical study of cultural products, such as fairy tales, language and cultural customs. G. H. Mead, John Dewey, Émile Durkheim, Ernst Cassirer and many others proceeded from the assumption that the nature of human consciousness is determined by sociocultural factors.

Thus, that which was "new" for psychology was not new for philosophy. The exception to this rule was the idea of monism. The social and the individual were *not* seen by Vygotsky as being mutually opposite:

> It is very naive to understand social only as collective, as the presence of a set of people. Social is also present where there is only one person and his personal experiences. Social is not outside of us, neither is it between people – it is in us, in the heads of these people (Vygotsky 1987, 131).

The social was not viewed within an "external-internal" paradigm. Developing this Vygotsky maintains merely monistic idea:

> All higher mental functions are internalised social relationships [...] Their composition, genetic structure, and means of action – in a word, their whole nature – is

social. Even when we turn to mental processes, their nature remains quasi-social...
(Vygotsky 1981,164–165).

The point, therefore, is not the "social origin of mind" but rather that the external and the internal are viewed as two *forms* of existence of human mind, as two modes of the *the same* higher mental (social) function.

Accordingly the famous idea of *mediation* could also be viewed from the monistic perspective: "…the central fact about our psychology is that of mediation" (Vygotsky 1982, 166).

All higher mental functions are mediated processes. A central and fundamental aspect of their structure is the use of the sign as a means of directing and mastering mental processes. This position very often is treated as a distinguishing feature of Vygotsky's "non-classical" psychology. The principle of mediation is opposite to the central principle of the so-called classical psychology based on dualistic stimulus–response model.

> …every elementary form of behavior presupposes a direct reaction to the task set before the organism (which can be expressed by the simple S–R formula). But the structure of sign operations requires an intermediate link between the stimulus and the response. This intermediate link is a second order stimulus (sign) that is drawn into the operation where it fulfills a special function; it creates a new relation between S and R (Vygotsky 1978, 39).

This looks like a sort of epistemological revision of the classical dualistic stimulus–response formula. However, looking from the philosophical point of view we could say that there is nothing new here. Ideas of *sign mediation* were widely discussed in Russian philosophy at the beginning of the century. Thus, in *Sistema sotsiologii* Pitirim Sorokin analysed the concept from many aspects. "The sign environment forms different types of behaviour" (Sorokin 1920, 185). More in a similar vein could be found in the conception of ethnic psychology developed by Gustav Shpet in the beginning of the 1920s.[2]

> The sphere of ethnic psychology is […] accessible to us through the understanding of a certain system of signs and, therefore, is comprehended only through the decryption and interpretation of these signs. These signs not only represent things, but are also messages about them. In other words, we deal with signs, which are not only indications to a thing, but express the meaning (Shpet 1989, 514).

In the philosophical theory of Pavel Florensky the sign was presented as a sort of *mediator* of the conscious life of an individual, a sort of "organ of communication with reality" (Florensky 1990, Vol. 2, 344).

This does not mean, of course, that Vygotsky simply borrowed certain ideas that were unknown to his contemporaries and applied them to psychology. The point is that, firstly, he was consciously searching for a monistic theory of mind, and secondly, that monism *was not seen in the fact of mediation.* Social relations and the higher forms of behaviour (which were for Vygotsky synonyous with "higher psychological functions") are mediated by signs and therefore possess the same psychological structure.

The Monistic approach of Vygotsky required that all higher functions be explained as *sharing one and the same origin and structure and develoingp according to the same law ("the general genetic law of development").*

> ...any function in the child's cultural development appears on the stage twice, on two planes. It firstly appears on social plane and then on a psychological plane. Firstly among people as an inter-psyhological category and then within the child as an intra-psychological category. This is equally true with regard to voluntary attention, logical memory, the formation of concepts and the development of volition (Vygotsky 1960, 44).

That was brilliant hypothesis and still remains a hypothesis[3]. At the same time, it encapsulated the monistic approach of Vygotsky. In some sense, it was a sort of "methodological monism" in psychology.

Looking to this from philosophical point of view I am bound to mention that there were certain deep inconsistencies within the approach. Methodologically, these inconsistencies were predetermined by the principal contradiction between the task (the creation of the *monistic* psychological theory) and the approach (a *dualistic* idea of existence of two subsystems, namely, man, i. e. psyche, consciousness, reactions, reflexes, responses etc. and the world of stimuli, social-cultural relations, etc.).

The consistent adoption of a monistic approach as a fundamental requirement for the analysis of mind was impossible without first destroying the initial postulate of the existence of two (external and internal) systems upon which the whole system of theoretical notions had been built. The main problem was that the methodology of analysis contradicted the approach to theory building. In short, it was impossible to maintain a monistic approach without changing the initial postulate.

With this in mind let us take a look at the psychological theory of activity that is very often treated as a continuation of Vygotsky's approach. I intend to show that this theory represents a different type of monistic approach, one which is, indeed, far from Vygotsky's original views.

Ilyenkov: Activity as Substance

The psychological theory of activity developed by A.N. Leontyev is very often viewed as if it belongs to the so-called "Vygotskian school" (Davydov

1996; Zinchenko 1995 and many others). Correspondingly, Ilyenkov, who supported thetheoretical positions of Leontyev, is presented as "the philosophical spokesman of the Vygotsky school" (Bakhurst 1991, 61). There are, indeed, some justifications for this. Thus, Ilyenkov wrote:

> Psychological definitions of man have their "being" not in the system of neurodynamic structures of his cortex, but in a broader [...] system of relations of man to man, mediated by things created by man to man [...] in relations of production of the objective-human world and the capacities corresponding to the organisation of his world (Ilyenkov 1984, 240).

Such an approach strongly resembles that of Vygotsky. However, there are some essential differences between the views of the two men concerning the question of the origins of human consciousness. These views represent *different types of monism* and for this reason they cannot be considered to constitute a *single* school or approach.

Let us start by briefly surveying the general principles of Ilyenkov's conception. He obviously follows the idea of an "organic whole" created in German classical philosophy and developed by Marx (more on this subject see Veresov, 1990).

> To *comprehend* a phenomenon means to establish its place and role in the concrete system of interacting phenomena in which it is necessarily realized [...] To *comprehend* a phenomenon means to discover the mode of its origin, the rule according to which the phenomenon emerges with necessity rooted in the concrete totality of conditions, it means to analyse the very conditions of the origin of phenomena.(Ilyenkov 1960, 177; quoted from Bakhurst 1991, 140).

To understand a phenomenon means to reconstruct the system (the organic whole) in which it necessarily appears. What then should be treated as the "organic whole" when human consciousness emerges? Ilyenkov explores the concept of "inorganic body of man" developed by Marx. "Humanity's inorganic body " is nature reconstructed by human labour, activity, *Tätigkeit*, embodied and objectified human capacities, "objectified social consciousness" (Ilyenkov 1964, 235).[4] The human mind, consciousness, therefore, does not exist within the human biological body or brain. Rather, it is a trait or feature of this "inorganic body" of the individual.

Such methodological principle obviously gave some possibilities to overcome the classical subject-object model and for opening up the way towards a monistic theory of mind.

The main role of such a theory comprised the concept of activity (*Tätigkeit, deiatelnost '*).[5] Activity for Ilyenkov was not a super-category or explanatory principle. On the contrary, and following Spinoza and Marx, activity was treated as a substance from which both subject and object derive.

The subject with its specifically human mental functions is not merely a passive recipient of incoming stimuli. The subject becomes a subject through activity. It should be analysed in terms of a *subject of activity*:

> All the specifically human mental functions are, without exception, [...] "internalized" modes and forms of man's external – sensuous, object-oriented (*chuvstennaia, predmetnaia*) – activity as a social being (Ilyenkov 1970, 89).

Human object-oriented activity as a substance has, in Ilyenkov's view, a quality of universality:

> The real structure of mental acts [...] is determined not by the structure and distribution of parts of the body and the brain of man, but solely by the external conditions of the *universal human actions* in the world of other bodies (Ilyenkov 1974, 53 – my italics, N.V.).

In some sense (and I hope that this will not be regarded as a gross exaggeration), according to Ilyenkov, the subject's mental acts and the subject itself are derivatives from external object-oriented activity.

On the other hand, the object (the wider, external world, including the natural world) is also viewed as given to the subject through the "prism" of activity. "...Nature 'in itself' is given to us if and only if it is transformed into an object, material or means of production, of human life" (Ilyenkov 1964, 42). Therefore:

> For human beings the whole of nature is idealised, not merely that part which humans directly produce and reproduce or which they exploit in utilitarian form (Ilyenkov 1974, 225).

Ilyenkov claims that the individual has access to the objects of nature only insofar as they are included, incorporated into and involved in the activity. The same is true of cultural objects:

> A thing [...] is only an objectified idea or form of the person's activity taken as a thing [...] All forms of culture are only forms of the activity of man himself" (Ilyenkov 1974, 183).

It is quite easy to see now what type of monistic approach Ilyenkov was advocating. "Thinking is an attribute of a substance" (Spinoza). "Thinking is an attribute of human activity" (Ilyenkov).

This becomes understandable when we treat the matter at a "psychological" level. The psychological theory of activity formulates a "substance-based" monistic approach with great clarity: "The activity (*deiatelnost', Tätigkeit* – N.V.) of a human being is the substance of his consciousness" (Leontyev 1977, 157).

One could claim that such an approach is a sort of continuation and even "concretisation" of Vygotsky's initial idea of the social origins of mind (i.e. that activity is the domain, the real "sensual body" of the social relations – see, for example Davydov 1998). But "social relations", according to Vygotsky, embrace more than *activity* and should not be limited to activity alone. Such a limitation may be fruitful at a philosophical level, but as an explanatory principle for psychological theory it leads to some unavoidable contradictions.

Thus, A.N. Leontyev claims:

> The process of internalisation is not the *transferral* of an external activity to a pre-existing, internal "plane of consciousness"; it is the process in which this internal plane is formed (Leontyev 1981, 56–57).

Consciousness is a derivative from practical activity. Activity is a goal-directed system of practical actions. But to be able to act the individual must already have some structures of consciousness. Otherwise he is simply not able to initiate and realise any form of systematic goal-directed activity.

The second contradiction is connected with the psychological structure of human consciousness. Repeating Vygotsky's position that the structure of consciousness includes meanings (*znachenia*) and personal senses (*lichnostnie smysli*), Leontyev wrote: "In contrast to meaning, the personal sense [...] does not have 'non-psychological' existence" (Leontyev 1977, 153). However, to say this means to presuppose that there is a component within the structure of consciousness which does not originate from the social relations outside the individual. This presupposition in some sense destroys the idea of the internalisation.

This does not appear to contradict Vygotsky's approach. Verbal communication, that is, speech, in the widest sense-affective (*affektivno-smyslovoi*) context, was seen by Vygotsky as an important source of the mental development.

We can now more easily see the essential differences between Ilyenkov's and Vygotsky's approaches. Thus, the "methodological monism" of Vygotsky and "substance-based monism" of Ilyenkov (and of the psychological theory of activity) are different approaches despite some similarities concerning the social origins of mind.

Vygotsky obviously adopts the classical Cartesian approach as he tries to overcome the gap between stimulus and response introducing a sort of methodological monism, employing some obvious "motives" from the Russian philosophy. By contrast, Ilyenkov applies a classical Spinozian view, introducing activity as a substance developed in a spirit of Hegel and

Marx. To say that they represent one school is to say that Descartes and Spinoza belong to the same philosophical school.

Let us ask the following question. If neither the "methodological monism" of Vygotsky, nor the "substance-based" approach of Ilyenkov brings any satisfactory solution to the problem of the monistic theory of mind, is it the case that such a theory is not possible?

The answer to this is "no". It simply means that the monistic approach in psychology should clearly understand that neither direct relations nor mediated relations between man and the world can be taken as a principle or can become a basis for a holistic conception of human consciousness. It would appear that no third way exists, as the relations between a person and the world can only be either direct or indirect (mediated). In some sense this is, indeed, the case. However, this is only so because we have chosen to proceed from the idea of two systems. The task, therefore, is to change this axiom, i. e. to start from the assertion that man and the social-cultural world together constitute a *single* system. This radical step was made by Merab Mamardashvili.

Mamardashvili: Consciousness and Culture as One System

Merab Mamardashvili defined his own philosophy as a "philosophy of consciousness". He contrasted his approach to that of Ilyenkov by describing Ilyenkov's philosophy as "too Hegelian" (Mamardashvili 1990, 35). Let us take a brief look at some of the ideas propounded by Mamardashvili which are relevant to the present paper.

First, he claims that human consciousness is not incorporated within the body of the individual, picturing it, instead, as a sort of "artificial state of mind" *(iskusstvennoe sostoianie)*.

> Man [...] has consciousness. This means that he has an opportunity to experience those things or states of mind *[sostoiania]*, which are not accessible by natural means as a consequence of merely physiological mechanism (Mamardashvili 1990, 43).

What types of states is he referring to? They are states which are in some way connected or combined with *symbols*. They are, therefore, within reach of the human being, who is involved in their "magnetic field lines".

Owing to the habit forming qualities of everyday experience, we attribute the acts of consciousness to the anatomic outlines of the man. But what kind of picture would we have, Mamardashvili asks, if consciousness were primarily placed *outside the individual* and represented a sort of spatial-field formation? The consequent metaphors and symbols of culture would contain more information concerning the properties of consciousness than any attempt to link behaviour with changes in the characteristics of the brain.

On this point Mamrdashvili's approach does not look different from Vygotsky's and Ilyenkov's. Nevertheless, he takes a step forward by introducing the idea of "spiritual instruments" within human consciousness.

Mental acts as such ("sincere feelings", "grief" etc.) cannot be maintained at their initial intensity. They dissipate, disintegrate, vanish without trace because in the nature there is no mechanism for the reproduction and realisation of specifically human attitudes, relations, desires or emotions. It is natural to forget and, at the same time, it is artificial to remember (Mamardashvili 1990, 88). We need, therefore, some *artificial devices* to keep such specifically human mental acts. The cultural phenomena (art, myth) are viewed as such devices. "Special products of art are as though add-on units to us, through which we in ourselves reproduce the man" (Mamardashvili 1990, 88).

They are a sort of "machines", created in such a manner as to bring us that which we cannot receive by a natural way, and which cannot be attained by simple extension of our natural mental and physical forces. Thus, both states of consciousness and the devices through which we are able to them are viewed as cultural components rather than natural ones.

Consciousness has its "body". This body possesses extension, volume, and movement. It is the collective "body" of a history offering to us certain environment of utensils and "tools of the soul" (Mamardashvili 1990, 184). Thus, "in a human and historical reality the external is internal, and the internal is external" (Mamardashvili 1990, 185).

The terms "internal" and "external" are applicable to the human consciousness to the same degree as they are to human culture. These terms, therefore, lose their status as absolute categories. We can thus see that, in developing Vygotsky's approach in a most original manner, Mamardashvili changes the initial postulate of human culture and human consciousness as comprising two separated interconnected systems. Consciousness ("internal", "individual", "subjective" and "external", "social") and culture (internal and external) make up a *single* system. This system *does not consist* of consciousness and the culture. Human consciousness *is* culture and human culture *is* consciousness. Consistent monism as the basis for a psychological theory of mind becomes possible.

Some Concluding Notes

The need for a monistic theory of human mind is viewed by modern psychology as a major contemporary issue. Attempts to construct such theory seem to lie outside the mainstream of modern psychological theorising. On the other hand, it is becoming increasingly clear that the causes of crisis in present-day world psychology are rooted in the very basics of its construction. The "heliocentric" approach to psychology, its "theory of relativity", should start from an understanding of both the limitations and applicability of the "dualistic approach". In this sense, the old (and often forgotten) names of philosophers, like Descartes, Spinoza, Kant, Hegel and Marx remain of essential importance and relevance. Psychology has not yet bridged the gap between Descartes and Spinoza, but that does not mean that a bridge cannot be built.

Comparing the various attempts to create the monistic theory of mind in order to develop this general approach we have to be very careful to attend to the philosophical and epistemological foundations of each. From these perspectives the picture looks surprisingly different. For example, Mamardashvili comes closer to Vygotsky than Ilyenkov. And this is not just a historical example.

The point is that there are two ways of developing any psychological theory. The first is to continue the search of interrelations *between* two systems (man–world, consciousness–culture, individual–social). This leads to a classical dualism, dressed in the clothes of modern philosophy. The second way is to start by asserting the existence of *a single system*, i.e. a monistic view of the basic conceptions of psychology. Time will show whether our science is ready to accept this as a basis for the theory of human consciousness.

Notes

[1] Here the term "methodologist" is used, according to Russian scientific tradition, to refer to study of general and metatheoretical issues that underline any investigation of psychological phenomena.

[2] From many historical sources we know that Vygotsky had read everything that Shpet had by then published (see Levitin, 1982).

[3] V. Davydov mentioned that "the cultural-historical conception of Vygotsky up until the present is not a theory, but rather a hypothesis" (Davydov 1998, 34). It should be mentioned that Vygotsky never used the terms "cultural-historical theory" or "sociohistorical theory" with respect to his own approach. The term "cultural-historical theory of Vygotsky" was introduced by A. Luria in early 1960s.

[4] It is better to say "non-biological body" because the world of human objects is a sort of "organic system".

[5] It is curious to mention that V. Davydov in the polemic around the status of the concept of activity wrote: "Yes, we need the monistic theory of human being" (Davydov, 1990, p. 281).

Literature

Bakhurst, D. (1991), *Consciousness and revolution in Soviet psychology; from the Bolsheviks to Evald Ilyenkov.* Cambridge: University Press.

Davydov, V. (1990), *Da, nam neobkhodima monisticheskaia teoriia chelovecheskogo bytiia.* In: *Deyatelnost': teorii, metodologia, problemy.* Moskva: Politizdat.

Davydov, V. (1996), *Teoriia razvivaiushchego obuchenia.* Moskva: Inton.

Davydov, V. (1998), *Poslednie vystupleniia.* Riga.

Dewey, J. (1896), The reflex arc concept in psychology. *Psychological Review,* 4, 357-370.

El'konin, D. B. (1989), *Izbrannye psikhologicheskie trudy.* Moskva: Pedagogika.

Ilyenkov, E. (1960), *Dialektika abstraktnogo i konkretnogo v "Kapitale"* Marksa. Moskva.

Ilyenkov, E. (1964), *Vopros o tozhdestve myshleniia i bytiia v domarksistskoi filosofii.* In: *Dialektika – teoria poznaniya.* Moskva: Politizdat, 21–54.

Ilyenkov, E. (1970), *Psikhika cheloveka pod "lupoi vremeni".* In: *Priroda,* 1, 87–91.

Ilyenkov, E. (1974), *Dialekticheskaia logika.* Moskva: Politizdat.

Ilyenkov, E. (1979), *Chto zhe takoe lichnost'?* In: *S chego nachinaetsia lichnost'.* Moskva: Politizdat, 183–237.

Ilyenkov, E .(1984), *Ob esteticheskoi prirode fantasii.* In: E. V. Ilyenkov, *Iskusstvo i kommunisticheskii ideal*, Moskva: Iskusstvo 1984.

Florensky, P. (1990), *Sochinenia,* Moskva: Pravda.

Levitin, K. E. (1982), *Lichnostiu ne rozhdaiutsia* [One is not born as personality]. Moskva: Progress.

Leontyev, A. N. (1977), *Dejatelnost', soznanie, lichnost'.* Moskva: Politizdat.

Leontyev, A. N. (1981b), The problem of activity in psychology. In J. Wertsch (Ed.), *The concept of activity in Soviet psychology.* New York: Sharpe, Armonk.

Mamardashvili, M. (1990), *Kak ia ponimaiu filosofiiu.* Moskva: Progress.

Shpet, G. (1989), *Sochineniia.* Moskva: Pravda.

Sorokin, P. (1920), *Sistema sotsiologii.* Moskva.

Veresov, N. N. (1990), *Obrazovaniie kak sposob razvitiya individa. Kontseptsiya Gegelia.* In: *Kultura, obrazovanie, razvitie lichhnosti.* Moskva: Institut Filosofii

Veresov, N. (1999), *Undiscovered Vygotsky.* Frankfurt am Main, Peter Lang.

Vygotsky, L. S. (1960), *Razvitie vysshikh psihicheskikh funktsii.* Moskva: APN.

Vygotsky, L.S. (1978), *Mind in society: the development of higher psychological processes*. Harvard University Press

Vygotsky, L. S. (1981), The genesis of higher mental functions. In J. V. Wertsch (Ed.). *The concept of activity in Soviet psychology*. Armonk, New York: Sharpe.

Vygotsky, L. S. (1982), *Sobranie sochinenii*. Tom 1, Moskva: Pedagogika.

Vygotsky, L. S. (1987), *Pskihologia iskusstva*. Moskva: Pedagogika.

Zinchenko, V. (1995), *Cultural-historical psychology and the psychological theory of activity: Respect and prospect*. In: J. V. Wertsch, P. del Rio & A. Alwares (Eds.). *Sociocultural studies of mind. Learning in going: Social, cognitive, and computational aspects*. Cambridge: Cambridge University Press, 37–55.

10

FOUNDATIONALISM AND ANTI-FOUNDATIONALISM: SEEKING ENCHANTMENT IN THE ROUGH GROUND

JAN DERRY

"As we found, however there is no privileged relationship between world and word. For any situation multiple descriptions are usually possible, and in principle there is no upper limit on our forms of descriptions. Nor did we find any ultimate means for ruling among competing descriptions, of declaring one as corresponding more 'truly' to the nature of reality than another"
(Gergen 1999, 34).

This statement expresses a sentiment commonly found in education and education research and coincides with a concern over what has been termed "abstract rationality". Abstract reason and truth in knowing are widely believed to belie the human condition which is always open to multiple perspectives and an imposition of a rationality is seen as party to a discourse of power concerned to subject participants to its rule.

In the literature on Vygotsky this concern is found in the discussion on the extent to which he believed in an abstract universal reason that ultimately all human thought would reach via a hierarchy of development. For instance,

Jay Lemke who identifies himself with the postmodernist critique of aspects of modernism, rejects arguments "for universally valid 'master narratives': meta-theories or discourses of any sort that aspire to set the terms of the conversation for everyone else." He argues for a reading of Vygotsky that discounts the idea of "abstraction itself as the highest form of reason".

> [D]espite the optimism that Lev Vygotsky undoubtedly shared with his times, I hope that he did not believe that abstract symbolic formulations were in themselves the highest goal of human meaning-making" (Lemke 1999, 91).

Like Lemke, Wertsch is concerned with an ambivalence in Vygotsky's writings. He presents Vygotsky as an Enlightenment Rationalist who "embraced human rationality as the telos of human development". Implying an identity between rationality and instrumentalism he adds, "as a Marxist he [Vygotsky] also viewed rationality as an essential tool for constructing a centrally planned economy and state" (Wertsch 1996, 25).

By contrast, Ilyenkov's thought-provoking piece The Concept of the Ideal (1977) offers a way of viewing the dilemma, of a dialogic construction of meaning versus universal rationality, in a different light. Gergen is concerned by a claim to a privileged relationship (or lack of it) between world and word. However, what is not dealt with in this conception of the problem of knowledge is the issue raised in Sellars attack on "The Myth of the Given". This is a technical philosophical argument, the gist of which is that knowledge by its very nature entails reason though not by the single abstract formalised universal reason opposed in modernist argument.

McDowell explains the following: "Sellars insists that the concept of knowledge belongs in a normative context. He writes: 'In characterising an episode or a state as that of knowing, we are not giving a logical description of that episode or state; we are placing it in the logical space of reasons, of justifying and being able to justify what one says.'" McDowell continues, by expanding the remit of Sellars' point, to urge: "[T]hough Sellars here speaks of knowledge in particular, that is just to stress one application of thought that a normative context is necessary for being in touch with the world at all, whether knowledgeably or not" (McDowell, 1996, xiv).

Moreover, for McDowell the realm of reasons (the normative context) that makes knowledge possible, exists outside individuals in the world itself, that is the social world which individuals inhabit. Ilyenkov has dealt with the nature of this world in his discussion of materialism and idealism, specifically in his rejection of a simple polar opposition.

A crucial issue in Lemke's, Gergen's and Wertsch's approach to this problem could be framed through a discussion of idea of foundationalism. On the one hand Gergen adopts an anti-foundationalist position and wishes to remain agnostic to an idea of a uniquely defined real for fear of placing limits on knowing. Yet there is an implicit foundationalism in the idea of the power attributed to discourse to construct the real, due in part to the absence of any consideration of the issues raised by McDowell's use of Sellars' attack on the "Myth of the Given." Unless the problem is confronted head on philosophically in the way that Sellars and McDowell have confronted it, foundationalism will never be expelled but find a place unnoticed in the logic of the argument.

This note begins with the question of foundationalism and anti-foundationalism and then moves on to expose some of the issues that underlie interpretations of Vygotsky. But before proceeding it should be noted that the terms foundationalism and anti-foundationalism are used loosely here to structure the argument and do not refer to the more technical philosophical discussion of which they are a part. More importantly, David Bakhurst's comprehensive work alerts us to many of the issues considered in this note. However what is developed here is an attempt to open up implicit assumptions in postmodernist concerns with the real and to address the question of reason as it is caricatured in critiques of Vygotsky.

Foundationalism and Anti-Foundationalism

In postmodernist thought foundationalism and anti-foundationalism are posed as a denial of human creativity on the one side and as an opportunity for infinite variety and creativity on the other. However two problems arise with this simple opposition.

First, anti-foundationalism conceived of in this way does not eradicate all elements of foundationalism, and second, it does not free human creativity to the extent that postmodernists imagine. Moreover it is hard to avoid the position, more or less vague, that underlying the whole project is an untheorised conception of freedom.

When foundationalism is understood as a denial of human creativity and understood as representative of logocentric rationality, anti-foundationalism allows the space for infinite human variety and creativity for postmodernists such as Gergen. But what is crucial here and missing from this use of anti-foundationalism, is that there is any material constraint on our thinking laid down by our cognitive activity in the world.

Foundationalism and anti-foundationalism are concerned with the way knowledge is obtained. The one starts from a secure ground of what is known to be true and builds on this. The other denies the existence of such a secure starting point. But this direct opposition has not been universally accepted. For instance Hegel, who was important to Ilyenkov, objected to it strongly. For Hegel there is not a pre-given foundation but that is not to deny the existence of foundation. Rockmore explains Hegel's position as follows:

> The justification is then, not already there, present from the beginning, so to say like something that is preserved and unchanged through the reasoning process. [...] the justification is created or produced during the development of the theory. [...] To begin, it is not enough to begin, for there is and can be no privileged beginning point. We [...] encounter the relation between system and history. The true only becomes true in and through its development, its real unfolding in the course of which it actualises itself (Rockmore, 1993, 63).

To put it simply, we start as an anti-foundationlist but, having built our foundations as we go along, we finish as foundationalists. As Neurath (1932) put it: "We are like sailors who have to rebuild their ship in the open sea, without ever being able to dismantle it in dry dock and reconstruct it from the best components." Both Hegel and Neurath were fully aware that their view of knowledge had a socio-cultural or historical dimension.

Creating and transforming the ground of knowledge as we go along, comes to have a central role (i.e. history). We will see below that this is crucial for an understanding of mind. Vygotsky's discussion of Spinoza's consideration about method shows clear evidence of an anti-foundationalism in his thought.

> A theory of method is, of course, the production of the means of production, to take a comparison from the field of industry. But in industry the production of the means of production is no special, primordial production, but forms part of the general process of production and itself depends upon the same methods and tools of production as all other production (Vygotsky 1997, 253).

Vygotsky endorsed Spinoza's argument that we should not commit ourselves to a search going back to infinity. To discover the best method for finding truth we do not need to find a method of finding a method:

> By such proceedings, we should never arrive at knowledge of the truth, or, indeed, at any knowledge at all. The matter stands on the same footing as the making of material tools, which might be argued about in a similar way. For, in order to work iron, a hammer is needed, and the hammer cannot be forthcoming unless it has been made; but in order to make it, there was need of another hammer and other tools, and so on to infinity. We might thus vainly endeavour to prove that men have no power of working iron. But as men first made use of the instrument supplied by nature to accomplish very easy pieces of workmanship, laboriously and imperfectly, and then, when finished, wrought other things more difficult with less labour, and greater perfection; and so gradually mounted from the simplest operations to the making of

tools, and from the making of tools to the making of more complex tools, and fresh feats of workmanship, till they arrived at making, with small expenditure of labour, the vast complicated mechanisms which they now possess. So, in a like manner, the intellect, by its native strength, makes for itself intellectual instruments, whereby it acquires strength for performing other intellectual operations, and from these operations gets again fresh instruments, or the power of pushing its investigations further, and thus gradually proceeds until it reaches the summit of wisdom (Vygotsky 1997, 254).

That thought and world are not separated by an unbridgeable epistemological chasm and that this places emphasis on development, as a non-linear process embedded in historical resources, provides an key line of enquiry for Vygotskian research. It suggests the importance of Hegel for Vygotsky. In particular that Vygotsky took on board Hegel's position that while we must be anti-foundationalist at the start we cannot but develop foundations for our knowledge as we proceed. Hegel rejected all a priori, or theoretical justification of claims to know prior to and apart from experience. As Rockmore put it, a philosophical system founds itself as it develops:

According to Hegel, philosophy, that he, like Kant, regards as the highest form of knowledge, and that he later in a famous passage in the Philosophy of Right will compare to an owl, can only take wing afterwards, or after the fact. The point is that for Hegel, knowledge, including philosophy, is not and cannot be a priori; on the contrary, it emerges in and is the product of collective effort of human beings over the course of recorded history to come to grips with their world and themselves (Rockmore, 1993, 85).

When the Hegelian dimension of Vygotsky's thought is acknowledged it becomes clear that Vygotsky's understanding of what a concept is and does, is far richer than the reason sometimes attributed to him. Far from having a decontextualised view of abstract rationality, Vygotsky's reason is ontological. Like a snowball rolling down a mountainside, his concept grows through the material it picks up in its descent.

Thus the concept does not arise from this as a mechanical result of abstraction – it is the result of a long and deep knowledge of the object. [...] Psychological research is disclosing that in a concept we always have an enrichment and deepening of the content that the concept contains (Vygotsky 1998, 53).

It is important to emphasise this aspect of Vygotsky's work, not only to avoid misapprehensions but also to appreciate the significance of his ideas for Ilyenkov. Vygotsky's characterisation of the nature of a concept offers the possibility of understanding the gap of (and mediation of) mind and world as creative. The concept is a result of a complex process of development in which both thought and the world are not categorically separated at any point.

In Hegel's view, the word [by which Vygotsky means concept] is existing vitalised thoughts. The connection between thought and word is not a primal connection that is given once and forever. It arises in development and it itself develop (Vygotsky 1987, 285).

Scientific concepts are not the apex of abstract rationality in the way that commentators such as Wertsch and Lemke suppose.

The foundationalism in relation to the "given" that we are discussing here has a reciprocal in the notion of apriorism in relation to mind. That is that the mind qua mind comes ready equipped with particular inherent capacities for knowing. Bakhurst stresses Vygotsky's attack on apriorism and "the idea that psychological faculties themselves exist prior to experience". Vygotsky, Bakhurst writes, "denies that the child enters the world naturally equipped with embryonic forms of higher mental functions [...] [H]e claims [that these] are irreducible to their primitive antecedents" (Bakhurst, 1991, 66). Higher mental functions are the realisation of human potential, but humans are by nature social animals and the realisation of this potential can only happen socially. At this point what arises is the extremely difficult problem of how the brain can be realised as mind only through activity.

Ilyenkov deals with this in a non-reductive way. Taking issue with the Kantian idea of " 'transcendentally inborn' forms of operation of the individual mentality as a priori 'internal mechanisms'", he insists upon "the self-consciousness of social man assimilated from without by the individual". In line with Vygotsky's argument he stressed that "[i]t is these forms of the organisation of social (collectively realised) human life activity that exists before, outside and completely independently of the individual mentality..." (Ilyenkov, 1977, 80–81).

On this question McDowell, who we will refer to in a moment, says: "The relevant conceptual capacities are drawn on, in receptivity. We should understand what Kant calls 'intuition' – experential intake – not as bare getting of an extra-conceptual Given, but a kind of occurance or state that already has conceptual content" (McDowell, 1996).

Once we move beyond the simple opposition of foundationalism and antifoundationalism and recognise the sociogenesis of mind, another simple opposition, namely that of idealism and materialism is called into question. This brings us directly to one of the most important contributions of Ilyenkov and one with contemporary relevance. On this issue writing with reference to Hegel's move from Kant, Ilyenkov wrote:

It will readily be appreciated how much broader and more profound such a positing of the question [the ideal and the material] is in comparison with any conception that designates as "ideal" everything that is "in consciousness of the individual" and "material" or "real", everything that is outside of the consciousness of the individual, everything that the given individual is not conscious of, although this "everything" does exist in reality, and thus draws between the "ideal" and the "real" a fundamental dividing line which turns them into "different worlds" that have "nothing in common" with each other. It is clear that given such a metaphysical division and delimitation, the "ideal" and the "material" cannot and must not be regarded as opposites (Ilyenkov 1977, 81).

As Bakhurst has pointed out, a similar view appears in the work of the contemporary philosopher McDowell, who alerts us to philosophical pitfalls posed by a conception of Mind and World which operates with and implicit "Myth of the Given".

McDowell's aim to re-address problems in modern philosophy raises issues that lie at the heart of the work of Vygotsky and Ilyenkov, namely the "second nature" and the materiality of thinking activity. A simple example of the materiality of thinking activity is that of tying a knot in a handkerchief as an aide-memoire, i.e. constituting a material thing as an ideal object. A more serious example of an ideal object is of course money, i.e. a thing of no intrinsic significance in itself but one that is the very stuff wealth; an ideal object which clearly has the most massive material implication. One of these implications is of course to condition the way we begin to think about the world in the first place. Reference to this aspect of money features prominently in Ilyenkov's argument concerning the materiality of the ideal. The implications of these arguments against polar oppositions of ideal and real, mind and world are far-reaching. They raise the importance of tradition, i.e. an already existing world of meaning into which the individual is born and with it the question of any mechanism of change – since changing something means working within its conditions of existence and expression.

According to McDowell the need to constrain spontaneity is vital; thought needs limits but these limits cannot be provided by an apriori "given". To prevent an oscillation between bare presence on the one side and recourse to coherentism on the other – that is using the coherence of arguments as the sole criteria of their validity – it is necessary to look elsewhere for constraint. McDowell follows a line of thought essentially similar to Ilyenkov. In rejecting a simple opposition between mind and world he is effectually following Ilyenkov's rejection of a simple opposition between ideal and material. McDowell talks of our "need [of] a conception of experiences as states of occurrence that are passive but reflect conceptual capacities". And when he talks he is similarly following a line of thought in Vygotsky. For his states of occurrence that are passive but reflect conceptual capacities bears all the hallmarks of Vygotsky's view of the development of concepts.

McDowell's demand for a passive form of experience is anticipated in Vygotskian view of the relation of everyday and scientific concepts. For Vygotsky scientific concepts by their very character require conscious operation and their meaning and reference is internal to a system of concepts rather than to an unwary (in contrast to a sense of scientific self referring) experience of the world.

That there may be a domain of knowing which is nuanced and not consciously acted on, but which is nevertheless rich in conceptual content, is often ignored by policy makers to the detriment of their intended aims and outcomes.

This is point is made in a powerful way by Dunne (1993) who begins his philosophic enquiries by considering the problem of professional education of teachers. Professional education in Britain is mainly funded by the state and as such has increasingly been subject to the control of administratively set targets and objectives. The stated purpose of these targets is to raise standards, but Dunne questions how such an end can be achieved by administrative measures which could tend to become instrumental. And particularly, how an artistic and expressive endeavour such as educating can be administered and by implication instrumentalised. Dunne is concerned with the nature of rationality in teaching and beyond this the nature of any rational practice. His work addresses not only contemporary agendas of professional education (including that of academics) but also the nature of theoretical knowledge itself. He argues that when the act of education is conceived instrumentally there is "no sense of the pedagogic relationship setting a field of psychic tension," or the fact that "something might be at work in the pedagogic situation which cannot simply be made the object of analysis but must rather be lived through". He talks of "a kind of subsoil which nourishes the fruit of explicit purpose but which is not itself the fruit" (Dunne1993, 5). Referring to Wittgenstein he makes the point that McDowell deals with – that we want constraint on the freedom of conceptual capacities to deploy concepts – "one might teach by this model on ice but hardly on the rough ground of the classroom."

It is precisely this "rough ground" that both Ilyenkov and McDowell speak to in recognising conceptual content/the space of reasons existing materially in the world prior to an individual's deployment of concepts. By conceiving of a world similarly to the way that Ilyenkov does in his work on the ideal, McDowell's aim is to recapture an idea of second nature which is all but explicit in Aristotle's account of the formation of ethical character. This will help "keep nature partially enchanted but without lapsing into pre-scientific superstition or rampant platonism" (McDowell, 1996, 85).

Gergen's appeal for an infinity of readings is made in response to a disappointment in what the material (as given) might offer. He states: "When committed to a language of materiality we lose a precious voice of enchantment [...] As we convert all human actions to 'mere material', they become flat and meaningless. Do we really wish to give up the discourse of mystery and deep significance" (Gergen, 1999, 223).

As Ilyenkov powerfully demonstrates, Gergen does not have to give up the discourse of deep significance (of normativity) by holding to the "mere material". It is only the crude undertheorised conception of material which Sellars attacks in the "Myth of the Given", that is disenchanted. A thorough going materialism cannot separate the human ability to think from the nature of which it is part and this was Spinoza's project worked out in Hegel and playing a part in the thought of Ilyenkov, McDowell and Vygotsky. The approach of all three rejects out of hand the infinity of readings that Gergen's idealist notion of material causes him to defend.

Literature

Bakhurst, D. (1991), *Consciousness and Revolution in Soviet Philosophy. From the Bolsheviks to Evald Ilyenkov.* Cambridge University Press.

Bakhurst, D. (1995a), *Lesson from Ilyenkov.* In: *Communication Review,* 1 (2), 155–178.

Bakhurst, D. (1997a), *Meaning, Normativity and the Life of Mind.* In: *Language and Communication,* 17 (1), 33–51.

Bakhurst, D. (1997b), *Activity, Consciousness and Communication.* In: Cole, M., Engestrom, Y and Vasquez, O. (eds) *Mind, Culture and Activity. Seminal Papers from the Laboratory of Comparative Human Cognition.* Cambridge University Press, Cambridge, 147–163.

Burgess, T. (1993), *Reading Vygotsky.* In: *Charting the Agenda, Educational Activity after Vygotsky.* edited by H. Daniels, Routledge.

Cartwright, N., Cat, J. and Fleck, L. (1996), *Otto Neurath: Philosophy between Science and Politics,* Cambridge University Press

Daniels, H. (1996), *An Introduction to Vygotsky.* Routledge.

Dunne, J. (1993), *Back to the Rough Ground: "Phronesis" and "Techne" in Modern Philosophy and in Aristotle.* University of Notre Dame Press, Notre Dame, London

Hegel, G.W.F.(1977), *Phenomenology of Spirit.* Miller, A.V. (trans.). Oxford University Press.

Hegel, G.W.F. (1975), *Hegel's Logic.* Wallace. W. (trans.). Oxford University Press.

Houlgate, S.(ed) (1998), *The Hegel Reader*, Blackwell

Kashap, S.P. (1987), *Spinoza and Moral Freedom.* State University of New York Press.

Gergen, K.J. (1999), *An Invitation to Social Construction.* Sage Publications, London.

Ilyenkov, E.V. (1977a), *Dialectical Logic, Essays on Its History and Theory,* Progress Publishers, Moscow.

Ilyenkov, E.V. (1977b), *The Concept of the Ideal. In: Philosophy in the USSR: Problems of Dialectical Materialism.* Progress Publishers, Moscow.

Lemke, J. L. (1999), *Meaning-Making in the Conversation: Head Spinning, Heart Winning, and Everything in Between.* In: *Human Development* 42.2.99

McDowell, J. (1996), *Mind and World.* Harvard University Press.

Pinkard, T. (1996), *Hegel's Phenomenology, The Sociality of Reason.* Cambridge University Press.

Rockmore, T. (1993), *Before and After Hegel; A Historical Introduction to Hegel's Thought,* University of California Press

Sellars, W. (1956), *Empiricism and the Philosophy of Mind,* in: Herbert Feigl and Michael Scriven (eds.), *Minnesota Studies in the Philosophy of Science, Vol. I: The Foundations of Science and the Concepts of Psychology and Psychoanalysis.* University of Minnesota Press. Net version: http://www.ditext.com/sellars/epm.html

Spinoza, B. (1993), *Ethics and Treatise on the Correction of the Intellect.* Everyman.

Vygotsky, L.S. (1987), *The collected works of L.S. Vygotsky,* Vol. 1, *Problems of general psychology,* Reiber, R.W. and Carton, A.S. (eds). Plenum Press.

Vygotsky, L.S. (1993), *The collected works of L.S. Vygotsky,* Vol. 2, *The Fundamental of Defectology,* Reiber, R.W. and Carton, A.S. (eds). Plenum Press.

Vygotsky, L.S. (1997), *The collected works of L.S. Vygotsky, Vol. 3, Problems of the Theory and History of Psychology,* Reiber, R.W. and Wollock, J. (eds). Plenum Press.

Vygotsky, L.S. (1998), *The collected works of L.S. Vygotsky,* Vol. 5, *Child Psychology,* Reiber, R.W. (ed). Plenum Press.

Wertsch, J.V. (1992), *The voice of rationality in a sociocultural approach to mind. In:* Mol (Ed) *Vygotsky and education: instructional implications and applications of sociohistorical psychology.* Cambridge University Press.

Wertsch, J.V. (1996), *The role of abstract rationality in Vygotsky's image of mind. In:* Tryphon, A. and Voneche, J. (eds) *Piaget-Vygotsky The Social Genesis of Thought.* Psychology Press, Erlbaum (UK) Taylor & Francis.

11

DIALECTICS AND DIALOGUE IN ILYENKOV – COMPARISON OF TWO APPROACHES

MATTI VARTIAINEN

I) Questions

The purpose of my paper is to compare two models or views with each other. Both of them aim at overcoming the Cartesian dualism, which separates the subject who knows from the object that is known. The other is the model of Ilyenkov (1984, see also 1977), describing how concepts are related to reality, and how they are developing. Ilyenkov wrote that the "object" or "subject matter" of Dialectical Logic is, in general, thought or thinking; Dialectical Logic is the science of thinking. When speaking about the development of thinking, crucial are its sources, development mechanisms, and the roles and forms of concepts or knowledge. The other model, I am referring to, is the knowledge creation model of Nonaka and Takeuchi (1995). It deals with the question of how new knowledge is created. Lately, I have been involved in studying and teaching knowledge management in the context of a research project in the field of new product design. When speaking about knowledge management, it is impossible to avoid the Nonaka–Takeuchi model of knowledge creation. My special interest in this paper is to compare, what kind of mechanisms and driving forces the two models provide for knowledge development and creation. So, I try to compare a philosophical approach with a work science and management approach.

I will start by describing their philosophical "subject matter". Secondly, I will view, how they define the concepts "concept" and "knowledge" and their dimensions. Thirdly, the models of thought and knowledge development will be compared. My basic task is to study, how Ilyenkov describes the development and use of concepts, and to ask the question, "What is the role of dialogue or communication in this process?" I will contrast his ideas to those raised in the discussion of knowledge creation in the context of learning organisations and knowledge management. In the Nonaka-Takeuchi model, the role of dialogue is emphasised in turning the tacit knowledge into explicit knowledge. Also, in other literature, the role of dialogue in transforming individual knowledge into collective knowledge has been widely discussed (e.g., Bohm 1996).

My method is a simple content analysis. I read two of Ilyenkov's texts (1977, 1984) and tried to construct his "model" of knowledge (concept) development. Then I read Nonaka's and Takeuchi's text (1995) and, finally, compared the two concepts.

II) The philosophical "Subject Matter"

In the *Dialectical Logic,* Ilyenkov (1994) defines his "object" or "subject matter" in general to be thought, thinking. He says that Dialectical Logic has as its aim the development of a scientific representation of thought in those necessary moments, and moreover in the necessary sequence, that do not in the least depend either on our will or on our consciousness. The critical question is, what are Thought's "moments" and "sequence"? Ilyenkov also defines the main problem of the "subject matter" referring to Descartes: "… the problem of the relationship of 'thought' to reality existing outside it and independently of it, to the world of things in space and time, the problem of

"Rationalism" and "Empiricism" traditions differ sharply with regard to (a) what constitutes the actual source of knowledge, and (b) method of obtaining knowledge. The first question is of special interest in this paper. Nonaka and Takeuchi provide "Japanese tradition" – whatever – it is as the synthesised answer to overcome Cartesian dualism. Ilyenkov provides an answer based on Dialectical Logic.

Rationalism	Empiricism	Synthesised views (Nonaka and Takeuchi)	Nonaka & Takeuchi's own view	Ilyenkov's preliminary view
- Source of knowledge: deductively by reasoning, product of ideal mental process, there exist a priori knowledge, absolute truth by reasoning - Science example: mathematics - Plato - Descartes	- Source of knowledge: inductively from sensory experiences, sensory experience the only bases, no a priori knowledge, everything has an intrinsically objective existence - Science example: experimental science - Aristotle - Locke	- Kant: the basis of knowledge is experience, but not the only one. Knowledge arises only when both the logical thinking of rationalism and sensory experience of empiricism work together. Human mind is active in ordering sensory experiences in time and space and supplying concepts as tool for understanding them - Hegel: knowledge begins with sensory perception, which becomes more subjective and rational through a dialectic purification of the senses, and at last reaches the stage of self-knowledge of the "Absolute Spirit" - Marx: Perception is an interaction between the knower (subject) and the known (object). In the pursuit of knowledge, both subject and object are in a continual and dialectic process of mutual adaptation. Object is transformed in the process of becoming known. Knowledge is obtained by handling things, or action, and its truth should be demonstrated in practice - Some form of interaction between the self and the outside world: Husserl, Heidegger, Sartre, Merleau-Ponty, Wittgenstein, James and Dewey (pragmatism)	Japanese tradition: (1) Oneness of humanity and nature. (2) oneness of body and mind – essential is to act in the world. Japanese epistemology tends to value the embodiment of direct, personal experience. (3) Oneness of self and other. Japanese view is collective and organic Nonaka and Takeuchi do not see the distinctions (subject vs object, mind vs body) as an either-or dichotomy, but mutually complementary. The cornerstone of the epistemology is the distinction of tacit and explicit knowledge.	Spinoza: Thought and extension are not two substances, but only two attributes of one and the same substance - After Schelling, the problem consisted in uniting dialectics as the true schema of developing knowledge and logic as the system of rules of thinking in general - According to Marx, labour is the process of changing nature by the action of social man, and is the "subject" to which thought belongs as "predicate"

III) What is Knowledge, and how it is created?

There are two dimensions in the knowledge creation (Fig. 1): epistemological and ontological dimensions (Nonaka & Takeuchi 1995). The epistemological basis is the distinction of tacit and explicit knowledge. The distinctive ontology is concerned with the levels of knowledge-creating entities (individual, group, organisational, and inter-organisational). A knowledge creation spiral emerges when the interaction between tacit and explicit knowledge is elevated dynamically from a lower ontological level to higher levels. From the ontological point of view, in a strict sense, *knowledge is created only by individuals*. ledge is elevated dynamically from a lower ontological level to higher levels. From the ontological point of view, in a strict sense, *knowledge is created only by individuals*. ledge is elevated dynamically from a lower ontological level to higher levels. From the ontological point of view, in a strict sense, *knowledge is created only by individuals*.

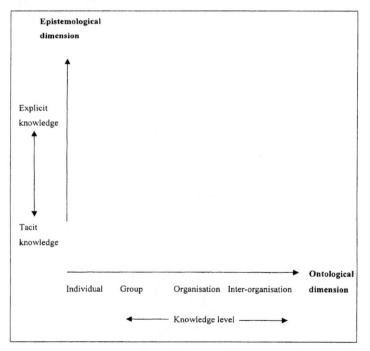

Figure 1. The two dimensions of knowledge creation (Nonaka & Takeuchi 1995, 56).

The four modes of knowledge conversion are created when tacit and explicit knowledge interact with each other. The four modes experienced by the individual are: socialisation, externalisation, combination, and internalisation. They constitute the "engine" of the entire knowledge-creation process. In addition, there are five conditions that enable or promote the spiral model in real work contexts. Knowledge is created through a five-phase process over time within the organisation.

What are Concepts and Knowledge?

According to Ilyenkov, Dialectical Logic must show how scientific thought develops, if it reflects, i.e. reproduces in concepts, an object existing outside our consciousness and will and independently of them. In other words, thought creates a mental reproduction of an object. What is then "concept" and how it is related to knowledge?

Ilyenkov refuses to define concept "concept" clearly. He says it is easy but would it be of any use? "Concept" could be understood as "state of brain substance", "external or internal, oral or written speech", "idea", "judgement", "sign" or "term defined through other terms". The concept could also be seen as accumulated knowledge, the "capital" of thought. He says it is better to start to consider "the gist of the matter". I understand that "the gist of the matter" is that the meaning of "concept" can be understood only by studying its development.

Nonaka and Takeuchi as work scientists are more simple and explicit. Knowledge is "justified true belief". They consider knowledge as a dynamic human process of justifying personal belief toward the "truth". There is a difference between information and knowledge. Information is a flow of messages, while knowledge is created by that very flow of information, anchored in the beliefs and commitment of its holder. This emphasises that knowledge is essentially related to human action. Both information and knowledge are created dynamically in social interaction among people.

Forms of Thinking and Dimensions of Knowledge

When discussing Hegel's contribution to the development of Dialectical Logic, Ilyenkov also deals with different forms of thinking. He said that Hegel was the first logician who threw aside the old prejudice that thought was presented only in the form of external or internal, oral or written speech. Language is, nevertheless, not the sole empirically observed form in which human thought manifests itself. Ilyenkov continues: "....man's actions, and so too the results of his actions, the things created by them, not only could, but must, be considered manifestations of his thought, as acts of the objectifying of his ideas, thoughts, plans, and conscious intentions." He cites Hegel by writing that thought in general "appears at first not in the form of thought but as feeling, intuition, imagination – forms that are to be distinguished from thought as form". This reminds me of Nonaka's and Takeuchi's epistemological point of view, which is based on Polanyi's (1966) distinction between explicit and tacit knowledge.

Explicit or "codified" knowledge refers to knowledge that is transmittable in formal, systematic language. Explicit knowledge can be articulated in formal language including grammatical statements, mathematical expressions, specifications, manuals, and so forth. This knowledge is easily transmitted across individuals.

A more important kind of knowledge is tacit knowledge, which is hard to articulate with formal language. It is highly personal, embedded in individual experience, context-specific and hard to formalise, making it difficult to communicate or to share with others. Subjective insights, intuitions, beliefs, value systems and hunches fall into this category of knowledge.

Tacit knowledge includes technical and cognitive elements (Fig. 2). The *technical element* encompasses the kind of informal and hard-to-pin-down skills or crafts captured in the term "know-how". At the same time, tacit knowledge contains an important *cognitive element*. Cognitive elements can be called mental models such as schemata, paradigms, perspectives, beliefs, and viewpoints. They help to perceive and define the world. It consists of schemata, mental models, beliefs, and perceptions so ingrained that we take them for granted. The cognitive element reflects our image of reality (what is) and our vision for the future (what ought to be).

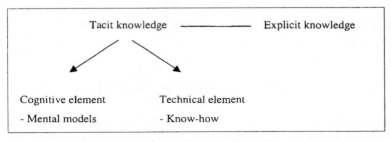

Figure 2. The division of Tacit Knowledge into cognitive and technical elements.

How tacit knowledge is created? *Polanyi (1966) contends that human beings acquire knowledge by actively creating and organising their own experiences.* This resembles Ilyenkov's description of Schelling's idea that the process of producing knowledge is done by the power of imagination. Or possibly, there is some similarity with Hegel's objective idealism. To know something is to create its image or pattern by tacitly integrating particulars. Therefore, scientific objectivity would not be a sole source of knowledge. According to Nonaka & Takeuchi (1995), tacit knowledge is *deeply rooted in an individual's action and experience, as well as in the ideals, values, or emotions* he or she embraces.

Development of Thought

In the seventh essay, Ilyenkov (1984) claims that Hegel could not explain from where thought originates. Thought is and to ask about its origin from something else was to ask a futile question. Thought is, it operates in man, and gradually arrives at awareness of its own activities, and of their schemes and laws. Labour only realises what the thinking spirit has found in itself in the course of utterance, in the course of dialogue with itself. Hegel"s conception is based on the idea that man thinks initially, and then only really acts. The scheme *"word – act – thing made by the act – again word"* (this time a verbally expressed report on what had been done) is repeated (Fig. 3). Further on, there is a new cycle according to the same scheme. The movement has the form of a spiral each turn of which both begins and ends at one and the same point, in a word.

As the alternative, Ilyenkov suggests the materialistic conception of development of thought. In this case, the question of the origin of thoughts is essential! The direction of the relationship of thought and reality is opposite to Hegel's view. Between the three concepts contemplating and thinking man and nature in itself, there is the mediating link of practice, labour and production, through which nature is transformed into thought, and thought into the body of nature.

In this connection, a new concept, "Ideal", comes to the picture. The well-known definition of "Ideal" is: "The ideal is the subjective image of objective reality, i.e. reflection of the external world in the forms of man's activity, in the forms of his consciousness and will". The ideal is not an individual, psychological fact, much less a physiological fact, but a socio-historical one, the product and form of mental production, writes Ilyenkov. How is then this "Ideal" formed? Ilyenkov answers based on Marx's and Engel's critics on the pre-Marxian materialism; "….the ideal could not be understood as the result and active function of labour, of the sensuously objective activity of social man, as the image of the external world arising in the thinking body not in the form of the result of passive contemplation but as the product and form of active transformation of nature by the labour of generations succeeding one another in the course of historical development". The "Ideal" is a cultural-historical product. The main point is the active aspect of the relation of thinking man to nature.

Ilyenkov provides a different view of the relationship of thought and reality (Fig. 3). He writes: "The ideal, as the form of social man's activity, exists where the process of the transformation of the body of nature into the object of man's activity, into the object of labour, and then into the product of labour, takes place". Ilyenkov describes the process of transformation in the following manner (my emphasis – MV): "The form of the *external thing* involved in the labour process is 'sublated' into the subjective form of objective activity *(action on objects)*; the latter is objectively registered in the subject in the form of the mechanisms of higher nervous activity; and then there is the reverse sequence of these metamorphoses, namely the *verbally expressed idea* is transformed into a *deed,* and through the deed into the form of an external, sensuously perceived thing, into a *thing."*

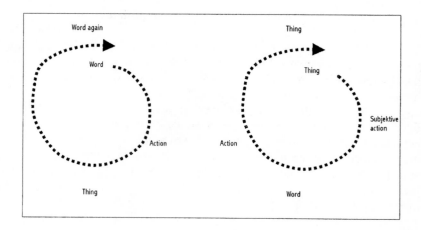

Figure 3. (a) Hegel's scheme of thought and reality, and (b) the materialist conception of action and thought.

What about the role of language in the transformation of the material into the ideal? External fact is expressed in language, but language of itself is as little ideal as the neuro-physiological structure of the brain. Language is only the form of expression of the ideal, its material-objective being. Ilyenkov writes: "The material is really 'transplanted' into the human head, and not simply into the brain as an organ of the individual's body, (1) only when it is expressed in immediately, generally significant forms of language (understood in the broadest sense of the word, including the language of drawings, diagrams, models, etc.), and (2) when it is transformed into an active form of man's activity with a real object (and not simply into a 'term' or 'utterance' as the material body of language)."

What about social interaction and communication? Marx said that man does not think in immediate unity with nature. Man only thinks when he is in unity with society, with the social and historical collective that produced his material and spiritual life. Abstracted from this context, he thinks as little as a brain isolated from the human body. Ilyenkov does not mention "dialogue" in this context. He nevertheless talks about "social man" and "social labour activity": "The ideal existed immediately only as the form (mode, image) of the activity of social man (i.e. of a quite objective, material being), directed to the external world", and: "The ideal [...] was the special function of man as the subject of social labour activity, accomplished in forms created by preceding development".

Nonaka and Takeuchi on Knowledge Conversion

Nonaka and Takeuchi (1995) emphasise that tacit and explicit knowledge are mutually complementary entities. How does transformation of the two types of knowledge occurs? Knowledge conversion, i.e., human knowledge is created and expanded through social interaction between tacit knowledge and explicit knowledge. This conversion is a "social" process between individuals and not confined within an individual. Is this the difference between Ilyenkov and Nonaka and Takeuchi: Ilyenkov emphasises practical activities while Nonaka and Takeuchi emphasise interaction, i.e., dialogue in transforming tacit knowledge into explicit in knowledge creation?

The four modes of knowledge conversion are (Fig. 4):

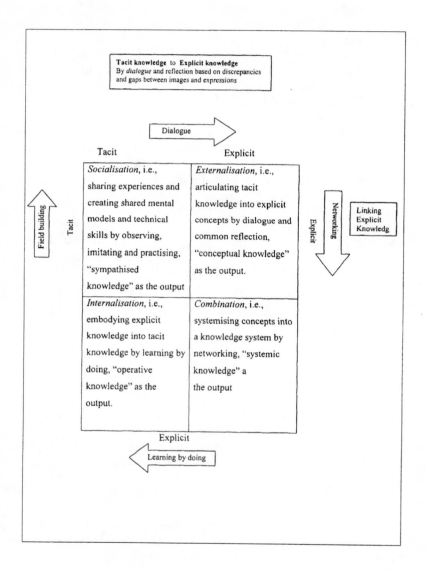

Figure 4. The Four modes of knowledge conversion (modified from Nonaka & Takeuchi 1995, Nonaka & Konno 1998).

1.   From tacit knowledge to tacit knowledge (socialisation). Socialisation is a process of sharing experiences and creating shared mental models and technical skills. An individual can acquire tacit knowledge directly from others without using language, i.e., by observing, imitation, and practice. The key point is common and shared experience. The socialisation mode starts by building a "field" of interaction. The output of socialisation is "sympathised knowledge".

Ilyenkov comments on the possibility to pass the ideal as such to another person, as the pure form of activity. He writes: "One can observe the activity of a painter or an engineer as long as one likes, striving to catch their mode of action, the form of their activity, but one can thus only copy the external techniques and methods of their work but never the ideal image itself, the active faculty itself. The ideal, as the form of subjective activity, is only masterable through active operation with the object and product of this activity, i.e. through the form of its product, through the objective form of the thing, through its active disobjectification." Although it is unclear whether or not we can identify "tacit knowledge" with "ideal", we can conclude that both models emphasise "practice" or "doing" as the pre-condition of knowledge transfer between persons. The emphasis is, however, different: Nonaka and Takeuchi underline "shared action" instead "individual action on object" by Ilyenkov.

2.   From tacit knowledge to explicit knowledge (externalisation). Externalisation is a process of articulating tacit knowledge into explicit concepts taking the shapes of metaphors, analogies, concepts, hypothesis and models. The output is "conceptual knowledge". They are mostly expressed in language. There are discrepancies and gaps between images and expressions helping to promote "reflection" and interaction between individuals. The externalisation mode is triggered by meaningful "dialogue or collective reflection". Among the four modes, externalisation holds the key to knowledge creation, because it creates new, explicit concepts! Metaphor is a way of perceiving or intuitively understanding one thing by imaging another thing symbolically. Once explicit concepts are created, they can then be modelled.

3.   From explicit knowledge to explicit knowledge (combination). Combination is a process of systemising concepts into a knowledge system. The output is "systemic knowledge". The combination mode is triggered by "networking" newly created knowledge and existing knowledge from other sections of the organisation. Different bodies of knowledge are combined and exchanged through such media as documents, meetings, telephone conver-

sations, and computerised communication networks. Refiguration of existing information is done through sorting, adding, combining, and categori-
sing of explicit knowledge.

4.   From explicit knowledge to implicit knowledge (internalisation). Internalisation is a process of embodying explicit knowledge again into tacit
knowledge. The output is "operative knowledge". It is closely related to "learning by doing" that triggers it. Experiences through socialisation, externalisation, and combination are internalised into individuals" tacit knowledge
bases in the form of shared mental models or technical know-how. For explicit knowledge to become tacit, it helps if the knowledge is verbalised or
diagrammed into documents, manuals or oral stories.

An organisation cannot create knowledge by itself. Individual tacit
knowledge is the basis of organisational knowledge creation. The mobilised
tacit knowledge is amplified through four modes of knowledge conversion
at higher ontological levels. It starts from individual level and moves up
through expanding communities of interaction.

IV) Conclusions and Discussion

Conclusions

It is evident that both Ilyenkov and Nonaka and Takeuchi want to overcome
the same basic and classical philosophical problem: the relationship of "the
thing in thought" and "the thing outside thought". The basic answer is the
same: "subject" and "object" are complementary, and the unity is created
through practice.

What kind of forms does Thought have? Ilyenkov denies to define the
concept "concept" clearly. He underlines the need to understand the concept's
development. Its highest form is the "ideal" as "the subjective image of
objective reality, i.e. reflection of the external world in the forms of man's
activity, in the forms of his consciousness and will." Nonaka and Takeuchi
are very clear: there are tacit knowledge, which is hard to articulate with
formal language, and explicit or "codified" knowledge that refers to knowledge
that is transmittable in formal, systematic language. Tacit knowledge is further
divided into cognitive and technical elements. These two forms transform
into each other during knowledge creation. Ilyenkov, however, agrees with

Hegel's distinction that thought may appear in the form of speech as well as in the form of feelings and intuitions.

How do thought and knowledge develop? There is at least one common feature in the two approaches: the development of thought and knowledge occurs in a cyclical manner. Ilyenkov emphasises "thing" or object oriented practice. Nonaka and Takeuchi add that human knowledge is created through social interaction between tacit and explicit knowledge and provide different mechanisms for knowledge conversion. The topic of my paper is "Dialectics and Dialogue in Ilyenkov". You may have wondered where the "Dialogue" stands? My conclusion is that it stands very far from Ilyenkov's model of concept development. He refers quite superficially to the "social man" and "social labour activity" without conceptualising "social" in more detail.

Are Nonaka and Takeuchi dialectical thinkers and practitioners? I would say yes! Ilyenkov clearly states that dialectical logic must show how thought develops if it is scientific and if it reflects, i.e. reproduces in concepts, an object existing outside our consciousness and will and independently of them. In other words, how it creates a mental reproduction of it, reconstructs its self-development, recreates it in the logic of the movement of concepts so as to recreate it later in fact (in experiment or in practice). In this meaning, Nonaka and Takeuchi show abilities to use dialectical logic.

Some Doubts

Ilyenkov moves on at least two levels: on the general philosophical level, and on the individual level, giving examples of how a person thinks. There is one more difficulty in interpreting Ilyenkov: it is sometimes difficult to con-clude whose voice he is using, his own or others". He does not always clearly separate and present his own stand to the subject matter.

Is it right to compare the Nonaka-Takeuchi-model of knowledge creation with Ilyenkov's description of dialectical logic as the science of thinking? It might be that the best way would be to analyse Nonaka's and Takeuchi's ideas from the view-point of a specific science, like cognitive science and psychology. Ilyenkov himself stated that only similar objects can be compared and contrasted. If we accept that the knowledge creation model in the work context is a special case of the development of thinking, the comparison can be made.

Literature

Bohm, D. (1996), *On dialogue*. London: Routledge.

Ilyenkov, E.V. (1977), *The concept of the ideal*. In: *Philosophy in the USSR. Problems of dialectical materialism*, 71–99. Moscow: Progress.

Ilyenkov, E.V. (1984), *Dialectical Logic: essays in its history and theory*. Moscow: Progress.

Nonaka, I. & Takeuchi, H. (1995,) *The knowledge-creating company. How Japanese companies create the dynamics of innovation*. New York: Oxford University Press.

Nonaka, I. & Konno, N. (1998) *The concept of "Ba": building a foundation for knowledge creation*. In: *California Management Review* 40, 3, 40–54.

Polanyi, M. (1966) *The tacit dimension*. New York: Doubleday & Co.

12

Denken, Sprache und Form.
Iljenkow und Bühler
– ein exemplarischer Vergleich

Janette Friedrich

Iljenkows Denken bereicherte und provozierte nicht nur die philosophischen Debatten seiner Zeit, sondern reichte auch in verschiedene sozialwissenschaftliche Disziplinen, wie die Psychologie und die Sprachwissenschaft, hinein. Er suchte in diesen Disziplinen vor allem Bestätigung und Verifikationsmöglichkeiten für seine Ideen. Die wohl bekannteste Zusammenarbeit dieser Art stellte Iljenkows Teilnahme an der Durchführung und Auswertung des sogenannten Meschtscherjakow-Experiments dar (vgl. Meschtscherjakow, 1971a, 1971b; Iljenkow, 1977b).[1]

Iljenkow trat jedoch nicht nur mit Psychologen sondern auch mit Sprachwissenschaftlern in einen Dialog, der sich vor allem um das Verhältnis von Denken und Sprache drehte. In den aktuellen Diskussionen wird dieses Problem oft ausschliesslich dem Gebiet der Psycholinguistik zugerechnet, jedoch für Iljenkow stellte es seinerzeit eine Herausforderung an das philosophische Denken dar. Betrachtet man die Geschichte der Diskussion um das Verhältnis von Denken und Sprache etwas näher, so fällt auf, dass gerade im ersten Drittel des 20. Jahrhunderts diese Problematik im Mittelpunkt einer grossen Anzahl von Veröffentlichungen stand.[2] Die hierbei diskutierten Themen unterscheiden sich deutlich von den heute in der Psycholinguistik vorherrschenden Debatten. Die Frage, ob Iljenkows Überlegungen zum Verhältnis von Denken und Sprache eine Fortsetzung der Diskussionen der 20/30er Jahre darstellen, kann in diesem Zusammenhang leider nicht untersucht werden und bleibt einer anderen Studie vorbehalten. Was im folgenden interessiert, sind, neben einer Rekonstruktion der Position Iljenkows, seine Bezüge auf die moderne Psychologie und Sprachwissenschaft. Diese Bezüge sind selektiv und zielen auf eine Traditionslinie – die Chomskys und Piagets. Es erscheint nicht uninteressant zu fragen, warum Iljenkow eine zweite, für das 20. Jahrhundert ebenso repräsentative Richtung insbesondere in den Sprachwissenschaften, unberücksichtigt liess. Durch die Untersuchung der Auslassungen des Autors soll also mehr über die Kerngedanken seiner Theorie erkundet werden. Zum anderen erhält man so Auskunft über den Kontext und den Zeitgeist der 60er/70er Jahre, denn Iljenkow ist nicht der einzige, der den Ideen Chomskys und Piagets einen privilegierten Platz in seiner Theorie einräumt.[3]

Zum Verhältnis von Denken und Sprache

Unter dem Titel *Überlegungen zum Verhältnis von Denken und Sprache,* zuerst 1977 in den *Voprosy filosofii* publiziert, hat Iljenkow seine Auffassung des Verhältnisses zusammengefasst.[4] Zum einen formuliert er hier eine klare Ablehnung der Gleichsetzung von Denken und Sprechen, zum anderen führt Iljenkow einen Sprachformbegriff ein, der es ermöglicht, Denken und Sprechen zu identifizieren. Für Iljenkow steht es ausser Frage, dass im realen Funktionieren der Sprache Formen existieren, die der spezifischen "Materie" der Sprache zugehören. Sie sind nicht ableitbar aus dem in der Sprache ausgedrücktem Inhalt, d.h. aus der Bewegung von Sinn und Bedeutung (vgl. Iljenkow 1977/1994, 287). Als Beispiel verweist er auf den Kasus, der in ganz unterschiedlicher Anzahl in den verschiedenen Sprachen auftritt. Für dieses Phänomen gibt es keinerlei rationale Erklärung. Die Kasusmorpheme sind der jeweiligen Sprache eigen und in diesem Sinne sind sie Sprachformen. Neben dem Verständnis der Sprachformen als arbiträre Formen einer natürlichen Sprache entwickelt Iljenkow eine zweite Sicht auf dieses Phänomen. Zu diesem Zweck spricht er von "Tiefenstrukturen der Sprache".

Der Begriff der Tiefenstrukturen der Sprache ist eindeutig von Chomsky entlehnt und Iljenkow versäumt nicht, darauf hinzuweisen. Die Tiefenstrukturen der Sprache unterscheiden sich von den variierenden Schemata in deren Gestalt sich diese Strukturen in den verschiedenen Sprachen realisieren, also in der Terminologie Chomskys, von den Oberflächenstrukturen der Sprache. Iljenkow folgt Chomsky nicht nur in der Gegenüberstellung von Tiefen- und Oberflächenstrukturen der Sprache sondern auch in der Behauptung, dass die ersteren einen Realitätscharakter besitzen. Für Iljenkow wie für Chomsky sind die Tiefenstrukturen der Sprache keine Abstraktion des Linguisten, sondern ihnen entspricht eine Realität. Sie existieren unabhängig davon, ob sie in einer besonderen Sprache realisiert sind oder nicht. Es scheint Iljenkow dabei wichtig zu sein, diese Unabhängigkeit der Sprachformen von den besonderen natürlichen Sprachen zu betonen. Auf der anderen Seite behauptet er jedoch, dass die Sprachformen das Resultat einer Abstraktion sind. Wir haben zu den Tiefenstrukturen der Sprache nur Zugang: "... indem man die 'Invarianten' sucht, die sich nicht anders ausdrücken als in der Vielfalt *rein formaler* Besonderheiten der nationalen Sprachen, d.h. durch Abstraktion (Absehen) von eben diesen Besonderheiten" (Iljenkow 1977/1994, 288).

Zwei Ideen erweisen sich als charakteristisch für den von Iljenkow verwendeten Formbegriff: Die Sprachformen besitzen nach Iljenkow einen Realitätscharakter und sind gleichzeitig das Resultat einer Abstraktion, da sie nicht ausserhalb der verschiedenen natürlichen Sprachen, also ausserhalb ihrer stofflichen Träger, existieren können.

In dem Jahrhundert, in dem für die Sprachwissenschaft nicht nur der Name Chomskys, sondern auch der Saussures und Humboldts steht, bezieht Iljenkow Position für Chomsky. Eine genaue und subtile Lektüre der Saussure-Schriften und seines Nachlasses hat in den letzten Jahren gezeigt, dass auch wenn *la langue* (die Sprache) immer wieder zum Zentralbegriff der Saussureschen Theorie erklärt wird, diese nicht den Ausgangspunkt seiner Untersuchungen bildete. Es ist nicht das formale Modell der Sprache *(la langue)*, sondern *les langues*, d.h. die natürlichen Sprachen, die Saussure zum Objekt seiner Sprachtheorie erhebt. Die Sprachen in ihren Besonderheiten, in ihrer existierenden Vielfalt sucht Saussure mit seinem Modell zu erfassen (vgl. Saussure 1997). Mit der seit einigen Jahren zu beobachtbaren Humboldt-Renaissance in den Sprachwissenschaften haben wir es ebenfalls mit einer Hinwendung nicht zum Formalen sondern zum Verschiedenen in den Sprachen zu tun (vgl. Humboldt, 1836/1998).

Man könnte also von einer zweiten, für das 20. Jahrhundert ebenfalls repräsentativen Richtung in den Sprachwissenschaften sprechen. Sie umfasst die Theorien, die im Gegensatz zu der Chomskys, die Verschiedenheiten der natürlichen Sprachen zu erklären und zu begründen suchen. Diese Richtung im sprachwissenschaftlichen Denken wird von Iljenkow weder verfolgt noch als relevant für seine Überlegungen wahrgenommen.

Freilich stimmt Iljenkow mit Chomsky nicht in allen mit dem Begriff der Tiefenstrukturen der Sprache zusammenhängenden Überlegungen überein. Einen ersten Unterschied sieht er in der Erklärung der Existenz der Tiefenstrukturen. Auf die Frage, wie die Tiefenstrukturen im Menschen existieren, geben Chomsky und Iljenkow eine unterschiedliche Antwort. Für Iljenkow erweist sich Chomsky als reiner Cartesianer, da er die Tiefenstrukturen als angeboren erachtet. Für Chomsky existieren die Tiefenstrukturen entweder in Gestalt morphologisch in den menschlichen Körper eingebauter Schemata des Gehirns oder als Schemata einer rein körperlosen Seele.

Plausibler erscheint Iljenkow dagegen Piagets Entdeckung der sensomotorischen Schemata. So sucht er zunächst, die Tiefenstrukturen Chomskys mit den sensomotorischen Schemata Piagets gleichzusetzen. Ein Vergleich drängt sich geradezu auf, da beide Denker den von ihnen diskutierten Formgebilden einen Realitätscharakter zusprechen. Ausserdem stimmen beide Autoren in der Behauptung überein, dass es Formen gibt (nach Chomsky Sprachformen, nach Piaget Handlungsformen), die unabhängig von und ontogenetisch vor unserem Sprechen in einer der natürlichen Sprachen existieren. Piaget zeigt, dass die sensomotorischen Schemata sich in der Ontogenese früher herausbilden als das Kind sprechen und die Rede verstehen kann. Ontogenetisch geht die Entwicklung des Denkens in Form des sensomotorischen Denkens der Entwicklung des sprachlichen Denkens voraus.

Damit hätten wir eine erste Antwort auf die Frage, warum Iljenkow in seiner Diskussion des Verhältnisses von Denken und Sprache gerade auf Chomsky und Piaget zurückgreift. Iljenkow sucht nachzuweisen, dass das Denken in der Tätigkeit des Individuums entsteht. Nach seiner Überzeugung spielt die Sprache in der Genesis des Denkens nur eine sekundäre Rolle:

> Und auf allen nachfolgenden Etappen des Lernens der Sprache vollzieht sich dieser Prozess nur durch "Versprachlichung" der eigenen, bereits geformten, schon vollzogenen und sich vollziehenden gegenständlichen menschlichen Tätigkeit, so dass die Logik der realen spezifisch menschlichen (zweckmässigen) Tätigkeit immer früher angeeignet wird als die linguistischen Redeschemata, als die "Logik der Sprache" und sie immer als Grundlage und Urbild der letzteren dient (Iljenkow, 1977/1994, 292–293).

Das ist eine der Hauptideen seiner Konzeption, die er durch die Ergebnisse des Meschtscherjakow-Experiments und die Arbeiten A.N. Leontjews bestätigt sah. In der Literatur wird der Versuch Iljenkows, eine Aneignungstheorie des Denkens zu entwickeln, immer wieder positiv hervorgehoben. Er wurde in der Psychologie insbesondere von den Vertretern der kulturhistorischen Schule aufgegriffen und fortgesetzt.[5] Wir glauben, dass die von Iljenkow vorgeschlagene Art der Betrachtung des Verhältnisses von Denken und Sprechen treffend als psychologisch-genetische charakterisiert werden kann.

In dem Text *Verhältnis von Denken und Sprache* finden wir allerdings noch eine andere Antwort auf die Frage, warum Iljenkow den Ideen Chomskys und Piagets einen zentralen Platz in seiner Theorie einräumt. Iljenkow schreibt: "Diese sensomotorischen Schemata, wie Piaget sie nennt, oder 'Tiefenstrukturen' wie sie die Linguisten bezeichnen, sind eben dasjenige, was die Philosophie von alters her logische Formen nennt, oder Formen des 'Denkens als solchem'"(Iljenkow, 1977/1994, 290). Diese Aussage Iljenkows ist weniger als Feststellung denn als Programm zu verstehen. Betrachten wir also näher was Iljenkow unter den "Formen des Denkens als solchem" versteht und welche Konzeption des Denkens er in seiner philosophischen Theorie entwickelt.

Iljenkows Konzeption des Denkens und der in ihr entwickelte Formbegriff

Eine Definition des Denkens, die uns gleichzeitig Auskunft über seinen Denkformbegriff gibt, entwickelt Iljenkow in den verschiedensten Texten (vgl. Iljenkow, 1962 ; 1974/1984; 1977a). In den *Überlegungen zum Verhältnis von Denken und Sprache* schreibt er exemplarisch: "... das Denken, auf allgemeinste Weise bestimmt, ist nichts anderes als die Fähigkeit, mit jedem beliebigen anderen Körper, der sich ausserhalb des eigenen Körpers befindet, gemäss seiner Form, Lage und Bedeutung in der ihn umgebenden Welt umzugehen" (Iljenkow 1977/1994, 291).

Iljenkow orientiert sich mit dieser Definition eindeutig an Spinoza und seiner Idee eines denkenden Körpers. Spinoza unterschied zwischen denkenden und nicht-denkenden Körpern, wobei das Kriterium der Unterscheidung ihre jeweilige Bewegungsform bildete. Die Bewegung des nichtdenkenden Körpers wird von seiner eigenen körperlichen Form bestimmt. Beim Zusammentreffen mit einem anderen Körper zerbricht er diesen oder er zerbricht selbst, so wie z.B. eine stetige Einwirkung von Wasser auf Stein eine Aushöhlung hinterlässt. Die Besonderheit von Spinozas denkendem Körper erblickte Iljenkow dagegen darin, dass er die Form seiner Bewegung im Raum gemäss den Formen eines anderen Körpers aktiv gestaltet. Man könnte demnach sagen, daß das Denken für Iljenkow eine besondere

Darstellung eines Körpers in einem anderen ist. Die Darstellung des Körpers A im Körper B ist die Reproduktion der äusseren Form von A in der materiellen Bewegung von B. B stellt in seiner Bewegung etwas dar, was mit seiner eigenen Gegenständlichkeit nichts gemeinsam hat. B erhält so etwas wie eine zweite Gegenständlichkeit – die Reproduktion der Form von A in seiner eigenen materiellen Bewegung als Körper. Diese zweite Gegenständlichkeit könnte man als funktionale Gegenständlichkeit bezeichnen (vgl. Friedrich, 1993, Kap. 1).

Eine ebensolche Definition des Denkens findet Iljenkow in der Beschreibung der sensomotorischen Schemata durch Piaget vorausgesetzt :

> Ein sensomotorisches Schema ist die durch die Bewegung in der Zeit entfaltete räumlich-geometrische Form eines Dinges; sie enthält nichts anderes. Es ist das Schema des Prozesses, der die Form eines Dinges reproduziert, d.h. die räumlich fixierte Form, die Geometrie des äusseren Körpers. Die Form des anderen (äusseren) Körpers ist als mit ihr übereinstimmende (ihr kongruente) Bewegungsform des Subjekts (d.h. des sich aktiv bewegenden Körpers) dargestellt. Es ist *ein* und dasselbe *Schema*, ein und dieselbe Kontur, nur einmal als simultan fixierte, erstarrte Kontur des Dinges; das andere Mal hingegen sukzessiv in der Zeit entfaltet, als Kontur der Bewegung, als Trajektorie dieser Bewegung, die eine räumlich fixierte Spur hinterlässt, an der sich diese Bewegung orientiert (Iljenkow 1974/1994, 290–291).

Im sensomotorischen Schema erscheint das Ding zum einen als Ding und zum anderen als Bewegungsform des Subjekts. Einmal ist es das Ding und das andere mal das Denken des Dinges.

Eine Korrespondenz zwischen Sein und Denken, zwischen dem Ding und seinem Denken ist hier behauptet. Das Schema des Dinges und das Schema seines Denkens fallen zusammen, sind kongruent. Mit einer solchen identitätsphilosophischen Annahme schliesst Iljenkow jedoch ein wichtiges Phänomen aus seiner Konzeption des Denkens aus.[6] Es handelt sich um den Widerstandscharakter der Realität. Er bringt dies selbst an mehreren Stellen indirekt zum Ausdruck. "Die Schemata der Handlung sind mit den Schemata der Dinge, der Objekte dieser Handlung, kongruent; anderenfalls könnte die Handlung, stiesse sie auf hartnäckigen Widerstand der Dinge, überhaupt nicht ausgeführt werden" (ebenda, 290). An anderer Stelle schreibt er: "Es ist dies vor allem die Fähigkeit, den eigenen Körper (seine Bewegung) so zu lenken, dass diese Bewegung verwirklicht werden kann, ohne auf ein unüberwindliches Hindernis, auf den Widerstand 'anderer Körper' (ihrer geometrischen, physikalischen, sowie aller anderen, bis hin zu semantischen und sittlichen, Parameter) zu stossen" (ebenda, 291).

Entweder das Subjekt bewegt sich gemäss der Logik der anderen und ordnet sie auf diese Weise seiner Handlung unter, oder es handelt nicht. Es scheint so als wenn Iljenkow eine dritte, real existierende Möglichkeit ausschliesst: nämlich zu handeln und in seiner Handlung am Widerstand der Realität oder des Anderen zu scheitern oder sie überwinden zu müssen.

Natürlich könnte man einwenden, dass es Iljenkow in seiner Konzeption des Denkens um ein grundsätzlich anderes Problem als den Resistenzcharakter der Realität ging. Er suchte in der Realität "Gegenstände" zu entdecken, auf die seine funktionale Definition des Denkens zutrifft. Er findet sie in der Welt der sozialen Körper. Der Mensch ist nicht nur von einer Welt natürlicher Körper, sondern auch von einer Welt sozialer Körper umgeben. Die sozialen Körper haben die Besonderheit zwei Logiken zu besitzen: zum einen eine gegenständliche Logik (ihre körperliche Form) und zum anderen eine soziale Logik. In ihnen sind die Logik ihrer Verwendung und ihrer Bedeutung objektiviert. Jeder Kulturgegenstand schreibt sozusagen die Tätigkeit mit sich vor, er enthält sie als zweite innere Kontur. Der Mensch reproduziert also nicht die äussere Form eines anderen Körpers, sondern die Logik des gesellschaftlich-menschlichen Denkens, die in den sozialen Dingen vergegenständlicht ist. Er nimmt am Gegenstand die Form der Tätigkeit wahr für die er produziert wurde und nicht die Form des Gegenstandes an und für sich.

Die Besonderheit der sozialen Körper resümiert Iljenkow in seinem Begriff des Ideellen, der einen Schlüsselbegriff seines Denkens darstellt und zu dem es seither eine Reihe sehr polemischer Stellungnahmen in der sowjetischen Philosophie gab.[7] Das Ideelle ist nach Iljenkow "... die Form des Dinges, doch ausserhalb dieses Dinges existierend und zwar in der Tätigkeit des Menschen als Form dieser Tätigkeit. Oder umgekehrt das ist die Form der Tätigkeit des Menschen, doch ausserhalb dieses Menschen als Form des Dinges" (Iljenkow 1979: 7, 148).

Methodologisch zieht Iljenkow zur Charakterisierung des Ideellen die Wertformanalyse von Marx heran. Marx widmete den größten Teil des 1. Bandes des *Kapitals* dem Nachweis, dass die Geld- oder Wertform eine von der handgreiflich reellen Körperform der Waren unterschiedene, nur ideelle oder vorgestellte Form sei, die voraussetzt und impliziert, dass die Waren im Warenaustausch als äquivalente ausgetauscht werden können. Die Wertform existiert einmal in Form der Dinge das andere mal in Form der Austauschtätigkeit. Damit erfüllt die Wertform die für das Ideelle als charakteristisch beschriebenen Merkmale (vgl. Friedrich 1993, Kap. 1.6.). Ausserdem finden wir hier den im ersten Paragraphen skizzierten Formbegriff wieder. Es handelt sich um eine Form, die nicht das Reflexionsprodukt eines Individuums ist, sie besitzt Realitätscharakter, sie existiert in Form der Tätigkeit des Individuums mit den Kulturgegenständen, sie existiert im Austausch der Waren. Gleichzeitig ist diese Form die ideelle Form der

Gegenstände, bedarf also einer Abstraktionsleistung des Subjekts. Jede beliebige Ware kann die Funktion der Geldware ausüben, kann als Austauschmittel gesehen werden. Dazu bedarf es der Abstraktion von seinem konkreten Sein als Ware.

Es erscheint an diesem Punkt interessant, Iljenkows Privilegierung des Formbegriffs in seiner Theorie des Denkens mit den Überlegungen anderer Theoretiker zu vergleichen, die ebenfalls auf die Unhintergehbarkeit des Formbegriffs hinauslaufen. Karl Bühlers Sprachtheorie bietet sich für einen kontrastiven Vergleich besonders an, da Bühler trotz seiner Kritik an der Verwendung des Formbegiffs in der Sprachtheorie diesen letztlich doch benötigt. Karl Bühler (1879–1963), Psychologe und Sprachwissenschaftler, ist bekannt geworden als Mitglied der Würzburger Schule, die sich mit Problemen der Denkpsychologie beschäftigte. Seine für die hier diskutierte Problematik interessanteste Schaffensperiode fiel in die zwanziger und dreissiger Jahre, während der er als Professor für Philosophie, Psychologie und angewandte Pädagogik an der Universität Wien arbeitete. Hier schrieb er die *Sprachtheorie* (1934), in der neben einer Kritik an der Gleichsetzung von Sprachzeichen und Geldzeichen eine kurze aber sehr treffende Charakterisierung der Funktion des Formbegriffs zu finden ist.[8]

Bühlers Ablehnung des Formbegriffs für die Sprachtheorie

Bühler schreibt:

> Und was das Begriffswort "Form" angeht, so mag es weiter leben in dem abgeblassten und nicht mehr spezifisch aristotelischen Sinn von "Klasse, Gruppe" und ausserdem so, wie man es nirgends im Leben oder in der Wissenschaft entbehren kann, wenn ad hoc und immer wieder wechselnd zwei Komponenten wie Stoff und Form opponiert werden sollen. In diesem relativen Sinne kann Höchstgeformtes wieder Stoff und Stofflichstes stets wieder Form sein für den Gestalter oder Theoretiker (Bühler 1936, 11).

Bühler kritisiert genau die Option des Formbegriffs, die für Iljenkows Konzeption des Denkens eine nicht zu unterschätzende Rolle spielt. Es handelt sich um die Opposition von Form und Stoff, die von Iljenkow als eine relative wahrgenommen wird. Für Iljenkow lässt sich die Opposition eindeutig an solchen Phänomenen wie der Wertform der Waren und der ideellen Form der Kulturprodukte ablesen. Die Form schlägt in den Stoff um, wie der Stoff in die Form. Die Ware kann als stofflich konkretes Arbeitsprodukt betrachtet werden oder als etwas, das in einer bestimmten Proportion gegen etwas anderes ausgetauscht werden kann, also als Wertform besitzend oder als Geldware auftretend. Genau das gleiche kann mit einem Kulturprodukt geschehen. Ich kann in einem Hammer das sehen, wofür er produziert wurde. Seiner Funktion nach dient er zum Einschlagen von Nägeln. Ich kann ihn ausgehend von seinen körperlichen Eigenschaften jedoch auch dazu benutzen, eine Seite meines Vortrages zu beschweren, damit sie vom Wind nicht davongetragen wird.

Was Bühler als Umschlagen des Stoffs in die Form und der Form in den Stoff bezeichnet ist nichts anderes als das, was Iljenkow mit dem Begriff des Ideellen konzeptualisiert. Das Ideelle ist die Form des Dinges aber ausserhalb des Dinges als Tätigkeit (Form → Stoff) und es ist die Tätigkeit aber in Form des Dinges (Stoff → Form). Bühler kritisiert die Verwendung solch eines Formbegriffs in der Sprachtheorie vor allem deshalb, weil sie eng mit einer psychologisch-genetischen Betrachtung des Verhältnisses von Denken und Sprache zusammenhängt wie sie auch von Iljenkow vorgeschlagen wurde. Weder die Kohärenz von Iljenkows Theorie noch die mit ihr ohne Zweifel verbundenen Erklärungspotenzen – was insbesondere die Prozesse der Aneignung des Denkens betrifft – sollen also im folgenden in Frage gestellt werden. Was an Bühlers Kritik des Formbegriffs interessiert, sind die Gründe für seine Ablehnung eines genetisch-psychologischen Standpunktes in der Sprachwissenschaft und die sich daraus ergebenden Konsequenzen für das Verständnis des Verhältnisses von Denken und Sprache. In seiner Argumentation geht Bühler als erstes auf die Versuche ein, das Geldzeichen mit dem Sprachzeichen gleichzusetzen und er bringt gegen das Aufmachen solcher Parallelen zwei Bedenken vor.

Der erste Unterschied zwischen dem Sprach- und dem Geldzeichen besteht nach Bühler darin, dass die Geldnote oder die Münze stofflich das Stück sein muss, welches einem offiziellen Druck- oder Prägeverfahren unterworfen war und aus ihm hervorgegangen ist. Die Dollarnote trägt eine Nummer, die nur diesem Stück eigen ist. Es handelt sich um so etwas wie ein polizeiliches Signalement, damit dieses Stück Papier im Bedarfsfall seine Echtheitsprüfung bestehen kann. Das Sprachzeichen besitzt im Unterschied zum Geld ein solches Signalement nicht. Es wird von vornherein in seiner konkreten lautlichen Realisierung wahrgenommen. Beim Hören eines Wortes kann man sofort unterscheiden, ob ein Mann, eine Frau oder ein Kind das entsprechende Wort aussprechen. Das wird am Klangbild der Stimme erkannt. Auch die Intonation, die Zusammensetzung des Wortes aus Silben, die benutzten Vokale usw. ermöglichen es, das Wort in seiner Einmaligkeit und konkreten Realisation zu erfahren. Der Unterschied des einen Wortes vom anderen wird, so betont Bühler, an seiner konkreten sinnlichen Realisierung wahrgenommen und nicht an einer Nummernreihe.

Für unsere Problematik bedeutet dies, daß jedes Sprachzeichen *an sich* eine von einem anderen Sprachzeichen unterschiedliche Existenz hat. Jedes Wort ist verschieden vom anderen, dazu braucht es kein individuelles Erkennungszeichen wie es bei der Dollarnote der Fall ist. Zur Sinnkrisis, die durch das Zeichen realisiert wird, gehört also nach Bühler die Wahrnehmung des Sprachzeichens als eines sinnlich konkreten Dinges. Im Unterschied dazu nimmt man bei der Betrachtung des Geldes nicht wahr aus welchem Papier es gemacht ist, sondern vielmehr das, wogegen man es austauschen kann. Auch wenn die Nummernreihe es ermöglicht, einen Fünfzigmarkschein vom anderen zu unterscheiden, ist es nicht sie, die am Geld wahrgenommen wird. Am Geld wird das gesehen, wogegen es ausgetauscht werden kann. Und damit wären wir beim zweiten Bedenken Bühlers gegen das Parallelsetzen von Geld und Sprache.

Das konkrete Wort ist ein Zeichending, der Dollar bleibt dagegen, so sehr er sich den Zeichendingen in seiner Papierform auch nähert, den Gütern verhaftet. Man kann ihn zwar nicht konsumieren, aber man erhält im Kaufakt etwas für das Geldzeichen. Dies – so Bühler – kann von den Sprachmünzen nicht behauptet werden. Die Verhaftung des Geldes im Reiche der Güter ist also sein wichtigstes Definitionsmerkmal. Der Warenaustausch ist die Existenzbedingung des Geldes. Die Existenz des Sprachzeichens hängt von etwas anderem ab. Ein Sprachzeichen existiert nur dann als solches, wenn bestimmte Eigenschaften des Zeichens, als die Eigenschaften wahrgenommen werden, an denen ihre Funktion, als Zeichen zu fungieren, gebunden ist.

Bühler zieht zur Illustrierung dieses Gedankens den mimischen Verkehr heran:

> Nach dem Ausweis älterer und neuerer Studien [...] ist es so im mimischen Verkehr, dass aus dem Fluss des kontinuierlichen Geschehens im Gesicht und an den gröberen Körperbewegungen des Menschen bestimmte *fruchtbare Momente* hervortreten, herausgeholt werden. Dies Verfahren ist Bildhauern und Malern, die menschlichen Ausdruck in Stein und Farbe fixieren, wohlvertraut ; dass es auch den Partnern des trivialen alltäglichen mimischen Verkehrs der Menschen wohlvertraut ist, wurde bewiesen in meinem Ausdrucksbuch. Psychologisch gesehen genau dasselbe geschieht am Klangbild des Wortes. Der aufnehmende Hörer gewinnt diesem Lautkontinuum bestimmte fruchtbare Momente ab für die unerlässliche Diakrise. Das ist es und gar nichts anderes, was man Phoneme nennt (Bühler, 1934/1982, 287).

Das heisst, in der Sprachtheorie stellt sich eine Frage, die sich in der Geldtheorie nie stellen würde. Hier wird gefragt, welches die Eigenschaften des wahrnehmbaren Stellvertreters (des Zeichens, des Wortes) sind, an welche die Vertretung gebunden ist. Anders formuliert heisst das: Welche Eigenschaften eines Zeichens sind es, die seine Diakrisis und damit Sinnkrisis realisieren? So gesehen geht es um die Entdeckung der Momente kraft derer ein Zeichen als Zeichen fungiert, d.h. hier liegt eindeutig eine semiotisch-deskriptive Fragestellung vor.

Bühler behauptet diese Fragestellung als zentral für die moderne Sprachtheorie. Dass er die semiotisch-deskriptive Fragestellung im selben Moment privilegierte, in dem die Phonologie geboren wurde, ist nicht zufällig, wird doch durch die Phonologie das erstemal die Frage nach der Relevanz des phonetischen Materials der Sprache für den Sinnbildungsprozess aufgeworfen.[9] Ausgehend von den Ergebnissen der Phonologie unterscheidet Bühler also zwischen einer semiotisch-deskriptiven und einer genetisch-psychologischen Fragestellung in der Sprachtheorie und gibt der ersteren ohne Zweifel die Priorität. Dies hat nicht unwesentliche Konsequenzen für die Bestimmung der Rolle des Subjekts in den Sozialwissenschaften.

Rekapitulieren wir noch einmal den kontrastiven Vergleich zwischen Iljenkow und Bühler im Hinblick auf das Problem des Verhältnisses von Denken und Sprache. Iljenkow untersucht die Bedingungen, die notwendig sind, damit ein Körper als denkender charakterisiert werden kann. Zu diesem Zwecke muß eine Kongruenz zwischen dem Ding und dem Denken des Dinges nachgewiesen werden. Diese Kongruenz sieht Iljenkow sowohl durch die sensomotorischen Schemata Piagets, wie auch durch die Kulturprodukte und die Tiefenstrukturen der Sprache garantiert. Sowohl die sensomotorischen Schemata wie auch die ideelle Form der Kulturprodukte sind jedoch nicht als Reflexionsprodukte des Individuums Bedingungen des Denkens. Sie sind es, ob das Individuum sich dessen bewußt wird oder nicht. An dieser Aussage ändert auch der Tatbestand nichts, dass das Individuum sich zur Erfassung z.B. der Sprachformen der Abstraktion bedienen muss. Chomsky hat das in seiner Theorie an mehreren Stellen klar zum Ausdruck gebracht. Er schreibt:

> Das will nicht heissen, dass er [der Sprecher – J.F.] sich der Regeln der Grammatik bewusst ist, nicht einmal, dass er sie sich bewusst machen kann, und auch nicht, dass seine Angaben über seine intuitive Sprachkenntnis notwendig richtig sind. Jede interessante generative Grammatik wird es grösstenteils mit mentalen Prozessen zu tun haben, die weit jenseits der Stufe aktueller oder selbst potentieller Bewusstheit liegen [...]. Somit stellt eine generative Grammatik den Versuch dar, das zu spezifizieren, was der Sprecher wirklich kennt, und nicht das, was er über seine Kenntnis berichten kann (Chomsky 1978, 19–20).

Der Sprecher, wie auch das Subjekt, das denkt, werden in den Konzeptionen Iljenkows, Piagets und Chomskys demnach zu einer eigenartigen Passivität verurteilt, was ihre Rolle bei der Untersuchung des Denkens und der Sprache betrifft. Es scheint, man kann – zugespitzt formuliert – das Denken und die Sprache unabhängig von dem untersuchen und erklären, was das Subjekt dem Forscher darüber zu berichten hat. Was Bühler betrifft so ist für seinen semiotisch-deskriptiven Ansatz das Gegenteil der Fall. Er schliesst das Subjekt als Bedingung der Forschung in die Sprachtheorie ein. Um zu erkennen, welche Eigenschaften des konkret wahrnehmbaren Sprachzeichens an der Sinnkrisis des Zeichens wirklich beteiligt sind, muss man untersuchen, auf welche Eigenschaften des Zeichens das Subjekt als Zeichenhaftes reagiert. Bühler drückt diesen Gedanken folgendermassen aus :

> Zu allem Zeichenhaften in der Welt gehören der Natur der Sache nach Wesen, die es dafür halten und mit ihm als Zeichenhaftem umgehen. Man muss also physikalisch gesprochen im objektiven Verfahren die geeigneten psychophysischen Systeme wie *Detektoren* verwenden, um zeichenhaft Wirkendes zu entdecken. Wo die Konkreta, welche Zeichenfunktion erfüllen, von handelnden Wesen produziert oder hergerichtet werden, wo diese Konkreta zu jenen Wesen im Verhältnis des Werkes zum Schöpfer oder [...] im Verhältnis der Tat zum Täter stehen, da kann man diese auch Zeichengeber nennen [...]. Die Sprachforschung stösst also im Axiom von der Zeichennatur der Sprache auf das Denkmodell des homo faber, eines Machers und Benützers von Geräten (Bühler 1934/1982, 47–48).

Bühler diskutiert das Subjekt offensichtlich als Formungsstation, als *homo faber,* als Produzenten von Werkzeugen und in diesem Sinne als Bedingung der Sprachforschung.

Es steht ausser Frage, dass in Iljenkows Konzeption das Subjekt und seine Fähigkeit, die Welt zu denken, im Mittelpunkt der philosophischen Begründung stehen. Doch sie werden dadurch erklärt, dass das Subjekt immer mit der Welt als schon-gedachter konfrontiert wird. Es sind die ideellen Formen, von denen das Subjekt in seiner kulturellen, sozialen und sprachlichen Welt umgeben ist, die Iljenkow ausführlich analysiert.

Bühler interessiert sich dagegen gerade für die Hervorbringung dieser gedachten Welt oder genauer für den Hervorbringer, den *homo faber.* Um zu erkennen, was am Sprachzeichen die Sinnkrisis garantiert, wendet sich Bühler dem sprechenden Subjekt zu und nicht den ideellen Formen. "Die Zeichen setzen psychophysische Systeme nach Art des menschlichen voraus. Man muss solche Systeme als *Detektoren* eingesetzt denken, sonst werden Zeichen im Weltgeschehen nicht manifest" (Bühler 1934/1982, 273). Das Subjekt wird zur Bedingung der wissenschaftlichen Erkenntnis erhoben.

Gleichzeitig hat man den Eindruck, dass Bühler in seinen Überlegungen von etwas redet, das man ebenfalls Form nennen könnte; es scheint, er entkommt dem Formbegriff nicht. Denn es ist nicht der *homo faber* an sich, der von ihm untersucht wird, sondern die Produkte seiner (z.B. sprachlichen) Tätigkeit. An der sinnlichen, jeweils konkreten und ihrem Charakter nach einmaligen Produktion eines Wortes oder eines Satzes interessieren die Merkmale, die signalisieren, dass es sich um *dieses* Wort, um *diesen* Satz handelt, d.h. die Merkmale, die garantieren, dass *das* Wort, *der* Satz verstanden werden. Die die Sinnkrisis garantierenden Momente sind nicht von der sinnlich, konkreten Realisierung des Wortes abtrennbar, es sind keine Zahlenreihen wie man sie auf die Banknote gedruckt vorfindet. Aus diesem Grunde scheinen sie sich auch von den von Iljenkow diskutierten ideellen Formen zu unterscheiden.

Während für Iljenkow die relative Opposition zwischen Form und Stoff wesentlich für die als Ideelles bezeichneten Phänomene ist, wird von Bühler diese Opposition für die Sprache in Zweifel gestellt. Ein Wort existiert nicht ohne die die Sinnkrisis realisierenden, stofflichen Merkmale des Wortes. Die sich daraus ergebende Frage, inwieweit Bühlers Überlegungen den von ihm kritisierten Formbegriff erweitern könnten, indem z.B. die Phoneme als Formgebilde betrachtet werden, bleibt zu diskutieren. Festgehalten werden soll jedoch, dass in Bühlers Sprachtheorie ein vom Formbegriff nicht zu trennendes Problem wieder auftaucht. Es handelt sich um die Existenz von Realitätsformen, die ohne das Zutun des Subjekts nicht als solche fungieren können. Einer psychologisch-genetischen Untersuchung dieser Realitäts-formen, wie wir sie bei Iljenkow finden, stellt Bühler eine semiotisch-deskriptive gegenüber. Ob die beiden Herangehensweisen einander ergänzen oder gegenseitig ausschliessen bedarf weiterer Untersuchungen.

Dass sich die Überlegungen eines Psychologen und Sprach-wissenschaftlers und die eines Philosophen zumindest indirekt in der Diskussion des Formbegriffs treffen, nährt jedoch die Hoffnung, dass die heute immer noch zu beobachtende Skepsis hinsichtlich der Fruchtbarkeit eines Dialogs zwischen den Vertretern der Sciences de l'homme und der Philosophie eine nur temporäre ist.

Notes

[1] Dieses Experiment und seine Interpretation wurden u.a. diskutiert von: Bakhurst 1991; Friedrich 1993; Jantzen, vgl. vorliegenden Band; Keiler 1997.

[2] Ich verweise hier exemplarisch auf einige Titel: Bally 1922; Binswanger 1926/ 1955; Brunot 1922; Cassirer 1946; Delacroix 1924; Piage, 1923; Sechehaye 1933/ 1969; Vygotskij 1934/1964.

[3] Es steht ausser Zweifel, dass die Linguistik in den 60er/70er Jahren von der Chomskyschen Theorie dominiert wurde. Was Piaget betrifft so wurde seine Erklärung der psychischen Entwicklung in diesem Zeitraum vor allem als strukturgenetische rezipiert und gefeiert. Seit den 90er Jahren wird Piaget mehr und mehr unter dem Gesichtspunkt des radikalen Konstruktivismus gelesen (vgl. Rusch/Schmidt 1994).

[4] Es existiert ein zweiter Text, der sich ebenfalls explizit mit diesem Thema auseinandersetzt, vgl. Iljenkow 1984.

[5] Auf die Beziehungen zwischen der kulturhistorischen Theorie und Iljenkow haben hingewiesen : Bakhurst 1995; Bronckart & Friedrich 1999; Keiler 1997 ; Jantzen 1991, 1994.

[6] Auf die identitätsphilosophischen Annahmen Iljenkows wurde schon des öfteren in der Literatur hingewiesen, vgl. Oittinen in diesem Band.

[7] Gegen den Begriff des Ideellen sprach sich vor allem D.I. Dubrovskij aus, der in dieser Diskussion einen naturalistisch-individualistischen Standpunkt vertrat und diesen durch die Ergebnisse der Neurophysiologie zu beweisen suchte (vgl. Dubrovskij 1983). Eine erste kritische Darstellung der sowjetischen Diskussion zum Begriff des Ideellen findet man bei Laitko 1989.

[8] Bühler kann nicht direkt als Repräsentant dieser zweiten, zur Chomskyschen Theorie alternativen Richtung in den Sprachwissenschaften bezeichnet werden. Dies nicht nur weil sein Werk ab Ende der 30er Jahre bis zu Beginn der 80er Jahre so gut wie nicht zur Kenntnis genommen wurde, sondern auch weil eine Diskussion seiner Sprachtheorie in ihrem oft eklektisch anmutenden Reichtum der Ideen m.E. noch am Anfang steht. Einen Versuch den Bühlerschen Eklektizismus ernst zu nehmen, findet man bei Vonk 1992.

[9] Bühler partizipierte in den 30er Jahren selbst aktiv an der Entwicklung der Phonologie. Er veröffentlichte 1931 in den Travaux du Cercle Linguistique de Prague einen Artikel, der sein Verständnis der von den Pragern und insbesondere von Trubetskoj entwickelten Phonologie darlegt (vgl. Bühler 1931). Dass dabei nicht unwesentliche Unterschiede zwischen ihm und den Pragern sichtbar werden, soll hier nur vermerkt werden (vgl. Friedrich 1999).

Bibliographie

Bakhurst, D. (1991),*The Meshcheryakow Experiment: Soviet Work on the Education of Blind-Deaf Children.* In : *Learning and Instruction,* 1991, 1, 201–215.

Bakhurst, D. (1995), *On the Social Constitution of Mind: Bruner, Ilyenkov and the Defence of Cultural Psychology.* In: *Mind, Culture and Activity,* 1995, 2(3), 158–171.

Bally, Ch. (1922), *La pensée et la langue.* In: *Bulletin de la Société de linguistique de Paris,* 1922, 23, 117–137.

Binswanger, L. (1926/1955), *Zum Problem von Sprache und Denken.* In: L. Binswanger, *Ausgewählte Vorträge und Aufsätze,* Band II: *Zur Problematik der psychiatrischen Forschung und zum Problem der Psychiatrie.* Francke Verlag, Bern, 308–345.

Bronckart, J.-P. & Friedrich, J. (1999), *Présentation.* In: L.S. Vygotsky, *La signification historique de la crise en psychologie.* Delachaux et Niestlé, Paris, Lausanne, 15–69.

Brunot, F. (1922), *La pensée et la langue. Méthode, principes et plan d'une théorie nouvelle du langage appliquée au français.* Masson, Paris.

Bühler, K. (1931), *Phonetik und Phonologie.* In: *Travaux du Cercle Linguistique de Prague,* 1931, 4, 22-53.

Bühler, K. (1934/1982), *Sprachtheorie. Die Darstellungsfunktion der Sprache.* Fischer-Verlag, Stuttgart, New York.

Bühler, K. (1936), *Das Strukturmodell der Sprache.* In: *Travaux du Cercle Linguistique de Prague,* 1936, 6, 3–12.

Cassirer, E. (1946), *L'influence du langage sur le développement de la pensée dans les sciences de la nature.* In: *Journal de psychologie,* 1946, 129–152.

Chomsky, N. (1978), *Aspekte der Syntax-Theorie.* Suhrkamp, Frankfurt/M.

Delacroix, H.(1924), *Le langage et la pensée.* Alcan, Paris.

Dubrovskij, D.I. (1983), *Problema ideal'nogo.* Moskva.

Friedrich, J. (1993), *Der Gehalt der Sprachform. Paradigmen von Bachtin bis Vygotskij.* Akademie-Verlag, Berlin.

Friedrich, J. (1999), *Karl Bühler – le passage de la psychologie à la linguistique. Une rencontre significative au début des années 30.* [Vortrag auf dem 8th International Conference on the History of Language Sciences, 14.-19. September 1999 in Paris.]

Humboldt, W. (1836/1998), *Über die Verschiedenheit des menschlichen Sprachbaues und ihren Einfluß auf die geistige Entwicklung des Menschengeschlechts.* Schöningh, Paderborn, München, Wien, Zürich.

Iljenkow, E. V., (1962) *Ideal'noe.* In: *Filosofskaja Enziklopedija,* tom 2. Moskva.

Iljenkow, E.V. (1974/1984), *Dialektitscheskaja logika. Otscherki istorii i teorii.* Moskva.

Iljenkow, E.V. (1977a), *Denken als Attribut der Substanz.* In: *Wissenschaftliche Zeitschrift der Karl-Marx-Universität Leipzig, Gesellschafts- und Sprachwissenschaftliche Reihe,* 1977a, 1.

Iljenkow, E.V. (1977b), *Stanowlenie litschnosti: K itogam nautschnogo eksperimenta.* In: *Kommunist,* 1977b, 2.

Iljenkow, E.V. (1977c/1994), *Überlegungen zum Verhältnis von Denken und Sprache (Sprechen).* In : E.V. Iljenkow, *Dialektik des Ideellen. Ausgewählte Aufsätze,* übersetzt von G. Richter. LIT-Verlag, Münster, Hamburg, 286–293.

Iljenkow, E.V. (1979), *Problema ideal'nogo.* In: *Voprosy filosofii,* 1979, 6, 7.

Iljenkow, E. V. (1984), *Gegel i germenevtika (Problema otnoschenija jazyka k myschleniju v konzepzii Gegel'ja).* In: E.V. Iljenkow, *Iskusstvo i kommunistitscheskij ideal.* Moskva.

Jantzen, W. (1991), *Psychologischer Materialismus, Tätigkeitstheorie, marxistische Anthropologie.* Argument-Verlag, Berlin, Hamburg.

Jantzen, W. (1994), *Am Anfang war der Sinn. Zur Naturgeschichte, Psychologie und Philosophie von Tätigkeit, Sinn und Dialog.* BdWi-Verlag, Marburg.

Keiler, P. (1997), *Feuerbach, Wygotski & Co. : Studien zur Grundlegung einer Psychologie des gesellschaftlichen Menschen.* Argument Verlag, Hamburg.

Laitko, H. (1989), *Zur Interpretation der Kategorie des 'Ideellen'. Aus der Diskussion.* In: *Sowjetwissenschaften, Gesellschaftswissen -schaftliche Beiträge,* 1989, 1.

Meschtscherjakow, A.I. (1971a), *Slepogluchonemye deti (Psichitscheskoe rasvitie v prozesse obutschjobija),* Doktorskaja dissertazija, Moskva.

Meschtscherjakow, A.I. (1971b), *Rasvitie sredstv obstschenija u slepogluchonemych detej.* In: *Voprosy filosofii,* 1971b, 8.

Piaget, J. (1923), *Le langage et la pensée chez l'enfant.* Delachaux et Niestlé, Neuchâtel, Paris.

Rusch, G. & Schmidt, S. (Hrsg.) (1994), *Piaget und der radikale Konstruktivismus.* Suhrkamp, Frankfurt/M.

Saussure, F. (1997), *Linguistik und Semiologie. Notizen aus dem Nachlaß.* Texte, Briefe und Dokumente gesammelt, übersetzt und eingeleitet von Johannes Fehr. Suhrkamp, Frankfurt/M.

Sechehaye, A., (1933/1969), *La pensée et la langue ou comment concevoir le rapport organique de l'individuel et du social dans le langage?* In: J.-C. Pariente (Hrsg.), *Essai sur le langage.* Minuit, Paris, 71-96.

Vonk, F. (1992), *Gestaltprinzip und abstraktive Relevanz: eine wissenschaftstheoretische Untersuchung zur Sprachaxiomatik Karl Bühlers.* Nodus, Münster.

Wygotski, L.S.(1934/1964), *Denken und Sprechen.* Akademie-Verlag, Berlin.

13

SEMIOSIS AND THE CONCEPT OF THE IDEAL

TARJA KNUUTTILA

1. Introduction

Reading Evald Ilyenkov's essay *The concept of the ideal* (1977a), one is easily overwhelmed by the different characterisations Ilyenkov gives to the ideal. It is as if one never got there, to the point, but is left circling around and around. Ilyenkov's short formulations like "The ideal form of a thing is not the form of the thing 'in itself', but a form of social life regarded as *the form of a thing* (ibid. 92)" are not very helpful either. But on second thought, one has to admit that the ideal cannot be given any *one* clarification or definition. If ideal is something that is in the process of continuous movement, being constantly born and reborn, made and remade, in the course of our different activities, then how could it be hypostatised, frozen into an object of definition? Maybe it can only be shown, pointed at, and then carefully followed – in its dialectical metamorphoses.

David Bakhurst approaches the concept of the ideal by asking, what the "problem of the ideal" is. It is, according to him, the problem of the status of immaterial properties in the material world (Bakhurst 1991, 175). An age-old, profound philosophical question.

Instead of getting lost in the philosophical subtleties of the question, I shall take a kind of a short cut. The phenomena of meaning and value are perhaps the first and foremost examples of the ideal phenomena. Ilyenkov himself draws heavily on Marx's analysis of the value-form in his attempt to pinpoint the concept of the ideal. He does not say that much about the phenomena of meaning, though this theme constantly recurs in his writings on the ideal. It is thus interesting, I think, to take up the theme of meaning, and ask, how the concept of the ideal relates to the findings of the study of the signs and meanings, semiotics.

In this paper, I am going to take up the concept of the ideal in the context of Umberto Eco's semiotic theory and his notion of the *encyclopedia*. By encylopedia, Eco means the totality of knowledge generated by humans, which is the cognitive background of any act of understanding or creation. Moreover, this knowledge is stored in our artefacts, which, for Eco, appear as an "enormous library composed of all books and encyclopedias – all papers and manuscripts, documents of all centuries, including the hieroglyphics of the ancient Egyptians and the inscriptions in cuneiform" (Eco 1994, 90). This resembles the way Ilyenkov invokes, in his essay on the ideal, the Hegelian vision of the "whole grandiose *materially established spiritual culture of the human race"* which "confronts the individual as the thought of preceding generations realised [...] in sensuously perceptible 'matter'..." (Ilyenkov 1977a, 81). Both views seem to stress how meanings can be found "objectified" from the artefactual sphere, but somehow this insight gets partly lost in Eco's subsequent semantic analysis. I will argue that the artefactuality and materiality of signs disappears in Eco's analysis, since something is missing from his otherwise sophisticated and careful semiotic view. And Ilyenkov's views on the ideal may help us understand what that something is. I will also argue, that even in Ilyenkov's materialist analysis it can be seen how easy it is to pass from the ideal on to idealism. This can happen once the ideal is conceived as a property of material things or of the world.

2. The Concept of the Encyclopedia according to Umberto Eco

It is widely agreed that most, if not all, sign-relations are at least partly conventional. Thus the concept of convention has been, and is, a very important one for semiotics. Too often, however, semiotic analyses become somehow stuck to the notion of convention as if it were a kind of ultimate explaining principle. It has proven difficult to approach especially the notion of sign and the purported "sign-systems" from any other angle. Umberto Eco is one of those, who have made an extensive use of the notion of convention in his semiotics, yet he sees clearly that semiotics has to deal with the genesis of signs and new conventions, too. But oddly enough, this insight leads Eco to divide his semiotic theory into two parts, to a *theory of codes* and to a *theory of sign production*. And Eco thinks that this is the way things should be (Eco 1976, 3). One may ask why.

At first sight, it would seem that Eco divides his theory into two because he is following the Saussurean tradition of distinguishing between a signification *system* and a communication *process*. But Eco denies that his distinction corresponds to the one between *langue* and *parole* (ibid. 4). Eco has something else in mind. He claims that

> ... *every act of communication to or between human beings* – or other intelligent biological or mechanical apparatus – *presupposes a signification system as its necessary condition*. It is possible, if not perhaps particularly desirable, to establish a semiotics of signification independently of a semiotics of communication: but it is impossible to establish a semiotics of communication without a semiotics of signification (ibid.,9).

In this, there is a strange asymmetry, which is certainly reflected in the practice of semioticians – Eco included. Semiotic study is often understood as a study of the different signifying systems, that is, of the different codes that our culture is supposed to be made of. From Eco's point of view, a culture appears to be a heterogeneous set of partly overlapping codes, which are of a different degree of organisation. Eco's analysis of the codes is basically componential and has its roots in structural semantics. Codes provide the rules according to which the elements of the conveying system are coupled with the elements of the conveyed system. In other words, codes generate as well as organise sign-functions, which correlate two functives, namely expression and content, together. But this is just a first approximation, because the functives are to be further analysed in their markers. So the sign-function becomes a relation between a given set of syntactic markers and a given set of semantic markers.

This idea of analysing signs into their semantic markers dominates the dictionary-based semantics, which Eco – even though his analysis is also componential – criticises with his concept of encyclopedia. Eco wants to show, that any dictionary is but an encyclopedia in disguise.

According to the theoretical concept of the dictionary, the meaning of linguistic expressions can be represented through a finite number of semantic *primitives* (which can be also called components, markers, properties, units or universal concepts... depending on the theory in question). In principle, the number of primitives could also be infinite – but obviously this makes the task of componential analysis impossible. So, at least ideally, the dictionary definition of a term should be composed of a limited number of primitives. Then the problems are, first, how to determine the primitives and, second, how to guarantee that their number is a finite one (Eco 1984, 49). Now Eco proceeds by claiming that the two questions cannot, presumably, be solved at the same time. As different researchers propose different primitives, one can legitimately ask, whether there actually are any primitives that are intuitively known to all speakers. And if there are not, then the primitives have to be interpreted, too. To make them interpretable, theory usually has to consider them as an unordered set and adopt cross-classificatory relations between primitives. But, the only way to limit the number of the primitives is to have the meaning relations hierarchically structured. Either, one has a limited number of uninterpreted primitives, or the primitives are interpreted, but the meaning relations are unordered and potentially infinite. Thus we have arrived at the encyclopedia.

The concept of encyclopedia preserves the idea of a componential analysis, but denies that signs could be analytically reduced into a limited number of meaning components in any sensible way. In the case of an encyclopedia then, it is not reasonable to talk about primitives any longer. On the contrary, as we saw above, any analysis of meaning is potentially endless – a sign can invoke a limitless number of markers. This is explained by the concept of an *interpretant* (by C.S. Peirce). The only way to explain what a given sign means is to give another representation. A sign's interpretant can thus be defined as "another representation which is referred to the same 'object'" (Eco 1976, 68). And, of course, the only means to establish an interpretant of the sign is by the way of using another sign, which in turn invokes another interpretant, and so on…

From this insight Eco proceeds to his idea of *model Q*, which is devised in accordance with M. Ross Quillian's proposal for a model for semantic memory (ibid., 122). Model Q is an n-dimensional network, where one can move a sign (which is taken as a *type*, for example "type A") by employing a series of sign-vehicles to any other place in the network, "from the center to the farthest periphery" (ibid.). These sign-vehicles, as interpretants, are included in the model as *tokens*, but each of them becomes, in its turn, a new type, for example, a "type B". One can think of Model Q as an intertextual space or an ever-growing hypertext, on which any point can be connected to another in a proper rhizomatic way. (In practice, though, no interpretative process is endless and this Eco explains by the fact, that some connections are statistically more probable than the others.)

In the contradistinction between dictionaries and encyclopedias, there is also something else at stake than whether the analysis of meaning is potentially limitless or not. Namely, the original insight behind the division between a dictionary and an encyclopedia is simply to distinguish between the knowledge of the semantics of a language and the knowledge of the real world, and it dates back, at least, to John Locke. He wanted to know which complex ideas we know from experience and which are acquired via other ideas. So, the "dictionaries relate words to other words" whereas "encyclopedias relate words to extralinguistic facts" (Haiman 1980, 333). Later, Russell thought that words could be divided in two classes. The so-called "object-words" get their meaning by direct association between a word and a thing. Then there are the dictionary words, the meaning of which we learn through verbal definition.[1]

Eco hopes to show with his concept of the encyclopedia that also this way of distinguishing between a dictionary and an encyclopedia is untenable. He seems to agree with Haiman "that the relations of sense in themselves are useless, unless the words are at some point anchored at reality" (ibid., 336). But, at the same time, rather unexpectedly, Eco wants do without the referent in his semiotics. For him, the theory of codes is concerned only with intensional semantics (Eco 1976, 59). Still he has numerous examples to show of how the analysis of meaning is not only dependent of the contextual but also extra-linguistic facts (see, e.g., Eco 1979a, 1979b, 1990).

How can this be achieved?

The point is that Eco tries to include also these factors in his semantic analysis. His aim is

> [...] to outline a theory of codes which takes into account even rules of discursive competence, text formation, contextual and circumstancial (or situational) disambiguation, therefore proposing a semantics which solves within its own framework many problems of the so-called pragmatics (ibid., 4).

Once all these things are represented in the language, or by the means of some other (coded or codable) signs, then it is possible to move in the semantic space without any referral to the real world. Encyclopedia becomes a self-sufficient, self-referring world of our semiotic systems. For Eco, language (or better – the intermixture of all our languages of different kinds) forms an "autoclarificatory system". A "sort of molecular landscape" emerges. In this landscape the "so-called 'things' are only the surface appearance assumed by an underlying network of more elementary units" (1976, 49). But this remains to be shown. According to Eco, our semantic universe, in its entirety, is unrepresentable. Only (small) parts of it can be analysed, on a temporary basis, owing to the fact the semantic universe is "highly mobile". These

Eco's positions are open to debate. Even if some "parts" of a supposed semantic universe were representable,[2] would these analyses then show, in
and of themselves, that such a totality or "whole" existed? Hardly. The conception of a self-sufficient semantic/semiotic universe, undergoing constant
change which results from the never ceasing semiosic process, is obscure, to
say the least. It is as if it were somehow self-moving and self-adjusting. No
wonder Eco has been accused of idealism – in spite of his contrary claims
(see, e.g., Carravetta 1998; Deely 1997).

The question is: how do the meaning-units ever become coded into the
semantic "space", and what keeps the coded (statistical) meaning relations
from collapsing and prevents this semantic/semiotic universe from turning
into a chaos? One surmises that this has something to do with the subjects
and the real material world, which were left out from the theory of codes.
Eco relegates the burden of explaining the relations between our semantic
systems and the external world to a theory of sign production. But he presents
his theory of sign production mostly in terms of individual work (see, e.g.,
critical remarks by Ponzio 1993, 34). The semiotic production is
predominantly apprehended according to an individualistic model of artistic
creation. Thus it becomes difficult to understand how (and why) the fruits of
this individual production ever become conventionalised, as part of our
culture? It appears to me that this is also the weak point of many other
interesting semiotic theories (think, for instance, of the theories of Julia
Kristeva and Roland Barthes). Rules and conventions are social, but the
breaking of the rules, inventing and creating, is something individual or
unique.

It appears, that the two component theories forming Eco's more general
semiotic theory do not make a pair. I suspect that this has something to do
with the fact that the theory of sign production is for Eco something secondary
in regard to the theory of codes (remember the asymmetric relation between
the signification system and the communication process). To quote Eco: "A
semiotics of sign production or code-changing is interested in the process by
which *a rule is imposed upon the indeterminacy of the source*" (1976, 126;
italics mine). In addition to artistic creation, Eco's theory of sign production
is mostly interested in arguing for the conventionality of also the iconic sign,
which is often thought to be in some natural or motivated relation with its
object (see, e.g., Caesar 1999, 67–69).

I mentioned already, how the global semantic system, as designed by
Eco, is both an idealistic and unrepresentable "construction". Eco does not
deny its uncertain ontological status but claims that it is only a regulative
idea, a methodological postulate. "Semiotics must proceed to isolate structures

as if a definite general structure existed (ibid., 129)", otherwise it could not be explained how meaning comes into existence.[3]   The validity of these Eco's claims depend, thus, on whether there are any other ways of explaining our linguistic competence. In particular, it is interesting to inquire *where* the meanings are generated, if not in some hypothetical "space"?

3. The Concept of the Ideal

Writing about the concept of the ideal, Ilyenkov expands much effort in explaining why the ideal cannot be located in consciousness. The dividing line between the "material" or "real" and the "ideal" cannot be drawn according to what is outside or inside the consciousness. Ideal phenomena are, thus, not mental phenomena nor situated primarily in the consciousness. Meanings, or the significance of things, are not projections of the mind onto reality (Bakhurst 1991, 177). They are, according to Ilyenkov, objective reality. Yet, the emergence of the ideal is dependent on conscious human beings. It is of our creation and, clearly, also something impalpable. Namely, where can you touch or see ideal? Nowhere, and still you are conscious of its presence.

Thus the existence of the ideal is not in doubt, but its objectiveness is. How can something that is sensuously imperceptible be objective? The answer Ilyenkov gives us is, that ideal is objective and, moreover, part of our objective reality, *since* it is something that is being objectified – or materialised – in our various activities. The notion of "objectification" seems to imply that something that was originally not objective, becomes it, by being "objectified". Maybe it is our thoughts that are being "objectified"? Then, at least the origin of the ideal is in mental? But this is exactly what Ilyenkov denies. What is the relation between our thoughts and reality? Finally, this question cannot be avoided, and Ilyenkov takes the challenge.

In his *Dialectical Logic* Ilyenkov (1977b) treats the question of the interrelations of thought and being, our ideas and the external world. The book can be read, in my opinion, also as a history of the concept of the ideal. In his first essay on "The Problem of the Subject Matter and Sources of Logic", Ilyenkov poses the question of

> [I]n what are such objects as "concept" ("idea") and "thing" related? In what special "space" can they be contrasted, compared and differentiated. Is there, in general, a "third" thing in which they are "one and the same" in spite of all their directly visible differences? (Ilyenkov 1977b, 18).

This is one formulation for the traditional epistemological question regarding our possibility of gaining truthful knowledge of the world. Only things of the same kind can be compared, thus it seems hopeless to try to confirm whether my idea of a thing corresponds with the thing itself. Am I destined always to "compare an idea of a thing with the *thing as an object of consciousness*, that is, not with the thing but with another idea of it" (Ilyenkov 1997c, 7)? Is there any third mediating term or factor that would somehow free us from the supposed prison of our consciousness?

In *Dialectical Logic* Ilyenkov investigates the thought of several philosophers from Spinoza onwards from the point of view of this question. Kant finds the third term from the space of representation. Once the thing has been transformed into a representation, it can be compared to another representation. Still, the things in themselves remain unknown. We have seen that the encyclopedia of Eco remains in the realm of representation and thus it is a Kantian construction though Eco does not, of course, believe in any a priori categorisations. As a sphere of interrelated representations, the concept of encyclopedia leaves the question of reference and the relationship of our representations to the surrounding world open. How, then, could our thoughts, or representations, ever get grip of the reality? An answer starts to take shape in the thinking of the German idealists. What if the thing in itself was a product of our consciousness?

In Hegel, this insight is already found in its full-fledged form. The thing in itself is not alien to our thought, since a thing for us and a thing in itself are moments of the same substance – the Spirit. In Hegel's analysis, the ideal plays the decisive part. The Spirit posits its "other", the material, objective world and reaches its self-consciousness in a "dialectical transformation of the ideal into the material and vice versa" (1977a, 73). But absolutising the ideal, in this way, as the self-evolving Spirit, Hegel's idealism is left without means to explain the possibility of thought itself (see Bakhurst 1991, 213).

For Marx too, the (collective) subject realises itself by way of objectification, but for him the material world is primary. "Prior to contemplation", writes Ilyenkov, "man acts practically with real things, and in the process of this activity all his representations are formed" (1997, 29).[4] The ideality is found from the social consciousness, which is materialised in the man-made culture and environment, in the humanised nature. Things, or better, our human environment, owe the ideality it manifests to the sensuous human aim-oriented activity (or labour), which is inherently collective. The objective sphere of the meanings or the significance of things becomes constructed in the labour process whereby a human being moulds her natural environment. The seeming gap between consciousness and the real world becomes bridged, because, actually, there was never any gap. And this is not achieved by losing the otherness of the material world into the thought, as happens in Hegel's system. Quite the contrary, it is exactly the otherness of the material world that makes thought possible, since in the process of changing her environment the human being (understood broadly also as a community of human individuals) becomes conscious of the world and herself. In the process of creating her environment a human being creates herself too – as she becomes an able inhabitant of the world of her own creation.

Thus the ideal, according to Ilyenkov, is not dependent on the mental for its existence. And mental itself is social in its origin. Consciousness and will will awaken in the individual as she finds herself confronted by the *materially established spiritual culture* of the humanity (ibid., 81). The specific forms of human activity follow rules and patterns, which, for the most part, do not have any genetic background, and, because of this, an individual is compelled to distinguish herself from her organic body. An individual gains – through the ideal, reified in the forms of collective labour – an outside view on herself, without which no self-consciousness or will would be possible. In this way ideality is something external and objective from the point of view of an individual even though she has been formed herself by it in her growing up into a member of a human society.

4. Semiosis as the Becoming of the Ideal

After the preceding exposition, one may, perhaps, ask what Umberto Eco's idealistic vision of the self-sufficient semantic universe has to do with Ilyenkov's materialistic conception of the ideal? Nevertheless, both Eco and Ilyenkov set out to solve the problem of culturally constructed meanings. Their basic insight is the same; meanings, or the ideal, are objective phenomena, the explanation of which does not need any recourse to mental phenomena. Quite the contrary. Mental phenomena should be explained with the help of intersubjective meanings, which are embodied in material things. Eco thinks that with the help of the interpretants, which are always materialised in some sign-vehicle, the meaningfulness of the cultural world can be approached in an empirically verifiable manner. Furthermore, for Eco "the subject of any semiotic enquiry" is nothing more than "the historical and social result of the world that a survey on Semantic Space makes available" (1976, 315).

This comes close to the opinion of Marx, who in his *Economic and Philosophical Manuscipts of 1844* writes: "We see how the history of *industry* and the established *objective* existence of industry are the *open book* of *man's essential powers*, the exposure to the senses of human psychology […]in the form of *sensuous, alien, useful objects…*" (Marx 1964, 142). Yet, Eco ends up sketching the signifying system as "an autonomous semiotic construct that has an abstract mode of existence independent of any possible communicative act it makes possible" (ibid.. 9). For some reason, the sphere of meanings becomes detached from its material embodiment in our actions and things – despite Eco's stated intentions.

In addition to the problem of the ontological status of his encyclopedia, Eco has the problem of not being able explain how the individual performances become part of the collective knowledge. Time and again, Eco invokes the notion of convention in his attempt at describing how the individual creation is dependent on the social – but it seems not work that well the other way around. And, indeed, Eco simply asserts, after a complicated analysis of the different forms of sign production, that, in the end, some of the innovations made become "publicly accepted".

It seems to me, that the above mentioned problems of Eco's semiotics are interrelated. In focusing on the culturally constructed artefacts and their supposed meanings, Eco loses sight of the *social* production process, or activities through which these artefacts are created. These activities are historical and local, and only in their context can the created meanings and the competencies be explained. Actually, there are no such things as meanings, existing independently of our life activities. Meanings are produced and reproduced, again and again, in the processes of our different activities – such is the life of semiosis, the process of meaning making and meaning engendering. No separate system of significations needs to be postulated, because it is precisely our shared labour, which carries them.

However, the temptation of hypostatising meanings and treating them, in idealistic manner, as something thing-like in themselves, is strong. The germ of this kind of thinking is already found from Ilyenkov himself. Repeatedly, he writes about the ideality as if it represented activity or its results, as if it were a some kind of spiritual or non-material "image", "stamp" or "imprint" laid on natural physical material or objects in labour process (see e.g., Ilyenkov 1977b, 253, 256, 280–282). When writing about the ideal as an "ideal image", Ilyenkov comes close to characterising the ideal as some kind of mental representation. This is not his intention, of course. According to Ilyenkov, ideality can be found from the relationships of representation where "one sensuously perceived thing performs the role or function of a representative of quite another thing […] which is in sensuous, bodily terms quite unlike it" (1977a, 84). This reminds one of the traditional, nowadays somewhat obsolete, definition of the sign as something that stands for something else.[5]

But, in the end, approaching ideality as a representation of some kind can be more deceptive than enlightening. Surely, it cannot be any mental representation without losing its distinctiveness but it cannot be any material representation either. "A person cannot pass the ideal as such to another person", Ilyenkov claims. "One can observe the activity of a painter or an engineer as long as one likes, striving to catch their mode of action [...] but one can thus only copy the external techniques and methods of their work but never the ideal image itself, the active faculty itself. The ideal [...] is only masterable through active operation with the object..." (ibid., 281). Thus it seems fair to say, that the ideal *dwells* in the relationship of representation, but that this relationship is always in a state of its becoming. It seems that the ideal is something fluid, flowing in the continuous stream of semiosis, where the meaning is constantly changing to its other.

Since the ideal is in the continuous movement, then, strictly speaking, ideality is no property of any individual thing. Specifically, it is not a property of a thing in the same way as the physical properties of a thing are. Let the activity which carries the thing die out and even the memory of it fade away, and nothing of the original ideality of the thing is left. But this should not lead us to think that ideality forms a sphere of its own, or, that it is involved only in certain kind of representations. Peter E. Jones (1999) claims, that ideal forms are derived "images" of material objects and processes and he makes ideal the property of words and symbols. This seems to me a very odd view. Firstly, words and symbols as artefacts are not very different from other man-made things. Abstracted from their use they, too, become mute. What else could the material traces of the dead, for us incomprehensible, languages teach us? Words, symbols and diverse representations are no privileged carriers of the ideal or significance. If they are treated us such, language becomes easily a mysterious totality, detached from our practical activities.

Secondly, the attempts to make the language somehow secondary to the practical tool-using activity seem to perpetuate the same tricky distinction between our thoughts/representations and the reality the dialectical thinking tries to evade. Trying to tell which events or things are primary, or "came first" – for instance tools or signs – seem to me futile. Any "first" genuine tool had to carry in itself already an elementary sign-function, too. Otherwise, it could not have been recognised as a tool of its kind, and it could not have preserved its function in a continued activity. The theoretical narratives of origin should not usually be interpreted as histories. The historical event or order is most often derived from a theoretical structure of some kind, consciously or not consciously subscribed (see e.g., Culler 1986).

If the ideal is not any property of a thing, then, can it be said that it is a property of the world? The answer depends, I think, on how we conceive the world. Bakhurst claims that Ilyenkov's notion of the ideal involves a wholesale idealisation of the natural world. "Through social forms of human activity man endows his natural environment with enduring significance and value, thus creating a realm of ideal properties and relations" (Bakhurst 1988, 37; see also Bakhurst 1991, 186–189). Once this step is taken, it becomes possible to think of the ideal, or the sphere of meanings, as a world of its own, which can be approached as a huge book of our civilisation, as a true encyclopedia, ready for reading. We can find the symptom of this shift in the way Bakhurst uses the metaphor of writing when trying to explain the idealisation of nature by human activity. "There is nothing mystical in this, he [Ilyenkov] insists, for ideal phenomena owe this objective existence to human beings [...] In the course of the transformation of nature by human action, meaning and value are *written* into nature" (Bakhurst 1995, 160, italics mine).

Seeing the ideal as some kind of a property of a thing, thus, leads one easily to think that it can be represented and, moreover, that it is especially prone to be represented by linguistic and symbolic means.[6] Once again, we see how a dividing line emerges, which separates the discursive realm from the practical and material activity, even though the concept of the ideal strives to overcome this kind of borderline.

Ilyenkov's "insight about artefacts", as Bakhurst puts it, should not be interpreted by relying predominantly on the artefacts having both material and ideal "form", which "insight" can, then, be generalised to the whole nature. In my opinion, there is no need to say that we live in a humanised world – it is merely a metaphor – instead of living in the material world. This one and the only world we inhabit has been and is being changed by our activities, and while living in it, we are also trying to make sense of it, and of ourselves, as part of it. I wonder how revealing it is to claim, like Ilyenkov does (on Bakhurst's reading), that we humans relate ourselves to a humanised nature as a *whole*. Do we ever *experience* nature or our environment as a totality and why should this supposed totality, nature, even be duplicated? We simply do not seem to act and perceive this way. Instead, we work in our environment in a piecemeal fashion trying to achieve our goals, and make sense out of it, by whatever means close at hand. The ideal dwells in this continuous labour of interpretation and meaning-making, and this process always leaves some traces of itself in our environment. In addition to the "insight about artefacts", the insight about interpretants is important. We can never catch the meaning, it always flies ahead of us, since in trying to express it we are reverting to just another representation.

Of course Bakhurst, in his interpretation of Ilyenkov, does not overlook this incessant movement of the ideal. Bakhurst stresses how "the ideal exists as a moment of the constant interchange between acting subject and environment" (Bakhurst 1991, 184). But both from the writings of Ilyenkov, as well as from Bakhurst's readings of it, a tension can be found between the ideal as a property of some thing and the ideal as movement. And the same kind of tension can also be found in the semiotic theory of Eco.

Behind this kind of internally conflicting theorising about meaning there seems to lie a vision of the world as a huge cluster of things, which are endowed with steady properties. Our use of language seems to perpetuate essentialistic thinking, even if we found essentialist idiom unsuitable for the phenomenon we strive to describe. The positive kernel of poststructuralist thinking is in the importance of finding different ways of talking and conceiving, and I do not see any reason why this should be seen as happening independently of our different knowledges and everyday practices in some textual space alone. There is a lot outside the text (of our discourses) but still linked to it by the most intricate and complex links.

Ilyenkov writes:

> The ideal form is a form of a thing, but a form that is outside the thing, and is to be found in man as a form of his dynamic life activity, as *goals and needs*. Or conversely, it is a form of man's life activity, but outside man, in the form of the thing he creates. "Ideality" as such exists only in the constant succession and replacement of these two forms of its "external embodiment" and does not coincide with either of them taken separately. It exists only through the unceasing process of the transformation of the *form of activity – into the form of a thing and back – the form of a thing into the form of activity* [...] Try to identify the "ideal" with any one of these two forms of its immediate existence – and it no longer exists (ibid., 98).

This is an apt characterisation of semiosis as well. The last sentence of the quotation is especially important. Doing justice to Ilyenkov's writings on the ideal amounts to understanding that if he was at pains in trying to explain what the ideal is, this was due to the evasiveness of the phenomenon he was trying to catch.

Notes

[1] For Russell, however, the distinction between knowledge by acquaintance and knowledge by description varies between people, depending on their life-experiences (Russell 1948, 65–70).

[2] It has been seriously doubted, whether even parts of our linguistic competence can be represented in any adequate way. John Searle (1979) has pointed out, how impossible it is to explicate all the background assumptions. The needed number of background assumptions grows every time one is able to construct one more deviant example.

[3] Since the publication of *A Theory of Semiotics,* Eco's views have become decidedly more Peircean than Saussurean. The inferential nature of the sign is stressed, and the importance of the notion of the code has diminished (Eco 1984). Yet, even in his latest book, Eco thinks that some kind of a signification system has to be postulated by the analysis of meaning (1997).

[4] And Ilyenkov continues: "The real object-related activity of a man who transforms the nature is in fact an act of identification or *coordination* of the form of man's activity with the form of a thing" (1997, 28, italics mine). Here Ilyenkov's Spinozean influences seem to manifest themselves. In *Dialectical Logic* Ilyenkov praises Spinoza's functional definition of thinking, which is action according to the shape of any other thing and thus, instead of inspecting what happens inside the brain, one should examine the real system within which this function is performed if one is to understand thinking (5 – 52).

[5] For a critique of this notion, see, for instance, Merrell 1995, xi–xii.

[6] It is not clear, whether the ideal is that which is represented by the "spiritual culture" of human race, or whether the ideal itself is that what (somehow) represents our "spiritual culture". Bakhurst, like Ilyenkov, is not clear on this point. On the one hand Bakhurst (1991) claims that "the emergence of this culture represents the idealization of nature as a whole" (189) but on the other hand he writes also that "[t]he ideal represents the entire edifice of the institutions of social life..." (188). Be that as it may, it seems that the attempts to identify ideal with representation, in any way, turn out more mystifying than revealing.

References

Bakhurst, David (1988), Activity, Consciousness and Communication. *The Quarterly Newsletter of the Laboratory of Comparative Human Cognition*, April 1988, Vol. 10, 2, 31– 39.

Bakhurst, David (1991), *Consciousness and Revolution in Soviet Philosophy. From the Bolsheviks to Evald Ilyenkov*. Cambridge: Cambridge University Press.

Bakhurst, David (1995), Lessons from Ilyenkov. *The Communication Review*. Vol. 1, 2, 155 –178.

Caesar, Michael (1999), *Umberto Eco. Philosophy, Semiotics and the Work of Fiction*. Bodmin: Polity Press.

Carravetta, Peter (1998), The Reasons of the Code: Reading Eco's "A Theory of Semiotics". In: Hugh J. Silverman (ed.) *Cultural Semiosis. Tracing the Signifier. Continental Philosophy IV*. New York & London: Routledge.

Culler, Jonathan (1986), *Ferdinand de Saussure*. Rev. ed. Ithaca: Cornell University Press.

Deely, John (1997), Looking back on "A Theory of Semiotics". In: Rocco Capozzi (ed.) *Reading Eco: An Anthology*, Bloomington: Indiana University Press.

Eco, Umberto (1976), *A Theory of Semiotics*. Bloomington: Indiana University Press.

Eco, Umberto (1979a), *Lector in Fabula*. Milano: Bompiani.

Eco, Umberto (1979b), Texts and Encyclopedia. In: J.S.Petöfi (ed.), *Text vs. Sentence: Basic Questions of Text Linguistics*. Hamburg: Buske.

Eco, Umberto (1984), *Semiotics and the Philosophy of Language*. London: McMillan.

Eco, Umberto (1990,) *The Limits of Interpretation*. Bloomington: Indiana University Press.

Eco, Umberto (1994), *Six Walks in the Fictional Woods*. Cambridge: Harvard University Press.

Eco, Umberto (1997), *Kant e l'Ornitorinco*. Milano: Bompiani.

Haiman, John (1980), Dictionaries and encyclopedias. *Lingua*, Vol. 50, 329– 357.

Ilyenkov, Evald (1977a), The Concept of the Ideal. Trans. Robert Daglish. In: *Philosophy in the USSR. Problems of Dialectical Materialism*, 71-99. Moscow: Progress.

Ilyenkov, Evald (1977b), *Dialectical Logic. Essays on Its History and Theory*. Trans. H. Campbell Creigthton. Moscow: Progress.

Ilyenkov, Evald (1997c), The Question of the Identity of Thought and Being in Pre-Marxist Philosophy. *Russian Studies in Philosophy*, Vol. 36, 1, 5–33.

Jones, Peter E. (1999), *Symbols, Tools and Ideality in Ilyenkov*. Internet document: http://geocities.com/Athens/9148/toolssi.html.

Marx, Karl (1964), *Economic and Philosophic Manuscripts of 1844*. Trans. Martin Milligan. New York: International Publishers.

Merrell, Floyd (1995), *Peirce's Semiotics Now: A Primer*. Toronto: Canadian Scholars' Press.

Ponzio, Augusto (1993), *Signs, Dialogue and Ideology*. Trans. Susan Petrilli. Amsterdam/Philadelphia: John Benjamins Publishing Company.

Russell, Bertrand (1948), *An Inquiry into Meaning and Truth*. 3rd impr. London: Allen and Unwin.

Searle, John (1979), Literal Meaning. *Expression and Meaning. Studies in the Theory of Speech Acts*. London: Cambridge University Press.

14

THE DIALECTICS OF THE IDEAL
AND SYMBOLIC MEDIATION

PETER JONES

"Without symbolisation, man cannot in general be
the active subject of social production"
– Evald Ilyenkov (1977a, 276).

Introduction

This paper seeks to explore some aspects of Ilyenkov's conception of the
"ideal" and to consider some of its implications for our understanding of the
process of symbolic mediation, a process which has great theoretical significance for contemporary cultural-historical and activity theory research.[1]
    The paper begins with a discussion of the reasons for Ilyenkov's turn to
Marx's *economic* work for answers to such a deeply *philosophical* problem
as that of ideality. This is followed by a closer investigation of Ilyenkov's
analysis of a "typical case" of ideality, namely the value form, accompanied
by a presentation of some of Marx's own commentary. The relevance of
these ideas to the process of symbolic mediation is then considered in detail.
Particular attention is devoted to the role and implications of what Ilyenkov

calls "the law of spiral-like development of a system of interacting phenomena". Finally, Vygotsky's conception of the "planning function of speech" is briefly examined in the light of this law.

1. Ilyenkov and Marx's *Capital*

It is well known that Ilyenkov had the highest regard for Marx's *Capital* not only for its concrete analysis of political economy but for its method of analysis of social formations. Most significantly for our purposes, Ilyenkov bases his approach to "the problem of 'ideality'", which "in its general form is equally significant for psychology, linguistics, and any socio-historical discipline" (1977b, 95), on Marx's analysis of the value form of the products of labour which provides "a concrete illustration of all the advantages of the dialectical materialist view of ideality" (1977b, 91). Ilyenkov describes the value form as "a typical and characteristic case of ideality in general" (1977b, 90–91), as "the most typical case of the idealisation of actuality, of the act of birth of the ideal" (1977a, 267). This turn to *Capital* in fact is made in line with a specific Marxian methodological principle (ably summarised by Bakhurst, 1991, 159ff). Ilyenkov seeks to develop a concept of ideality not by constructing an empirical generalization capturing those properties common to all known ideal forms but by a detailed analysis of this one "typical and characteristic case" already laid out in *Capital*. In this work "the dialectic of the transformation of a thing into a symbol, and of a symbol into a token, is [...] traced [...] on the example of the origin and evolution of the money form of value" (Ilyenkov 1977a, 273).

We need to emphasise, however, that an approach to the general problem through this "typical case" does not involve the kind of extended analogy between monetary exchange and, say, communicative "exchange', or between exchange-value and linguistic meaning or "value", to be found in e.g. Rossi-Landi (1974), or Baudrillard (1981). Analogy has its place as a heuristic, of course, in scientific investigation but as a guiding principle and method of analysis it remains at the level of comparison of surface form rather than penetrating to the level of essential connection, causation, and internal self-movement.[2] Ilyenkov's point, then, is that scientific analysis of this one case will reveal the *essence of the matter – the law-governed process by which ideal forms, whatever the particular domain of social activity in question, arise within human social being,* and will thereby disclose the irreducible and distinctive function, the very raison d'etre, of the ideal or symbolic sphere.[3]

Something more should perhaps be said as to what makes the money form of value "a typical and characteristic case".[4] First of all, of course, it has "literally all those characteristics which traditional philosophy and theology attributed to "spirit" – universality, incorporeality, the ability to evade all the most subtle forms of physico-chemical detection" (Ilyenkov, 1991, 241). Secondly, we have to do with a large-scale, and thoroughly completed, socio-historical process at that stage of development in which "all the really necessary conditions of its emergence and evolution are *retained* and all the more or less accidental, purely historical conditions of its emergence are absent" (Ilyenkov, 1982, 210). Thirdly, the value form is a phenomenon proper to social *being*, or, crudely speaking, the "economic base", demonstrating that ideality is an integral component of social production itself and not a "superstructural" or "ideological" phenomenon.

And then, of course, there is Marx's method of analysis of the phenomenon, which recommends itself on a number of counts. Firstly, Marx's approach exemplifies the materialist orientation in which the ideal is taken to be the reflection of things emerging in objective, reality-transforming activity. This is not a mechanistic or metaphysical materialism which would treat ideality (and therefore human thought and language) as essentially psychological, rooted in higher nervous activity or, God forbid, in some innate, biological "module" in the Chomskyan style.[5] The ideal is treated as an objective social product and form and "exists not in the head but with the help of the head in the real objective activity (activity on things) of man as the active agent of social production" (Ilyenkov, 1977a, 261). Secondly, Marx develops a systemic approach to the problem, analysing ideality as a property and function of the workings of the entire social metabolism: "Its existence and functioning as a symbol consequently does not belong to it as such but only to the system within which it has acquired its properties" (1977a, 273). Thirdly, there is the celebrated Marxian method of "ascent from the abstract to the concrete" (Ilyenkov, 1982, 1997; Bakhurst, 1991). Marx's theoretical system reproduces the dialectical logic of development of the value form from the "cell" or "concrete universal" – the commodity as a unity of use-value and exchange-value – through a necessary series of ripenings into exchange-value, money, capital, etc.[6]

With these general points in mind, let us now pass on to a closer look at the details of Marx's analysis and the concept of symbolic mediation which emerges from it.

2. The Significance of Marx's Analysis of the Value Form

Marx treats the commodity as a double-sided entity having a *use-value* and an *exchange-value*. Use-value is a function of the natural properties of the thing which are realised when the thing is used in production or in individual consumption. Exchange-value is realised in the *circulation* process in which commodities are bought and sold prior to their use. Exchange-value has nothing to do with the naturally conditioned useful properties of things but derives solely from the relative amounts of *abstract* human labour objecti-fied within them. This is why Marx distinguishes between the "natural form" of the commodity (as a use-value) and its "value form" (as an exchange-value) (1976, 138). While use-values "constitute the material content of wealth, whatever the social form may be" (1976, 126), the value form is entirely due to the particular social form – commodity production – within which use-values are produced. While nature as well as *concrete* labour is the source of use-value, exchange-value is purely the result of the particular social form which the labour process takes under capitalism. It is what Marx calls "a simple social form" (1976, 195), and it is the value *form* which is *ideal:*

> Not an atom of matter enters into the objectivity of commodities as values; in this it is the direct opposite of the coarsely sensuous objectivity of commodities as physical objects [...] their objective character as values is therefore purely social (Marx, 1976, 138–139, and cf. the detailed discussions in Ilyenkov, 1977b, 1991).

The production and exchange of commodities is a historical *precondition* for the emergence of the money form of value which at first *mediates* the exchange of goods already produced:

> The pattern of commodity-money circulation is [...] expressed by the formula C–M–C. The commodity (C) appears in it as both the *beginning* and the *end* of the cycle, and money (M) as its *mediating link*, as the "metamorphosis of the commodity" (Ilyenkov, 1977a, 244).

Here, money "plays the part of middleman [...] as the medium of exchange" (Marx, 1973, 193). How and why does money arise and enter the exchange process? Ilyenkov summarises Marx's answer:

> It arises as a means of resolving the contradictions maturing in the course of the circulation process, and within it (and not inside the head, though not without the help of the head), as a means of satisfying a need that has become immanent in commodity circulation (Ilyenkov, 1977a, 268).

The problem is that commodity production as a generalised social form of production (not to mention *capitalism,* its highest form) is impossible as long as exchange-value is manifest only in the localised and accidental acts of reciprocal, direct exchange of commodities in the market. Progress is possible only if that common social substance inherent in commodities can take a form which is independent of the particularised shapes of the whole mass of use-values and in which it can appear and be measured directly in its pure, stable, socially valid state. The problem is resolved "by one commodity 'being expelled' from their equal family and being converted into the immediately social standard of the socially necessary expenditure of labour" (Ilyenkov, 1977a, 268–269). In short, one commodity "obtains the privilege of representing, symbolizing, the exchange value of all other commodities, i.e. of becoming *money*" (1973, 167).

Money, then, is a *symbol*. It is the "exchange value which is separated from commodities and exists alongside them as itself a commodity" (1973, 145), in which "all properties of the commodity as exchange value appear as an object distinct from it, as a form of social existence separated from the natural existence of the commodity" (1973, 145). Money is the "universal equivalent" (1973, 142), the immediate and direct form or embodiment of exchange-value per se. Marx emphasises, crucially for our purposes, that "exchange value as such can of course only exist symbolically" (1973, 154). Consequently, one commodity (typically gold), in becoming money, becomes the *ideal image, ideal form* or "the symbol of the commodity as commodity, of the commodity's exchange value itself" (1973, 144). "Such a symbol", Marx explains, "presupposes general recognition; it can only be a social symbol; it expresses, indeed, nothing more than a social relation" (1973, 144).

But, still, why does the circulation process posit a *symbolic* mediator? Marx is careful to fend off idealist interpretations of the process: "this symbol, this material sign of exchange value, is a product of exchange itself, and not the execution of an idea conceived *a priori*" (1973, 144). The secret of the symbol lies not in something outside exchange but in fact in the contradictory inner nature of the commodity as a doublet of use-value and exchange-value.[7] As an exchange-value the commodity is a pure economic form, a quantity of abstract labour on account of which it "differs from itself as a natural, material thing" (1973, 188). Consequently, a "mediation is required to posit it as an exchange value" (1973, 188). The labour time contained in the commodity "must not be expressed in its immediate, particular product, but in a mediated, general product" (1973, 167). Now, the exchange-value of a particular commodity is its proportional *relation* to the general sum of socially necessary labour time. But "nothing can express a relation without relating to one particular thing, and there can be no general relation unless it relates to a general thing" (1973, 205). Labour time, "being a general object, [...] can exist only symbolically, and hence only as a particular commodity which plays the role of money" (1973, 168). Thus, the socially general, abstract labour embodied within the commodity can "exist only symbolically" because it is in fact only the form of a relation between all commodities, presented separately from the things which are actually in this relation – "just as, in general, relations can be established as existing only by being *thought*, as distinct from the subjects which are in these relations with each other" (1973, 143).

Money, then, is an *abstraction*, embodying not the "sensuously perceived image" of the commodity "but rather its essence, i.e. the law of its existence within the system that in general creates the situation being analysed" (Ilyenkov, 1977a, 272). The money commodity mediates the connection between commodities through its symbolically embodying their relation to the entire world of commodities, or, more exactly, to the general, indeed, universal substance of exchange-value – abstract labour. With its appearance on the scene, *particular* commodities can only relate to one another through the *universal* (itself, of course, a particular commodity), through which they also each relate to themselves.

Furthermore, the process of idealisation of value does not end with the appearance of the commodity in its "transformed form" as money.[8] The process continues to develop according to its immanent dialectic until a particular inversion takes place between elements and functions within the now symbolically mediated system. In the simple process of circulation already examined, money performs the two functions of measure of value and medium of circulation. From this process there arises "the third function of money" now described by a new movement $M - C - C - M$ "in which money appears not only as *medium*, nor as *measure*, but as end-in-itself, and hence steps outside circulation" (Marx, 1973, 215). As the process runs its inexorable course, money, initially the "middleman", becomes the very starting point and precondition of the entire process of commodity production and exchange, dominating and reconstructing it in the specific shape of capital:

> at a certain point in the self-closing cyclical movement $C - M - C - M - C - M...$ and so on, money ceases to be a simple "intermediary", the means of circulation of the mass of commodities and suddenly discloses an enigmatic faculty for "self-expansion". Schematically this phenomenon is expressed in the formula as follows: $M - C - M$ (Ilyenkov, 1977a, 244–45).

Now the roles of the commodity and money are reversed. The commodity – "the *real starting point* of the process as a whole" – takes up the position which money had and becomes "*intermediary* and *means* of the transient *metamorphosis of money"* (1977a, 245); the mediated becomes the mediator. Furthermore, this transformed system now develops according to a higher law:

> a historically posterior result [in this case, capital, PEJ] arising from the entire preceding development does not remain merely a passive result, merely a consequence. Each newly arisen (higher) form of interaction becomes a new universal principle dominating all historically preceding forms, transforming them into secondary external forms of its specific development (Ilyenkov, 1982, 209).

The consequences for relations within the system are radical:

> This new and higher (historically later) system of concrete interaction begins to preserve and actively reproduce, by its own movement, all the really necessary conditions of its movement. It generates, as it were, out of itself everything that was originally created by the previous development and not by itself (1982, 209–210).

As a result of this newly developed dynamic "commodities, money, "free" labour force ... are no less products of capital, consequences of its specific movement, than they are its historical premises, the conditions of its emergence" (1982, 115). This dialectical "flip over" within the system is a manifestation of the *"law of spiral-like development of a system of interacting phenomena"* (1982, 116, my emphasis) governing nature, society, and thinking itself. This law "poses some specific difficulties for thought" (1982, 116) inasmuch as it produces a "logical circularity in definitions" (1982, 117) of phenomena due to their being mutually dependent, interlocking aspects of a complex organic unity. So, for example, one cannot understand capital without understanding money, but at the same time money itself is a form of appearance of capital. It also creates a situation where the relationship between *essence* and *appearance* of phenomena seems reversed. Hence, money as capital (i.e., the symbolic existence of value) appears to be the source and creator of value itself although, in essence, it is human activity – real, living labour – which remains the only source of value. The action and properties of the symbolic forms of value are ultimately governed by, and continue to manifest, albeit in contradictory and increasingly mediated fashion, this inescapable and determining law at the heart of the dynamic of the system.

3. General Properties of the Process of Symbolic Mediation

On the basis of this discussion of Marx's analysis of money, and the ideas which Ilyenkov draws from it, it may be worth trying to identify some ideas of potentially general significance for the investigation of symbolic forms. These ideas should be taken as starting points for investigation, of course, rather than ready made conclusions.

1)   A thing is converted into a symbol due to its specific emergent role as mediator within "an already formed system of relations between people mediated by things" (Ilyenkov, 1977a, 272).

2)   The symbolic function is a necessary expression or reflection of contradictions immanent in that "already formed system". While the symbol does not create the matter or substance (e.g. value) which it represents, its generation and incorporation into the process which it mediates gives a new form of appearance to the things involved in that process and creates a new and additional link in the causal chain of action and reaction within the system as a whole.[9]

3)   Symbolic mediation arises through the self-differentiating dynamic of productive activity, which appears as a cyclical movement through opposites: real – ideal/concrete – abstract/ particular – universal, etc. Symbolic mediation can only be understood by analysing the dialectical logic of development of that system within which the symbol is generated. In fact, when looking at the symbol, one is actually looking at this system of human activity itself in a special "transformed form" (Mamardashvili, 1992), but one in which the origins of the symbol and its interconnections and mediations with social practice are not immediately evident. To put it another way, while the dialectic of development of social production leads to its being symbolically mediated, this does not make social production itself, or the law of its own self-development, a symbolic phenomenon *per se*.

4)   The symbol is the objective form of existence of an *ideal form* or *ideal image*. It is ideal because, within the dynamic of the system, it acts as the form not of itself but of something else which it represents, reflects, or whose place it takes. The relation between the symbol and what is symbolized is therefore one of *identity,* but identity through *difference* (since the symbol is different, separate, and independent from what it symbolizes).

5)   The symbolic function of the thing (its meaning) does not derive from its natural, material properties but is a purely social product. Money and language are ideal, not material (*pace* Wertsch, 1998, e.g. 30–

31), although they are "based in an autonomous material" (Marx, 1973, 188). The material properties of the forms of symbolic mediation must not therefore blind us to their ideal function. Moreover, "the material body of the thing is brought into conformity with its function" (Ilyenkov, 1977a, 273).

6) The ideal is an *abstraction,* representing not the "sensuously perceived image" of the commodity "but rather its essence, i.e. the law of its existence within the system that in general creates the situation being analysed" (Ilyenkov, 1977a, 272, quoted above). The symbol is (as Marx says of money) "a means to accomplish this abstraction" (1973, 142).

7) The symbol, generated by an already established system of activity as a "middleman", reacts back on that system. From the middle of the process the symbol moves to the beginning, the whole system turning upside down in accordance with the "law of spiral-like development".

At this stage we should perhaps introduce a clarification in relation to Marx's conception of symbolization. We have seen that Marx repeatedly refers to money as a symbol. However, he also attacks the suggestion that money (or indeed value itself) is a "mere symbol" in the sense that its function as universal equivalent depends on mere *convention,* subjective whim, or on the authority of the state or some other power. In this respect, the symbolic function of money differs from that of a token, such as paper money, whose relation to value is purely conventional and arbitrary. But he appears to see the "real" symbol (money) as a precondition for the "mere symbol", and in a certain relation with it. Thus, he argues that the money symbol, once developed, "can in turn be replaced by a symbol of itself. *It then becomes the conscious sign of exchange value"* (1973, 144, my emphasis). Marx clearly spells out the implications of confusing these two stages of symbolic mediation:

> The fact that money can, in certain functions, be replaced by mere symbols of itself, gave rise to another mistaken notion, that it is itself a mere symbol [...] if it is declared that the social characteristics assumed by material objects, or the material characteristics assumed by the social determinations of labour on the basis of a definite mode of production, are mere symbols, then it is also declared, at the same time, that these characteristics are the arbitrary product of human reflection (1976, 184–186 and see also the discussion in Ilyenkov, 1977a, 270–271).

Ilyenkov takes up Marx's idea, attacking the reduction of "value and its forms *to pure symbolics,* to the naming of relations, to a conventionally or legally instituted sign" (1977a, 270, my emphasis). He also widens his attack to include those typically idealist philosophical systems which "proclaim the forms of expression of the ideal in speech, in terms and statements, to be conventional phenomena, behind which, however, there stands something mystically elusive" (1977a, 270). Such views consider the ideal simply as "a symbol or sign of immaterial relations (or connections as such, connections without a material substratum" instead of as "a symbol of the social relations between people" (1977a, 270).

Ilyenkov's point seems to be that ideality is not the relation between a symbol or sign and an idea, since this begs the question of the nature and origin of the idea itself. On the contrary:

> By "ideality" or the "ideal", materialism has to mean that quite specific – and identifiable by strict criteria [*strogo fiksiruemoe*] – correlation between (at least) two material objects (things, processes, events, states) within which one material object, while remaining itself, takes on the role of *representative of the other object*, or, more exactly, of the universal nature of this other object, the universal form and law of *this other object* (1991, 253).

Still more can be said about Marx's treatment of the money form of value. This concrete, historical materialist analysis of one "typical" case of ideality, as Ilyenkov in fact shows, gives clues to Marx's general approach to the nature of human thought and language. Money, as Marx insists (see above), is "a product of exchange itself, and not the execution of an idea conceived *a priori*". As Ilyenkov puts it, it arises "not inside the head" and yet "not without the help of the head". What kind of help does the head provide? Tracing Marx's explanation, Ilyenkov argues that the actual use of gold as a medium of circulation (i.e. for payment) grows out of an earlier stage in which it "functioned as money purely ideally" (1977a, 271). At this stage, the exchange of commodities was mediated not by money as cash, but by calculating how much gold each commodity was worth. Here, gold "does not enter bodily into the exchange" but "is all the same involved in the act of exchange, since it is also present only *ideally,* i.e. in the idea, in the mind of the commodity-owners, in speech, on paper, and so on" (Ilyenkov, 1977a, 269). Ilyenkov is not offering a psychological explanation of money since the calculation must be done "not only in the head of the individual but in the conception held by society (directly, the conception held by the participants in the process of buying and selling)" (Marx, *Grundrisse,* in Ilyenkov, 1977a, 271–272). Nevertheless, *ideal* gold must function as an *ideal* measure of value in an *ideal* act of exchange before it can become *real* money. This is how Marx himself sums up the whole process:

> The product becomes a commodity, i.e. *a mere moment of exchange.* The commodity is transformed into exchange value. In order to equate it with itself as an exchange value, it is exchanged for a symbol which represents it as exchange value as such. As

such a symbolized exchange value, it can then in turn be exchanged in definite relations for every other commodity. Because the product becomes a commodity, and the commodity becomes an exchange value, *it obtains, at first only in the head, a double existence. This doubling in the idea proceeds (and must proceed) to the point where the commodity appears double in real exchange: as a natural product on one side, as exchange value on the other.* I.e. the commodity's exchange value obtains a material existence separate from the commodity (1973, 145, my emphasis).

So real money (the real, objectified symbol of exchange-value) is necessarily preceded by ideal money, by the idea of money, as it were. Here we see another case of the "circularity of definitions" resulting from the "law of spiral-like development", this time in the contradictory relation between being and thinking: on the one hand, money is a product of exchange and not the idea; on the other, real money logically depends on the idea of money. The solution to the problem of circularity lies in tracing "the act of birth of the ideal from the process of social man's objective-practical activity" (Ilyenkov, 1977a, 270). From this point of view, the idea of money is not "conceived *a priori*" but is a reflection in people's heads of a real state of affairs outside consciousness. More specifically, the idea is a full part of the solution to the problem "immanent in the sphere of circulation". Thought itself is here seen as a necessary and irreducible link in the chain of development of social being, as a moment of the self-development of the system of material production.[10] Ilyenkov's general formulation of the situation is characteristically paradoxical:

In thinking [the ideal] is generated before the contradictions will be resolved in reality i.e. before its own objective realisation. This original position, when the image is born earlier than the object which it reflects, also creates the whole difficulty of the problem of the ideal, unresolvable for metaphysical materialism with its version of the theory of reflection. The object as an immediately visible thing does not yet exist while its image is already there (1991, 210).

Indeed, this explains why Marx is able to present the logic of development of the money form of value through a detailed analysis of a series of verbally expressed equations expressing the different stages in that evolution (cf Jones, 1991 for detailed discussion). So the passage of money into reality is itself mediated by "the head", in particular by language. While money involves the idealisation of a relatively narrow sphere of human economic activity, language functions as the idealisation of any and all actuality and as the midwife of other ideal forms, including money itself.

4. The Law of Spiral-like Development of Interacting Systems

From Marx's concrete analysis of a "typical case", Ilyenkov draws a general conception of the dialectics of ideality in human social production. The ideal exists within *material* production as an image of things involved in production. The image reacts back on its material matrix creating "internal interaction" through which "actual development assumes the form of a circle or, to be more precise, of a spiral which extends the scope of its motion all the time, with each new turn" (Ilyenkov, 1982, 115). This spiral movement manifests the "dialectics of all real development, in which the universal necessary condition of the emergence of an object becomes its own universal and necessary consequence" (1982, 115). The result is a "dialectical inversion in which the condition becomes the conditioned, the cause becomes the effect, the universal becomes the particular" (1982, 115).

As noted above, the law creates a real contradiction within the sociohistorical process, as well as a contradiction in the theoretical elucidation of that process. Accordingly, it creates a contradiction at the very centre of Marxist theory and philosophy. As Ilyenkov explains: "On the one hand, the proposition advocated by any kind of materialism asserts that matter (objective reality) is primary, whereas consciousness is a reflection of this reality, that is, it is secondary" (1982, 252). Hence Marx's formulation of his own philosophical position: "the ideal is nothing other than the material when it has been transposed and translated inside the human head" (cited from *Capital,* in Ilyenkov, 1977a, 252). On the other hand, "if one takes abstractly a single isolated fact of man's goal-directed activity, the relation between consciousness and objectiveness is the reverse" (1982, 252) as is the case in Marx's well known definition of human labour: "The labour process ends in the creation of something which, when the process began, already existed in the worker's imagination, already existed in an *ideal* form" (*Capital,* in Ilyenkov, 1977a, 276–277, my emphasis). Here: "What is primary [...] is consciousness, the ideal plan of activity, while the sensual objective implementation of this plan is something secondary or derivative" (1982, 252).

Thus the "concrete-universal law" (Ilyenkov, 1997, 333) of the reflection of being into consciousness is in direct contradiction with the fact of goal-directed labour activity. This contradiction has in fact led some commentators to the conclusion that Marx's position is inconsistent and logically flawed. Newman and Holzman, for example, argue that Marx's account of the labour process given above shows a "functionalist bias" and that it is "both philosophically (analytically) and empirically (descriptively) inaccurate", allowing "the old philosophical-theological argument of first cause back into play" (1993, 47–48).

However, Ilyenkov considers such arguments to be the result of formal, metaphysical reasoning. They fail "to grasp the role of practice" and to "see the real mediating link between objective reality and consciousness" (1982, 252). Specifically, such arguments miss "the whole chain of mediating links" between reality and consciousness, and leave out "the necessity thanks to which consciousness, arising as a special reflection of objective reality, is transformed into a relatively independent sphere of activity and exercises a reverse influence on objective reality" (1997, 333–334). Once again we come up against "a dialectical transformation of cause into effect, which stems from the spiral-like character of any development of mutually conditioning phenomena" (1982, 125).

But precisely how and why does this dialectical inversion take place in symbolically mediated systems? The whole issue should be extensively investigated. Meanwhile, let us try to draw some initial clues from the discussion in Marx and Ilyenkov. We have seen that the process of symbolic mediation is one in which the universal or essential law-governed interconnection of things acquires "an existence based in an autonomous material of its own" (Marx, 1973, 188), i.e. in the symbol. The symbol immediately embodies the common, social interconnections and relations between people in the course of production. It reflects the concentrated power of the social collectivity into itself and this reflection of *all* into *one* effects an inversion within the dynamic of social practice.[11] Marx explains the economic manifestation of this phenomenon, in a rather cryptic passage which should be followed up, by appeal to a general law of mediation:

> the movement, or the relation, which originally appears as mediatory between the extremes necessarily develops dialectically to where it appears as mediation with itself, as the subject [*Subjekt*] for whom the extremes are merely its moments, whose autonomous presupposition it suspends in order to posit itself, through their suspension, as that which alone is autonomous (1973, 331–332).[12]

Mediation, he argues, brings about this transformation because the mediator is the middle term (the "intermediary situation [*Mitte*]") and (in the case of exchange-value) as such "always appears as the economic relation in its completeness" since it "comprises the opposed poles, and ultimately always appears as a one-sidedly higher power vis-a-vis the extremes themselves" (1973, 331).

However we interpret these remarks, it is difficult to overestimate the importance of understanding, and analysing, this dialectical transformation between the material and the ideal within human activity. Ilyenkov sees the source of "diverse idealist conceptions" in their viewing the apparent dominance of symbols or thought "in a one-sided manner, only from the standpoint of active reverse effect of social consciousness in all its forms on social being, on the sphere of economic relations between men and of men to nature" (1982, 125). The Hegelian conception was, Ilyenkov argues, based squarely on this "abstract absolutisation of [...] the active reverse effect of thought on all other spheres of activity" (1982, 125). But exactly the same could be said about many contemporary (particularly "postmodern") conceptions in social, political and cultural theory whose advocates are unable to see or think beyond "discourse" to the "sensuously objective activity of the millions of people who by their labour created the body of culture" (1977a, 236).

Conceptions of this kind, Ilyenkov argues, are the product of an uncritical acceptance of the real, contradictory appearance of things (cf 1977a, 246). Specifically, those abstractions "that quite precisely expressed (described) the forms and schemas of the flow of thought in all forms of its concrete realisatio" are taken for "schemas of the process that had created the whole diversity of human culture, in which they were discovered" (1977a, 236). In sum, the logical relation between the primary "substance" (material practice) and its internal, symbolic or ideal moments and dimensions (thinking, language, "discourse") is turned upside down. This pervasive inversion "is not simply an analogy with what happens in the world of relations founded on value, but the same social process, only in the sphere of mental rather than material production" (1977a, 243).

One could perhaps say, adapting Marx's words above, that the privileging of language or discourse is due to the fact that the word, as symbolic mediator, "always appears as the social relation in its completeness" (1973, 331). However, what is not understood (to use Ilyenkov's comment on money, 1977a, 246) is that "a property is ascribed to it that in fact belongs to quite another process that is *expressed* ("reflected") in its form". The finished conversion of (symbolic) mediator into mediated is taken as a simple fact, a given, and made into the theoretical starting point. Hence, discourse appears to have the power to create social processes and forms in its own (arbitrary, "power"-related) image.

In this connection it is interesting to compare Ilyenkov's conception of the ideal with Voloshinov's (1973) "ideological" which, at first glance, sits well with Ilyenkov's "ideality":

> Any ideological product is not only itself a part of a reality (natural or social), just as is any physical body, any instrument of production, or any product for consumption, it also, in contradistinction to these other phenomena, reflects and refracts another reality outside itself (1973, 9).

Where the two thinkers differ sharply, however, is in their view of the relationship between ideality/ideology and material productive activity. For Ilyenkov ideality language functions as a necessary internal moment within activity which is thus cast as a dialectical unity of material and ideal sides in interaction, manifesting the "law of spiral-like development". Voloshinov, on the other hand (and despite the undoubted merits of his conception), firmly situates the whole problematic of the relationship of "ideological" to material within a mechanistic (and therefore most un-Marxian) conception of the base-superstructure opposition. He sees ideology, by which he means all symbolic activity and not just those forms of consciousness which reflect the economic organisation of society, as "the immediate superstructure over the economic base" (1973, 13). And so the "base" – the labour process – is purged of "ideology", and therefore also of language and consciousness, altogether. Paradoxically, the money form of value, being a symbol, i.e "ideological", would be part of the superstructure in Voloshinov's terms. Voloshinov, further, argues that the "laws of semiotic communication are directly determined by the total aggregate of social and economic laws" (1973, 13). Neither the origin and role of the symbolic (and of thinking) within material productive activity, nor the "active reverse effect" of social consciousness (and therefore spiral development) are considered. The "ideological" is confined to the superstructure and never turns back into material practice. Voloshinov's definition of communication via signs has, consequently, a rather idealistic ring to it:

> The understanding of a sign is, after all, an act of reference between the sign apprehended and other, already known signs; in other words, understanding is a response to a sign with signs. And this chain of ideological creativity and understanding, moving from sign to sign and then to a new sign, is perfectly consistent and continuous: from one link of a semiotic nature (hence also of a material nature) we proceed uninterruptedly to another link of exactly the same nature [...] This ideological chain stretches from individual consciousness to individual consciousness, connecting them together (1973, 11).

In contrast, the Marxist view is that the ideal is not a "superstructure" over the "base" since human labour is itself necessarily dependent on the ideal plane, and, consequently, on symbolic activity. At the same time, language and other symbolic forms are the products of labour activity. Labour as the precondition and also the consequence of language: once more this "circularity in definitions" reflecting the "'circular' nature of interaction" (Ilyenkov, 1982, 116–117), a circularity that cannot be broken "by any sophisticated logical procedures or semantic manipulations with concepts and their definitions" but requires a "genuinely historical approach" (1982, 117). We have seen something of this approach in the discussion of the evolution of money, but what would it look like in the case of language? Let us, finally, turn to a consideration of the function of the verbal symbol in human activity by exploring Vygotsky's conception of the "planning function of speech".

5. Vygotsky and the "Planning Function of Speech"

Vygotsky's account of the "planning function of speech" in effect provides us with a detailed analysis of the origins and development *within activity* of the ability to act on the ideal plane. His analysis accords "symbolic activity a specific *organizing* function that penetrates the process of tool use and produces fundamentally new forms of behaviour" (1978, 24). This process of penetration is shown to involve a transformation of the structure and dynamic of activity which is intimately linked to the mediating function of words. It is indeed the word (or, strictly speaking, "word meaning") which Vygotsky takes as the basic "cell" or *unit of analysis* for verbal thinking and its evolution within activity. Ilyenkov's "genuinely historical approach" to the ideal is exemplified, then, in the form of Vygotsky's "genetic method".[13]

Vygotsky argues that the word (or sign) emerges initially against the background of already established activity. The child's speech "accompanies the child's actions and reflects the vicissitudes of problem solving in a disrupted and chaotic form" (Vygotsky, 1978, 28). At this stage speech "remains in a structural relation of subordination to action" (Vygotsky, 1984, 35). Speech follows activity and the child "fixes in words the result of activity or its separate moments" (1984, 34). Expressing himself in rather different terminology, Vygotsky argues that the sign enters an already formed relation between "stimulus" and "response" as an "intermediate link" (1978, 39). It is "drawn into the operation where it fulfills a special function; it creates a new relation between S and R" (1978, p. 39).[14] The initial stage, then, does not manifest a real integration of speech within activity. The "relation between speech and action is a dynamic one" (1978, 27), however, and so: "At a later stage speech moves more and more toward the starting point of the process, so that is comes to *precede* action. It functions then as an aid to a plan that has been conceived but not yet realized in behaviour" (1978, 28). Vygotsky explains that this shift within the activity cycle "means not only a temporal advance of speech in relation to action, but also a change in the functional centre of the whole system" (1984, 35).Thus: "When speech is moved to the starting point of an activity, a new relation between word and action emerges. Now speech guides, determines, and dominates the course of action; the *planning function of speech* comes into being in addition to the already existing function of language to reflect the external world" (1978, 28). The result is that "the child who uses speech divides the activity into two consecutive parts. She plans how to solve the problem through speech and then carries out the prepared solution through overt activity" (1978, 26).

The development of the planning function of speech is, of course, bound up with profound changes in the nature of word meaning which Vygotsky traced in detail (his "natural history of the sign", 1978). From embodying the simplest empirical generalizations (or "notions", Ilyenkov, 1982) recording the general features of the phenomenon as already experienced, the word becomes a vehicle for the concept whose content involves the compression of complex cognitive actions (Ilyenkov, 1991, 91) and which can serve the child "as a really generalized image of reality, an image with which he could act instead of with the immediately tangible reality" (1997, 91).[15]

This account of the planning function of speech sits very well with Ilyenkov's general picture of the "law of spiral-like development". This should not really surprise us, since Vygotsky, like Ilyenkov, made a conscious attempt to absorb the method of *Capital,* and his analysis is clearly informed by an understanding of the "truly dialectical character of the development of functional systems" (1986, 88).[16] It is strange, then, that Vygotsky's conception of symbolic mediation should have been misinterpreted in some quarters as the product of an (un-Marxian) privileging of the role of language in human life activity.[17] By the same argument Marx would be guilty of overemphasising money or capital at the expense of the commodity or, more fundamentally, the labour process in general. What Vygotsky's work shows us is that it does not make sense to abstractly counterpose the word to activity, as if it were a question of choosing one over the other. The word, as the symbolic substance of planning, is the *perfection* of activity; its power derives from its function as the "transformed form" of activity. Through the movement of symbolically mediated practice, language comes to abstract and distill the necessary connections and relations between people and things.[18] The word becomes the "social relation in its completeness", embodying the extremes or opposing poles (subject/object; action/social relation) of social practice. Through language the specific operations and actions which constitute the parts of a complex goal-directed activity are guided, directed and integrated by an *ideal image* of the aims and structure of the whole activity to which the parts are subordinated. In this way, "the form itself of the activity [...] is transformed for man into a special object with which he can operate specially without touching and without changing the real object up to a certain point" (1977a, 278) and the human labour process proper – "labour in a form in which it is an exclusively human characteristic" (Marx, 1976, 283–284) – comes into being.[19]

This ideal plane, like the activity of Marx's architect (1976, 284), is neither superstructure nor ideology but its differentiated existence within the activity cycle does contain the seeds of the division of mental and manual labour without which superstructural and ideological phenomena would be impossible.

The Vygotskian perspective, therefore, helps us to understand the path of development of *"conscious ideality"* in Ilyenkov's terms (1977b, 87), that is, how it can be that human action is conscious but not based or founded on consciousness. Vygotsky's account also shows that the logic of the individual psychological mastery of the means of symbolic mediation reproduces in essence the social logic of genesis and evolution of ideal forms. This intimate connection between the Vygotskian and Ilyenkovian accounts serves as a powerful reminder that we must not artificially counterpose the social and the *psychological,* or the *social* and the *individual,* since the development of the individual as an acting and thinking being is in fact the social process itself.[20]

This interpretation of the role of language encourages the following speculation about its historical development. One could imagine that once language is generated within the system of social production, perhaps as "a very rare exception to the rule" (Ilyenkov, 1982, 199) of social intercourse and communication, the internal structure of the system of social life as a whole gradually undergoes our familiar dialectical inversion. Language penetrates the entire social organism, unleashing the potential of socially organised production and thereby permitting the revolutionising of all spheres of life activity and social relations and creating new spheres and new activities into the bargain. In other words, language-mediated activity, in accordance with the "law of spiral-like development", would displace *all other forms of activity,* making all human activities language-dependent and thereby helping to constantly re-create the necessary conditions for language throughout the whole of social existence.

6. Conclusion

The paper has presented a discussion of the relevance of Ilyenkov's conception of ideality to our understanding of symbolic mediation. I hope to have shown that Ilyenkov, aided by his own deep insight into Marx's work, developed a set of ideas full of intriguing implications and conceptual keys for our understanding of language and other symbolic systems. In particular, I have argued that Ilyenkov's conception of the "law of spiral-like development" is a crucial ingredient in an explanatory, materialist account of the role and power of symbols within social life. Ilyenkov also shows us the value of returning to Marx's work as a theoretical and methodological support for enquiry into the most difficult problems. On this basis alone, I would argue that the rich seam of Ilyenkov's thought is far from exhausted.

Notes

[1] The process of symbolic mediation clearly figures prominently in Vygotsky's work (e.g., 1962, 1978) and has already been discussed with great insight in such works as Bakhurst (1991), Wertsch (1985, 1991), and Lee (1985, 1987).

[2] In relation to language, Marx himself specifically warned against spurious analogies with money and monetary circulation: "To compare money with language is not less erroneous [than to compare it with blood, PEJ]. Language does not transform ideas, so that the peculiarity of ideas is dissolved and their social character runs alongside them as a separate entity, like prices alongside commodities. Ideas do not exist separately from language" (1973, pp. 162–163).

[3] It is not easy, however, to distinguish between what belongs to the general law and what to the circumstances of its operation in a particular instance. Elsewhere (Jones, 1998, in press) I have argued that the complicated relationship between Ilyenkov's general formulations of the problem of the ideal and the specifics of Marx's theory of value has given rise to some misunderstandings in recent interpretations of the concept such as that of Bakhurst (1991), Cole (1996), and Engeström (1996).

[4] Cf Novikov (1999, 85) who denies that there can be typical or untypical forms of ideality.

[5] Cf Ilyenkov (1991, 270–274) for comments on Chomsky.

[6] We should note at this point the general relevance to this whole discussion of Marx's parenthetical comment on his own treatment: "It will be necessary later [...] to correct the idealist manner of the presentation, which makes it seem as if it were merely a matter of conceptual determinations and of the dialectic of these concepts. Above all in the phrase: product (or activity) becomes commodity; commodity, exchange value; exchange value, money" (1973, 151).

[7] Cf Here Ilyenkov (1982, 258): "The value concept expresses the inner relation of the commodity form rather than the external relation of one commodity to another".

[8] On Marx's concept of "transformed form" see particularly Mamardashvili (1992).

[9] Furthermore, those contradictions which give rise to the symbol are not overcome with its emergence but are carried over into the new symbolically mediated system, cf. Ilyenkov (1982).

[10] This point is beautifully expressed in Mamardashvili's work, e.g.: "The fact is that Marx had his own way of describing social systems: in each case, he would construct his investigation in such a way that from the beginning he had to do with systems actualizing and functioning through consciousness, i.e. such that they contained reflection as a necessary element" (1986, 103).

11 Cf. the quite brilliant discussion of the same phenomenon in Mamardashvili (1992). He argues for a "transformation of the internal relations of the complex system, a transformation which takes place at a particular level within the system and which conceals the true character and direct interconnectedness of these relations behind indirect forms of expression. These latter forms, being the product and outcome of the transformations worked on the action of connections within the system, at the same time have an independent life within the system in the form of separate, qualitatively whole phenomena, 'objects' alongside others. It is this 'material existence' that constitutes the whole problem of the transformed form" (1992, 270).

12 Marx continues: "Thus, in the religious sphere, Christ, the mediator between God and humanity – a mere instrument of circulation between the two – becomes their unity, God-man, and, as such, becomes more important than God; the saints more important than Christ; the popes more important than the saints" (1973, 332).

13 Vygotsky's choice of word meaning as a unit of analysis has been much discussed, and often criticised (cf Bakhurst, 1991; Lee, 1985, 1987; Wertsch, 1985). While I believe that much of the criticism is misplaced, I would also suggest that it is actually the *word*, and not *word meaning*, which constitutes Vygotsky's unit, for the same reason that Marx's starting point is the *commodity* and not *exchange-value*.

14 Vygotsky stresses that "the term 'drawn into' indicates that an individual must be actively engaged in establishing such a link" (1978, p. 39).

15 "An abstraction, fixed in a word or term is only the 'antediluvian' (as Marx would have said) precondition for the arising of the concept, the historical condition of its emergence, but not the real condition of its real being" (1997, 80).

16 On the relation between Vygotsky's method and that of Marx see, for example, Lee (1985, 1987).

17 Brushlinsky and Polikarpov (1990), for instance, criticise Vygotsky's "sign-centred" (*znakotsentriskii*) approach from the standpoint of Rubinshteinian activity theory. Cf also Wertsch (1985, 29) who argues: "Whereas Marx clearly emphasized the emergence of socially organized labor and production as the key to distinguishing humans from animals, Vygotsky considered the emergence of speech to be equally important. In this connection he made his most important and unique contributions but also *departed in significant ways from the ideas of Marx and even Engels*" (my emphasis).

18 Cf also Mamardashvili (1992, 278): "The syncretic nature of the transformed form allows the system to work [...] summarily (*summarno*)", that is "without taking into account or actually manifesting all its connections".

19 See Lee (1985, 71; 1987, 96) for discussion of the same issue.

20 Here I follow Marx: "It is above all necessary to avoid once more establishing 'society' as an abstraction over against the individual. The individual *is* the *social being*" (1975, 350).

References

Bakhurst, D. (1991), *Consciousness and Revolution in Soviet Philosophy: From the Bolsheviks to Evald Ilyenkov.* Cambridge: Cambridge University Press.

Bakhurst, D. (1995), *Lessons from Ilyenkov.* In: *The Communication Review,* 1995, 1, 155–178

Bakhurst, D., *Meaning, normativity and the life of the mind.* In: *Language & Communication,* 1997, 17, 33–55.

Baudrillard, J. (1981), *For a Critique of the Political Economy of the Sign.* Telos Press

Brushlinsky, A.V. & Polikarpov, V.A. (1990), *Thinking and Social Interaction* [Myshlenie i obshchenie]. Minsk University Press.

Cole, M. (1996), *Cultural Psychology: A Once and Future Discipline.* Cambridge, Mass.: Harvard University Press.

Engeström, Y., *Interobjectivity, ideality, and dialectics.* In: *Mind, Culture, and Activity,* 1996, 3, 259–265.

Fairclough, N. (1992), *Discourse and Social Change.* Polity Press.

Ilyenkov, E.V. (1977a), *Dialectical logic: Essays on its History and Theory.* Moscow: Progress.

Ilyenkov, E.V. (1977b,) *The concept of the ideal.* In: *Philosophy in the USSR: Problems of Dialectical Materialism,* 71–99. Moscow: Progress.

Ilyenkov, E.V. (1982), *The Dialectics of the Abstract and the Concrete in Marx's "Capital".* Moscow: Progress.

Ilyenkov, E.V. (1991), *Filosofiia i kul'tura* [Philosophy and culture]. Moscow: Politizdat.

Ilyenkov, E.V. (1997), *Dialektika abstraktnogo i konkretnogo v nauchno-teoreticheskom myshlenii.* [The dialectic of the abstract and the concrete in scientifico-theoretical thinking]. Moscow: Rosspen.

Jones, P.E. (1991), *Marxism, Materialism, and Language Structure.* Sheffield: Pavic

Jones, P.E. (1988), *Critical Discourse Analysis as Social Theory.* In: *Proceedings of the Association of Media, Communications, and Cultural Studies,* 1998.

Jones, P.E. (1998), *Symbols, Tools and Ideality in Ilyenkov,* paper presented at the 4th International conference of ISCRAT, Aarhus University.

Jones, P.E., in press, *The Ideal in Cultural-Historical Activity Theory: Issues and Perspectives.* In: S. Chaiklin, ed, *The Theory/Practice of Cultural-Historical Psychology.* Aarhus: Aarhus University Press.

Lee, B. (1985), *Intellectual Origins of Vygotsky's Semiotic Analysis*. In: J.V. Wertsch, ed, *Culture, Communication and Cognition: Vygotskian Perspectives*. Cambridge: Cambridge University Press, 66–93.

Lee, B. (1987), *Recontextualizing Vygotsky*. In: M. Hickmann, ed, *Social and Functional Approaches to Language and Thought*. Orlando: Academic Press, 87–104.

Lektorsky, V.A. (ed.)(1999), *E.V.Il'enkov: lichnost' i tvorchestvo*. [E.V.Ilyenkov: Personality and creativity]. Moscow: "Iazyki russkoi kul'tury".

Mamardashvili, M. K., *Analysis of Consciousness in the Works of Marx*. In: *Studies in Soviet Thought*, 1986, 32, 101–120.

Mamardashvili, M.K. (1992), *Kak ia ponimaiu filosofiiu* [How I understand philosophy]. 2nd edition. Moscow: Progress.

Marx, K. (1973), *Grundrisse*. Harmondsworth: Penguin.

Marx, K. (1975), *Early writings*. Harmondsworth: Penguin.

Marx, K. (1976), *Capital*, Vol. 1. Harmondsworth: Penguin.

Newman, F. & Holzman, L. (1993), *Lev Vygotsky: Revolutionary Scientist*. London: Routledge.

Novikov, A.A. (1999), *The Problem of the Ideal: Traditions and Innovations*, in: Lektorsky (ed). 1999, 74–86.

Rossi-Landi, F. (1974), *Linguistics and Economics*. In: T.A. Sebeok (ed), *Current Trends in Linguistics* Vol 12, The Hague: Mouton.

Voloshinov, V.N. (1973), *Marxism and the Philosophy of Language*. New York: Seminar Press.

Vygotsky, L.S. (1962), *Thought and Language*. Cambridge, Mass: MIT Press.

Vygotsky, L.S. (1978), *Mind in Society*. Cambridge, Mass: Harvard University Press.

Vygotsky, L.S. (1984), *Orudie i znak v razvitii rebenka* [Tool and sign in child development]. In: *Sobranie Sochinenii* [Collected Works], Vol. 6, (A. V. Zaporozhets, ed.). Moscow.

Wertsch, J.V. (1985), *Vygotsky and the Social Formation of Mind*. Cambridge, Mass: Harvard University Press.

Wertsch, J.V. (1991), *Voices of the mind: A sociocultural approach to mediated action*. London: Harvester Wheatsheaf.

Wertsch, J.V. (1998), *Mind as Action*. New York: Oxford University Press.

15

Social and Physical Form: Ilyenkov on the Ideal and Marx on the Value-Form

Andrew Chitty

E.V. Ilyenkov's philosophy represents an extraordinarily ambitious attempt to use the idea that human social activity has determinate "forms" to achieve three different goals: an account of the categories of thought, an account of our knowledge of the natural world, and an account of human consciousness.[1] Overarching these goals, and incorporating them, is another: that of giving an account of mind based on social activity.

Ilyenkov's conception of the ideal, or of ideality, plays a central role in this project. We could go as far as to say that for Ilyenkov "ideality" is the most fundamental feature of human mindedness. By demonstrating that ideality is an objective yet non-physical feature of social activities, and of the things used and produced by social activities, Ilyenkov aims to show that an elementary human mindedness inheres in these activities and things, which makes possible the fully-fledged human mindedness that characterises individual reflective human beings.

Understanding Ilyenkov's account of mind, therefore, depends on gaining a clear grasp of his conception of the ideal. Yet, notoriously, that conception has proved an elusive one to pin down. In this article, I shall attempt to elucidate some aspects of Ilyenkov's conception of the ideal by taking as a cue his statement, in his article *The Problem of the Ideal,* that "the ideality of the value-form is an extremely typical and characteristic case of ideality in general" (DI, 207; CI, 90–91).[2] This suggests that Ilyenkov develops his account of the ideality of human activities and the things involved in those activities by generalising from Marx's account of the value-form of commodities.[3] And in fact in this article, which is his fullest exposition of the concept of the ideal, Ilyenkov – after attacking his opponents and commenting on the notion of the ideal in Plato, Kant and Hegel – presents his own account of the ideal precisely through a discussion of Marx's account of the value-form. My procedure here will be to comment in detail on this presentation, adopting the working assumption that in it Ilyenkov is in fact generalising from Marx's value-form to arrive at his concept of the ideal. This will lead to some conclusions about the nature of Ilyenkov's generalisation from Marx, and about the conception of the ideal that results from it.

1. The Varieties of the Value-Form

Ilyenkov begins his discussion as follows:

> In his analysis of money – that familiar yet mysterious category of social phenomena – Marx formulated the following definition: "price or the money-form of commodities is, like their value-form in general, a form distinct from their palpable real bodily form, therefore only an ideal or represented form". Here Marx describes as "ideal" nothing more or less than the value-form of the products of labour in general. (DI, 198 – 199; cf. CI, 85).[4]

What exactly is the "value-form" of a product, which Marx contrasts here (and elsewhere) to its bodily form? Ilyenkov proceeds to a brief summary:

> According to Marx, the ideality of the form of value consists not, of course, in the fact that this form represents a mental phenomenon existing only in the brain of the commodity-owner or theoretician, but in the fact that, here as in many other cases, the corporeal palpable form of the thing (for example, a coat) is only a form of expression of a quite different "thing" (linen, as a value) with which it has nothing in common. The value of the linen is represented, expressed, "embodied" in the form of the coat, and the form of the coat is the "ideal or represented form" of the value of the linen (DI, 199; CI, 85).

Ilyenkov is referring to Marx's exposition of the form of value in chapter 1 of *Capital,* in which he examines the ways in which the values of commodities are expressed, that is, the ways in which a commodity can be worth something or other. If one commodity is worth a certain amount of another commodity or commodities then the commodities stand in what Marx calls a "value relation", in which the value of the first is expressed in terms of a quantity of the other(s). The sentence that describes this relation is called a "value expression".[5] Marx begins his exposition with the simplest kind of value relation, in which the value of one commodity is expressed in terms of a certain amount of one other commodity: for example the relation of 20 yards of linen being worth one coat. Here the coat plays what he calls the role of the "equivalent", that is, the commodity in terms of which the value of the linen is expressed. Ilyenkov quotes from a paragraph in the later editions of *Capital* which contains the heart of Marx's analysis of this simple value relation:

> Hence in the value relation, in which the coat is the equivalent of the linen, the coat-form counts as value-form [i.e. as the form of value – AC]. The value of the commodity linen is therefore expressed in the body of the commodity coat, the value of one commodity in the use-value of another. As use-value the linen is something sensibly different from the coat; as value it is the same as the coat, and therefore looks like the coat. Thus it acquires a value-form different from its natural-form. Its value-being appears in its sameness with the coat, just as the sheep-like nature of the Christian does in his sameness with the Lamb of God (MEW 23, 66, Marx 1976a, 143).[6]

This paragraph of Marx's deserves close examination, an examination which I shall use as a starting point for a brief exposition of his account of the value-form as a whole. The linen is a use-value, that is, an object useful for satisfying human wants or needs. As such it is a physical object and has characteristics which are quite distinct from those of the coat.[7] But if the linen is conceived simply from the point of view of its value, i.e. of what it is worth, rather than from the point of view of its usefulness for satisfying human wants directly, then its qualitative difference from the coat disappears. The linen's value is the same as the coat, so considered purely as a thing-with-value – or, as Marx puts it, considered as a value – the linen itself is the same as the coat.[8] If we now distinguish between the magnitude of the linen's value (i.e. the fact that it is worth one coat rather than two or three) and the form in which its value is expressed in the value relation (i.e. the fact that it is worth a certain number of coats rather than, say, a certain quantity of iron), and if we leave aside the magnitude, we can say the following: the linen's value has the form of a coat, so, considered as a value, the linen itself has the form of a coat.[9]

Here what must be meant by the word "form" is the perceptible outer expression or appearance of an inner content, rather than a shape superimposed on a matter which is indifferent to it.[10] In other words, we must think of form in the way we do when we distinguish the outer form (perceptible aspects) and inner content (meaning) of a linguistic utterance, rather than when we distinguish the form (shape) and matter (material) of a statue.[11] It is in this sense that the linen, considered as a value, has the form of a coat. In fact Marx can now say that the linen has two forms. Considered as a use-value, it has a physical form: namely the totality of its physical characteristics, for they "express" its usefulness in a perceptible way. This physical form is what Marx calls its "bodily form" or "natural form", although the second of these terms is something of a misnomer since these physical characteristics include both those that belong to its materials by nature and also those which have been given to it in the process of making those materials into linen. Considered as a value, by contrast, the linen has a form quite distinct from its own physical form, namely that of the totality of the physical characteristics of the coat.[12] This is its "value-form". As Marx puts it in a passage in the first edition of *Capital*:

> In that [the linen] *equates* [*gleichsetzt*] itself with [the coat] *as value* – while at the same time *distinguishing* itself from it as use-object, what happens is that the coat becomes the appearance-form of linen-*value* as opposed to linen-*body*: its *value-form* as distinguished from its *natural-form* (MEGA II.5, 30; Marx 1976b, 20).

It is worth emphasising that the term "value-form" in these passages combines two distinct senses. On the one hand the coat's physical form is the value-form of the linen in that it is the outer expression of the value of the linen. Here "form" refers to a certain aspect of the value of the linen (namely its outer expression as opposed to some other aspect of it). I shall call this the "attributive" sense of the term "value-form". But on the other hand the coat is the value-form of the linen in that it is the outer expression of the linen *as value*, as opposed to its outer expression as use-object. Here "form" refers to a certain kind of form *of the linen itself* (namely its "value" form as opposed to its physical form). I shall call this the "predicative" sense of the term "value-form".[13] The key to the transition between the first sense and the second is the move between thinking of the commodity as *having* a value (in which case the value-form is the form of the value that the commodity has) and thinking of it as *being* a value (in which case the value-form is the form of the value that the commodity is, the form of the commodity itself *qua* value). Marx alternates freely between these two ways of thinking about value, as can be seen in the last quotation: if "linen-value" there is interpreted as the value of the linen then the term "value-form" following it means the form of that value, but if "linen-value" means the linen itself (considered as value), then "value-form" means the form of the linen itself (again considered as value).

To sum up then, for Marx the linen acquires a value-form by virtue of being worth a certain amount of a commodity of another kind. This is a value-form in both the attributive and the predicative sense: it is a form of the linen's value, but in so far as the linen is considered as a value it is also a form of the linen itself. Because of this the linen itself has two kinds of form: as a useful object it has its own physical form, but as a value it has the physical form of another commodity. This, its value-form, is completely distinct from its own physical characteristics.[14] It consists in the physical characteristics of a qualitatively different commodity.

There is one more point to make about the transition from the attributive to the predicative sense of "value-form". I have said that this transition depends on the linen being "considered as a value". But in turn, the linen becomes something that it is appropriate to "consider as a value" only through its being related to the coat by the value relation itself. Suppose we use a truncated form of the value expression, saying that "20 yards of linen are worth something" without having any idea of what it is worth. Then it is only in an implicit sense that we can think of the linen as a value, as a thing-with-value, for we cannot say anything about what that value is. By contrast, when we say "20 yards of linen are worth one coat", we give the linen's value a form in our statement. We can now say what the linen's value is. This enables us to think of the linen itself explicitly as a value. In turn we can thereby think of the form of its value as a form of the linen itself, as a value-form of the linen in the predicative sense. These are logical facts about what is entailed by the value expression as opposed to its truncated form, and psychological facts about what is involved in taking these expressions seriously. But Marx thinks of them as reflecting ontological facts about what is involved in the value relation itself. Outside the value relation the linen is a value only in a potential sense. The value relation gives a form to the linen's value. It thereby *realises* the linen as a value; it constitutes it as a value in a full sense, so that it is appropriate to consider it as a value. In turn this constitutes the form of the linen's value as a form of the linen itself, alongside its physical form. So through constituting the linen as having a value-form in the attributive sense, the value relation constitutes it also as having a value-form in the predicative sense. This set of claims is implicit in both of the above quotations from Marx, but it is clearest in a passage from the first edition of *Capital* which is the direct forerunner of the paragraph in the later editions from which Ilyenkov quotes:

> Thus through the *relative value expression*[15] the *value* of the commodity acquires firstly a *form different from its own use-value*. The use-form of this commodity is, e.g., *linen*. But it possesses *its value-form* in its *relation of sameness with the coat*. Through this relation of sameness the body of another commodity, sensibly different from it, becomes the mirror of its own value-being, of its own value-character. In this way it gains *a value-form different, independent and autonomous from its natural form* (MEGA II.5, 630–631; Marx 1978, 137).

Clearly, it is the value-form in the predicative sense that is of interest to Ilyenkov, since it is in this sense that the value-form is the non-physical form of a thing and so can serve as a model for the general idea that things can have non-physical forms, or what he calls "ideal forms". Accordingly, in what follows I shall focus on the predicative sense, and when I use the term "value-form" it will be with this sense in the foreground.

If it is the value-relation that constitutes the linen as having a value-form, then we need to know something about what this relation consists in. What is it, exactly, for 20 yards of linen to be worth one coat, or for the value of 20 yards of linen to be one coat? In the view I shall assume here, it is for it to be the case that 20 yards of linen can "normally" be exchanged on the market for one coat. The assertion that they can normally be so exchanged involves a quantitative and a qualitative claim: a claim about the magnitude of the linen's value and a claim about its form. With regard to the quantitative claim, Marx recognises that in individual transactions commodities are often exchanged at above or below their value (for example, that 20 yards of linen are often exchanged for more than or less than the one coat which they are actually worth), and even that the average quantity of the commodity for which a commodity is exchanged in the market may deviate from its value for a period of time. However his view is that the mechanisms of supply and demand tend to drive the rates at which commodities are actually exchanged towards their values.[16] At any rate, some such equilibrating mechanism is necessary in order to be able to define the value of a commodity in a way that distinguishes it from the rate at which it can as a matter of act be exchanged in the market at any one time. So for a commodity to have a given value-magnitude is for it to be normally exchangeable for a certain *quantity* of another commodity. With regard to the qualitative claim, similar points apply. For a commodity to have a given value-form is for it to be normally exchangeable for a certain *kind* of commodity, in whatever quantity, although in individual transactions, or even for a period of time in the market as a whole, it may be exchanged with other kinds of commodity.

The value of a commodity is therefore constituted as what it is, as having the magnitude and form that it does, by the long-term behaviour of the market as a whole, that is, by the totality of the individual acts of offering-to-exchange-for, declining-to-exchange-for, and actually exchanging that make up this behaviour. Value is an objective feature of a commodity in the strict sense that the commodity possesses that feature independently of any one individual's ways of perceiving it or acting towards it, although not of course independently of the way that all individuals in the market do over a long period of time. Marx reinforces the claim that the magnitude of the value of a commodity is an objective feature by arguing that this magnitude is determined by the amount of labour-time currently needed to produce the commodity (relative to the amount currently needed to produce a unit of the commodity that plays the role of equivalent). But we do not need to accept this argument to appreciate that the magnitude and form of a commodity's value are objective in the stated sense.[17]

Up till now, I have restricted the discussion of the value-form to the simplest kind of value relation, one in which the value of a commodity is expressed in terms of a quantity of one other commodity. This is the form that value would take in a two-commodity market where exchange consisted in bartering one kind of commodity for the other. But in the last two paragraphs this restriction has begun to look strained. In order to complete this exposition, we need to see how Marx expands his account to include the familiar case where the value of commodities is expressed in terms of money.

Every commodity that has a value, has a particular value-form. The value-form of a certain amount of linen is a coat, the value-form of a certain amount of corn is (say) iron, and so on. However Marx distinguishes between different *kinds* of value-form.[18] If a certain amount of linen stands in a value relation in which its value is expressed in terms of a certain amount of just one other commodity, as in the discussion so far, then the linen is said to have the "simple value-form". If the linen's value is expressed in terms of alternative quantities of various commodities (for example, 20 yards of linen are worth 1 coat, or 10 lb. of tea, or 2 ounces of gold etc.) then the linen has the "expanded value-form". If its value, along with that of all the other commodities in the market, is expressed in terms of a quantity of one particular commodity, while that commodity's value is expressed in terms of alternative quantities of every commodity on the market, then that commodity is called the "universal equivalent", and the linen has the "universal value-form". And if by social custom a single commodity (such as silver or gold) comes to play the role of universal equivalent, then that commodity is called the "money-commodity" and the linen has the "money-form". Furthermore, Marx sees these four kinds of value-form as developmental stages in a single process rather than as alternatives alongside each other. In a fully developed market the kind of value-form in play is the money-form.

It should be added that in each of these four cases Marx describes not only the commodity whose value is expressed in the value relation but also the equivalent commodity as having a value-form, calling the former a "relative value-form" and the latter an "equivalent-form". Thus a commodity can have either the relative or the equivalent versions of the four different kinds of value-form.[19] In particular, it is important to distinguish the relative and equivalent versions of the most developed kind of value-form, the money-form: if 20 yards of linen are worth 2 ounces of gold then linen has the relative money-form (also called the "price-form") and the gold has the equivalent money-form (or simply the "money-form" for short).[20]

Finally, we can use the phrase "the value-form as such" to indicate of a commodity that it has a value-form, without specifying exactly what that value-form is, or even of what kind or version it is. Thus to say that a certain amount of linen has the value-form as such is to say that its value has *some* form, or equivalently that it itself *qua* value has some form, without saying anything further about what that form is. From what has been said above, it follows that for a commodity to possess the value-form as such is just for it to be (normally) exchangeable in the market for some quantity of some other commodity (or commodities). In short, it is for it to be exchangeable as such. As Marx says, "a commodity is in general *exchangeable* with another commodity insofar as it possesses a *form* in which it *appears as value*" (MEGA II.5, 631; Marx 1978, 137).[21] We can add that since Marx defines a commodity as a thing which is both a use-value and a value, and since it is having a value-form that makes a useful thing into a value in the full sense, we can say that it is having the value-form as such, or being exchangeable as such, that makes a thing into a commodity in the full sense. Hence Marx's (and Ilyenkov's) occasional use of the term "commodity-form" as an equivalent for "the value-form as such".

Ilyenkov – to return to his account – affirms Marx's account of the value-form of commodities and in particular the idea that the value-form of a commodity is an objective feature of the commodity, yet a feature that is completely distinct from its physical form.[22] But what is noticeable about Ilyenkov's account of the value-form is that he treats the equivalent versions of it as paradigmatic. This fact is disguised by his use of quotations from Marx which refer to the relative value-form, but it can be demonstrated as follows.

Ilyenkov, like Marx, thinks of the value relation as a relation of representation: "the value of the linen is represented, expressed, 'embodied' in the form of the coat" (DI, 199; CI, 85, quoted above). In this relation it is the equivalent commodity (coat) that represents, and the other commodity (linen) – or rather its value – that is represented. For Ilyenkov this "representing" is a crucial aspect of the value-form. Yet when he subsequently refers to it he consistently portrays the commodity that has the value-form (or else that value-form itself) as representing another commodity (or its value). For example he says that the value-form is perceived "as the form of an external thing, not as its palpable bodily form, but as the form of another equally palpable bodily thing that it represents (expresses, embodies)" (DI, 200; CI, 86).[23] This makes sense only if the thing that has the value-form is the coat rather than the linen, for it is the coat that represents, expresses or embodies the linen, or more exactly its value, rather than vice versa. It follows that on such occasions he must be thinking of the value-form in question as an equivalent form.

In Marx, as I have presented him, the term "value-form" refers primarily to the relative version of that form and only derivatively to the equivalent version. In Ilyenkov, by contrast, it seems that the priority is reversed, so that when he uses the term "value-form" we should assume that it is primarily the equivalent version that he has in mind. In the context of a fully developed market this means the (equivalent) money-form. In fact in *The Problem of the Ideal* Ilyenkov's first example of an ideal form existing outside the head is precisely the money-form, in the shape of the "hundred talers" with which Kant illustrates his refutation of the ontological proof for the existence of God (DI, 181 – 185; CI, 74 – 77).[24]

2. Market Exchange and Abstract Labour

In turn, however, Ilyenkov thinks of the (equivalent) value-form of the commodity as representing not just another commodity or its value but something that lies beyond these, namely a form of human activity. Speaking of the value-form as an "objective ideal form", he says that what is expressed in it, what it "represents", is a definite social relation between people themselves, which in their eyes assumes the fantastic form of a relation between things. In other words, what is "represented" here is the form of people's activity, the form of life activity which they realise together, which has taken shape completely spontaneously "behind the back of consciousness" and is objectively fixed in the shape of the relation between things described above, as a thing. From this, and this alone, arises the ideality of such a "thing", its "sensuous-supersensuous" character (DI, 200; CI, 86).

From what has been said so far, it might be surmised that the "social relation between people" or the "form of people's activity" that is represented by the value-form of the commodity is market exchange, for it is the social practices of market exchange over time that constitute things as having a value-form, whether relative or equivalent.[25] However a few sentences later Ilyenkov appears to undermine this expectation by saying instead that what is represented is a form of *labour*:

> What is embodied and "represented" here is the definite form of labour, the definite form of human objective activity, that is, of the transformation of nature by social man (DI, 200; CI, 86).

Furthermore, in his subsequent restatements Ilyenkov consistently reasserts that the value-form represents a form of labour. For example:

> The value of a thing presented itself as the objectified[26] labour of man, and therefore the value-form turned out to be nothing else but the objectified form of this labour, as a form of human life activity, which appeared to men in the form of the thing they had transformed (DI, 209; CI, 92).[27]

To clarify how for Ilyenkov the value-form can represent both a social relation between people and a form of labour, we need to return to the passage in Marx from which he draws the phrase about social relations between people and relations between things. Again, the clearest version of this passage is not the well-known one in the section on commodity fetishism in the later editions of *Capital*, but its forerunner in the first edition. There Marx begins by asserting that products are constituted as values of particular magnitudes only by their incorporation into our "intercourse":

> The fact that the products of labour, such useful things as coat, linen, wheat, iron etc. are *values*, *definite magnitudes of value*, and in general *commodities*, are properties which of course pertain to them only in *our intercourse* and not by nature like, for example, the property of being heavy or being warming or nourishing (MEGA II.5, 637; Marx 1978,142).

He now goes on to characterise that intercourse, which must presumably be identified with market exchange, in terms of a "social relation between the producers". Commodity fetishism then consists in misconstruing the value-magnitude and the value-form of commodities as properties that they have by nature when in fact they are properties that they have only by being incorporated into this social relation:

> Now the fact that e.g. *20 yards of linen = 1 coat* or *20 yards of linen are worth 1 coat* only expresses the fact that [...] tailors and weavers enter into a definite *social relation of production*. It is a *definite social relation between the producers*, in which they *equate* [*gleichsetzen*] their different types of labour *as human labour*. It is not less a *definite social relation between producers*, in which they *measure* the magnitude of their labours *by the duration of expenditure of human labour-power*. But *within our intercourse these social characters* of their own labours *appear* to them

as *social natural-properties*, as *objective* determinations *of the products of labour themselves*, the sameness of human labours *as a value-property* of the products of labour, the *measure* of the labour by the socially necessary labour-time as *the magnitude of value* of the products of labour, and finally the social relation between the producers through their labours appears as a *value-relation* or *social relation between these things*, the products of labour (Ibid.).[28]

If we leave aside again the issue of the magnitude of value, it is noticeable here that Marx presents the value-form (as such) of the products *both* as something constituted by the "social relation" between the producers *and* as an expression of a "social character" of the labours involved in making them. How is this possible?

For Marx, it is possible because the specific social character in question, which he calls here "the sameness of human labours" but elsewhere the character of being "universal human labour", "abstract universal labour" or simply "abstract labour", is inseparable from the social relation of market exchange.[29] In any society with a division of labour, individual acts of labour have a social character *in general*: that means to say, they function as a part of the totality of acts of labour in the society in producing the totality of goods that will fulfil the wants and needs of the members of that society. What distinguishes abstract labour from other kinds of labour is the specific way in which this "insertion" into the totality of labours is achieved. This is its *specific* social character, "the specific form in which labour obtains a social character" (MEW 13, 20; Marx 1970, 32).[30] In a society in which everyone agreed democratically how to divide the tasks that needed doing, for example, an individual act of labour would obtain its social character by virtue of the fact that in performing it the worker would be implementing such an agreement. In a commodity-producing society, by contrast, there is no such advance agreement. The labours of different producers are co-ordinated to form a totality that meets the wants and needs of society as a whole only through the signals of the market, and a given act of labour gains its place within this totality only through the sale of its products on the market. If its products fail to sell, then it is redundant from the point of view of this totality and fails to find such a place in it. Abstract labour is labour that gains its social character in this way.

Thus abstract labour is labour whose specific social character, or (as I shall now say) specific social form, consists in its gaining its social character through the sale of its products on a market.[31] In particular, this must be a market with a money-commodity, since only through the comparative pricing of different products in terms of the same commodity that occurs in such a market it is possible to co-ordinate a multiplicity of labours. The term "abstract" is appropriate for such labour because by selling the product for money its producer proves that the particular labour that went into making it is substitutable for any of the labours that have gone into the other products on the market, since all products are for sale in exchange for some quantity or another of money, and the producer can therefore use some quantity or another of this particular labour to obtain any other product instead of having to make that other product. In the sense that it can be substituted for all those other labours, this labour has a "sameness" with them, and an "abstractness" from its particular characteristics as the production of its own particular product.

A central feature of abstract labour is that it gains its social character in two stages. In a first stage, individuals labour to produce products which they think will be saleable, and in the second stage they actually sell them.[32] In the first stage their labours are "private", in that it is not yet certain whether they will actually function as part of the totality of labours in society, in other words whether they do have a social character. It is only when a products is sold that the labour that made it is assured a place in the totality of labours, that its social character is confirmed. So in the case of abstract labour:

> The point of departure is not the labour of individuals as social, but on the contrary the particular labours of private individuals, i.e. labours which only prove themselves as universal social labour by the supersession of their original character in the exchange process. Universal social labour is not a ready-made presupposition but an emerging [*werdendes*] result (MEW 13, 31-32; Marx 1970, 45).

We can make the "emerging" or "coming to be" quality of abstract labour explicit by distinguishing between what I shall call "actual" and "latent" abstract labour. A given act of labour is constituted as "actual abstract labour" by the fact that its product is sold in the market. It is constituted as "latent abstract labour" by the fact that it is carried out with the *aim* of selling its products on the market. The specific social form of abstract labour is one which any given act of labour acquires at first latently, through its orientation towards the sale of its product, and then actually, through the successful sale of that product. The sale of the product is the realisation of its labour as abstract labour.[33]

To describe the sale of products as the "realisation" of the labour that went into them as abstract labour, and this labour as already "latently" abstract in advance of the sale, is not just a matter of terminological whim. By describing market exchange as the realisation of the activities of producing goods for the market, it expresses the dependence of market exchange on these activities: the fact that over the long term the social relation of market exchange cannot sustain itself unless it forms part of a more inclusive social relation made up of the totality of the activities of production-with-the-aim-of-exchange and of exchange itself in a multi-product market. I shall call this inclusive social relation the "production-for-exchange relation". It is this social relation, rather than the social relation of market exchange alone, that must be seen as endowing things with the value-form. And this relation is inseparable from labour that has the specific social form of being abstract labour. For members of a society to engage in the production-for-exchange relation is for their labour to have the (emerging) form of abstract labour, and vice versa.[34]

So Ilyenkov's claim that the value-form represents both a "definite social relation between people" and "a definite form of labour" is vindicated by Marx's account of the form of labour in question. The value-form "represents" both of these in the sense that things acquire the value-form, whether relative or equivalent, by virtue of being incorporated into the production-for-exchange relation, or to put it another way, by virtue of being the products of labour that has the specific social form of (actual) abstract labour. So if a product has the value-form, this is a sign that has been incorporated into that social relation, or equally that it has been produced by labour with that specific social form.

However the move from seeing the value-form as constituted by a social relation to seeing it as constituted by a specific social form of labour has some cost. For just as the value-form of the product is completely distinct from its physical form, so that for example if the market were abolished products would lose their value-form without any change to their physical form, so the same must be true of the specific social form of the labour that constitutes it. It must be completely distinct from the physical form of that labour, that is, from those of its characteristics in virtue of which its products have the physical properties that they do.[35] Marx says that

> none of these private labours in its natural form possesses this specific social form of abstract human labour, just as little as the commodity in its natural form possesses the social form of a mere coagulation of labour, or of value [...] the *social form* is a form which is different from the natural forms of the actual useful labours, foreign to them, and abstract (MEGA II.5, 41; Marx 1976b, 32).[36]

So although Marx (and Ilyenkov) can say that the value-form is constituted by, and so "represents", a form of labour, the form in question cannot be a physical form. It is significant that, in summarising Marx's view, Ilyenkov does not acknowledge this point. In the passages quoted above he simply says that the value-form represents or objectifies a "form of labour", or a form of "the transformation of nature by social man". He does not specify that the form in question is a specific social form rather than a physical form of labour.

3. Ilyenkov and Ideal Forms

With this point I conclude my summary of Marx's theory of the value-form and of Ilyenkov's account of it, and turn to look at how Ilyenkov generalises that account to his own account of ideality, so that the value-form can be seen as a "typical and characteristic case of ideality in general" (DI, 207; CI, 90–91, quoted above).

In the light of the account of the value-form given above, a natural way to think of this generalisation as working is as follows. What Ilyenkov extracts from Marx's account of the value-form, and generalises to produce his own account of the ideal, is the idea that social relations between people can constitute the things that are incorporated into them as having features which are distinct from their physical properties and yet objective in the sense stated earlier. So the social relation of production-for-exchange constitutes the things that are produced and exchanged within it as values and as possessors of the value-form. Similarly, we could say that the social relation of giving constitutes the things that are given as gifts, or as having "the gift-form". In general, the ideal forms of things would be those features which they have only by virtue of being incorporated into some social relation or other.[37]

Let us call the interpretation of Ilyenkov's ideal forms arrived at here the "constitution by social relations" interpretation.[38] A number of objections could be raised against the view that it is true to Ilyenkov's own conception, but I believe that there is one that is decisive. This is that in this interpretation there is no necessary connection between a thing having an ideal form and it, or its form, "representing" other things. It is true that a gift, or its gift-form, can be said to "represent" the social relation of giving. But it would be stretching the meaning of representation to say that it "represents" all other gifts. By contrast, Ilyenkov insists that "representing" other things is an essential characteristic, not only of the value-form, but of ideality in general:

> This relation of representation is a relation in which one sensuously perceivable thing, while remaining itself, performs the role or function of representative of quite another thing, or, to be more precise, of the universal nature of that other thing, that is, of something "other" which in sensuous, bodily terms is quite unlike it, and thereby acquires a new plane of existence, and it was this relation that in the Hegelian terminological tradition gained the title of "ideality" (DI, 197; CI, 84).

It is true that Ilyenkov goes on to present his own conception of ideality (which he identifies as Marx's, portraying himself merely as its interpreter) as superseding Hegel's. But he immediately makes it clear that in this supersession the element of representation is preserved, for in turning from Hegel to Marx, he begins by pointedly quoting Marx's statement that "price or the money-form of commodities is, like their value-form in general [...] an *ideal or represented* form" (DI, 198–199, quoted above; emphasis added).[39] As we have seen Ilyenkov understands the representation in question as the representing not just of a social relation or of a form of human activity, but also of other physical things.[40] So clearly Ilyenkov places himself within "the Hegelian terminological tradition" that he describes here.[41]

I therefore propose to outline a different view of the way in which Ilyenkov generalises from Marx's theory of the value-form, leading to a different interpretation of his ideal forms. As starting point, notice that Ilyenkov repeatedly insists that the ideal is not simply a form of things, nor for that matter simply a form of social activity. It is a form of social activity embodied as the form of a thing. Ideality achieves existence "only as a reified and reifiable form of activity – as a form of activity that has become and is becoming the form of an object" (DI, 203; CI, 88). The ideal is to be grasped as "the form of dynamic activity of social man that is embodiable in things [...] As activity under the form of a thing, or conversely as a thing under the form of activity, as a 'moment' of this activity, as its fluid metamorphosis" (DI, 204; cf. CI, 89). Most explicitly of all:

> The ideal form is a form of the thing, but outside this thing, in man as a form of his dynamic life activity, as goals and needs. Or conversely, it is a form of man's dynamic life activity, but outside man, as a form of the thing created by him. "Ideality" itself exists only in the constant alternation of these two forms of its "external embodiment" without coinciding with either of them taken separately. It exists only through the unceasing process in which the form of activity transforms itself into the form of the thing, and conversely – the form of the thing into the form of activity (of social man of course) (DI, 222; CI, 98.)[42]

These two aspects of the ideal are so closely related that it is impossible to grasp the ideal through either of them alone, for:

> As soon as it is fixed as the "form of a thing" it begins to tease the theoretician with its "un-thinglikeness", its "functional" character, and appears only as a form of "pure activity", as *"actus purus"*. On the other hand, as soon as one attempts to fix it "as such", purified of all the traces of material palpable corporeality, it turns out that this attempt is fundamentally doomed to failure, for after such a subtraction there will be nothing but a transparent emptiness, a formless vacuum (DI, 201 – 202; CI 87).

In defining ideal form as a form at once of things and of activity, Ilyenkov's usage departs from that of Marx, who understands the value-form strictly as a form of things, and abstract labour as a form of labour that constitutes things as having this form. However despite this revision it is not difficult to see Ilyenkov's conception of the ideal form here as a generalisation of Marx's view of the relation between one specific *kind* of value-form of the commodity, namely the (equivalent) money-form, and the abstract form of the labour that creates commodities. For in Marx's view each of these forms depends on the other. The abstract form of labour is realised by the exchange of its product for the money-commodity. But by definition the money-commodity is a commodity in which the role of universal equivalent is bound up with a particular physical form, and this binding-up is maintained only through the practice of exchanging products for things of that particular physical form. So labour can only realise itself as abstract labour insofar as there is a commodity that has the (equivalent) money-form, against which its products can be exchanged, while at the same time a commodity can only have and retain the money-form insofar as the products of labour are exchanged for it. The abstract form of labour and the money-form therefore depend on each other. Abstract labour depends on the money-form in that it is constituted as latent abstract labour through its orientation to the acquisition of money, and is realised as actual abstract labour through that acquisition. But the money-form itself depends on abstract labour in that a given kind of commodity is only endowed with this form through such a realisation of abstract labour, continually repeated. We could say that abstract labour both realises itself through the money-form and expresses itself in the money-form.[43] In that it realises itself through the money-form it depends on the money-form; in that it expresses itself in the money-form the money-form depends on it.[44]

Furthermore, we can say exactly the same of the production-for-exchange relation. In general we can say that things are endowed with the value-form by virtue of being incorporated into the production-for-exchange relation. However in the case of one specific kind of value-form, the (equivalent) money-form, things are not so simple. The money-form is constituted by the production-for-exchange relation and yet that relation also presupposes the money-form. For unless at any particular time there is one commodity that has the money-form, so that all products can be exchanged for that commodity and all labours can be oriented towards the exchange of their products for it, the production-for-exchange relation cannot be sustained. So in the case of the money-form we cannot say simply that it is constituted by a social relation of production-for-exchange that is independent of it. Rather the production-for-exchange relation both realises itself through and expresses itself in the money-form.

It is the close interdependence of the form of abstract labour (or the production-for-exchange relation) with the money-form that, in Marx, is chiefly responsible for the more sophisticated forms of fetishism. On the one hand in the money-form a particular physical form, that of gold for instance, is closely bound up with a certain kind of value-form, namely the universal equivalent form. On the other hand, the money-form as a whole is closely bound up with the form of abstract labour. The result is not just a tendency to explain the peculiar features of the money-commodity purely in terms of its physical characteristics, an example, like the ordinary commodity fetishism described above, of what might be called "physical fetishism". It is also a reverse tendency to explain them purely in terms of the form of labour, or the social relation, which realises itself through that commodity, what might be called "relations fetishism". The interdependence of the money-form of the commodity and the abstract form of labour is close enough that it would have been legitimate for Marx to see them as simply aspects of a single form of the overall process of the economic interchange between human beings, nature and other human beings, a form which cannot properly be grasped as a form of things alone or of labour alone. And in fact he did give a single name to a more developed version of such a form, namely "capital". So it is significant that Ilyenkov's declaration of the futility of trying to grasp the ideal just as a form of a thing or just as a form of activity echoes, no doubt deliberately, Marx's remark on the "naïve astonishment" of economists trying to understand capital, when "the phenomenon that they have just ponderously described as a thing soon appears as a social relation and, a moment later, having been defined as a social relation, teases them once more as a thing" (MEW 13, 22; Marx 1970, 35). The alternation of physical fetishism and relations fetishism in economists trying to grasp the nature of capital recurs, according to Ilyenkov, in philosophers trying to grasp the nature of the ideal.

My suggestion, then, is that we should see Ilyenkov's account of the ideal as a generalisation of one specific aspect of Marx's theory of the value-form, namely his account of the simultaneous realisation and expression of the form of abstract labour in the money-form of the commodity. In this light Ilyenkov's focus on the equivalent value-form, and specifically the money-form, in his account of Marx becomes comprehensible, since on the present view it is the money-form, rather than the value-form in general that he takes as the starting point from which to generalise in order to reach his account of that ideal form. Accordingly it is the money-form that he should see as the "typical and characteristic case" of the ideal form of things.

How exactly, though, can Ilyenkov generalise Marx's highly specific account of the relation between abstract labour and the money-form to a more general account of the realisation and expression of the forms of human activity in the forms of things? To illustrate how this could be done, let us take the case of an activity that is closely associated with a particular kind of thing, as for example the standard activity of cutting is with knives.[45] This activity can only be done well with a knife, and people only learn to do it by practising with knives. But at the same time human beings only make and maintain knives because this kind of activity goes on. So if we look at the cutting-form of activity and the knife-form of things as a whole, across the whole of society, each of these forms depends on the other. From this point of view what we have here is really a single form, the "cutting/knife-form": a form of activity which realises itself through but also expresses itself in a form of things.

Furthermore, this form is a unified one across the whole of society. Through processes of imitation and mutual correction, operating under the pressures of physical necessity, a society normally develops a roughly standard way of cutting and a roughly standard size, shape and composition of knife.[46] As unified across a society, the "cutting/knife-form" acts as a norm that guides individuals in their actions of cutting, making and repairing knives. This means that the cutting/knife-form will be more or less adequately realised in individual actions and individual things. Some actions succeed better than others as actions of cutting, and some particular things make better knives than others. And when an action does possess the cutting-form, or a thing the knife-form, it does so objectively, in the sense of "objective" stated above.

Thus the cutting-form of a given individual action is distinct from, although related to, the action's physical form as a whole (which I define as the totality of the physical movements and the intentions involved in the action). It consists in those aspects of the physical form which enable the action to count, by the standards of this society, as a proper action of cutting. Similarly, the knife-form of a given thing consists in those aspects of its physical form which make it count, by the same standards, as properly a knife.

So although the cutting-form and the knife-form are objective forms distinct from the physical forms of the individual actions and things that have them, they are also related to those physical forms. In a given society, they "supervene" on the physical forms: that is, whether or not an action has the cutting-form or a thing the knife-form is determined by its physical form. Yet they are forms which those actions and things have only by virtue of belonging to a collective social practice. In a society where cutting and knives were unknown, a metal shard from a fire might accidentally take the physical shape of a knife, but it would not have the knife-form. As Ilyenkov says:

> The humanly created form of the thing, taken out of the process of social life activity, out of the process of man-nature metabolism, is also simply the material form of the thing, the physical form of an external body, and nothing more (DI, 223; CI, 99).

Likewise someone might accidentally, on one occasion only, engage in an action that looks like cutting to us, but it would not have the cutting-form. It is not just that people in that society would not have words for "knife" or "cut". It is that the socially constituted forms of things and of actions that those words name would not exist, so that individual things and actions could not take those forms.[47]

If we understand Ilyenkov's account of the structure of an "ideal form" in this way, we can see how it makes sense to say that this form cannot be grasped either as a form of things or as a form of activity. The knife-form as a form of things is intelligible only in the context of actions with the cutting-form, and the cutting-form as a form of actions is intelligible only in a world in which there are things with the knife-form. The two forms have to be seen as aspects of a single form. I have said that this single form acts as a "norm" which individual things and actions match more or less adequately, so it cannot be identified with the physical form of any single thing or action. Rather, it exists only in the totality of things and actions that more or less adequately have the form, and in the social processes of imitation and correction whereby individuals reproduce that form in the things they use and in their actions.

Understood in this way, Ilyenkov's ideal forms are akin to Plato's ideas or forms, for they serve as norms which individual things or actions realise more or less well, and in fact Ilyenkov sees himself as salvaging what is true in Plato's objective idealism.[48] The difference is that by seeing his ideal forms as sustained by social activity in interaction with nature Ilyenkov can locate them entirely within the material world.[49]

More immediately, though, we can see that Ilyenkov's account of the structure of an ideal form can indeed be a generalisation of Marx's account of the interrelation between the form of abstract labour and the money-form of the commodity. For the basic shape of the two-way relation in each case is very similar: the form of activity has to make use of the form of the thing in order to realise itself, but the form of the thing only comes into existence through the form of activity.

4. Social Form and Physical Form

This interpretation of Ilyenkov's notion of an "ideal form", and thus implicitly of his notion of ideality as such, has focused only on activities associated with a particular kind of thing which is used in the activity, and which is an artefact made by human beings. An immediate task would be to extend the account to other kinds of activity: for example activities like celestial navigation, which use a kind of thing (a star) that is not an artefact; like knife-making, which are associated with a particular kind of thing as the thing they make rather than the thing they use; or like promising, which are not associated with any particular kind of thing.[50] A further task would be to ask whether, under this interpretation, Ilyenkov's ideal forms can fulfil his claim that they are prior to, rather than consequences of, human "consciousness and will" (DI, 212; CI, 94).[51] I shall not attempt any of these tasks here, but instead finish by commenting, from the point of view of the present interpretation, on one crucial issue in the comparison between Marx's value-theory and Ilyenkov's theory of ideal forms. This is the issue of the relationship between social form and physical form in the two thinkers.

Suppose we use the general term "social form" to cover Marx's value-form, Marx's form of abstract labour, and Ilyenkov's ideal form. For both Marx and Ilyenkov social form is always distinct from physical form in the sense that things and actions have the social forms that they do only by virtue of the system of interaction between humans, nature and other humans of which they are a part; if they were taken out of that system then they would lose their social form. Yet for both, social form supervenes on physical form. That is, the physical form of a thing or action, once it is placed within that system, will determine what social form it has: "determine" it in the strict sense that this physical form (in conjunction with the current state of the system of interaction in which it is placed) will dictate what its social form must be, so that from the physical form (and the state of the system) one can deduce the social form. If a commodity, such as a piece of linen, is produced in a given market society at a given time, then its physical characteristics (in conjunction with the current state of the system of production and exchange, and in particular the labour-time currently necessary in the system to produce something with those physical characteristics) will dictate what, if any, value-magnitude and value-form it has. So, given the current state of the system of production and exchange in which it is placed, the physical characteristics of the piece of linen will determine its value-magnitude and value-form. If the former were to change then the latter would too.[52] Likewise it is the physical characteristics of a thing that determine whether it can count, in our society, as a knife.

In this respect, Marx and Ilyenkov look similar. But if we consider the converse relation, then an important difference emerges between them. In Marx's theory of the value-form, if one considers a thing or activity in a given society, its social form generally does not determine its physical form, that is, its physical form cannot be deduced from its social form. The physical form of an act of labour cannot be deduced from knowing that it has the social form of abstract labour, and the physical form of a thing cannot be deduced from knowing either that it has the value-form as such, or that it has a certain kind or version of value-form (simple, expanded, universal, or money; relative or equivalent), or even that it has a certain particular value-form (e.g. a coat, iron). This is because, for each of these social forms, there is a multitude of physical activities or things that could take that form in a given society. Any one of the mass of useful products available in a society can take the price-form, for example, and any labour that produces one of those products can take the form of abstract labour. So in a given society one can deduce very little about the physical form of an activity or a thing from knowing its social form. In Ilyenkov, by contrast, there is not the same many-to-one relation between physical forms and social forms. Instead there appear to be a vast number of ideal forms such as the "cutting/knife-form", each closely related to a physical form of activities and things. Accordingly in a given society one can deduce a great deal about the physical form of a thing or activity from its ideal form.[53]

Now there is one point at which this divergence between Marx and Ilyenkov disappears. This is in the case of the (equivalent) money-form. For in a given society one *can* deduce the physical form of a commodity by knowing that it has the money-form, since by definition this is a kind of value-form which is bound up with a particular kind of physical thing. So in this one case we can say that, in a given society, the physical form of a thing and its social form are mutually determining (that one can deduce either from the other), as they are in general in Ilyenkov.[54]

This parallel between the entanglement of physical and social form in Marx's money-form and Ilyenkov's ideal form of things is really only a result of interpreting the latter as a generalisation of the former in the way that I have done, so it should not come as a surprise. Nevertheless it has several important consequences.

Firstly, the fact that this parallel holds only between Marx's money-form and Ilyenkov's ideal form of things, and not elsewhere between Marx's and Ilyenkov's social forms, helps to explain Ilyenkov's failure, noted above, to point out that the form of labour which constitutes commodities as having the value-form is a social rather than a physical form of labour. The entanglement of social and physical form that obtains in the case of Marx's money-form sets it apart not only from the other kinds of value-form but also from the form of abstract labour. The form of abstract labour is not closely connected with its physical form in the way that the ideal form of an activity and its physical form are, on the view proposed here, for Ilyenkov. So here there is an important disanalogy between Marx's account of the value-form and abstract labour and Ilyenkov's account of ideal forms. Wanting to present his account so that Marx's could be seen as one particular instance of it, Ilyenkov needed to gloss over this difference. This, I suggest, can explain his silence on the fact that the form of labour that constitutes commodities as having the value-form is a "specifically social form", not a physical form, of labour.

Secondly, the entanglement of ideal and physical forms in the present interpretation of Ilyenkov's ideal forms clarifies the difference between this interpretation and the "constitution by social relations" interpretation described above. Clearly there is some similarity between these two interpretations. In each case ideal forms are in some sense "socially constituted". The central difference, though, is that in the "constitution by social relations" interpretation the existence of social relations (i.e. forms of social activity) is taken for granted, and these social relations are then taken to constitute the ideal forms of things. By contrast in the present interpretation the ideal forms of human activities do not exist independently of the ideal forms of the things which are used in those activities. Rather, an ideal form of activity can realise itself only through the corresponding ideal form of things. An activity can properly realise itself as cutting only through the use of a knife, even though a thing can only be a knife by virtue of its suitability for cutting. There is an interdependence here which is not present in the "constitution by social relations" interpretation. So when we say that ideal forms are "socially constituted", we mean not that the ideal forms of things are constituted by forms of social activity that are independent of them. Rather, the ideal forms of *both* things and activities are constituted in conjunction with each other by the overall process of interaction between humans, nature and other humans. Here "society" must be understood as this process in its entirety (it must be understood, as it were, "ecologically"), whereas in the "constitution by social relations" interpretation it is understood simply as an interaction between humans.

The interdependence of the ideal form of the thing and the ideal form of the correlative activity helps to explain why these forms have to be bound up closely with the respective physical forms of thing and activity. In the "constitution by social relations" interpretation they do not need to be so bound up. Because the existence and stability of the form of social activity is taken for granted, it can impose an ideal form onto a thing that may have very little connection with its physical form, as the example of the "gift-form" illustrates. This form can be associated with a very wide range of physical things: all the kinds of things one can give as gifts. By contrast, when an ideal form of activity (such as cutting) can realise itself only through the corresponding ideal form of things, then the ideal and physical form of the thing must be much more closely connected. For in order to be able to engage in cutting one must be able to identify the kind of thing that cutting uses, and to identify it in advance of beginning to cut with it. And for this to be possible, the ideal form of the thing must be closely bound up with its physical form, so that the former can be recognised from the latter. It is as if giving could only be realised through the fact that the thing given had, independently of the fact of its being given, a particular physical form. To put it metaphorically, the ideal forms of activities have to be "anchored" by the correlative ideal forms of things, through those ideal forms being closely bound up with their physical forms.[55] Since this is not the case with giving, it follows that on the present view the "gift-form" is not an example of what Ilyenkov means by an ideal form.

Thirdly, because of the way that the physical and ideal forms of things are bound up in this interpretation of Ilyenkov's ideal forms, I believe that it can account, as the "constitution by social relations" interpretation cannot, for the centrality of the idea of "representing other things" in Ilyenkov's view of the ideal. To revert to the example of knives, it could be said that a knife "represents" all other knives in a way that a gift does not represent all other gifts, and a leaf does not represent all other leaves. For in a particular thing that has the knife-form that form shows up in its physical characteristics, in its possession of a reasonably sharp blade, a handle of the right kind of size and shape, and so on. By virtue of those characteristics, the thing, simply as a physical object, presents itself to us, as members of a society characterised by the cutting/knife-form, as something that can be used for cutting. It "represents" cutting. But thereby it also presents itself as a substitute for any other knife, in that one could cut with it instead of with another knife. So in a sense, as this physical object, it "points to" or "represents" every other knife, and thus even "knifehood" as such. By contrast a gift, as a physical object, does not represent every other gift, because its properties as a physical object do not single it out as a gift.[56] But equally a leaf does not (in our society) represent all other leaves, because although its physical properties do single it out as a leaf there is no standard form of activity in that society with respect to which, as so singled out, it presents itself as a substitute for them. It is the entanglement of social form and physical form in the knife, absent in the case of both the gift and the leaf, that enables it to "represent". A particular knife, through its ideal form, represents other things with that form, and thus that form itself, as well as the form of activity with which all those things are correlated. Indeed, this roughly matches the way in which the money-commodity, through its money-form, represents all the other commodities for which it can be exchanged, and thus the value-form that is common to them all, as well as the form of abstract labour which is common to the labour that has produced each of those commodities.[57]

Fourthly, the parallel between Marx's money-form and Ilyenkov's ideal forms can be taken beyond the mere fact that in both social form and physical form are bound up together, in the sense that can each be deduced from the other. For in Marx this binding is a consequence of a process whereby a social form (the universal equivalent form) of things, which initially has no particular relation to the physical form of those things, gradually "moulds" that physical form in its own image. For this form tends to attach itself to the kind of thing whose physical properties suit the ideal form, such as gold or silver, and to physically transform the thing to which it attaches itself, as when gold is coined in order to serve its function as money-commodity better. This "real subsumption" of physical form by social form is one which Marx in his theory of value describes only in the case of the money-form, although elsewhere he describes a similar moulding of the physical form of labour by the social form of labour-employed-by-capital, which is a development of the form of abstract labour.[58] But something akin to such a "real subsumption" is characteristic of Ilyenkov's ideal forms in general, as they have been interpreted here. The cutting/knife-form, for example, continually moulds individual actions and also individual things so as to bring them into conformity with that form, through the processes of imitation and correction mentioned above as applied to the activities of cutting and of making, repairing, and preserving knives. It is true that Ilyenkov does not talk of individual actions and things becoming progressively more adequate to their ideal forms over time, but it would be quite natural for him to extend his account in this way. If he did then here again a feature that is specific to the money-form in Marx would become one common to the ideal forms of things in general in Ilyenkov.[59]

Finally, it has already been mentioned that for Marx the interconnection of physical form and value-form in the case of the money-form, and the close connection of this form with the form of abstract labour, leads not only to what I have called "physical fetishism" but also to a reverse kind of fetishism, "relations fetishism", and that Ilyenkov thinks that philosophers make analogous errors in their efforts to define the ideal as just the form of a thing or just as the form of an activity. Recognising that for Ilyenkov in a similar way the ideal form and the physical form of a thing are interconnected, and the ideal form of a thing is connected with that of the correlated activity, helps us to see how he can generalise Marx's notion of fetishism in order to turn it against philosophers who have rival concepts of the ideal. Such a generalisation can also be turned against interpretations of Ilyenkov's own concept of the ideal. Ilyenkov himself clearly thinks of his positivist opponents as falling prey to a certain kind of physical fetishism in their attempts to identify the ideal with brain events: this is "a fetishism of nervous tissue, of neurones, axons and DNA" (DI, 218; CI, 97).[60] But equally it may not be too far-fetched to suggest that the "constitution by social relations" interpretation of Ilyenkov's concept of the ideal falls prey to the reverse kind of fetishism, relations fetishism. Here this can remain only a suggestion, for a proper investigation of Ilyenkov's conception of fetishism is beyond the scope of this article.

To sum up, this investigation of Ilyenkov's account of the ideal as a generalisation of Marx's value theory has led to the conclusion that this generalisation focuses on the relation of mutual dependence between abstract labour and the money-form, a mutual dependence which is reproduced in the relation between the ideal forms of activities and the correlated ideal forms of things in Ilyenkov. A further conclusion is that the specific kind of entanglement between social form and physical form that characterises the money-form also characterises Ilyenkov's ideal forms in general. The interpretation of Ilyenkov's ideal that results differs substantially from the "constitution by social relations" interpretation which at first sight suggests itself, but it is one that can make sense of a number of things that Ilyenkov says about the ideal, as well as about Marx. In particular, it can explain the strong connection he asserts between the ideal and the idea of representation. Needless to say, it is an interpretation that would require much more elaboration in order for us to ask whether it can provide the foundations of a genuinely social account of mind.

Notes

[1] I am grateful to Chris Arthur and Joseph McCarney for comments on an earlier draft of this paper.

[2] The article originally appeared in 1979 as *Problema ideal'nogo* (The Problem of the Ideal), and was reprinted in 1991 as *Dialektika ideal'nogo* (The Dialectic of the Ideal). I have used the German translation by G. Richter of the latter as *Dialektik des Ideellen* (Iljenkow 1994, referred to here as DI). In translating Richter's German into English I have been closely guided by the partial English translation of the article by R. Daglish as *The Concept of the Ideal,* which was published before the full article appeared in Russian (Ilyenkov 1977a, referred to here as CI).

[3] Of course this is not to deny the influence of other antecedents, most obviously of Hegel's account of "objective spirit", in the formation of Ilyenkov's concept of the ideal.

[4] The Marx quotation is from *Capital* Volume 1 (MEW 23, 110; Marx 1976a,189). Unless otherwise mentioned, passages from *Capital* are from the fourth edition, on which MEW 23 and Marx 1976a are based. However in the passages cited in this article there are no significant differences between the second, third and fourth editions (what I call the "later editions"). In the present instance Ilyenkov quotes from Marx in the original German, but where he quotes in Russian Richter reproduces Marx's original German text. In translating Marx's German into English for this article I have used the standard translations listed in the bibliography as guides.

[5] It is important to see that the value relation itself involves an "expression", albeit of a non-linguistic kind, of a commodity's value. This "expression" is itself expressed linguistically when that relation is described in a value expression. This may explain why Marx does not distinguish as clearly as I have here between a value relation and the value expression that describes it.

[6] Ilyenkov quotes only the last three sentences of the paragraph, beginning "As use-value..." (DI, 199; CI, 85). I have reproduced the whole paragraph so as to make Marx's sense clearer and to serve as a basis for the following discussion.

[7] Marx typically identifies the commodity's status as a use-value with its status as a physical object: for him the "existence of the commodity as a use-value coincides with its natural palpable existence" (MEW 13, 15; Marx 1970, 27).

[8] "Same" and "sameness" in the quotation from Marx translate *gleich* and *Gleichheit*. It seems clear that the sameness or identity that Marx has in mind is qualitative identity (having the same qualities, as have two identical twins) rather than numerical identity (being the very same thing, as are the Morning Star and the Evening Star). A few sentences later he says that the linen "as value-thing, is as like [*gleich*] the coat as one egg is to another" (MEW 23, 67; Marx 1976a, 144).

[9] Marx makes the distinction between the form and magnitude of value most clearly in the first edition of *Capital*. See MEGA II.5, 630-1; Marx 1978, 137. NB The

expression "a coat" should be understood as having the broad sense of "an unspeci-
fied number of coats exactly like the one in question'. If the linen's value were to
double or triple, its value would have a different magnitude, but would still have the
form of "a coat" in this broad sense.

[10] Cf. Inwood (1992, 108): "In aesthetics, the *Form* of a work of art is its perceptible outer appearance [...] in contrast to its inner content".

[11] Hegel distinguishes between form as counterposed to content *(Inhalt)* and form
as counterposed to matter *(Materie)*, in a way that corresponds roughly to the distinction made here, in his *Science of Logic* (Hegel 1986, 88–95; 1969, 450–6) .

[12] Note that this totality of physical characteristics does not include the coat's number (the fact that it is one coat rather than two or three). It might have been more
consistent for Marx to define the form of the linen's value as including both the
physical characteristics and the number of the coat, since surely the linen's value is
expressed in both of these together. As so defined, the form of the linen's value
would include its magnitude, rather than being contrasted to it. However I follow
Marx's terminology on this point.

[13] Grammatically, the difference is that in the attributive sense of the phrase "the
value-form of the linen" the word "form" modifies "value" (giving the meaning
"the form of the value of the linen"), whereas in the predicative sense "value" modifies "form" (giving the meaning "the value-kind of form of the linen"). The distinction can be marked, in English or German, by using "form of value" *(Form des
Werts)* for the attributive sense and "value-form" *(Wertform)* for the predicative, but
Marx almost invariably uses the latter term even when an attributive sense is clearly
present, and I have preferred to follow his usage in my translations and commentary,
preserving the double sense of "value-form" that this involves. The terminology of
"attributive" and "predicative" is borrowed from Geach (1976), who uses it to make
a somewhat analogous distinction.

[14] So the relation between the value-form (in the predicative sense) and the physical
form of a commodity can in fact be thought of as a relation between superimposed
form and indifferent matter, on the model of the form and matter of a statue. This
form-and-matter sense of "form" always lurks in the background when the predicative sense of the term "value-form" is in play. But see note 54 below.

[15] It looks as if Marx should have said "in the value relation" here, as he did in the
later editions (MEW 23, 66; Marx 1976a, 143, quoted above). See note 5 above.

[16] See section 2 of Marx's *Wage-Labour and Capital* (MEW 6, 402–407; CW 9,
205–215).

[17] However the definition of value given here does presuppose that there is *some*
process that, over time, pushes the actual quantities of other commodities for which
a commodity is exchanged towards the "normal" level that constitutes its value-
magnitude. Likewise with regard to its value-form. If the actual ratios in which a
commodity was exchanged for others varied completely randomly over time, then
that commodity would not have a value as the term is defined here.

[18] Marx calls them simply different value-forms, since he does not make the terminological distinction that I make here between a particular value-form (e.g. a coat, iron, or corn) and a kind of value-form (i.e. simple, expanded, universal or money).

[19] Strictly speaking the equivalent-forms are not "value-forms", since in the relevant value relation the value of the equivalent commodity is not expressed, i.e. its value does not have a form. However if the value relation is thought of as reversible, so that if A is worth B this entails that B is also worth A (and Marx implies from the start that this is the case by using the "=" sign to stand for "is worth") then every value relation does "indirectly" give a form to the value of the equivalent, and in this sense it can be said that the equivalent-forms are value-forms.

[20] Marx's own terminology is not always consistent, but it broadly conforms to that adopted here.

[21] Cf. MEGA II.5, 38; Marx 1976b, 29, where Marx uses "value-form" and "form of exchangeability" as equivalent terms.

[22] Marx goes so far as to speak of a commodity's relation with that other commodity in which its value is expressed as "haunting" the head of the commodity (MEW 23, 110; Marx 1976a, 189).

[23] For another example, see DI, 205; CI, 89.

[24] In his 1962 encyclopaedia article *Ideal'noe* (The Ideal), an amended version of which is translated as essay 8 of his *Dialectical Logic*, Ilyenkov's treatment of the value-form as an example of ideality focuses almost exclusively on the (equivalent) money-form. There he says that the money-commodity is transformed "into the *representative of any other body* [...] In other words, it is the *external embodiment of another thing*, not [of] its sensuously perceived image but rather [of] *its essence*, i.e. the *law* of its existence within the system" (Ilyenkov 1977b, 272).

[25] In what follows, I shall take it that when Marx and Ilyenkov refer to social relations between people they have in mind "interactional relations", that is, ones that consist in each case of two or more individuals thinking of and acting towards each other in a certain standard pattern of complementary ways over some period of time. Examples apart from market exchange would be friendship, vassalage and democracy. "Social practices" captures roughly the same idea, although it does not carry the same implication of complementarity. Such relations are of a different kind from the "relations between things" that Ilyenkov refers to in the quotation above, namely value relations, which consist simply in one commodity being worth a certain amount of another. Marx typically uses *Beziehung* for the former kind of relation and *Verhältnis* for the latter (or for the former in so far as it is realised through the latter).

[26] DI has "*vergesellschaftete*" (socialised) here, but given the context this looks like a mistake for "*vergegenständlichte*" (objectified). This would allow Ilyenkov to be making exactly parallel points about value and the value-form in the passage. CI has "reified" in both places.

27 Cf. a passage shortly before this one, where Ilyenkov says that in *Capital* the value-form is the reified form of "labour, as physical human labour transforming the physical body of nature" (DI, 207–208; CI, 91).

28 The equivalent passage in the second edition is at MEW 23, 86–87; Marx 1976a, 164–165, culminating in the assertion that in the value-relation, "It is nothing but the definite social relation between men themselves which assumes here, for them, the fantastic form of a relation between things".

29 The account of abstract labour in the following paragraphs follows that given in the 1920s by the Soviet economist I.I. Rubin (Rubin 1973, 13–158). See also Arthur 1979. To substantiate the account I rely, as does Rubin, on Marx's *Contribution to the Critique of Political Economy* and the first edition of *Capital*. It is clear from his terminology and examples that Ilyenkov was familiar with both of these texts of Marx's. I am not aware of whether he knew Rubin's work.

30 Marx himself sometimes, as in this quotation, uses the term "social character" to mean what I have called "social character in general" (and from now on call just "social character'), but sometimes to mean what I have called "specific social character'. It is usually clear from the context which he has in mind.

31 Marx calls abstract human labour a "specific social form" of labour at MEGA II.5, 41; Marx 1976b, 32, quoted below. It is worth noticing that the term "social form of labour" can also be read in an attributive sense, to mean "form of the sociality of labour" (as opposed to the form of some other feature it has), as well as in a predicative sense, to mean "social form of labour itself" (as opposed to its physical form). The transition from the attributive to the predicative sense is legitimate if labour is thought of as essentially social. In this article I use the term in the predicative sense.

32 In my exposition of the value-form and the form of abstract labour I follow Marx in initially conceiving the market as one in which individuals sell the products of their own labour (see MEW 23, 123; Marx 1976a, 203). Marx's view is that in its fully developed form the market becomes a capitalist market, in which the roles of producer and seller are divided between wage-labourer and capitalist, but this development does not substantially affect the concepts of value-form or abstract labour.

33 This realisation is connected to the realisation, described above, of the product as a value, although the present realisation is accomplished in time by the act of sale, whereas that one was brought about logically by the fact of exchangeability.

34 Here Marx reconciles the concept of "alienated labour" which was central to his 1844 writings with that of "social relations of production", the key concept of his later theory of history. For abstract labour is the successor-concept to alienated labour.

35 No doubt those properties will include intentional as well as behavioural ones, but I shall not go into that here.

36 Marx attempted to highlight this point in the later editions of *Capital* by defining labour's property of being abstract labour in contrast to its property of being "concrete labour", i.e. of being labour that produces use-values (MEW 23, 61; Marx 1976a, 137). Unfortunately this conflates the distinction between labour's specific social form and its physical form with a distinction between the property of being labour as such and the property of being labour of a particular physical form. The result has been a persistent failure in readers of Marx to recognise that abstract labour is a specific social form of labour.

37 Such a generalisation of Marx's account of the value-form is suggested by Anton 1974, from whom I have taken the example of a gift. Anton presents his suggestion in terms of "constitutive rules", rules which state what one has to do, for example, for one's action to count as giving, or for the object of the action to count as a gift. But I take it that a constitutive rule is itself simply a formulation of the internal structure of a social relation (or, in Anton's terminology, of a social practice). To be understood properly, Anton's article needs to be read in conjunction with chapter 8 of Austin 1962.

38 It is the interpretation which I believe David Bakhurst adopts in his account of Ilyenkov's ideal, the most substantive to have appeared in English (Bakhurst 1991, 175–215). Despite my differences with it, I am greatly indebted to Bakhurst's account.

39 In the light of the above discussion, from Ilyenkov's point of view Marx should really have said "an ideal or representing form". At points like this a tension becomes apparent between Ilyenkov's conception of the ideal and the more conventional way in which Marx himself uses the word.

40 Bakhurst (1991, 182–183) recognises that for Ilyenkov the ideal intrinsically involves representation, but construes this exclusively as a matter of the representation of a form of human activity.

41 Whether Ilyenkov is correct in attributing his own meaning of the word "ideal" to Marx and Hegel as well is a question that can be left aside here. What matters is how Ilyenkov himself understands the word.

42 Cf. the corresponding passage in *The Ideal* (Ilyenkov 1977b, 264–265), and the abbreviated forms of this characterisation of the ideal at DI, 201 (CI 87) and DI, 209 (a passage not included in CI). It should be noticed that in the present quotation Ilyenkov alternates between using "ideal form" in a predicative sense (the ideal form of the thing or activity, as opposed to its physical form) and in an attributive sense (the form of the ideality of the thing or activity) in this passage. Normally he uses "ideal form" in the predicative sense.

43 The idea that self-realisation and self-expression are interconnected in Hegel's thought is a central theme of Taylor 1975. See especially chapter 3.

44 Marx comes close to expressing this mutual dependency when he describes the related mutual dependency of abstract labour and exchange, saying that "on the one hand commodities must enter the exchange process as objectified universal labour

time, on the other hand the objectification of the labour time of the individual as universal is itself only a product of the exchange process" (MEW 13, 32; Marx 1970, 45). Here he includes a quantitative dimension from which I have abstracted. For a discussion of the mutual dependency of abstract labour and exchange see Rubin 1973, 148–151. For its original formulation by James Steuart, the 18th century economist whom Marx described as the first person to identify, with his term "industry", the concept of abstract labour (MEGA II.5, 43; Marx 1970, 58), see Steuart 1966, book 2 chapter 1, "Of the reciprocal connection between trade and industry".

[45] "Activity" in the generic sense (the sense in which Ilyenkov uses it) means continuing or repeated human action in general. "An activity" means a particular kind of such generic activity. By "the standard activity of cutting" I mean the kind of cutting that one normally does with knives (although one could also do it with a ruler or one's finger), as opposed to the kinds of cutting that one normally does with scissors, axes or one's teeth. By "cutting" in what follows I mean this kind of cutting.

[46] If this is doubted as a matter of empirical fact we could make it an analytical claim by defining a society as a group of people who sustain more or less unified forms of activity and of the things used in those forms of activity.

[47] What if someone taught themselves to cut for the first time, and then passed the trick onto others? Then we would have to talk of the form of cutting coming into existence in that society.

[48] See DI, 186 (CI, 78) and DI, 206 – 207 (CI, 90).

[49] In *The Ideal* Ilyenkov apparently uses the term "ideal image" (which is dropped in *The Problem of the Ideal*) as an alternative to "ideal form" when he wants to emphasise the normative dimension of the ideal. For example, "the individual realisation of the ideal image is always linked with some deviation or other, or rather with concretisation of the image, with its correcting in accordance with specific conditions, new social needs, the peculiarities of the material, and so on" (Ilyenkov 1977b, 281). The connection between Ilyenkov and Plato is especially apparent in such passages.

[50] The case of celestial navigation is especially important, since here there can be no process whereby the thing is shaped so that it matches its ideal form. So here the form of activity can "express" itself in the ideal form of the thing only in the sense that it selects certain independently existing features of the thing which are relevant to the activity and treats those as the essence of the thing. For some comments by Ilyenkov on this case, see DI, 221 (CI, 97) and Ilyenkov 1977b, 256–267.

[51] Cf. DI, 219 (CI, 97) and Ilyenkov 1977b, 284–285. Clearly a great deal here will depend on whether we can make sense of a social form like the cutting/knife-form acting as a "norm" independently of the "consciousness and will" (in Ilyenkov's understanding of those terms) of the individuals whose actions and artefacts take that form.

[52] In a similar way, if an utterance is made in the course of a conversation in English then, given the current state of the English language and the particular context of the utterance, the physical characteristics of the utterance will determine its meaning. If its physical characteristics were changed then its meaning would change, too. Yet outside a linguistic system the utterance would not have any meaning at all.

[53] Ilyenkov never tells us what the criteria are for individuating ideal forms, but they appear to be fairly fine-grained. He in effect gives "bread" and "house" as examples at Ilyenkov 1977b, 276. However, since he also suggests that ideal forms are the real ground of Kant's categories (DI, 189–190; CI, 79–80; Ilyenkov 1977b, 283), he appears committed to the existence of a hierarchy of forms. Thus "bread" and "house" would be sub-forms of a higher-order form such as "product'. The determination of physical form by ideal form could not hold for such higher-order forms.

[54] To the extent that physical form determines social form, and especially to the extent that this determination becomes mutual, the possibility of conceiving the relation of social form to physical form as a relation of superimposed form to indifferent matter recedes and disappears (see note 14 above). It should be added here that to speak of a "mutual determination" of physical and social form when the social context is *given* is not to deny the fundamental asymmetry between the two forms: namely that a thing's social form exists only by virtue of its social context whereas it has its physical form whether or not it is in that context.

[55] I have implicitly suggested here that the same thing holds in reverse, i.e. that the ideal form of an activity needs to be closely bound up with its physical form, in order for it to "anchor" the ideal form of the thing. It would take a further argument to substantiate this. The line of thought of the last two paragraphs was suggested to me by some remarks made by H.-G. Backhaus in criticism of a "constitution by social relations" interpretation of Marx's value-form (Backhaus 1980, 115–116).

[56] What if it is something clearly manufactured to be a gift, for example in that it has "Greetings from Helsinki" emblazoned on it? This aspect of its physical form may suit it to being made into a gift, but it does not constitute it as a gift, whereas the physical form alone of a thing is enough (in the right society) to make a thing a knife.

[57] See again the quotation from Ilyenkov in note 24 above.

[58] See the relevant sections of his *Results of the Immediate Process of Production* (Marx 1976a, 1023–1038). The term "real subsumption" comes from this text.

[59] At this point it is worth mentioning that a likely philosophical inspiration for Marx's notion of real subsumption, in which the physical form of labour is remoulded so that it becomes an adequate expression of its social form, is Hegel's description of the process whereby some part of objective reality becomes the adequate expression of its concept, and that Hegel's term for the resulting unity is "the idea". For Hegel, "the idea is the unity of the concept and objectivity" (Hegel 1986, 464; Hegel 1969, 756).

60 Here the error lies not in identifying ideal form with the physical form of the thing used in activity but in identifying it with the physical form of the brain of the actor, so the analogy with Marx's physical fetishism is somewhat loose. But Ilyenkov shows that he thinks it is valid by immediately comparing this error with the error of thinking that a diamond that has not yet been discovered has a value by virtue of its physical characteristics (DI, 218; CI, 97).

Bibliography

Anton, A. (1974), *Commodities and Exchange: Notes for an Interpretation of Marx*. In: *Philosophy and Phenomenological Research*, 34, 355-385.

Arthur, C. (1979), *Dialectics and Labour.* In: *Issues in Marxist Philosophy*, vol. 1: *Dialectics and Method*, eds. J. Mepham and D.-H. Ruben. Brighton.

Austin, J.L. (1962), *How to do Things with Words*. Oxford.

Backhaus, H.-G. (1980), *On the Dialectics of the Value-Form.* In: *Thesis Eleven*, 1.

Bakhurst, D. (1991), *Consciousness and Revolution in Soviet Philosophy: From the Bolsheviks to Evald Ilyenkov*. Cambridge.

Geach, P.T. (1976), *Good and Evil.* In: *Theories of Ethics*, ed. P. Foot. Oxford, 64–73.

Hegel, G.W.F. (1969), *The Science of Logic*, tr. A.V. Miller. London.

Hegel, G.W.F. (1986), *Werke*. Band 6: *Wissenschaft der Logik II*. Frankfurt-am-Main.

Ilyenkov, E.V. (1977a), *The Concept of the Ideal.* In: *Philosophy in the USSR: Problems of Dialectical Materialism*. Moscow, 71–99 (partial translation by R. Daglish of *Problema ideal'nogo*, in: *Voprosy Filosofii*, 1979, 6, 128–140 and 7, 145–158) [CI]

Ilyenkov, E.V. (1977b), *Dialectical Logic: Essays on is History and Theory*. Moscow.

Iljenkov, E.V. (1994), *Dialektik des Ideellen.* In: *Dialektik des Ideellen. Ausgewälte Aufsätze*. Münster, 154-223 (translation by G. Richter of *Dialektika ideal'nogo*, in: *Filosofia i Kultura*, ed. A.G. Novochatko. Moskva, 1991, 229-270, which reprints *Problema ideal'nogo,* in: *Voprosy Filosofii*, 6, 128-140 and 7, 145-158) [DI]

Inwood, M. (1992), *A Hegel Dictionary*. Oxford.

Marx, K. and Engels, F. (1956–), [MEW] *Werke*. Berlin.

Marx, K. and Engels, F., 1983–, [MEGA] *Gesamtausgabe*. Berlin.

Marx, K. and Engels, F. (1975–), [CW] *Collected Works*. London.

Marx, K. (1970), *Contribution to the Critique of Political Economy*. Moscow.

Marx, K. (1976a), *Capital*, volume 1, tr. B. Fowkes. Harmondsworth.

Marx, K. (1976b), *The Commodity* (chapter 1 of the first edition of *Capital* volume 1). In: *Value: Studies by Marx*, tr. A. Dragstedt. London, 7–70

Marx, K. (1978), The Value-form (appendix to the first edition of *Capital* volume 1). *Capital and Class*, 4, 130-150.

Oittinen, V. (2000), *Iljenkow, Kant und die Dinge an sich.* [In the present volume]

Oittinen, V. (1992), *Aporien des Ideellen. Zur Dialektik-Konzeption Ewald Iljenkows*. In: *Dialektik*, 1992, 1, 141–149.

Rubin, I.I. (1973), *Essays on Marx's Theory of Value*. Montreal.

Steuart, J. (1966), *An Inquiry into the Principles of Political Economy*, 2 vols., ed. A.S. Skinner, Edinburgh

Taylor, C. (1975), *Hegel.* Cambridge.

16

ILYENKOV AND THE LOGIC OF *CAPITAL*

PERTTI HONKANEN

1 Marx, Hegel and Ricardo

It may well be appropriate, as we are in Helsinki, to begin with a famous quotation from *Flüchtlingsgespräche* by Bertolt Brecht. The play is set at one of the restaurants in the nearby railway station. It is there that Ziffel, a refugee, and Kalle, a Finnish worker, meet and end up discussing various issues. At one point, Ziffel, talking about Marxism, brings up in passing the issue of "inferior Marxism without Hegel or lacking Ricardo etc" (Brecht 1990, 83). This may serve as a preliminary starting point in classifying various trends and schools in Marxist thinking. There is Marxism without Hegel and Ricardo, with Hegel but without Ricardo, and finally without Hegel but with Ricardo. It is, indeed, not so easy to find Marxism with both Hegel and Ricardo.

The relation to Ricardo or Hegel can often be seen as a dividing line between philosophical and economical interpretations of Marx's work. Economists are, of course, more acquainted with Ricardo while philosophers are at home with Hegel. Personally, I am more of an economist than a philosopher, and I am therefore looking at Marxism above all from the viewpoint of the economic theory of capitalism.

The Hegel/Ricardo-duality also reflects the duality of qualitative and quantitative analysis in Marx's economic theory. As we speak about the substance of economic categories and their interrelations, we end up discussing about Marx's dialectics and Hegel's impact on it. On the other hand, when a Marxist economist considers the capitalist economy as a system of quantitative relations, he soon forgets Hegel and finds much in common with the Ricardian deductive way of thinking.

In my opinion it is justified to say that the Marxism of the II International, the Kautskyan Marxism, was Marxism without Hegel and without Ricardo. At the time there was very little interest in studying the method of *Capital*. Essential manuscripts and drafts by Marx were not known. Mathematical economics generally was only just emerging, and more so when we speak of Marxian economics or other schools outside the mainstream.

Gronow (1986, 14) notes that the Kautskyan Marxism "neglected almost totally the analysis of the value form of a commodity and of labour power, and consequently its theoretical position can be claimed to be closer to classical political economy than to Marx's critique of it". This may be an exaggeration, but I agree with the idea that there was a tendency to interpret Marx's *Capital* in a left-Ricardian spirit. But even the Ricardian way of thinking was at a fairly primitive stage compared to modern mathematical analysis.

Nowadays the picture is very different. The publication of *Grundrisse* and other manuscripts have given an impetus for studying the genesis and the method of Marx's *Capital*. This line of research flourished in the 1970s, and the works of Reichelt (1973), Rosdolsky (1972), and Zelený (1972) are known to a generation of students. In addition, many economists have used linear and matrix algebra as tools in the investigation of Marxian economics, especially the theory of value and growth. The neo-Ricardian theory of Piero Sraffa gave a strong inspiration to this line of research. There are attempts to integrate the Sraffian and Marxian frameworks of analysis (e.g. Abraham-Frois 1979). Today we can "choose" between different interpretations and reconstructions of Marxian theory of capitalism. Besides, there are Hegelian or even super-Hegelian interpretations of the *Capital*. For example the "capital-logics" school has underlined the importance of Marx's analysis of value form and the dialectical method of Marx (see Backhaus 1995). There are many other books and articles on Marx's method acknowleding and analysing the Hegelian contribution to it (e.g. Murray 1988, Smith 1998). The discussions go beyond the problem of value form into the entire structure of Marx' *Capital*. So Arthur (1998) stresses important parallels between the Hegelian logic and the concepts of the second volume of *Capital* investigating the circulation of capital.

On the other hand, the interpretation of Marxian value theory in the form of linear equations or matrix algebra generally leads to completely ignoring or even rejecting the dialectics and the Hegelian roots of Marx's method. It is openly Marxism without Hegel but with Ricardo. And even if the method and the way of thinking is not mathematical, there is some research explicitly rejecting the Hegelian dialectics. An example of this line of reasoning is the so-called analytical Marxism. Elster claims that Marx's views of Hegelian origin "are of little or no intrinsic interest" and that "the dialectical method can be stated in ordinary 'analytical' language" (Elster 1985, 4, 37). Rosenthal goes further still arguing bluntly that the presence of the Hegelian formulae in *Capital* "has absolutely nothing to do with any adoption on Marx's part of a 'dialectical method'" (Rosenthal 1998, x) and that "the actual scientific discourse of *Capital* must be quite free to any distinctively Hegelian aspect" (37).

In general, the "mathematical school" of Marxian economics has much in common with the neo-Ricardian or Sraffian line in economics. The Grand Lady of (post-)Keynesian thought, Joan Robinson, ridiculed the "Hegelian stuff and nonsense" (Robinson 1973, 265) in Marxism. This apparently is – consciously or unconsciously – the guiding line for many of those who are at present trying to give a mathematical form to Marxian theory of value and reproduction. This has important consequences, as it is very difficult – or impossible – to develop the Marxian economic categories in the framework of pure deductive models. They are simply taken as given in mathematical constructions. A characteristic feature of these studies is ordinarily the neglect of any monetary theory.

As to Soviet Marxism, studying the relation of Marx and Hegel was, of course, legitimate in view of the well-known advice given by Lenin in his *Philosophical Notebooks*: it is necessary to study the whole of Hegel's *Logic* in order to fully grasp Marx's *Capital*. But the publication of these notebooks only began in 1929. Lenin himself claimed in the notebook aphorism that so far no Marxist had really understood Marx. The realisation of Lenin's advice is quite another thing than its publication, and the atmosphere in the Stalinist period – at least until 1950s – was not favourable to creative thinking.

On the other hand, the contribution of Soviet (and GDR-) Marxism to the mathematical formulation of Marxian economic theory was fairly modest. Quaas (1992, 131) even characterises the relation of many scholars in the GDR to the mathematical formulation of economic problems as "hostile". The mathematical formulation of the theory of value was discovered in the West, and it was there that heated discussions on the "transformation problem" (transformation of values into prices of production) took place. So the

"Ricardian" influence on Soviet Marxism was slight. In general, it may be possible to classify the Soviet Marxism as Marxism *more* with Hegel and *less* with Ricardo.

Due to ideological differences Soviet Marxism and Western academic Marxism developed in relative isolation. There were not many connections. As to political economy, the works of Western scholars were in the Soviet literature usually subsumed into the heading of "left radicalism" or "revisionism". It was only during the "perestroika", we could witness the emergence of a somewhat softened and more differentiated attitudes.[1] But equally the Western research usually ignored the Soviet studies irrespective of their validity.

2) Logical and Historical

Evald Ilyenkov's work *Dialektika abstraktnogo i konkretnogo v "Kapitale" Marksa* is an exception to the rule. It was translated into many languages, and it is cited in many studies on Marx's method. Even now Ilyenkov's book is regarded as an early and original contribution to the study of Marx's method. The fact that it is not saturated with the liturgy to typical to Soviet literature. Quaas (1992, 28) notes that even 30 years after its publication, the work is inspiring. He, however, criticises it for overestimating the dialectics of abstract and concrete in the whole system of Marxian dialectics.

Next I shall concentrate on the relation between the logical and the historical in Marx's *Capital*. Ilyenkov touches upon this topic in the fourth chapter of the shortened version, and in the fifth chapter of the original, uncensored version of his book *Dialektika abstraktnogo i konkretnogo* (Iljenkow 1976, 200–220; Ilyenkov 1997, 278–300), under the heading "Logical development and abstract historicism". There are no essential differences between the two versions of the chapter.

The debate partly originates in Engels's review of Marx's work *Contribution to the Critique of Political Economy,* and in his annex to the third volume of *Capital*, published by Kautsky after his death. In the *review* Engels sees the logical method as "the historical method, only stripped of the historical form and interfering contingencies" (MEW 13, 475). In the annex Engels sees the transformation of values into prices of production "as not only a purely logical, but also as a historical process, and its reflection in the thought, as the logical succession of its inner connection" (MEW 25, 905). In this annex Engels states that the Marxian law of value is generally valid, so far as economic laws in general are valid, in the whole period of simple commodity production (MEW 25, 909). The annex gives the impression that the first chapters of *Capital* touch only "simple commodity production" and that only thereafter Marx begins the study of truly capitalist production.

So it was Engels who laid down the foundation for the discussion of the logical and the historical in Marx's work. But Engels's formulations are controversial, and the Marx's comments concerning the issue in the *Grundrisse*, are not entirely compatible with them.

These statements give terrain to different interpretations of Marx's *Capital* and the relation of the logical and the historical analysis in it. Especially Engels's annex nourishes the comprehension of *Capital* as a study of different stages of capitalism and the idea, that the object of study in the theory of value formulated in the first chapters of *Capital* is "simple commodity production", not capitalism. This view has been criticised especially by the "capital-logics" school.

In Kautsky's *Marx's Oekonomische Lehren* such an interpretation is present both explicitly and implicitly. Of course, Kautsky's booklet is a popular presentation of Marx's doctrine, and not a methodological study, but we should note the following interesting judgement in the preface of the book: "The *Capital* is an essentially historical work" (*"Das Kapital ist ein wesentlich historisches Werk"*, Kautsky 1906, xi).

It is interesting to find an analogous formulation in a Soviet compendium: "The method of Marx is characterised before all by profound historicism" (Rosenberg 1983, 8). Criticising the "logical" interpretation of *Capital* as one-sided, Chepurenko (1988, 197) admits that the Soviet literature was dominated by the one-sided claim of "historicism" of Marx's method. Consequently there are grounds to classify the orthodox Soviet interpretation of *Capital* more as historical than logical. But it is important to note that also many "Western" explanations of Marx's method are "historical", e. g. the contributions by Paul M. Sweezy, Ronald Meek and Ernest Mandel. Sweezy (1946, 20) for example stresses "the historical character of Marx's thought" in his sketch about Marx's method, and also the title of his work *The Theory of Capitalist Development* puts the emphasis on this aspect of understanding[2] (see discussion in Sekine 1984, 74–76).

But there are interpretations underlining more the logical method than the historicity of Marx's method. The so-called "capital-logics" school is a clear example of this line of thought. Also Althusser rejected "historicism" in Marx' *Capital* (Althusser 1970, ch. 5). In this connection Ilyenkov seems to be an exception among Soviet scholars, because he quite emphatically underlines the logical method: according to him Marx "favoured the logical method of critique and the logical method of looking at the reality" (Iljenkow

1976, 201; Ilyenkov 1997, 279). This statement is strengthened by the comment, that the historical method plays a subordinated, auxiliary role in Marx's critique. (Iljenkow 1976, 204; Ilyenkov 1997, 284.). Of course, he was able to rely on Marx's arguments in the *Grundrisse* to the effect that the sequence of categories in the theory of capital does not follow a historical sequence.

But the problem is not solved when by underlining either the historical or the logical method in Marx's dialectics. What is the interrelation between the logical and the historical in the economic theory of capitalism? And I wish to stress the words "theory of capitalism". When we state that capitalism is a specific historical stage of economic/social formations, or when we demand that different social phenomena must be studied in their historical context, the issue remains unsolved. The fact that Marx studied the history of capitalism and the theoretical history of political economy is not an answer to the question, either. The main issue here is: what is the place of the *history of capitalism* in Marx's *economic theory*, or what is their mutual relationship. Also Ilyenkov is somewhat ambiguous here – or rather he does not formulate the problem in this manner.

In this context we should have a closer look at how Ilyenkov characterises Marx's object of study : "historical inception, development and decline" of capitalist production (Iljenkow 1976, 220; Ilyenkov 1997, 300). These words echo the conventional understanding of Marx's *Capital* as a theory of the *history* of capitalism. The same words we find in Lenin's short article on Marx' theory. "An investigation into the relations of production in a given historically defined society, in their inception, development and decline – such is the content of Marx's economic doctrine." (LPSS 26, 60). We find almost the same expression in a review, cited by Marx in the postscript to the second edition of the *Capital*: "[...] laws that regulate the origin, existence, development, death of a given social organism [...]" (MEW 23, 27).

The conventional view is that Marx's *Capital* contains not only a general theory of capitalist relations of production, but also a theory of the history of capitalism, a theory of its "origin, development and decline", expressed in a familiar way. The difference seems to be only in the emphasis: either the logic of capital or the history of capitalism, and in various ways of explaining their interrelation or unity. According to a common Marxist belief the history of capitalism can be deducted from the logic of capital. In a German polemics of 1970s defending the theory of state-monopoly capitalism, we find the following – in my opinion quite confused – formulation accentuating the unity of logical and historical analysis: "[...] the logical analysis of fundamental structures, necessary connections, relations, laws, categories is in its content, in its substratum always a historical analysis" (Jung 1979, 112).

3) The Uno School

A radical break with this tradition is represented by the Uno school from Japan. Unoists try to formulate on the basis of Marx's theory a logic of pure capitalism, cleaned from all historical features and contingencies. The history of capitalism is quite another field of study, which must be carried on two levels: a theory of the stages of capitalism and the concrete history of capitalism. Unoists see that Marx's essential task was to formulate a pure theory of capitalism, but he was not quite consequent in his work, and consequently Marx's theory is mixed and even confused with various propositions, belonging into the realm of the history of capitalism.

Kozo Uno's (1897–1977) work is not well known outside Japan, but at present he has followers also in the Western academic world.[3] Sekine (1997) has formulated on the basis of Uno's theory a comprehensive theory of capitalist economy with the title *An Outline of the Dialectic of Capital*. The Unoist program is quite ambitious. According to Albritton (1986, 2), he wishes "to present Uno's approach as a complete paradigm, which gives clear and consistent answers to all fundamental issues of Marxist theory". Uno himself calls his solution an "overhauling and complete restatement of *Capital* as a theory of pure capitalism" (Uno 1980, xxvi). The building blocks of the theory are essentially the same as in Marx's theory, but they are rearranged and on many points reinterpreted. Because Sekine builds an explicit analogy with Hegel's *Logic* and the dialectic of capital, the school may be characterised even as "super-Hegelian".[4]

Unoists also criticise a "residue of classical value theory" in Marx's *Capital* (See Itoh 1988, 71). They lay even more stress on the analysis of value-form than the capital-logics school: Sekine's *Dialectic of Capital* begins with a doctrine of circulation, not of production. But he also lays stress on mathematical and deductive formulations of the theory, and there are reasons to evaluate the Unoist theory as Marxism with *very much* of Hegel and *also* with Ricardo.

We may well ask, is it really possible to separate the history of capitalism and the logic of capital (or the theory of pure capitalism)? Such a separation seems justified, because capitalism has universal features and the basic concepts of capitalism seem to reflect a specific totality. Therefore, it is justified to say that there are essential theoretical categories and laws of capitalism which can be formulated disregarding the history of capitalism and its various stages. The Unoists explicitly reject the conception that Marx's theory is a theory of the "inception, development, and decline" of capitalism (see Sekine 1975, 849). On the contrary, they formulate the theory of capitalism as a self-contained theoretical system. They see pure capitalism "in perpetual motion, without beginning or an end" (ibid., 857).

But once we make this separation, we cannot adapt the categories and laws of pure capitalism directly to the history of capitalism. A central thesis of the Unoists is that there is a need for a theory of stages of capitalism mediating between the pure theory and the history of capitalism. The two different levels of analysis should be not mixed, and a third level of analysis – the stage theory – is necessary to mediate between pure theory and concrete history. Uno himself and his followers have outlined the stage theory in an effort to formulate some explicit criteria on how separate the different stages. Accordingly, Albritton defines the mercantilist, liberalist, imperialist and consumerist stages of capitalism (Albritton 1991).

The idea of different stages of capitalism is, of course, not new. Marx himself analysed the peculiarities of manufacturing and large industrial phases of capitalism. There are theories of imperialism and state-monopoly capitalism. Fordism and post-Fordism are popular concepts introduced by the regulation school. The on-going discussion on globalisation can also be seen in this context. But the difficulty lies in defining the connections between the general theory and the stage theory of capitalism – and still more in formulating the general theory. It is not difficult either to detect an obvious defect of the "capital-logics" school: when stressing the logical interpretation of *Capital,* it was not able to find a fruitful way to investigate the concrete reality and the history of capitalism.

Albritton (1986 and 1991) especially criticises the logical-historical interpretation of Marx's *Capital,* considering it as a source of various evils, having in the end led to a deterministic, mechanical and economistic theory of society. He emphasises the incorrectness of the logical-historical method, claiming that the connection between theory and history in it is too close and too direct. "The law of value is either seen as an abstracted history or capitalist history is seen as the concretisation of the law of value. The result is weakened theory, reductionist history or both." (Albritton 1986, 35)

Albritton formulates the problem in a fairly abstract and metaphoric way, the contradiction of value and use-value as starting point. In pure capitalism use-values are idealised, "value is always permitted to be victorious in overcoming use-value obstacles". But at the level of stage theory and concrete history "use values are not so easily tamed". The motion of value only partially subsumes the material reproduction of social life. So labour-power always resists when being commodified. (Albritton 1991, 14, 15 and 1986, 39) The logical-historical method overestimates the capability of value to subdue the use-value obstacles, and even Marx himself is not free from such a tendency. According to Albritton, there need be no presupposition that capital's logic is always in the last instance the determining factor in social life.

Unfortunately, it is not possible to deal in any greater depth with the various aspects of this discussion, but I shall present, as an example, a problem, which I call the "Marxist-feminist dilemma". Some feminist researches have accused Marx's theory of being sexist and patriarchal (see e.g. Barrett 1987). More concretely, they claim that Marx assumed the so-called male-breadwinner model in his economic theory. A closer look reveals that there are passages or gaps in Marx's works, that might justify these accusations. But when the problem is stated in the context of pure theory of capitalism, it can be said that the gender relations belong to the history (and prehistory) of capitalism. The law of value and other categories of pure economic theory are compatible with various forms of sexual relations or family types, also with matriarchy. But in the concrete history of capitalism, specific forms may prevail, and it is the task or concrete studies to analyse them and their interrelations with economic development. The law of value can adapt itself to various family types or gender relations. The general or pure economic theory are not to explain these relations – they belong to the realm of more concrete historical and sociological studies, as do the domestic labour or biological reproduction.[5] The aim here is not to defend apparent defects in Marx's thinking or to underestimate the feminist argumentation but to define more precisely the object of study in a Marxist economic theory.

I would also like to stress the difference between economic theory and sociological theory. If Marx's *Capital* is seen as a general sociological theory, it is asking too much from it. Marx's *Capital* is above all an analysis of economic categories – and so is the Unoist *Dialectic of Capital*. The points of connection – the *interface* in computer language – between general economic theory and specific sociological (or political, socio-political etc.) studies require a very careful definition.

A more familiar problem is the so-called "immiserisation theory" (theory of growing misery) of Marx, more exactly the "general law of capitalist accumulation" formulated in 23rd chapter of the 1st volume of

Capital. It is generally understood as some kind of prophecy by Marx, although also other interpretations of the chapter exist. This understanding is closely connected with the historical interpretation of *Capital:* the law is seen as a proof of the ultimate decline and collapse of capitalism. But the Unoist pure theory of capitalism abstains from such prophecies. The relative surplus population is seen as a part of the cyclical development of capital, but there is no chronic or advancing unemployment on the level of pure theory. The problem of "immiserisation" belongs to the analysis of the history of capitalism, and in Unoist judgement Marx's theory at this point is strongly influenced by the experience of economic development in England in the 19th century.

I would like to call this problem the "breakdown dilemma" in Marxist theory. If the abstract theory postulates a breakdown of capitalism due to economic or social contradictions, it is soon running into difficulties. If the breakdown does not take place, or if we cannot predict its timing, the theory is obviously invalid, and so are the assumptions of the theory. The Unoist theory tries to solve this problem by relegating the breakdown problem to a historical (and philosophical) level of discussion, beyond the economic theory of pure capitalism. Some kind of breakdown theory is often – if not always – implicit in the historical interpretation of Marx's *Capital*, and this Unoists are refuting.

The Unoist interpretation and reconstruction of Marx's economic theory – and his method – is interesting and ambitious. It remains to be seen, if it can serve as a guiding line to fruitful studies and analysis of capitalist reality.

Conclusions

A short and simplified classification of various interpretations of Marx's *Capital* shows that the Kautskyan Marxism, ordinary Soviet Marxism, and many Western works (Sweezy, Mandel, Meek) emphasise the historical interpretation of capital. On the other side of the line are the capital-logics school, Althusserian Marxism and the Uno-Sekine school emphasising the logic of *Capital.* I would include also Ilyenkov in this group, although we can put some question marks should be left to this classification. Ilyenkov is not so radical or polemic in stressing the logical method of Marx as particularly the Unoist school. He did not make a clear break with the logico-historical interpretation – but we cannot identify him with the conventional historical interpretation of Marx's *Capital.* (See Table below.)

Historical and logical interpretations of Marx's *Capital*	
PRINCIPALLY HISTORICAL:	*PRINCIPALLY LOGICAL:*
Kautsky ordinary Soviet Marxism Sweezy Mandel Meek	"Capital-logics" school Uno-Sekine school Althusser Ilyenkov

This classification of course does not coincide with Hegel/Ricardo-classification, from which I began. But it is clear that the logical interpretation of *Capital* gets inspiration from the study of Hegelian dialectics. In this picture Althusser is an exception. Althusser is also an example of another controversial dimension in interpretations of Marx: the problem of Marx's anthropology and humanism. In my opinion Althusser's "theoretical anti-humanism" is hard to defend, and the spirit of Ilyenkov's work is very far away from it.

But at a more general level, I think that logical interpretations of *Capital* underline the theoretical integrity and coherence of Marx's economic theory better than the historical interpretations, sometimes leading to some kind of dissolution of the theory, to overstressing of Marx's prophecies, and to deterministic and economistic views. It can also be said that it is important to see the contradictions of the logical and historical aspects of the theory, and not only their unity, as the logico-historical interpretation of Marx's *Capital* does.

Discussion on Marx's method will continue and in this context the work of Ilyenkov is a distinguished landmark. In view of the present discussions his work *Dialektika abstraknogo i konkretnogo* is quite interesting, although some weaknesses and traces of conventional Marx-interpretation can be spotted, as I have noted.

Notes

[1] As an example we can see the work of Chepurenko (1988) which treats various schools of western Marxism critically but not in a hostile manner. In Chepurenko's book there are also self-critical comments about "dogmatic layers and scholastic theorising in Soviet social research" (8).

[2] Meek sees that Marx's theory of value can be considered under the three headings of Pre-Capitalist Society, Early Capitalism and Developed Capitalism. "The task of analysis of value as Marx understood it, was to solve these basic [logical] problems in terms of the relations of productions of appropriate 'historical' stage which was under consideration." (Meek 1967, 99). This clearly is an example of a historical interpretation of *Capital*.

[3] Of Uno's works, only a condensed version of his "principles" has been translated into English (Uno 1980). The main sources of this discussion are the works of Albritton (1986 and 1991), and Sekine (1975, 1980, 1984, 1997). See also Itoh 1988 and the collection *A Japanese Approach to Political Economy* (1995).

[4] Sekine even speaks of "exact correspondence between the dialectic of capital and Hegel's Logic" (Sekine 1980, 150).

[5] Commenting such discussions Julkunen (1997) notes: "In the theory of value the bearers of living labour do not have a materiality like gender. The theory of value does not answer to the question, why capital – or its representatives – treat men and women differently."

Literature

Abraham-Frois, Gilbert & Berrebi, Edmond (1979), *Theory of Value, Prices and Accumulation. A mathematical integration of Marx, von Neumann and Sraffa.* Cambridge: Cambridge University Press

Albritton, Robert (1986), *A Japanese Reconstruction of Marxist Theory.* Houndmills: Macmillan

Albritton, Robert (1991), *A Japanese Approach to Stages of Capitalist Development,* New York: St. Martin's Press

Althusser, Louis & Balibar, Étienne (1970), *Reading Capital,* London: NLB (original Lire le Capital 1968)

Backhaus, Hans-Georg (1997), *Dialektik der Wertform. Untersuchungen zur marxschen Ökonomiekritik,* Freiburg: Ça ira Verlag

Barrett, Michèle (1987), *Marxist-Feminism and the Work of Karl Marx,* in: *Feminism and Equality.* Oxford: Basil Blackwell

Brecht, Bertolt (1990), *Flüchtlingsgespräche,* Frankfurt am Main: Suhrkamp Verlag

Chepurenko, A. Iu. (1988), *Idejnaia bor'ba vokrug "Kapitala" segodnia.* Moskva: Izdatel'stvo polititicheskoj literatury 1988

Elster, Jon (1985), *Making Sense of Marx,* Cambridge: Cambridge University Press

Gronow, Jukka (1986), *On the Formation of Marxism. Karl Kautsky's Theory of Capitalism, the Marxism of the Second International and Karl Marx's Critique of Political Economy.* In: *Commentationes Scientiarum Socialium* 33. Helsinki

Iljenkow, E.W. (1979), *Die Dialektik des Abstrakten und Konkreten im "Kapital" von Karl Marx,* Westberlin: Das europäische Buch Literaturvertrieb GmbH (original: *Dialektika abstraktnogo i konkretnogo v "Kapitale" Marksa* 1960)

Ilyenkov, E. V. (1997), *Dialektika abstraktnogo i konkretnogo v nauchno-teoreticheskom myshlenii,* Moskva: Rossiiskaia politicheskaia entsiklopediia

Itoh, Makoto (1988), *The Basic Theory of Capitalism. The Forms and Substance of the Capitalist Economy.* Houndmills: The Macmillan Press

A Japanese Approach to Political Economy. Unoist Variations (1995). Houndmills: MacMillan

Julkunen, Raija (1997), *Minun Marxini kohtaa feminismin,* in: Jukka Heiskanen (ed.), *Marx ja villi länsi.* Marxilainen foorumi -julkaisusarja 20. Helsinki: Demokraattinen Sivistysliitto ry.

Jung, Heinz & Schleifstein, Josef (1979), *Die Theorie des staatsmonopolistischen Kapitalismus und ihre Kritiker in der Bundesrepublik Deutschland. Eine allgemeinverständliche Antwort.* Frankfurt am Main: Verlag Marxistische Blätter

Kautsky, Karl (1906), *Karl Marx' Oekonomische Lehren,* Stuttgart: Verlag von J. H. W. Dietz Nachf. (original 1886)

LPSS = Lenin, V. I. *: Polnoe sobranie sochinenii,* Moskva: Politizdat

Meek, Ronald L. (1967), *Economics and Ideology and other Essays. Studies in the Development of Economic Thought.* London: Chapman and Hall Ltd

MEW = Marx, Karl & Engels, Friedrich: Werke, Berlin: Dietz Verlag

Murray, Patrick (1990), *Marx's Theory of Scientific Knowledge.* Atlantic Highlands, N. J.: Humanities Press International, Inc. (original 1988)

Quaas, Friedrun (1992), *Das Transformationsproblem. Ein theoriehistorischer Beitrag zur Analyse der Quellen und Resultate seiner Diskussion.* Marburg: Metropolis Verlag

Quaas, Georg (1992), *Dialektik als philosophische Theorie und Methode des "Kapital". Eine methodologische Untersuchung des ökonomischen Werkes von Karl Marx.* Frankfurt am Main: Peter Lang

Reichelt, Helmut (1973), *Zur logischen Struktur des Kapitalbegriffs bei Karl Marx.* Frankfurt am Main: Europäische Verlagsanstalt (original 1970)

Robinson, Joan (1973), *Collected Economic Papers,* Vol. 4, Oxford: Basil Blackwell

Rosdolsky, Roman (1972), *Zur Entstehungsgeschichte des Marxschen "Kapital". Der Rohentwurf des Kapital 1857–1858,* Band I & Band II, Frankfurt am Main: Europäische Verlagsanstalt (original 1967)

Rosenberg, D. I. (1983), *Kommentarii k "Kapitalu" K. Marksa.* Moskva: Ekonomika

Rosenthal, John (1998), *The Myth of Dialectics. Reinterpreting the Marx–Hegel Relation.* Houndmills: MacMillan Press Ltd

Sekine, Thomas T. (1975), *Uno-Riron: A Japanese Contribution to Marxian Political Economy.* In: *Journal of Economic Literature* 1975, 13, 847– 877

Sekine, Thomas T. (1980), *An Essay on Uno's Dialectic of Capital,* in: Uno, Kozo: *Principles of Political of Economy. Theory of Purely Capitalist Society,* Brighton: Harvester Press

Sekine, Thomas T. (1984), *The Dialectic of Capital. A Study of the Inner Logic of Capitalism.* Tokyo: The Yushindo Press

Sekine, Thomas T. (1997), *An Outline of the Dialectic of Capital.* Vol. 1. & Vol. 2. Houndmills: MacMillan

Smith, Tony (1993), *Marx's Capital and Hegelian Dialectic Logic,* in*: Marx's Method in Capital. A Reexamination.* Atlantic Higlands, N. J.: Humanities Press

Sweezy, Paul M. (1946), *The Theory of Capitalist Development. Principles of Marxian Political Economy.* London: Dennis Dobson Limited (original 1942)

Uno, Kozo (1980), *Principles of Political of Economy. Theory of Purely Capitalist Society.* Brighton: Harvester Press (original *Geizai genron* 1964)

Zelený, Jindřich (1972), *Die Wissenschaftslogik bei Marx und "Das Kapital".* Frankfurt am Main: Europäische Verlagsanstalt (original *O Logické Strukture Marxova Kapitálu* 1962)

17

Bemerkungen zu "Die Leninsche Dialektik und die Metaphysik des Positivismus" von E. W. Iljenkow

Wladislaw Hedeler

Die Studie über die Leninsche Dialektik und die Metaphysik des Positivismus von Ewald Wasiljewitsch Iljenkow – es sollte das erste postum veröffentlichte Buch des Philosophen sein – ging am 23. Juli 1980 in Satz und am 4. Oktober 1980 in Druck. Lew Naumenko, der das Geleitwort zu dieser Publikation verfasste, erinnerte an das Talent, die Leidenschaft und die Vielseitigkeit des am 21. März 1979 verstorbenen Philosophen und unterstrich, dass Iljenkow die materialistische Dialektik als "Logik revolutionären Denkens und revolutionärer Aktion" verstand und handhabe. Buchstabe und Geist Leninschen Philosophierens leben in dieser Streitschrift des kämpferischen Materialisten Iljenkow auf:

> Und auch in dem letzten Buch, das von Lenins Auffassung von Materie und Bewusstsein, Sprache und Denken, Wahrheit und Widerspruch, vom Wechselverhältnis von Spontaneität und Bewusstheit, von Philosophie und Naturwissenschaft, handelt, ist der eigentliche Gegenstand die Vorbereitung der Menschen auf die grösste aller historischen Leistungen – die Schaffung des Kommunismus (Naumenko 1980, 4).

Ein Gedanke, der im Nekrolog über Iljenkow (vgl. Iljenkow 1979a, 182–184) eher zurückhaltend formuliert worden war, rückte nun in den Vordergrund:

> Die parteiliche Unversöhnlichkeit gegenüber der dem Marxismus-Leninismus feindlichen Ideologie, gegenüber jeglichen Versuchen der Falsifikation grundlegender Errungenschaften des marxistisch-leninistischen philosophischen Denkens, durchdrang sein gesamtes Schaffen (Iljenkow 1979a, 184).

Lenins Definition der Dialektik und deren Ausarbeitung beim Aufbau der neuen sozialistischen Gesellschaft – eine in Iljenkows Studien in der Regel abgeleitete Fragestellung wurde gewissermassen zum zentralen Forschungsthema aufgewertet. David Bakhurst hat in seiner Arbeit über die Sowjetphilosophie (Bakhurst 1991, 123–134) eine Erklärung für diesen "Rückfall in den Dogmatismus" angeboten, die an dieser Stelle aufgegriffen und diskutiert werden soll.

Das Erbe des über die Grenzen des Landes hinaus bekannten originellen Denkers und Schulbildners[1] Iljenkow, der als "kritischer Marxist" oder als "Neohegelianer" galt, sollte möglichst schnell in das Flussbett des offiziellen Marxismus-Leninismus zurückgeführt werden. Es ging nicht um eine Reform, sondern um die Konsolidierung des stagnierenden Sowjetsystems. Die Betonung der unerschütterlichen Prinzipien und der Parteilichkeit jeglicher Wissenschaft stand oben an. Ohne willkürliche Eingriffe war diese vehement betriebene Instrumentalisierung nicht zu haben. Die Zensoren knüpften in der Regel dort an, wo die Selbstzensur des Autors Ansatzpunkte bot.

Meines Erachtens ist es ein Fehler, die zweifellos vorhandenen, aber nicht belegbaren Eingriffe in den Text[2] nur unter einem philosophischen Blickwinkel (wie es Bakhurst tut) zu sehen. Die entscheidenden "Schlachten an der philosophischen Front" begannen Anfang der 80er Jahre auf dem Feld der Philosophiegeschichte. Es ist in diesem Zusammenhang angebracht, an die von Evert van der Zweerde vorgeschlagene Periodisierung sowjetischer philosophischer Kultur zu erinnern (vgl. van der Zweerde 1997).

Was sowjetische Philosophen in den Jahren der Marginalisierung und Professionalisierung (1967–1975) dachten, in Zirkeln diskutierten und für die Schublade schrieben, bildete in den darauffolgenden Jahren der Stagnation (1967–1985) den Stein des Anstosses für etliche öffentlich ausgetragene Kontroversen. Der Schlagabtausch über das Erbe von Nikolaj Fjodorovitsch Fjodorow reichte von der Drucklegung 1980 bis zur Auslieferung der Werkausgabe des russischen Philosophen im Jahre 1982. Juri Davydow legte im August 1982 ein Buch über Probleme der Moralphilosophie[3] vor, die harsche Antwort im *Kommunist* (vgl. Petropawlowskij 1983) erfolgte umgehend. Da der Vertrieb von Aleksej Losews Buch über Vladimir

Solovjow 1983 nicht mehr verhindert werden konnte, begnügte man sich damit, das Buch jenseits der Hochschulzentren zu verkaufen. Im Mai–Juli 1983 begannen im Wissenschaftlichen Rat der Philosophischen Fakultät der Staatlichen Moskauer Universität die Debatten über das im gleichen Jahr veröffentlichte *Filosofskij Enziklopeditscheskij Slowar*. Viele Artikel, hiess es in einem 1985 publizierten Bericht über die Auseinandersetzungen, "stehen in krassem Widerspruch zur Lehrmeinung".[4] Kaum vorstellbar, dass Iljenkow in dieser Situation für die "prinzipienfesten" Konservativen Partei ergreift.

Der Philosophiehistoriker A. I. Wolodin, dessen zwei aufeinander-folgende Abhandlungen über Lenins *Materialismus und Empiriokritizismus* 1982 und 1985 neues, der Forschung unbekanntes Material über die Rolle dieses Buches in der Auseinandersetzung innerhalb der russischen Sozialdemokratie vorstellten, hat Iljenkows Studie, genau so wie es die offizielle Lesart vorschrieb, rezipiert. Iljenkow liefert den Beweis, hob Wolodin hervor, dass Lenins Buch "heute nicht einfach fortlebt, sondern mehr und mehr – unter dem Einfluss neuer Anforderungen der sich entwickelnden Wirklichkeit und Wissenschaft – ihr theoretisches Potential eröffnet."[5] Den Hinweis darauf, dass einige Überlegungen von Iljenkow mit den von ihm vorgetragenen kompatibel sind, wird man bei Wolodin vergebens suchen.

Die Leistung der Interpreten ist, gemessen an der Botschaft die sie zu vermitteln haben, nebensächlich, die Nuancen unwichtig, ihre Namen austauschbar. Typisch für die in der Sowjetunion verfassten marxistisch-leninistischen Kommentare zu Lenins *Materialismus und Empiriokritizismus* ist das beständige "Aktualisieren" von drei thematischen Schwerpunkten der Auseinandersetzung mit der bürgerlichen Ideologie. Eine Illustration hierfür ist der von Igor Narski am 31. Mai 1973 vor Propagandisten an der Sonderschule des Zentralkomitees der Sozialistischen Einheitspartei Deutschlands gehaltene Vortrag *Über die Aktualität von Lenins "Materialismus und Empiriokritizismus"*. Im Parteilehrjahr der SED 1973/74 wurden anhand dieses Vortrags "Das Prinzip der Parteilichkeit in der Philosophie"; "Naturwissenschaftliche Erkenntnisse und ihre philosophische Interpretation" und das "Beispiel der Auseinandersetzung mit der bürgerlichen Philosophie und dem Revisionismus" behandelt (vgl. Narski 1973).

Gemessen an diesen Vorgaben fiel Iljenkows Buch aus dem Rahmen. In drei Kapiteln über den "Machismus als Philosophie der toten Reaktion", das "positive Programm des russischen Positivismus" und die "Dialektik als Logik der Revolution" kommentiert Iljenkow Lenins Kritik an der "Modephilosophie". Die Redakteure sahen sich veranlasst, dem Leser Fingerzeige zu geben und Hilfestellung anzubieten, um Iljenkows Polemik folgen zu können. Die Fussnote zu Iljenkows Aussage

Hier liegt die Wurzel des Idealismus in seiner zeichensymbolischen Variante. Wenn man von der individuellen Erfahrung ausgeht, wenn man sie zum Ausgangspunkt und zur Grundlage der Erkenntnistheorie erklärt, dann ist Idealismus unvermeidlich. Aber er ist ebenfalls unvermeidlich, wenn man sich auf die kollektive Erfahrung stützt,

lautet: "Damit dem Leser die in diesem Buch vertretene Position deutlicher wird, empfehlen wir ihm die Abhandlung von Iljenkow *Dialektitscheskaja logika* (M., 1974), besonders die Abschnitte zwei, sieben und acht" (Iljenkow 1980, 37).[6] Diese Abschnitte enthalten u.a. Iljenkows Kritik der von Narski und B. M. Kedrow formulierten Auffassungen zum Thema (vgl. Kedrow 1983).

Iljenkow bediente im Buch *Leninskaja dialektika i metafisika positiwisma* mehr oder weniger die Klischees, Losungen und Feindbilder der offiziellen KPdSU-Geschichtsschreibung. Tabuisierte Themen, wie die Schicksale der von Iljenkow vorgestellten Philosophen, blieben selbstverständlich tabu. Das Buch enthält aber auch Beispiele für Kompromissformeln und Hinweise auf zaghafte Versuche, Neuland zu betreten. Die Leitung des Akademieinstitutes, an dem Iljenkow in den letzten 5–6 Lebensjahren tätig war, versuchte das zu verhindern, übte Druck auf die Philosophen aus und initiierte Kampagnen zur Disziplinierung der "Abtrünnigen" (vgl. Chamidow 1995, 214).

In Kenntnis dieser Situation möchte man meinen, dass das antiquierte Bild vom "allwissenden Parteiführer und Funktionär der russischen und internationalen Arbeiterbewegung", das die Iljenkow zugeschriebene Studie vermittelt, eher die Vorstellungs- und Gedankenwelt der Auftraggeber, als die des Philosophen widerspiegelt. Lenin hatte zum Zeitpunkt der Niederschrift von *Materialismus und Empiriokritizismus* das Wesen der Hegelschen Dialektik und der Dialektik des *Kapital* vollständig erfasst, schreibt Iljenkow. In den *Philosophischen Heften* hat Lenin nur einige Details seiner bereits zuvor entwickelten und im Feuer der Praxis erprobten Theorie konkretisiert (Iljenkow 1980, 28).

Lenins Entwicklung, dessen Weg als Theoretiker von der politischen Ökonomie zur Philosophie führte war aber komplizierter. Wie W. Adoratski 1930 in einer über die philosophischen Studien Lenins verfassten Skizze feststellte:

Leider besitzt das Lenin-Institut bei weitem nicht alles, was Lenin über philosophische Fragen geschrieben hat. Es fehlen die Briefe an Lengnik (1899) mit einer Kritik der Kantianer. Es fehlen drei *Hefte Notizen eines Durchschnittsmarxisten über Philosophie* (1906) mit einer Kritik der Philosophie Bogdanows. Es fehlt das Material der Vorarbeiten zu *Materialismus und Empiriokritizismus* (1908). Endlich fehlen ganz die Konspekte der Frühzeit, in der Lenin mit dem Studium der Grundwerke des Marxismus begann: also die Konspekte zum *Kapital,* zum *Anti-Dühring* und zu den anderen Werken philosophischen Charakters (Adoratski 1930, 231).

An dieser vom Verfasser an anderer Stelle (Hedeler 1994) kommentierten Quellenlage hat sich auch nach Veröffentlichung des Sammelbandes *W. I. Lenin. Neiswestnye dokumenty* (Moskwa 1999) nichts geändert. Lenin ist bereits 1894 in seinen frühen Arbeiten mit einer glänzenden Charakteristik des dialektischen Materialismus hervorgetreten, notierte Adoratski in dem bereits zitierten Aufsatz. "Schon in jungen Jahren" hatte Lenin alle grundlegenden Werke von Marx und Engels gelesen, studiert und sich zu eigen gemacht. "Auf allen Gebieten der marxistischen Theorie", fasste Adoratski zusammen, "verstand es Lenin, den theoretischen Gedanken wesentlich weiterzuführen. Auch in der Philosophie verliess ihn diese Fähigkeit nicht" (Adoratski 1930, 231).

Iljenkows Lesart ist eine Modifikation dieser glorifizierenden Auslegung des Leninschen Nachlasses. Weil Bogdanow in den Denkschemata von Mach "eine 'philosophische Begründung' seiner Position fand, begann er noch überzeugter und konsequenter in diesem Sinne zu denken und zu handeln. Und das führte ihn bald von Lenin, vom Bolschewismus, von der bewusst angewandten materialistischen Dialektik weg" (Iljenkow 1980, 57). Platter geht es wirklich nicht mehr.

Vergleichbare Ungereimtheiten und Brüche in der "Beweisführung" sind in Iljenkows Buch häufig anzutreffen. Würde Iljenkow der o.g. "Argumentationslinie" wirklich folgen, müsste ihm die Tatsache, dass die Unterscheidung der politischen Fraktionen der russischen Sozialdemokratie zu Lebzeiten Lenins nicht mit den Unterschieden in den philosophischen Auffassungen deckungsgleich war, völlig gleichgültig sein. Sie ist es jedoch nicht. Iljenkow hob hervor, dass die bequeme Formel von der wechselseitigen Bedingtheit von "falscher Theorie" und "fehlerhafter Politik" nicht auf die Kontrahenten Lenin, Aleksandr Bogdanow und Georgi Plechanow zutrifft. Hinzu kommt, dass Bogdanow und Plechanow bestimmte Fraktionen innerhalb des bolschewistischen bzw. menschewistischen Flügels unter dem Dach der russischen Sozialdemokratie verkörperten.

Es ist bedauerlich, dass Iljenkow diesen aufschlussreichen Zugang, den das VI. Kapitel "Empiriokritizismus und historischer Materialismus" von Lenins Werk ermöglicht, nicht weiter verfolgt. Wäre er den eingeschlagenen Weg zu Ende oder wenigstens ein Stück weiter gegangen, hätte er, wie später Wolodin, tradierte Sichtweisen der Parteigeschichtsschreibung in Frage stellen müssen. Diese "Inkonsequenz" wird auch im Zusammenhang mit der originellen, aber letzten Endes nicht durchgehaltenen Kritik, die Iljenkow gegen die Machisten vorbringt, deutlich.

Diese "Konterpropaganda" ist eingebettet in eine Auseinandersetzung mit Jakov Bermans[7] Buch *Die Dialektik im Lichte der modernen Erkenntnistheorie* (1908) und den utopischen Romanen *Ingenieur Menni* und *Roter Stern* von Bogdanow.[8] Lenin hat sich nur sehr flüchtig (im Briefwechsel mit Maxim Gorki) zu den utopischen Romanen, die in Russland ein lebhaftes Echo fanden, geäussert. Nachdem sich die Gruppierung um Lenin im Kampf der Fraktionen gegen Bogdanow durchgesetzt hatte und letzterer sich aus der aktiven Politik zurückzog, erlosch Lenins Interesse an Bogdanow als Theoretiker. Lenin hatte das Interesse an Bogdanows weiteren, die Philosophie "überwindenden" Arbeiten schon lange verloren. Im Januar 1913 schrieb er an Gorki, Bogdanows neue "Philosophie der lebendigen Erfahrung" nicht zu kennen. "Wahrscheinlich derselbe Machismus in neuem Gewande...", mutmasste Lenin.[9] Er hatte andere Sorgen, als sich mit Bogdanow zu beschäftigen. Lenins kurzer Meinungsaustausch im September 1920 mit Bucharin über das von W. Newski[10] für die 2. Auflage von *Materialismus und Empiriokritizismus* zu verfassende Nachwort und die in diesem Zusammenhang vorgebrachte Kritik an Bogdanow zeugt nicht von Sachkenntnis (vgl. Lenin 1936, 431–432).

In den letzten zehn Jahren hat das Bogdanow-Bild in der Sowjetunion bzw. Russland ernsthafte Korrekturen erfahren (vgl. hierzu Hedeler 1999). Bogdanows Bücher über die Fragen des Sozialismus und über die Tektologie wurden aufgelegt und unbekanntes Archivmaterial publiziert. Diese Materialien, darunter Bogdanows Aufzeichnungen, die während der fünf Wochen dauernden Haft im Inneren Gefängnis der GPU vom 8. September bis 13. Oktober 1923 entstanden, erklären, warum sich Bogdanow aus der Politik in die Medizin "zurückzog". Im September 1923 begann eine Kampagne gegen den "Idealisten" Bogdanow, dem u.a. vorgeworfen wurde, eine parteifeindliche Gruppe organisiert und geleitet zu haben.[11]

Neben der Auftragsarbeit hatte sich Iljenkow auch weiterhin mit seinem eigentlichen Thema beschäftigt. In der Einleitung zum postum publizierten Aufsatz *Problema idealnogo* mitteilte die Redaktion der *Woprossy filosofii:*

Am Manuskript, das wir veröffentlichen, arbeitete Ewald Wasiljewitsch bis zuletzt. Darin entwickelt und vertieft der Autor Ideen, die in seinen früheren Arbeiten zum Thema enthalten sind. Die Redaktion der Zeitschrift hält das Manuskript für gründlich und ausserordentlich interessant, obwohl es eine bestimmte Etappe in der Ausarbeitung des Problems des Ideellen widerspiegelt und strittige Thesen und Überlegungen enthält, die weiterer Konkretisierung bedürfen (Iljenkow 1979c, 128).

Naumenko, der auch die 1984 in zweiter erweiterter[12] Auflage veröffentlichte Sammlung *Dialektitscheskaja logika* einleitete, schrieb den Denkweg Iljenkows als von Marx über Hegel zu Lenin verlaufend fest. Er tat dies mit ausdrücklichem Hinweis auf Iljenkows letzten fertiggestellten Artikel *Woinst-wujuschtschij materialism – snatschit dialektitscheskij*. Dieser Artikel, der als *"otscherk* 15" in den Sammelband *Dialektitscheskaja logika* Aufnahme fand, ist mit dem gleichnamigen Artikel, der aus Anlass des 70. Jahrestages der Veröffentlichung von Lenins *Materialismus und Empiriokritizismus* im Heft 6/1979 der theoretischen Zeitschrift der KPdSU *Kommunist* erschienen war (Iljenkow 1979b), nicht identisch.

Naumenko geht auf die Unterschiede in den vorliegenden unterschiedlichen Fassungen nicht ein. Er erläutert auch nicht, warum die in den *Woprossy filosofii* Heft 6/1979 veröffentlichte Skizze über eine der wichtigsten Kategorien der Philosophie, betitelt *Problema idealnogo* (Iljenkow 1979c), nicht in die zweite erweiterte Auflage des Sammelbandes *Dialektitscheskaja logika* aufgenommen wurde.

Wie die Bearbeitung von philosophischen Artikeln erfolgte, zeigt der Vergleich des im *Kommunist* veröffentlichten Aufsatzes mit der Broschüre *Leninskaja dialektika i metafisika positiwisma*.

Im *Kommunist* ist von dem "genialen Buch" Lenins die Rede und von der Bedeutung des Buches für die Geschichte des Jahrhunderts (vgl. Iljenkow 1979b, 47). Die Kennzeichnung "genial" fehlt in der Broschüre, in der das Buch nur in seiner Rolle für die "intellektuelle Geschichte" des Jahrhunderts untersucht wird (Iljenkow 1980, 7). Diese "Einschränkung des Geltungsbereiches" wurde nicht in die *Kommunist*-Fassung übernommen. Die Formulierung in der Broschüre, dass Lenin sich "Fragen der Philosophie" (Iljenkow 1980, 7) zuwandte, genügte der *Kommunist*-Redaktion nicht. Im theoretischen Organ der KPdSU ist davon die Rede, dass Lenin "alle entscheidenden Probleme, mit denen die marxistische Philosophie konfrontiert war" genau skizziert hatte (Iljenkow 1979b, 47).

Die in der Broschüre enthaltene sachliche Polemik gegen Karl Kautsky, Plechanow und den Idealismus wird im *Kommunist*-Artikel "populärer" und in einem verhältnismässig rüden Ton dargeboten (vgl. Iljenkow 1980, 24 und Iljenkow 1979b, 49).

An die aus der "Einleitung" der Broschüre entnommenen Passagen schliessen sich im Artikel Überlegungen aus dem dritten Kapitel an, was zur Folge hat, dass die für Iljenkow wichtigen Methodik-Kapitel keine Erwähnung finden. Für den Grossteil des *Kommunist*-Artikels (Iljenkow 1979b, 51–53; 56–59) findet sich in der Broschüre keine Entsprechung. Wie hier zuspitzend umgeschrieben oder den Bitten der Redaktion, die Polemik schärfer zu betonen, entsprochen wurde, zeigen die Seiten 130 bis 134 der Broschüre, deren überarbeitete Fassung im *Kommunist*-Artikel auf den Seiten 54–55 nachgelesen werden kann. Im *"otscherk* 15" im Sammelband *Dialektitscheskaja logika* (2. Auflage), der wie der Herausgeber schreibt, mit dem gleichnamigen *Kommunist*-Artikel identisch ist, fehlt diese polemische Passage (vgl. Iljenkow 1984, 297).

Was Iljenkow wirklich geschrieben hat, kann man nur raten. Auch jene zwei Seiten, die Ausfälle gegen die opportunistischen Theoretiker der II. Internationale enthalten, wurden nicht aus dem *Kommunist* in den "*otscherk* 15*"* übernommen.[13] Das ist nicht die einzige vom Redakteur kommentarlos vorgenommene Streichung, die auch als Wiederherstellung einer der ursprünglichen Vorlage aus der Feder des Philosophen nahekommenden Fassung interpretiert werden kann. Die Tilgung rüder Passagen bleibt Kosmetik.[14] Schönheitspflaster ändern nichts an der Aussage. Der *Kommunist*-Artikel endet mit einigen Absätzen, die auch im Schlusskapitel der Broschüre[15] enthalten sind.

Notes

[1] Vgl. hierzu Eichler und Schneider 1996.

[2] Dem Autor ist der Umfang der "Bearbeitung" von Iljenkows Broschüre nicht bekannt.

[3] Ju. N. Davydow, *Etika ljubwi i metafisika swoevolija.* Moskva 1982.

[4] So *Obsushdenije* 1985, 62. Vgl. auch den ausführlichen Bericht in *Westnik Moskovskogo Universiteta,* Serija 7, Filosofija, 1987, Heft 2, 58–87.

[5] Wolodin 1982, 137. In der zweiten erweiterten Auflage, die 1985 unter dem selben Titel erschien, nennt Wolodin Iljenkow in einem Atemzug mit einer Reihe von sowjetischen Autoren, gegen die Iljenkow polemisierte, darunter I. S. Narski und B. M. Kedrow (Wolodin 1985, 222).

[6] In den von der Redaktion empfohlenen Abschnitten der *Dialektitscheskaja logika* werden folgende Themen untersucht: Das Denken als Attribut der Substanz; Zur Frage der dialektisch-materialistischen Kritik des objektiven Idealismus; Die materialistische Auffasssung vom Denken als Gegenstand der Logik.

[7] Jakow Aleksandrowitsch Berman (1868–1933) – Philosoph, Jurist, 1890 Absolvent der juristischen Fakultät der Moskauer Universität. Nach 1917 Mitglied der KPR(B), seit 1922 Hochschullehrer für Staats- und Rechtstheorie an Moskauer Hochschulen.

[8] 1984 erschien in Berlin in deutscher Übersetzung *Der rote Planet* und 1989 *Ingenieur Menni.*

[9] In: W. I. Lenin, *Werke,* 35:47–50.

[10] Nevski, Wladimir Iwanowitsch (eigentlicher Name Kriwobokow, Feodossij Iwanowitsch, 1876–1937) – Historiker, 1924 Direktor der Lenin-Bibliothek. Im Mai 1937 widerrief er seine Aussagen gegen Bucharin und wurde erschossen.

[11] Bogdanows Aufzeichnungen über die Haft in: Bogdanow 1995, 18–65.

[12] Die zweite Auflage wurde um drei Skizzen erweitert: *Logika „Kapitala"; Abstraktnoe i konkretnoe w dialektitscheskoj logike; Dialektitscheskaja wsjaimoswjas logitscheskogo i istoritscheskogo.* Dazu kam noch ein Kapitel *Dialektika i sowremennost* (enthält die Skizzen *Woistwujuschtschij materialism – snatschit dialektitscheskij; Dialektika i mirowossrenie*).

[13] Vgl. Iljenkow 1979b, 58–59 und Iljenkow 1984, 302 (Auslassung zwischen dem 4. und 5. Absatz).

[14] Vgl. Iljenkow 1984, 296, und Iljenkow 1979b , 54 (Absatz 3).

[15] Vgl. Iljenkow 1980, 173–174 und Iljenkow 1979b, 60.

Literatur

Adoratski, W., *Über die philosophischen Studien Lenins.* In: *Unter dem Banner des Marxismus,* April 1930

Bakhurst, David, *Consciousness and Revolution in Soviet Philosophy. From the Bolsheviks to Evald Ilyenkov.* Cambridge 1991

[Bogdanow, A. A.], *Neisvestnyj Bogdanow.* Kniga 1. *Stati, doklady, pisma i wospominanija 1901–1928 gg.* Zsgst. von N. S. Antonowa und N. W. Drosdowa. Moskwa 1995

Chamidov, A., *Iljenkow.* In: *Russkaja filosofija. Malyj enziklopeditscheskij slovar.* Moskva 1995

Davydow, Ju. N., *Etika ljubwi i metafisika swoewolija.* Moskwa 1982.

Eichler, K. D. und Schneider, U. J. (Hrsgg.), *Russische Philosophie im 20. Jahrhundert.* Leipzig 1996.

Filosofskij Enziklopeditscheskij slovar. Moskva 1983.

Hedeler, W., *Lenins Aneignung des Marxismus.* In: Th. Bergmann u. a. (Hrsgg.), *Lenin. Theorie und Praxis in historischer Perspektive.* Mainz 1994,163-181.

Hedeler, W., *Alexander Bogdanows Utopie einer kommunistischen Gesellschaft.* In: *Vielfalt sozialistischen Denkens.* Ausgabe 5. Berlin (Hg. Helle Panke e.V.) 1999.

E. W. Iljenkow [*Nekrolog*]. In: *Woprossy filosofii,* 1979, Heft 6, 182–184 [= Iljenkow 1979a]

Iljenkow, E. W., *Materialism woinstvujuschtschij – snatschit dialektitscheskij. K 70-letiju wychoda w swet knigi W. I. Lenina "Materialism i empiriokritizism".* In: *Kommunist,* 1979, 6. [= Iljenkow 1979b]

Iljenkow, E. W., *Problema idealnogo.* In: *Woprossy filosofii,* 1979, Heft 6, 128–140 [= Iljenkow 1979c]

Iljenkow, E. W., *Leninskaja dialektika i metafisika positivisma. Rasmyschlenija nad knigoj V. I. Lenina "Materialism i Empiriokritizism".* Moskwa 1980

Iljenkow, E. W., *Dialektitscheskaja logika.* 2. Auflage, Moskwa 1984.

Kedrov, B. M., *Kak isutschat knigu W. I. Lenina "Materialism i empiriokritizism"* (4. erweiterte Auflage). Moskwa 1983.

Lenin, W. I., *Obmen sapiskami meshdu Leninym i Bucharinym po powodu stati W. Newskogo "Dialektitscheskij materialism i filosofija mertwoj reakzii".* In: Lenin, W. I., *Filosofskie tetradi.* Moskva 1936

Lenin, W. I., *Werke,* Berlin: Dietz Verlag 1958 ff.

Narski, I. S., *Die Aktualität von Lenins "Materialismus und Empiriokritizismus".* (Vorträge zu philosophischen Themen.) Berlin 1973

Naumenko, K. L., *K tschitatelju.* In: Iljenkow 1980.

Obsushdenie "Filosofskogo Enziklopeditscheskogo slovarja". In: *Westnik Moskowskogo Uniwersiteta*, Serija 7, Filosofija, 1985, Heft 1

Petropawlowskij, R., *Po powodu odnoj knigi*. In: *Kommunist*, 1983, Heft 8, 102–114.

W. I. Lenin. Neisvestnye dokumenty 1891-1922. Moskva 1999.

Wolodin, A. I., *"Boj absoljutno neisbeshen"*. Moskwa, 1982 [zweite Auflage 1985].

van der Zweerde, Evert, *Soviet Historiography of Philosophy*. Dordrecht 1997.

18

Ильенков и Спиноза

А. Г. Новохатько

Известно, что все люди талантливы, одни более, другие менее. Но есть люди с *духовной* гарантией, способные выносить, выдерживать напряжение противоречия своей эпохи.

С тех пор, как 21 марта 1979 года трагически оборвалась жизнь выдающегося философа Эвальда Васильевича Ильенкова прошло уже два десятилетия. За эти годы были изданы и переизданы важнейшие его произведения – книги, статьи, письма. Появились воспоминания, исследования о нем – в России и за рубежом. Уже нет государства, в котором жил и мыслил Э. В. Ильенков, но интерес к его личности, творчеству не ослабевает.

Как могло бы показаться с формальной точки зрения, доклад следовало озаглавить иначе – "Спиноза и Ильенков". Но вопрос приходится все же ставить именно так. Дело в том, что Ильенков инициировал ряд новых, совершенно оригинальных аспектов исследования идей Спинозы, коих до него в "Этике" не видел никто. Обозначим некоторые из них.

Принцип историзма – одно из основополагающих завоеваний классической немецкой диалектики – генетически связан, в понимании Э.В.Ильенкова, с интерпретацией существа теоретических воззрений Спинозы. Как именно? Ход мысли Э.В.Ильенкова таков.

Историзм как философский (теоретико-познавательный) принцип возникает впервые не в XIX веке, а в конце XVIII, и не в результате развития биологии (эволюционное учение Дарвина) или политической экономии (разработанный и применный Марксом в "Капитале" и примыкающих к нему работах логико-диалектический анализ исторического развития форм материального производства), причем, можно сказать, до, вне и независимо от этих наук, а именно в ходе разработки и обоснования тончайших спекулятивно-метафизических систем, созданных Фихте и молодым Гегелем. Ильенков и показал, что предпринятый в фихтевском "Наукоучении" (1794 г.) анализ природы сознания – со времен Аристотеля одна из наиболее фундаментальных разработок той проблематики, которую сегодня принято относить к ведомству теоретической психологии – и стал колыбелью исторического взгляда на вещи.

В "Наукоучении" Фихте и в иенской "философии духа" Гегеля историзм впервые, в понимании Ильенкова, предстал в виде глубоко продуманного и систематически реализованного принципа. В этих трудах весь мир психических (духовных) явлений был развернут как мир, *возникающий и развивающийся во времени*. Всю немецкую классику пронизывает идея *непрерывного совершенствования* отдельной души в координатах Духа, которое выковывается в их антиномической диалектике так, что каждая человеческая душа ("Я") уже в самый момент своего рождения необходимо вовлекается в общую историческую логику выработки всей духовной культуры, задающей собою *объективную меру* для развития человеческой индивидуальности. Общее направление развития человечества – не плоская эволюция от хорошего к лучшему, а трагедийно-противоречивый и объективно-закономерный вектор свободы и духовного бессмертия. Обывательски-казенный взгляд на бессмертие души, казалось, был навсегда дискредитирован.

Кстати, глубокий русский мыслитель Чаадаев в связи с этим однажды тонко заметил: "Без слепой веры в отвлеченное совершенство невозможно шагу ступить по пути к совершенству, осуществляемому на деле. Только поверив в недостижимое благо, мы можем приблизиться к благу достижимому. Без этой светящейся точки, которая сияет впереди нас в отдалении, мы шагу не могли бы ступить среди глубокой окружающей нас тьмы [...] На пути, ведущем к абсолютному совершенству, расположены все те маленькие совершенства, на которые могут притязать люди [...] Христианское бессмертие есть жизнь без смерти. А совсем не то, что обыкновенно воображают: жизнь после смерти".

Даже фрагментарное обнаружение содержательной исторической связи между явлениями и фактами, т.е. в мире изучаемых естествознанием вещей самих по себе, возникло лишь к середине XIX века. Таким образом, историзм как центральная проблема современной психологии не может быть удовлетворительно понят без обращения к фихтевскому наследию.

Тонкость, однако, состоит в том, что ядро "Наукоучения", его основные принципы суть прямая альтернатива воззрениям Спинозы.

Якоби, современник Фихте, как-то признался, что он впервые нашел доступ к наукоучению, представив себе идею, обратную спинозизму. Во второй половине XX века Ильенков не только актуализировал проблему "антиспинозизма Фихте", но и придал ей новый разворот тем, что не удовлетворился метким наблюдением Якоби. Дело, таким образом, не исчерпывается формальным оборачиванием одной системы в другую. Обычно этим чисто внешним соотношением и ограничиваются в понимании сути наукоучения Фихте.

Суть в том, что Фихте целый ряд проблем развернул глубже Спинозы именно потому, что уже "Наукоучение" 1794 года открывало новый теоретико-познавательный пласт – процессуальную антитетику Абсолютного.

Характерен упрек Гегеля Лейбницу в связи с проблемой Абсолюта и природой зла: "...Если Лейбниц отвечает: "Бог это сделал", то это не ответ. *Мы желаем знать определенное основание этого закона.* Такие общие определения звучат благочестиво, но неудовлетворительны" (Гегель. Соч., т. XI, М., М.-Л., 1935, стр. 353).

Фихте как раз взялся исследовать и "благочестивое", и "удовлетворительное" определенное основание вопроса, на который Лейбниц дал облегченный вариант ответа. Гегель формулирует этот вопрос в предельно острой логической форме: "Почему и как в Абсолютном и его решениях есть конечность ?" ...

С проблемой Абсолюта, кстати, связаны последующие "исправленные" (1798) и совершеннно "новые" версии наукоучения.

Неразработанность в системах Спинозы и Лейбница понятийной диалектики, отражающей безусловные (абсолютные) грани соотношения телеологии и причинности, впервые и высветил Фихте, причем гораздо раньше Гегеля.

Именно Фихте взялся за подвижно-рефлектированную разработку вышеуказанной "определенности" в понятийной деятельности Я, за выявление способов обнаружения Абсолюта в конечном, т.е. в целеполагающем человеческом сознании. Фихте, подчеркивает Ильенков, "восстанавливая исходное понятие картезианства, разрушенное Спинозой, – понятие "свободной воли", – стремится преодолеть спинозизм на его собственной почве, то есть принимая во внимание все те факты, которые Спиноза делает исходным пунктом своей концепции интеллекта и воли, но стараясь "вывести" ("дедуци-ровать") все эти факты *как следствия* (как "условия возможности") априорно предзаложенной "разумной воли", как внешние проявления "Я" ("лучшего" – трансцендентального Я), как формы его "реализации" в чувственно-эмпирическом мире" ("Вопросы философии", 1977, № 5, стр. 146–147).

На гегелевском отношении к Фихте хотелось бы остановиться подробнее. Гегель был согласен с Фихте – да, формирование ("дедукция") сознания определяется по праву из самой его сути, из себе-тождественности самосознания, из Я = Я, а также вследствие модификации объекта, Не-Я.

Но почему в таком случае остаются за скобками, почему оказываются растворенными в активности Я основания его (этого Я) собственной деятельности, объективирующей себя и только себя (свою субъективность), почему исчезает на деле *объективно-идеальный* момент самосознания? Реального перехода в противоположность у Фихте-то и нет. Поэтому вышеуказанное единство переводится у него в модус морального полагания, или лучше сказать – *бытия в долженст-вовании.*

Гегелевский диагноз короток: размыта *абсолютная* грань единства Я и Не-Я, сознания и предмета. Сила воображения, рождающая настоящее из будущего, единственная творческая (психическая) способность, "раскручивающая" все циклы самосознания, имеет один роковой изъян – она *не помнит* действительной истории своей самодеятельности, не в состоянии удержать эти исторические циклы в себе.

Вот почему, исследуя вопрос об основаниях личностного развития человека, Гегель вынужден отдать в конце концов предпочтение не продуктивной силе воображения, а – *возникающей из интеллекта памяти.* Вследствие этого у Гегеля практически полностью исчезает "трансцендентальная" лексика Канта и его последователей. Созна-тельный поворот к Спинозе был, таким образом, внутренне обоснован, а если иметь в виду назревшую потребность возникновения психологии как науки – даже неизбежен.

Потому и психология деятельности рождалась исторически в лоне философии самосознания.

Ильенков показал, что *исторический* взгляд Фихте на развитие человеческой психики возник благодаря именно тому, что в самих теоретических основоположениях "Наукоучения" (и стоящих за ними реальных фактах становления сознания и самосознания!) *предположены* прямо противоположные исходные принципы спинозизма, которые затем и рассматриваются внутри фихтевской системы как её собственный результат.

Историзм метода – это его диалектичность, способность выдерживать напряжение противоречия и, говоря позднейшим гегелевским языком, разрешать его.

Отсюда, кстати, у Ильенкова обостренный интерес к логико-гносеологическим спорам в современной теоретической физике (ждут публикации материалы его полемики с акад. Фоком о причинности в квантовой механике), к острым дискуссиям в советской экономической науке, в эстетике и педагогике в 1960–70-е гг., отсюда, наконец, более глубокое, чем у таких первоклассных профессиональных психологов, как Рубинштейн и Леонтьев, проникновение в проблемные миры Выготского и Пиаже.

Так, например, гениальность Л.С. Выготского Э.В.Ильенков видел именно в том, что тот "вышел на Спинозу" и потому открыл новые горизонты для психологической науки.

Спинозизм Выготского дал великолепные результаты в конкретных психологических исследованиях. Душа не может выполнить никакого намерения, если не вспомнит о нем. Намерение всегда опирается на память, оно лишь раб памяти, цитирует Выготский слова Шекспира. Но особенно великолепны размышления Выготского о "жребии" и свободе воли:

> В этом пункте нашего исследования перед нами открывается философская перспектива. Впервые в процессе психологических исследований появляется возможность средствами психологического эксперимента решить в сущности чисто философские проблемы и эмпирически показать происхождение свободы человеческой воли. Мы полагаем сделать это в другой работе, посвященной специально философии. Мы не можем не отметить, что мы пришли к тому же пониманию свободы и господства над собой, которое в своей "Этике" развил Спиноза (Выготский Л.С. Соч., М., 1983, т. 3, стр. 290–291).

Опорный (исходный) пункт спинозизма, навстречу которому мысль Выготского шла неуклонно, через экспериментально-психологический материал, можно сформулировать так: первое, что на деле составляет бытие человеческой души, есть идея. Но это не высший способ познания. Сущность вещи постигается только тогда, когда из знания отдельной вещи вытекает возможность *всеобщей формы знания,* или самосознания, ибо, как говорит Спиноза, просто понаслышке, там, где не предшествовало собственное понимание, никто никогда не может достичь знания.

Любые человеческие намерения не только предполагают наличие у нас памяти, но и требуют деятельного ее участия. В этой связи Выготский ссылается на исследования своих сотрудников о законченных и незаконченных действиях. Прерванные незаконченные действия запоминаются в два раза лучше, чем действия законченные, в то время как, например, с восприятием – наоборот, незаконченные зрительные образы запоминаются хуже, чем законченные. Собственные действия и собственные зрительные образы запоминаются, подчиняясь разным закономерностям.

Наши намерения забываются именно потому, что существуют разные по своей природе виды памяти, обусловливающие наш выбор. Богатейший психолого-педагогический экспериментальный материал Выготского подтверждает спинозовскую мысль о том, что *душа не может сделать ничего по своему решению, если она не вспомнит, что нужно сделать.*

Но самое любопытное заключается в том, что это возможно только потому, что человеческая душа есть часть "бесконечного интеллекта Бога", так что говоря: "человеческая душа воспринимает отдельную вещь", мы на деле говорим лишь только то, что Бог, поскольку он выражается природой человеческой души (т.е. составляет ее сущность), имеет ту или другую идею. Душа ("мыслящая *вещь*"), т.о., всегда существует в интеллекте Бога как идея *отдельной вещи,* которая самой человеческой душой постигается лишь отчасти, сиречь – *не адекватно.* "*Объектом идеи, составляющей человеческую душу, служит тело*", т.е. известный актуальный модус протяжения, утверждает Спиноза в знаменитая тринадцатой теореме "Этики" (ч.II). Душа и тело не просто связаны воедино, ибо сама тайна такого "единства" – в адекватном познании.

Но именно *в вопросе о природе психических способностей "спинозизм" Гегеля как бы улетучивается.* Ильенков здесь восхитительно точен: Гегель сознательно стоит на фихтевской точке зрения, и, можно сказать, до максимально возможного для нее внутреннего предела ее усиливает, но при этом "креативные" функции силы воображения сохраняет – за "понятием".

Характерно, что в вопросе о природе памяти и ее соотношении с воображением и мышлением Э.В.Ильенков опирается не на Гегеля, а на Спинозу – точно так же, как и в вопросе о свободе воли. По крайней мере, такой выбор он сделал в статье "Три века бессмертия" к юбилею Спинозы.

Обратимся к гегелевским размышлениям. "Один из действительно самых трудных пунктов учений о Духе, остававшийся до сих пор совершенно без внимания, заключается в установлении места и значения памяти, - в выяснении ее органической связи с мышлением. Память, как таковая, сама есть только внешний способ, одностронний момент *существования* мышления"(Гегель. Соч., М., 1956, т. III, стр. 275). "Превращение дела памяти в дело воображения есть деградация" (Гегель. Соч., т. XI, М., 1935, стр. 182).

И поскольку мы мыслим посредством имен, память имеет дело не с образом уже, а с продуктом самого интеллекта, "интеллигенции". Она ставит произвол силы воображения на место: "Упражнение памяти есть поэтому первый *труд* пробудившегося духа как духа. Давать, изобретать имена есть *непосредственный* изобретающий произвол. В *памяти* сначала исчезает этот произвол"(Гегель. Работы разных лет. Т.1, М., 1970, стр. 295). Память для Гегеля – точка прорыва орудийной деятельности человека. Память не связана (в отличие от воображения) с внешним предметом деятельности – она сохраняет имя Я как некоторую "*вещь*" для Я в первичном акте *труда*. За это Гегель, как известно, удостоился похвалы от Маркса.

Шаг вперед, который намеревается сделать Гегель в сравнении со Спинозой, важно понять прежде всего. Спиноза ясно понимал, что любой акт целеполагания причинно обусловлен, однако суть дела заключается в том, что через акты целеполагания (и их осуществления в труде) человек придает предметам и силам природы другие функции и формы, которые в природе самой по себе, без вмешательства человека, спонтанно никогда бы не возникли. Человек своей деятельностью вызывает на себя силы природы, это дает ему шанс познать более глубокие причинные связи и отношения в ней. Тонкость в том, что человек при этом *ничего* не добавляет "от себя" к сущности природы, к ее собственным закономерностям. Однако, вмешательство в природу целеполагающей деятельности человека, которая, как справедливо считал Спиноза, также причинно обусловлена (т.е. вполне закономерна), открывает возможность выявить и извлечь из этой причинности и закономерности новые, ранее не обнаруживавшиеся связи, свойства и потенции самой бесконечной Природы, но уже вовлеченной в систему человеческой деятельности.

Ильенков же в данном пункте не случайно возвращается к Спинозе и потому даже тайну языка видит в атрибутивной природе мышления, выводит из мышления. А не наоборот.

Это предрассудок, будто воображение более высокая духовная способность, чем память, неустанно подчеркивает Гегель. Память выполняет, скорее, *именно своей репродуктивностью* продуктивную, базисную, роль в развитии психики. Репродукция, автоматизм, привычка, навык и т.д. предполагают память и опираются на неё как на всеобщую форму удержания всеобщих ситуаций. С психологической точки зрения тут – перевод *целеполагающей (сознательной) формы действования* в форму бессознательного, слепого, автоматического поведения.

Функции памяти, т.е. специфически субъектной деятельности, ответственной за *репродуктивный,* воспроизводящий аспект деяния, в истории новоевропейской философии – за исключением позиции Спинозы! – противостоит (в рамках единой, общей для них целостности, конкретности) функция продуктивная, *мыслящая,* производящая, т.е. такая субъектная деятельность, которая сообщает смысл, разумность действованию, иначе говоря, – она ответственна за т.н. "логику истории".

Память связана с языком, консерватором действования, генетически: она выступает как *неподвижный момент движения разумности,* если использовать аристотелевский взгляд на природу космического "Ума". Память – накопитель, собиратель предметного содержания действования, аккумуляция всеобщего.

Продуктивная, "творческая", функция разумного действования – есть взятие на себя инерции репродуктивного движения, сиречь – *перевод его в форму разумности* без умаления объёма и мощи этой инерции. Данный аспект деятельности Гегель называл "хитростью разума", способностью принимать на себя или хотя бы улавливать "логику истории".

Поэтому для Спинозы (как и для Аристотеля) не имеет принципиального значения форсированное противопоставление "продуктивной" и "репродуктивной" сторон деятельности, гипертрофированное в кантианстве.

Функции бессознательного – в сознании, репродукции – в творчестве у человека берет на себя память. Спиноза проблему памяти ставит в контекст проблематики, вскрывающей природу "интеллекта". При этом память непосредственно увязывается с воображением ("имагинацией"). Если человеческое тело подверглось однажды действию одновременно со стороны двух или нескольких тел, то душа, воображая впоследствии одно из них, тотчас будет вспоминать и о других, – настаивает Спиноза.

Формируя воображение, человек *одновременно* формирует и развивает и свою память. Вместе с тем память по отношению к воображению – всегда *предположена*. Вот и весь секрет, с точки зрения Спинозы. "Отсюда ясно, что такое *память*. Она есть не что иное, как некоторое сцепление идей, заключающих в себе природу вещей, находящихся вне человеческого тела, происходящее в душе сообразно с порядком и сцеплением состояний человеческого тела" – читаем мы в "Этике". Только тут есть одна любопытная тонкость. Память есть прежде всего некоторое "сцепление идей". Но идеи, согласно Спинозе, суть только такие состояния человеческого тела, которые заключают в себе как природу этого тела, так и природу тела внешнего. Идеи – это целостности, которые заключают в себе единство противоположностей. Память тем самым всегда обречена зацеплять оба вышеуказанных момента именно в силу того, что она *своим родом из идеи*. Иными словами говоря, память имеет "интеллектное" происхождение. Однако это вовсе не означает, что память сама по себе способна вывести человеческую душу на постижение вещей в их "первых причинах" – даже если предположить, что ей обеспечена со стороны человеческого тела возможность бесконечно сцеплять идеи внешних по отношению к нему тел.

Память (как и воображение, "имагинация") – своего рода предчувствие интеллекта, симптом возможности его обнаружения, можно, наконец, сказать, что память есть ищущий себя интеллект, или интеллект, нуждающийся в "очищении" (срв. гениальный замысел незаконченного шедевра Спинозы – "Tractatus de intellectus emendatione"), но ни в коем случае не есть самый этот *интеллект как таковой*. Мера развития интеллекта определяет меру развития памяти (да и других способностей души), а не наоборот. Мысля, человек *вспоминает* сообразно тому, как, каким способом он на деле привык "сцеплять" и соединять между собой различные образы вещей.

Вот почему душа от мышления одной вещи тотчас переходит к мышлению другой, не имеющей с первой никакого сходства. Всякий переходит от одной мысли к другой, настаивает Спиноза, смотря по тому, как привычка расположила в его теле образы вещей. Солдат, например, при виде следов коня на песке тотчас переходит от мысли о коне к мысли о всаднике, а отсюда – к мысли о войне и т.д. Крестьянин же от мысли о коне переходит к мысли о плуге или поле.

Показательно, что в понимании природы психических способностей, и прежде всего соотношения интеллекта, воображения и памяти, Спиноза стоит неизмеримо выше Декарта. Ильенков блистательно проанализировал и эту историко-философскую и одновременно теоретико-психологическую проблематику. Дело в том, что согласно Декарту, человеческое тело, как и все органические тела, есть машина, автомат. И вся разница между естественными автоматами и искусственными (т.е. созданными людьми) состоит лишь в степени, иначе говоря, носит лишь количественный характер. Подобно тому, как поломанные часы означают их смерть, так и разрушение человеческого тела может привести к его смерти. Поэтому удаление души есть следствие, а не причина смерти, считает Декарт, и подчеркивает, что не душа порождает в теле жизнь, а наоборот, телесная жизнь есть условие соединения души и тела – так что жизнь в теле существует до того, как с ним объединилась душа, и прекращение этой жизни происходит также до того, как душа отделяется от тела.

Вот почему принципиальное отличие человека от животного заключается в том, что человек помимо тела имеет разумную душу, которая даже гипотетически не может рассматриваться как продукт протяженной материи. Животные – это живые, но неодушевленные тела, и души они не имеют. Вполне можно допустить, что она создана Богом как сила, дополняющая материальную субстанцию, однако Декарт этот ход мысли оставляет для богословских дискуссий, не вмешиваясь в них, а сам предпочитает двигаться в несколько ином направлении.

Да, душа связана с телом связана весьма специфически. Она присутствует в нем не так вульгарно, как матрос присутствует на своем корабле, однако и не так тонко, чтобы был невозможен объективный, научно-методически корректный анализ такой связи, которую Декарт терминологически жестко обозначает как "композиционное единство", unio compositionis. В отличие от окказионалистов, Декарт в соответствии с избранной им логикой (методом) исследования никогда не назвал бы это "чудом", разве что в фигуральном смысле.

Душа и тело связаны бесконечно многими отношениями, но их ядро, главное место пересечения их всех, их взаимодействия сосредоточено непосредственно в одной небольшой частице тела, в своего рода седалище души – т.н. "шишковидной железе". Это центральный и к тому же единственный непарный орган в мозгу, полагает Декарт. В нем душа как сама воздействует на тело, так и испытывает на себе телесные влияния. И только *память,* "memoria" выпадает из этой системы взаимодействия, поскольку Декарт вынужденно, в силу своей дуалистической методологии, рассматривает ее скорее как материальный процесс, нежели психический. Что же касается проблемы воображения, вгляд Декарта на нее восхищает нас и сегодня остротой анализа.

Прежде всего Декарт твердо стоит на той точке зрения, согласно которой построение образа вещи есть активный способ деятельности души, а не тела."Уже достаточно хорошо известно, что ощущает душа, а не тело" – пишет он в своей "Диоптрике". (Р.Декарт. Рассуждение о методе. С приложениями "Диоптрика", "Метеоры", "Геометрия". М., 1953, стр. 92–93). Ощущение трактуется Декартом не как продукт пассивного восприятия, но как способ и результат действования ума и воли человека. Душа есть универсальное, активное начало в человеке. Активность действования пронизывает все способы проявления духовной жизни человека – от утонченных чисто интеллектуальных актов до простейших образов восприятия и первичных ощущений. Даже самый элементарный чувственный образ Декарт отказывается рассматривать как пассивный отпечаток, тавро внешнего воздействия. Вот почему никоим образом не следует полагать, что для восприятия ощущения душа должна созерцать образы, направленные предметами к мозгу, "как обычно думают наши философы...".

Рисунок или гравюра не тождественны отражаемой реальности, но они дают нам представление о ней. И вообще "во многих случаях, чтобы получить наиболее совершенные изображения и лучше представить предмет, нужно, чтобы изображения не походили на этот предмет" (там же, стр. 95). Образ внешней вещи человек строит, воспроизводя логику ее существования в объективном мире вне человека. При этом образ может возникнуть даже на основе знака или слова, ничего общего не имеющих с вещью. Более того, именно наличие такого разрыва есть необходимое условие входа человека в более универсальный мир значений, в царство идеальных форм.

Душа, управляющая органами чувств, своей активностью может заместить недостачу или полную утрату человеческих сенсорных возможностей – например, зрения. Поэтому слепые "как бы видят руками, и их палка представляет собой какое-то шестое чувство, данное им вместо зрения" (там же, стр. 71). Суть всей позиции Декарта в данном случае состоит в том, что раз ум человека универсален, т.е. способен строить свои действия по осознанию и осуществлению самостоятельно выработанной цели в соответствии с неповторимо складывающейся ситуацией, то он не может быть воспроизведен в виде запрограми-рованного машинообразного действия. Вернее, такое действие воспроизвести можно, только оно схватывает не самый ум, а лишь один из вариантов его воплощения. Исчезает, остается неуловимым при этом то, что Аристотель называл энтелехийностью.

Антропологическая проблема (на языке картезианства – "психофизическая проблема") – специфически-историческая форма проявления более глубокой проблемы *субстанциальной противоречивости* мышления (cogitatio) и протяжения (extensio), совершенно по-разному решаемой Декартом, окказионалистами и Спинозой.

Окказионализм Гейлинкса-Мальбранша и философия Спинозы – два исторических варианта разрешения картезианского дуализма.

Сам Рене Декарт мучительно размышлял над неразрешимыми затруднениями своего антропологического учения. Незавершенная книга Ильенкова о Спинозе затрагивает и эту проблематику. В своих работах 1970-х годов, связанных с исследованиями А.И.Мещерякова в области тифлосурдопедагогики, "поздний" Ильенков склоняется к решающему выводу, что философия Спинозы – теоретический ключ, открывающий тайны *человеческой зоопсихики* как фундамента в развитии высших психических функций личности, и настаивает на аналогии с выявленной в "Капитале" К.Маркса диалектикой формы стоимости (товар как основа понимания природы денег и капитала, а не наоборот).

С формальной стороны Спиноза, разумеется, последователь Декарта или, по крайней мере, подготовлен им.

Э.В.Ильенков впервые поставил вопрос в совершенно иной плоскости: оригинальность, глубина философских интуиций Декарта раскрывается и постигается в гораздо более полном объеме именно через призму основных понятий спинозовской "Этики". Спиноза, таким образом, выступает как подлинный отправной пункт развития новоевропейской философии, включая и ее кульминационную фазу – классический немецкий идеализм от Канта до Гегеля.

Спиноза, развивая вслед за Декартом проблему научного метода, формулирует ее как производную от единой (и единственной) универсальной субстанции, от Deus sive Natura. Это означало, что любой предмет природы, в том числе и такой "предмет", как человек со своим собственным внутренним миром, *адекватно* познается не из себя и не через выявление своего сходства с окружающими его телами (или со сколь угодно большим количеством других тел). Наоборот, адекватную идею о себе самом человек может создать только на пути мыслящего познания закономерности своих действий именно и исключительно внутри Deus sive Natura, – так что критерием высшей формы истинного познания любого предмета, т.е. высшей формой истинности вещи, может быть, согласно Спинозе, только выявление связи этой вещи прежде всего с *одним-единственным* предметом, с субстанцией, с бесконечной природой.

> Только отправляясь от идеи субстанции, мыслящее тело может понять как самое себя, так и и ту действительность, внутри которой и с которой оно действует, о которой оно мыслит [...] Поняв же способ своих действий (т.е. мышление), мыслящее тело как раз и постигает субстанцию как абсолютно необходимое условие взаимодействия с внешним миром (Э.В.Ильенков. *Диалектическая логика. Очерки истории и теории*. М., 1974, стр. 44).

В этом своеобразие спинозовского учения о единстве, об универсальности научного метода. В этом же состоит и отличие точки зрения Спинозы от картезианской: любой познаваемый предмет высвечивается сквозь призму универсальных законов природы, т.е. таких ее *собственных* законов , которым она сама подчиняется как целое. Дело, разумеется, не в "общих законах природы" как некоей системе абстракций, а в возможности нашего ума опираться на атрибутивно-мыслящее обнаружение природы. Это прекрасно понял и демонстративно проанализировал Ильенков в своей программной статье "Понимание абстрактного и конкретного в диалектике и формальной логике", где существо научного метода Спинозы интерпретируется как *процесс последовательной мысленной реконструкции вещи*, который "совершается не по правилам силлогистики, а по "норме истины", по норме согласия, единства мышления и протяженности, интеллекта и внешнего мира"(см. сборник "Диалектика и логика. Формы мышления". М., Изд-во АН СССР, 1962, стр. 181–188).

Ильенков, безусловно, не первый в истории новоевропейской философии мыслитель, защитивший мировоззренческую репутацию Спинозы, но он первый и, пожалуй, единственный, кто открыто и доказательно подтвердил не только логическую состоятельность спинозистских принципов, но и их преимущество в общем методологическом контексте развития науки XX века.

Спиноза для Ильенкова не кумир и не просто близкий по убеждениям мыслитель. Они оба – в личностном отношении родственные натуры:

Ильенков имел спинозовский склад души. Этим далеко не в последнюю очередь объясняется его внутреннее влечение к автору "Богословско-политического трактата" и "Этики".

Весьма любопытную оценку Спинозы можно найти в гегелевских "Лекциях по истории философии":

Современный мир представляет собою по своему существу власть связи и, благодаря этому, индивидууму абсолютно необходимо вступать в эту связь внешнего существования. В каждом сословии возможен только один общий способ существования, и лишь *Спиноза составляет исключение из этого правила.* Так, например, в прежние времена храбрость носила индивидуальный характер; современная же храбрость состоит в том, что каждый действует не по-своему, а полагается на связь с другим, и лишь эта связь дает ему его заслугу […] *Существенным для философа является верность своей цели* (Гегель. Соч., т. XI, стр.214).

Философ Ильенков и философия Ильенкова соответствуют этому гегелевскому критерию.

19

Iljenkow, Kant und die Dinge an sich

Vesa Oittinen

Wenn Iljenkows Lieblingsphilosophen aus der vormarxistischen Zeit vor allem Hegel, aber auch Spinoza waren, so war sein Verhältnis zu Kant eher gespannt. Ich möchte hier Iljenkows Kant-Rezeption hauptsächlich von dem Gesichtspunkt her betrachten, wie er die bekannte "Ding an sich"-Problematik behandelt und welche Folgen dies auf seine Philosophie hat. Andererseits handelt es sich bei der stiefmütterlichen Auslegung Kants mitnichten um eine blosse Idiosynkratie Iljenkows, sondern um eine durchgehende Tendenz in der sowjetischen Philosophie überhaupt, eine Tendenz, deren Wurzel sich bis auf Lenin, Plechanow und der linken Kritik an dem Neukantianismus-Flirt der II. Internationale am Ende des vorigen Jahrhunderts zurückverfolgen lassen. Aber dies wäre eigentlich schon eine andere Geschichte.

Gehen wir gleich *in medias res.* In der *Dialektischen Logik,* das sich wohl als das Hauptwerk Iljenkows charakterisieren lässt, stellt er im ersten Teil eine kurze Geschichte des dialektischen Denkens in der Neuzeit dar. Nachdem er den Dualismus von Descartes (*Otscherk* 1) und den Monismus Spinozas (*Otscherk* 2) dargestellt hat, geht er in der dritten "Umschau" dazu über, die Rolle der klassischen deutschen Philosophie bei der Schaffung einer "Grossen Logik" zu analysieren:

> Eben in der deutschen klassischen Philosophie wurde die Tatsache klar erkannt und scharf formuliert, dass alle Probleme der Philosophie als einer besonderen Wissenschaft [*kak osoboj nauki*] sich auf einer oder anderen Weise um die Frage kreisen, *was das Denken sei und welches seine Verhältnisse zur äusseren Welt seien* (Iljenkow 1984, 55).

Die Darstellung fängt mit Kant an, denn gerade in der Person des grossen Königsbergers trete die neuzeitliche Philosophie in eine neue Phase des Verständnisses und der Lösung ihrer spezifischen Probleme ein. Kant, fährt Iljenkow fort, strebte danach, alle grundlegenden aber zugleich einander widerstreitenden Denkprinzipien der Epoche in ein System zusammenzufassen. Dabei "legte er ungewollt nur deutlicher das Wesen der Probleme bloss, die man nicht mit den gewährten, der Philosophie bekannten Methoden lösen konnte" (Iljenkow 1984, 55). So wurde Kant zu einem Vorbereiter der dialektischen Logik.

Das von Iljenkow gebotene Bild der Vorgeschichte der dialektischen Logik ist insofern konventionell, weil ein altes Klischee marxistischer – somit auch sowjetischer – Philosophiegeschichtsschreibung hier ununterbrochen fortwirkt. Diese Klischee besteht darin, Kant, Fichte, Schelling und Hegel als einander ablösende Phasen der "klassischen deutschen Philosophie" zu betrachten. Hegel sei der Gipfelpunkt, der *Non plus ultra* der "vormarxistischen Philosophie". Die Zählebigkeit dieses Schemas, das in den Lehrbuch-Darstellungen der Sowjetzeit immer wieder wiederholt wurde, ist umso merkwürdiger, als darin eigentlich nichts spezifisch Marxistisches steckt. Vielmehr wird hier die Tradition einer bürgerlichen, ja konservativen Interpretation quasi fortgesetzt, deren typischer Vertreter Richard Kroner mit seinem Buch *Von Kant zu Hegel* (1921) ist (vgl. Dietzsch 1990, 7).Wie der deutsche Marxist Steffen Dietzsch bemerkt, war Kroner ein Hegel-Verehrer, der sich bemühte, "nur diejenigen Strukturen in der Entwicklung des klassischen Idealismus von Kant bis Hegel zu akzentuieren, die im Begriffsspiritualismus Hegels gipfeln" (ebenda, 55). Die sowjetmarxistische Interpretation betrachtete die klassische deutsche Philosophie ähnlich eindimensional-stadial[1] wie der Idealist Kroner, nur mit dem Unterschied, dass man die Klassikern nun "auf die Fussen stellte" und Antizipationen der materialistischen Dialektik bei ihnen suchte.

Dass man die Philosophiegeschichte als einen geradezu teleologischen Prozess betrachtete, hat verständlicherweise auch Proteste hergorgerufen. Merab Mamardaschwili beispielsweise vertrat in seinen Moskauer

Vorlesungen April 1982 (die aber erst 1997 publiziert wurden) trotzig einen
der offiziösen Deutung gerade entgegengesetzten Standpunkt:

> Unter den vielen Vorurteilen, die uns verhindern, zu verstehen was auf den Seiten
> der Kantschen Arbeiten gesagt wird, ist einer, dass man Kant als eine Stufe zu etwas
> betrachtet. Die gewöhnliche Formel lautet: Kant ist der Stammvater der klassischen
> deutschen Philosophie [...] Aber vom Kant darf man nicht sagen, dass er der Abra-
> ham war, der Isak erzeugte [...] Er bildet überhaupt keine Stufe zu irgend etwas
> (Mamardaschwili 1997, 11).[2]

Das ist nicht Iljenkows Position, denn er hat nicht vom herkömmliches phi-
losophiegeschichtliches Schema abgewichen. In seinen Augen ist Kant eben
"eine Stufe zu etwas", nämlich zur materialistischen Dialektik. Der Ver-
dienst Kants bestand darin, die Unzulänglichkeit der alten formalen Logik
nachzuweisen. Ihr Geltungsbereich beschränkt sich nur auf die analytischen
Urteile; die synthetischen bleiben ausserhalb ihres Anwendungsgebiets, da
sie im Prädikat zum Subjekt etwas zufügen, was da vorher nicht gab, und so
im Urteil einen Widerspruch formulieren:

> Mit anderen Worten, die allgemeine [d. h. formale – V. O.] Logik hat nicht das
> Recht, der Urteilskraft Rekommendationen zu erteilen, da diese Kraft das Recht hat,
> unter den Bestimmungen des Begriffs solche Tatsachen zu subsumieren, die direkt
> und unmittelbar diesen Bestimmungen *widersprechen* (Iljenkow 1984, 60).

Iljenkow akzeptiert Kants Unterscheidung zwischen empirischen und wis-
senschaftlich-theoretischen Begriffen, wobei nur den letztgenannten Allge-
meingültigkeit und Notwendigkeit eigen ist. Zwar erfasst Kant diese Allge-
meingültigkeit apriorisch, als Bedingung der Erfahrung, er zieht jedoch den
richtigen Schluss, dass man neben einer allgemeinen Logik noch eine spe-
zielle Logik entwerfen muss – eine Logik, die uns zeigt, wie verschiedene
Vorstellungen in eine Einheit des Mannigfaltigen vereinigt werden.

Dies geschieht durch Kategorien, und laut Iljenkow ist Kant denn auch
der erste, der "die hauptsächlichen *logischen* Formen des Denkens in den
Kategorien zu sehen beginnt"(Iljenkow 1984, 66). Er zitiert Kants
Formulierung, nach der wir uns "keinen Gegenstand *denken* [können], ohne
durch Kategorien" (*KdrV* B 165), und fährt fort: "Also, eben Kant (und nicht
Hegel, wie man gemeindlich denkt und sagt) sah den hauptsächlichen Inhalt
der Logik in den kategorialen Bestimmungen der Erkenntnis" (Iljenkow 1984,
67).

Gleichzeitig aber meinte Kant, dass "die Kategorien nichts anderes
sind, als universelle Formen (Schemen) der Erkenntnistätigkeit des Subjekts,
rein logische Formen des Denkens" (Iljenkow 1984, 67). Laut Iljenkow sei
Kant damit tatsächlich wieder in eine "absolute Kritiklosigkeit" gefallen, da
er meinte, dass es genüge, die Kategorien der alten Metaphysik (d. h.

Ontologie) in eine Logik umzuwandeln. "Praktisch lief dies zuweilen in einer
blossen Umbenennung 'ontologischer' Begriffe zu 'logischen' hinaus"
(ebenda, 69). So erweist Kant sich in der Darstellung Iljenkows als der Mann,
der zwar den ersten Schritt zu einer neuartigen, dialektischen Logik getan
hatte, aber auch nur den ersten.

Seine Unzufriedenheit mit Kant präzisiert Iljenkow folgendermassen:

> Nach Kant sind die Kategorien rein logische Formen, Tätigkeitsschemen des Intel-
> lekts, die das in der sinnlichen Erfahrung Gegebene (die Wahrnehmungen) mit der
> Form des Begriffs verbinden [...] Für sich genommen sind die Kategorien leer [...] In
> keinem Falle darf man die Kategorien als abstrakte Bestimmungen der Dinge an sich
> zu verstehen, wie diese Dinge ausserhalb des Bewusstseins der Menschen existieren
> [...] Sie kennzeichnen auf einer allgemeinen (abstrakt-allgemeinen) Weise nur den
> *denkbaren* Gegenstand (Iljenkow 1984, 69).

Eben deshalb ist Kants transzendentale Logik "eine *blosse Logik,* bloss eine
Lehre vom Denken. Ihre Begriffe (Kategorien) sagen uns absolut nichts darüber, wie es steht in der Welt ausserhalb der Erfahrung" (ebenda, 70). Kant
verfällt in einen Agnostizismus, in die "Behauptung, dass es überhaupt unmöglich ist, eine für den gegebenen Zeitpunkt mindenstens verhältnismässig
befriedigendes, einheitliches wissenschaftlich begründetes Weltbild zu
konstruieren" (ebenda, 71). Mit anderen Worten, die Kantsche Reform der
Logik findet nur auf dem gnoseologischen Niveau statt. Sie muss mit einer
weiteren ergänzt werden, die auch das Ontologische berührt.

Iljenkow und Kants Dialektik

Es ist mir nicht bekannt, inwiefern das ursprüngliche Manuskript der *Dialektischen Logik* bei der Herausgabe verkürzt worden ist, doch scheint mir,
dass man nicht nur editorische Zugriffe dafür beschuldigen kann, dass Iljenkows Wiedergabe der Dialektik Kants merkwürdige Auslassungen enthält
und sogar entstellend ist.

Mit "Dialektik" verstand Kant bekanntlich lediglich eine "Logik des
Scheins" (*KdrV* B 86), die daraus resultiert, dass man die an sich bloss
formalen Vernunftprinzipien "materiell" anzuwenden versucht (*KdrV* B 88).
Kant unterschied dabei mehrere Arten des dialektischen Scheins: die
Paralogismen der rationalen Seelenlehre, die Antinomien der reinen Vernunft
und die metaphysischen Gottesbeweise.

Von diesen Formen des dialektischen Scheins greift Iljenkow nur die
Antinomien auf. Die anderen von Kant analysierten dialektischen

Trugschlüsse lässt er in seiner Darstellung ausser Acht. Das mag noch aus Raumgründen verständlich sein, weitaus mehr problematisch aber ist es, wenn Iljenkow merkwürdiger Weise auch der Tatsache vorbeigeht, dass es bei Kant nur von *vier* Antinomien der Vernunft die Rede war. Er behauptet demgegenüber, dass Kant sich überhaupt alle Kategorien als polare Gegensätze vorstellte:

> Im Instrumentarium des Verstandes gibt es, wie die transzendentale Logik zeigte, gegensätzliche Kategorienpaare, d. h. in gegensätzliche Richtungen gehende [*wsaimno protiwonaprawlennych*] Schemata der Denktätigkeit. Zum Beispiel, es gibt nicht nur die Kategorie der Identität, die den Intellekt zur Suche von gleichartigen, invarianten Bestimmungen in verschiedenen Objekten richtet, sondern auch die ihr polare Kategorie von Unterschied, die gerade in entgegengesetzte Richtung führt [...] Neben dem Begriff der Notwendigkeit gibt es den Begriff von Zufall usw. usf. Jede Kategorie hat eine ihr gegensätzliche Kategorie, die mit ihr nicht vereinigt werden kann ohne Verletzung des Gesetzes vom Widerspruch (ebenda, 74)

Einige Zeilen später formuliert Iljenkow noch entschiedener:

> Und jede Erscheinung, die in der Erfahrung gegeben ist, kann immer mit Hilfe von jenem oder dann diesem, ihm direkt gegensätzlichen kategorialen Schemas interpretiert werden [...] Also, von jedem Gegenstand oder Objekt im Weltall kann man immer zwei einander ausschliessende Gesichtspunkte äussern... (ebenda, 74 – 75).

Dies ist schon eine sehr freie Auslegung der Ansichten Kants, die keineswegs sachgerecht angesehen werden kann. Ich hebe hier nur zwei Pointen hervor:

1) Kant erblickte die Antinomien vor allem in der *Vernunft*, die "dialektisch" zu irren beginnt sobald sie den Boden der Erfahrung verlässt und sich in spekulativen Ausflügen wagt. Man kann von einer Antinomität des blossen *Verstandes* bei Kant eigentlich[3] nicht sprechen, weil die grundlegende Bedingung für die Entstehung von Antinomien, nämlich das in der Verstandeseinheit Gegebene bis zum Unbedingten fortzusetzen, die Sache der Vernunft ist (vgl. *KdrV* B 397 ff.). (Nebenbei bemerkt: auch Hegel sah später – ganz im Gleichklang mit Kant – bekanntlich eben den *Verstand* als den Hort undialektischer Denkweise an; das Denken als Verstand, schrieb er, "bleibt bei der festen Bestimmtheit und der Unterschiedenheit derselben gegen andere stehen", während die *Vernunft* über feste Bestimmungen hinausgeht und zuerst als Dialektik, danach aber auch als Spekulation hervortritt; vgl. Hegel 1986: VIII, 169 ff.).

2) Die zweite, und wichtigere, Pointe ist, dass man bei Kant nirgends eine solche "Zwei-Gesichtspunkte-Lehre" wie ihm Iljenkow aufzwingt, finden kann. Wohl stellt Kant in der *Kritik der reinen Vernunft* auch eine Kategorientafel auf, wo man die von Iljenkov benannten Kategorien findet

(*KdrV* B 106 ff.) – aber eben *nicht* in der Form der ausschliessenden Gegensätzlichkeit, wie Iljenkow behauptet. Die Kategorien bilden bei Kant keine polaren Gruppen von zwei, sondern Triplizitäten von drei Gliedern. Beim Betrachten der Kategorientafel, wo er die Kategorien in vier Klassen (die der Quantität, Qualität, Relation und Modalität) gruppiert hat, notiert Kant, wie die von ihm vermerkte Tatsache, dass in jeder Klasse von Kategorien eine gleiche Zahl, nämlich *drei*, sind, bemerkenswert ist und "zum Nachdenken auffordert".

Dass Iljenkow eine philosophiegeschichtlich nicht stichhaltige Behauptung von der angeblichen polaren Gegensätzlichkeit Kantischer Kategorien – entgegen der von Kant selbst deutlich hervorgehobenen Triplizität – aufstellt, kommt ohne Zweifel daher, dass er Kant von einem ganz bestimmten Gesichtspunkt aus liest. Für Iljenkow ist es wichtig zu zeigen, dass Kant nicht nur ein Vorläufer von Hegel, sondern auch der marxistischen Widerspruchsdialektik ist.[4] Dass die Dialektik vor allem eine Lehre von den Widersprüchen sei, ist eine dem sowjetischen Diamat typische Vorstellung, deren Wurzel bis auf Plechanow und Lenins *Philosophischen Heften* zurückgehen. Sie folgt zudem Hegel darin, dass die dialektischen Widersprüche nicht als eine bloss gnoseologische (d. h. im Erkenntnisprozess sich geltend machende), sondern auch eine ontologische Rolle spielen sollten. Die "Widerspruchsdialektik" will eben die in den Dingen objektiv existierende Einheit und den Kampf der Gegensätze in den Griff bekommen.[5]

Dieses leidige Ding an sich....

Kant wäre also – laut Iljenkow – der "Erfinder" des dialektischen Widerspruchs, der jedem Ding zugrunde liegen soll. Andererseits aber meinte Kant, dass die Antinomien lediglich wegen der Mangelhaftigkeit (der Endlichkeit) des erkennenden Subjekts entstehen und dass es in der realen Welt keine Widersprüche gäbe (oder wir jedenfalls das nicht wissen könnten).

Will man also Kant in das stadiale Schema der Philosophiegeschichte pressen und zeigen, dass die Entwicklung doch in eine Widerspruchsdialektik vom Typus Diamat resultiert, sind besondere Deutungsoperationen vonnöten. Die Dialektik wird bei Kant ja nur im *negativen* Sinne verstanden, als keine echte Erkenntnis. Die dialektische "Logik des Scheins" entsteht daraus, dass wir auf die Dinge, wie sie an sich sind, unsere Bestimmungen anwenden, die aber nur im Bereich der Erscheinungen gültig sind. Es scheint daraus zu folgen, dass eine im *positiven* Sinne (als Logik der Wirklichkeit) verstandene Dialektik und der Kantische Ding-an-sich-Begriff einander notwendigerweise ausschliessen. So mindestens dachte Hegel, der sein Programm einer positiven Dialektik mit einer vernichtenden Kritik an Ding an sich verband.

Laut Iljenkow ist diese Ablehnung des Dings an sich auch für das Programm einer materialistischen Dialektik verbindlich. Er sieht sich benötigt, ähnlich wie Hegel, den Kantschen Dualismus abzustreifen, um das Dialektische bei ihm besser herauszupräparieren – das heisst, die Komplementarität von Gnoseologie und Ontologie soll aufgehoben werden:

> Aber die Kantische "Dialektik" wies eigentlich auf keinen Ausgang, auf keinen Weg der *Lösung* der ideellen Konflikte. Sie konstatierte lediglich, dass der Ideenkonflikt ein natürlicher Zustand der Wissenschaft sei, und rät den zwistenden Parteien überall diese oder andere Form des Kompromisses aufzusuchen, nach dem Regel "Leb und lass leben" [...], denn ihr seid beide Gefangene der subjektiven Interessen, und eine objektive, für alle gemeinsame Wahrheit ist euch jedenfalls unerreichbar... (Iljenkow 1984, 78–79)

Um meine Darstellung nicht allzu viel zu komplizieren, gehe ich hier nicht darauf ein, wie auch dieses Zitat eine höchst verzerrte Wiedergabe der Resultate der Kantschen Antinomienlehre bietet (Kant hat z. B. nie die wissenschaftliche Wahrheit als "Kompromiss" betrachtet!). Der Kantsche Dualismus, den Iljenkow hier unerträglich findet, rührt letzten Endes von Kants Weigerung her, die Antinomien als eine ontologische Tatsache hinzunehmen.

Hier interveniert nun der nächsthöchste Denker auf der philosophischen Leiter, Fichte:

> Der Dualismus, auf den Kant insistierte als einen ewigen, nicht zu überwindenden Zustand der geistigen Kultur, schien dem revolutionär eingestellten Fichte lediglich ein Ausdruck der Schüchternheit und Inkonsequenz des Denkens in der Ausführung seiner Prinzipien zu sein. Die Logik kann nicht zwei sich gleichzeitig ausschliessende Systeme rechtmässig begründen [...] Und Fichte sucht und findet die fundamentale Inkonsequenz der Kantschen Lehre vom Denken in dem Ausgangsbegriff, den Kant bewusst zum Grund aller seiner Konstruktionen legte, in dem Begriff vom "Ding an sich"... (ebenda, 80).

Ganz im Gleichschritt mit Fichte findet Iljenkow, dass das Kantsche "Ding an sich" der eigentliche Stein des Anstosses ist:

> In der Tat, in dem *Begriff* eines "Dinges, wie es vor und ausserhalb aller möglichen Erfahrung existiert", steckt eine von Kant nicht bemerkte Sinnlosigkeit: zu sagen dass *Ich im Bewusstsein* ein Ding *ausserhalb des Bewusstseins* habe, ist gleich wenn ich sagen würde: es gibt in der Tasche Geld, das ausserhalb der Tasche sich befindet... (ebenda, 80 – 81).

Iljenkow meint sogar, Kant neige zur Ansicht, dass das Ich, das Subjekt des
Denkens, auch ein Ding an sich sei (ebenda, 82),[6] und fährt fort:

> Eben darum erweist es sich beim Versuch, ein System aller Bestimmungen dieses
> Ichs – eine Logik als ein System der logischen Parameter des Denkens – zu schaffen,
> dass ein solches System durch und durch widersprüchlich, d. h., sich selbst zerstö-
> rend ist [...] Hier verliert selbst die Idee der Logik als einer Wissenschaft ihren Sinn.
> Denn alle Schlussfolgerungen, die man gewinnt wenn man das Denken *des Denkens*
> (als "Ding an sich", als Noumenon) betrachtet, werden nicht den mindesten Zusam-
> menhang haben mit dem Denken der *Dinge, die in der Anschauung und den Vorstel-
> lungen gegeben* sind. Keines der Sätze der Logik (d. h. des Denkens vom Denken)
> würden eine zwingende Kraft fürs Denken der Dinge, d. h. für das Denken des
> Naturwissenschaftlers, haben (ebenda, 82).

Aus diesen Sätzen geht klar hervor, dass Iljenkow die Kant-Kritik der deutschen Transzendentalphilosophie mindestens in ihrem Grundzug teilt. Sowohl der klassische deutsche Idealismus als auch der Neukantianismus lehn-
ten Kants Ding an sich ab, in dem man lediglich eine dem Aufbau eines
einheitlichen Systems hinderliche Inkonsequenz des Königsberger Denkers
sah. Im Klartext: Die Forderung des "Denken des Denkens" ist Gnoseologie,
während das "Denken der Dinge" zur Ontologie gehört. Sie zusammen-
zubringen bedeutet also, den Unterschied zwischen Ontologie und Gnoseologie und mit ihn den "Dualismus" vom Ding an sich und Erscheinung, deutlicher: von Objekt und Subjekt zu überwinden.

Meines Erachtens ist diese Weise, Kant zu interpretieren, für Iljenkow
in vieler Hinsicht verhängnisvoll. Das Wichtigste ist, dass Iljenkow damit
den bei Kant vorhandenen materialistischen Ansatz ignoriert. Dies sabotiert
seine eigene, zweifellos ehrlich gemeinte Intention, den marxistischen
Materialismus besser und kluger als bisher zu fundieren. Tatsächlich ist es
ein Vorurteil, in Kant nur einen Idealisten zu erblicken. Abgesehen davon,
dass Kant selbst immer bemüht war, den gegen ihn gerichteten Idealismus-
Verdacht vorzubeugen – man erinne sich nur an den "Widerlegung des
Idealismus" betitelten Zusatz in der zweiten Auflage der *Kritik der reinen
Vernunft* (B 274 ff.), den Kant hineinschob, um Garves Behauptungen über
die angebliche Nähe des Kritizismus zum Berkeleyanismus hinfällig zu
machen –, auch die innere Logik seiner Philosophie spricht dagegen. Wie
Steffen Dietzsch zusammenfassend formuliert, glaubte Kant "mehrfach
deutlich gemacht zu haben, dass es eben *keinen* ontologischen Bruch zwischen
den Erscheinungen und den Dingen (an sich selbst) gibt, sondern dass man
jene Trennung bloss *erkenntnistheoretisch* machen muss..." (Dietzsch 1990,
28).

Heute weiss man, dass die in der Herrschaftsperiode des Neukantianismus weitverbreitet gewordene Auslegung Kants als einen Idealisten eher

eine Karikatur ist.[7] Aber sogar aus dem Horizont des Marxismus der 70er Jahre gesehen lässt es sich sagen, dass Iljenkows Kant-Deutung an veralteten, von der linken Flügel der II. Internationale ererbten Klischees leidet. Eine mehr sachgerechte Interpretation Kants hatte sich nämlich schon damals auch im Umfeld des Marxismus durchzusetzen begonnen. So schrieb Hans-Jörg Sandkühler schon 1976 vom "transzendentalen *Erkenntnismaterialismus*" Kants (Sandkühler 1976, 256), und auch in der sowjetischen Philosophie hatte man sich ungefähr gleichzeitig um ein differenzierteres Kant-Bild zu bemühen begonnen.[8]

Aber nun zurück zur Ding-an-sich-Problematik. Wie wir sahen, soll darin laut Iljenkow "eine von Kant nicht bemerkte Sinnlosigkeit" stecken. Das ist keine gerechte Kritik, denn die Erkenntnis ist bei Kant immer eine Synthese von sinnlichem "Inhalt" (Materie) und intellektueller Form. Es sind die ausserhalb uns liegenden Dinge, die diesen Inhalt bzw. diese Materie liefern, indem sie unsere Sinnlichkeit affizieren. Gerade bei diesem Akt des Affizierens aber werden sie "Dinge für uns", also Erscheinungen. Es wäre demnach einfach töricht, zu fordern, dass man von den Dingen wie sie an sich sind, etwas wissen müsste, denn sobald wir etwas über sie wissen, sind sie schon "Dinge für uns" geworden. Ich als Erkenntnissubjekt habe also nach Kant keineswegs "im Bewusstsein ein Ding ausserhalb des Bewusstseins", wie Iljenkow interpretiert, sondern ich habe im Bewusstsein nur die Erscheinung des Dings, das an sich ausserhalb meines Denkens bleibt. Das "Ding an sich" spielt somit in der kritischen Philosophie eher die Rolle eines leeren Grenzbegriffes – es weist auf die Quelle unserer sinnlichen Erfahrung hin, von dem wir an sich, d. h., *vor* der Erfahrung, noch nichts sagen können, obgleich wir seine Existenz nicht bezweifeln brauchen oder müssen.[9]

Die deutschen Idealisten, und unten ihnen vor allem Hegel, aber wollten gerade aus dem Grenzbegriff des Kritizismus einen "richtigen" Begriff machen, einen Begriff mit bestimmtem Inhalt. Das ist gleichbedeutend mit der Forderung, dass man von den Dingen schon *vor* der Erfahrung etwas wissen soll. Das wiederum ist nur möglich, wenn man eine ursprüngliche Übereinstimmung bzw. Identität von Subjekt und Objekt postuliert, denn nur so kann Objektives ein ursprüngliches Besitz des Subjektiven sein.

Wie man sieht, es geht beim Kantschen "Ding an sich" um keine Kleinigkeiten, sondern um die berühmt-berüchtigte Grundfrage der Philosophie selbst. Wenn Iljenkow im Gefolge des nachkantischen Idealismus – Fichte, Schelling und Hegel – auch deren Kritik am "Ding an sich" akzeptiert, so muss die innere Logik seiner Argumentation ihn *nolens volens* auf dem Pfade der Identitätsphilosophie führen. Man muss dies besonders einschärfen, denn Iljenkow selbst sagt sich natürlich auf verbalem Niveau vom Idealismus der deutschen klassischen Philosophie los. Als er in der *Dialektischen Logik* dahin kommt, über Schellings Identitätsphilosophie – und also über eine Position, die faktisch auch die seinige ist – sich zu äussern, vermeidet er merkwürdiger Weise den Kern des Problems, die ontologischen Folgen des Subjekt-Objekt-Identitätspostulats. Statt dessen weist er darauf hin, dass diese ursprüngliche Identität Schellings sich nicht begrifflich ausdrücken lässt (denn sie ist ja ein ursprünglicher Akt). Somit verliert die Philosophie den Status der höchsten Wissenschaft und die Kunst tritt an ihrer Stelle. Schelling kann aus solchen Voraussetzungen ausgehend keine neue Logik aufbauen und sein Vorschlag zur Lösung des Problems sei aus *diesem* (sic!) Grunde abzulehnen (vgl. Iljenkow 1984, 99–109).

Etwa dreissig Seiten später tangiert Iljenkow in der *Dialektischen Logik* noch einmal das Problem einer Identitätsphilosophie, und diesmal gibt er zu verstehen, dass diesbezügliche Konstruktionen Schellings und Hegels nichts mit seinem eigenen Standpunkt zu tun habe, denn schliesslich waren Schelling und Hegel Idealisten, er, Iljenkow, aber ein Materialist. Auf Feuerbachs Kritik stützend, schreibt Iljenkow:

> Die sogenannte Philosophie der absoluten Identität ist tatsächlich eine Philosophie der Identität des Denkens mit sich selbst [...] Darum steckt unter der grandios tiefsinnigen Konstruktion der Hegelschen Philosophie tatsächlich eine leere Tautologie: wir denken die uns umgebende Welt so, wie wir sie denken. Demnach hat die Schelling-Hegelsche Philosophie nicht nur keine "absolute", sondern in der Tat keinerlei Identität vom Sein und Denken überhaupt feststellen können, denn auf "das Sein als solches", auf das freie, selbständige, autarke Sein, das ausserhalb und unabhängig vom Denken existiert, wird hier einfach nicht Rücksicht genommen. Es bleibt etwas gänzlich Jenseitiges und Unbestimmtes. Das fundamentale Prinzip des Kantschen Dualismus bleibt somit unberührt. Man betrachtet vom Anfang an den denkenden Geist als allem Sinnlichen, Körperlichen, Materiellen etwas gänzlich Gegensätzliches, als ein besonderes immaterielles Wesen... (ebenda, 140).

Ich würde diese Sätze Iljenkows nicht einfach als eine Idealismus-Kritik lesen. *De facto* wirft er hier den deutschen Identitätsphilosophen vor, dass sie nicht identitätsphilosophisch genug waren. Es erweist sich, dass sogar Hegel, Iljenkovs Lieblingsphilosoph, nicht ganz den Dualismus Kantscher Provenienz los wird, einen Dualismus, dessen Wurzel in dem leidigen Dinge an sich liegen.

Marxismus als Identitätsphilosophie

Iljenkows Überzeugung ist, dass erst die marxistische Philosophe das lästige Kantsche Ding vom Hals gekriegt hat dank der materialistischen Umstülpung der Hegelschen Erbe. Die Vereinigung des Hegelschen Historismus und der Tätigkeitsidee mit dem Materialismus habe es dem Marxismus ermöglicht, in der gegenständlich-historischen Praxis des Menschen die endgültige Lösung der alten philosophischen Probleme zu finden. Diese neue, die bisherige Philosophie revolutionierende Sichtweise wäre zum erstenmal in den Feuerbach-Thesen von Marx klar formuliert. Iljenkow referiert Lenins Hegel-Exzerpte aus den *Philosophischen Heften*, in denen Lenin – ganz im Geiste des von Marx in den Feuerbach-Thesen formulierten Gedankens, dass der Idealismus bisher "die *tätige* Seite" entwickelt habe, während der Materialismus kontemplativ geblieben sei – darauf hinwies, wie Hegel in seinem Verständnis der Rolle der Praxis Marx ganz nahe kam.[10] Dann kommentiert Iljenkow:

> Als ein praktischer Akt bezieht das Denken *die Dinge ausserhalb des Bewusstseins* in seiner Bewegung ein, und dann erweist es sich, dass die "Dinge an sich" sich dem Diktat des denkenden Menschen unterwerfen; sie bewegen sich und verändern sich gehorsam nach den Gesetzen und Schemata, die das Denken ihnen diktiert. Also nicht nur der "Geist" bewegt sich nach den logischen Gesetzen, sondern auch die Welt der "Dinge an sich" . Folglich erweist die Logik sich als eben *auch* eine Erkenntnistheorie *der Dinge,* und nicht nur als eine Theorie der Selbsterkenntnis des Geistes (Iljenkow 1984, 200).

Diese Worte sind nicht als ein blosses Hegel-Referat zu verstehen, sondern geben unmissverständlich Iljenkows eigene Marxismus-Deutung wieder. Es ist die Position, die in der bekannten Formulierung vom "Zusammenfallen der Logik, Dialektik und Erkenntnistheorie" fixiert wurde – einer Formulierung, die man in den *Philosophischen Heften* Lenins trifft[11] und die Iljenkow zu seiner eigenen Devise erhoben hatte. Da Lenin in den Schriften Iljenkows stets als oberste Auktorität *in philosophicis* figuriert, entsteht damit eine seltsame Kombination: einerseits vermittelt Iljenkow durch seine ständige Berufung auf Lenin den Eindruck, er sei ein typischer Repräsentant des sowjetischen philosophischen Establishments, für den die ideologische Reinheit das Wichtigste sei, andererseits aber liegt der eigentliche philosophische Kern seiner Botschaft weit abseits des herkömmlichen Marxismusverständnisses.

   Wohl scheint Iljenkow sich auch hier von der Identitätsphilosophie zuerst zu distanzieren. Er unterstreicht, dass "[d]er Unterschied zwischen den Formulierungen Hegels und Lenins *prinzipiell* ist" (Iljenkow 1984, 201).

Denn während Lenin in den *Philosophischen Heften* notierte, dass die Logik
nicht nur die Lehre "von den äusseren Formen des Denkens ist, sondern von
den Entwicklungsgesetzen 'aller materiellen, natürlichen und geistigen Dinge',
d. h. der Entwicklung des gesamten konkreten Inhalts der Welt unb ihrer
Erkenntnis..." (ebenda, 200),[12] könne bei Hegel von keiner Entwicklung der
"natürlichen Dinge" die Rede sein. Für Hegel gibt es nämlich keine
geschichtliche Entwicklung in der Natur. Darum, fährt Iljenkow fort,

> ist die Meinung grob falsch, dass die Bestimmung der Logik als eine Wissenschaft
> von den Entwicklungsgesetzen "aller materiellen, natürlichen und geistigen Dinge"
> nur ein von Lenin wiedergegebener oder sogar nur von ihm zitierter Gedanke He-
> gels sei. Nichts dergleichen. Er ist *Lenins* eigener *Gedanke,* den er bei kritischer
> Lektüre des Hegelschen Passus formuliert hatte (ebenda, 201).

Welche unter Iljenkows sowjetischen Adversarien diese "grob falsche Meinung" vertreten hatten, ist mir beim Niederschreiben dieser Zeilen nicht bekannt, und es ist auch nicht in diesem Zusammenhang wichtig. Wichtig ist,
dass Iljenkow hier den Unterschied zwischen Hegel und Lenin auf einen
einzigen Punkt reduziert – nämlich auf die Frage, ob es eine (historische)
Entwicklung auch in der Natur gebe oder nicht. An der Hauptfrage aber, die
Frage nach dem Subjekt-Objekt-Identität oder -Koinzidenz, geht er ganz still-
schweigend vorbei. Dadurch entsteht der Eindruck, als ob Lenin ein direkter
Nachfolger von Hegel wäre, uneins nur in einigen eher nebensächlichen Fra-
gen.
        Nach all dem Gesagten bleibt der Status eines "identitätsphilosophischen
Marxismus", wie Iljenkow ihn vertritt, unklar und zwitterhaft. Entgegen
Iljenkows eigenen Beteuerungen ist der Materialismus in seiner Position
keineswegs eindeutig. Wie paradox es immer klingen mag, Kant ist mit seinem
Beharren auf "Dinge an sich" tatsächlich materialistischer (im
erkenntnistheoretischen Sinne) als Iljenkow. Denn der gnoseologische
Dualismus von Dinge an sich und Erscheinungen baut auf einer strikten
Unterscheidung von objektiven und subjektiven Quellen unserer Erkenntnis,
auf der Einsicht dass das Sein vom Denken durchaus unabhängig ist. Nach
Kant weist der Grenzbegriff des Dings an sich auf einen irreduziblen
ontologischen Rest hin, der uns nötigt, den "Dualismus" von Subjekt und
Objekt aufrechterhalten.
        Mehr noch: eben dieser Dualismus ist – wieder paradoxerweise – die
notwendige Voraussetzung dazu, dass wir von der "Objektivität der
Aussenwelt" überhaupt sprechen können, denn "Objekt" und "Subjekt" sind
ja korrelative Begriffe: ohne Subjektivität keine Objektivität und vice versa.[13]
Auch der Materialist müsste also demnach auf *gnoseologischem* Niveau auf
den "Dualismus" von Subjekt und Objekt festhalten, um *ontologisch* die

objektive Einheit der Welt begründen zu können. Oder anders ausgedrückt: *"Dualismus" und "Monismus" schliessen einander nicht aus, sondern setzen vielmehr einander voraus.*[14] Nicht so bei Iljenkow. Beim Lesen seiner Texte kann man immer wieder ein Oszillieren feststellen, wenn von Objektivität bzw. Subjektivität die Rede ist. So schreibt er z. B. an einer Stelle der *Dialektischen Logik*, dass

> Schelling und Hegel gingen von der These einer ursprünglichen Gegensätzlichkeit von nicht-körperlichem Denken und nicht-denkendem Körper aus, um dann als Resultat zur Einheit der Gegensätze zu gelangen. Das ist eben der falsche Weg des Spiritualismus. Der Materialist wiederum [hier verweist Iljenkow natürlich auch auf sich selbst – V. O.] soll von der faktischen, unmittelbaren Einheit (Ungeteiltheit) des menschlichen Individuums ausgehen, um zu verstehen und zu zeigen, wie und warum im Kopf dieses Individuums die Illusion von der angeblichen Gegensätzlichkeit des Denkens und des körperlichen Seins entsteht.

Unmittelbar nach diesen Sätzen fährt Iljenkow fort:

> Die Illusion von der Gegensätzlichkeit des denkenden Geistes und des Körpers ist überhaupt also ein rein subjektives Faktum, d. h. ein Faktum, das nur im Kopf des menschlichen Individuums existiert, ein rein psychologisches Faktum (Iljenkow 1984, 143).

Soll es mit dieser Formulierung ernst gemeint sein, so verlieren die Begriffe "Subjektivität" und "Objektivität" ihren präzisen Sinn, den sie noch beibehalten würden, wenn man nicht die Dinge an sich über Bord geworfen hätte.

Macht die Praxis das "Ding an sich" obsolet?

Ich werde hier nicht alle die möglichen Weisen auflisten, mit denen eine derartige "identitätsphilosophische" Lesart des Marxismus den ursprünglichen materialistisch gemeinten Ansatz sabotiert, zumal ich in meinen früheren Arbeiten auf einige schon hingewiesen habe. [15] Hier mag es genügen, als Beispiel eines der wichtigsten Fragen der angestrebten neuen dialektischen Logik, die Frage der Kategorien, aufzugreifen. Für Kant waren – eben als konsequente Folge seines "Dualismus" – die Kategorien lediglich "subjektive Bedingungen des Denkens" (*KdrV* B 122), oder wie Rolf-Peter Horstmann präzis formuliert: "Kategorien sind für Kant Begriffe mit einer epistemologischen Funktion; sie haben keine metaphysische Bedeutung in dem Sinn, dass sie den ontologischen Begriffen zuzurechnen wären. Bei Hegel sieht das ganz anders aus. Für ihn haben die Kategorien oder Denkbestimmungen, wie er sie nennt, eine eminent ontologische Funktion und Bedeutung. Sie bestimmen, was ein Gegenstand in Wirklichkeit ist" (Horstmann 1997, 191).

Auch in dieser Frage nimmt Iljenkow Stellung für Hegel und gegen Kant. Er kritisiert überhaupt die Hervorhebung der Rolle der Gnoseologie, in der er nur einen Versuch der Neukantianer sieht, einen extremen Subjektivismus ins Feld zu führen.[16] Statt dessen sollte die Gnoseologie in die Ontologie aufgehen, und dies geschieht dadurch, dass die Gesellschaftlichkeit als Mittler zwischen Gnoseologie (bzw. Subjekt) und Ontologie (bzw. Objekt) gesetzt wird. Nach Iljenkow werden im Marxismus

> die Denkformen und Kategorien nicht als einfache Abstraktionen aus unhistorisch verstandenen Sinnlichkeit verstanden, sondern vor allem als im Bewusstsein wiedergespiegelte allgemeine Formen der sinnlich-gegenständlichen Tätigkeit des gesellschaftlichen Menschen (Iljenkow 1984, 185).

Diese allgemeinen Formen der gesellschaftlichen Tätigkeit hat Iljenkow in mehreren seinen Schriften als Analogie des Marxschen Wertbegriffes betrachtet.[17] Ganz wie der Wert der Waren etwas Ideelles ist, der nur in der Tätigkeit und in den gesellschaftlichen Verhältnissen des Menschen existiert, zugleich aber objektiv-allgemein ist, so sind auch die anderen Denkbestimmungen, Ideen bzw. Kategorien auf ähnliche Weise sowohl objektiv als subjektiv:

> Das Individuum denkt nur insofern er schon die allgemeinen (logischen) Bestimmungen angeeignet hat, die historisch vor ihm und ganz von ihm unabhängig existiert haben [...] Marx und Engels sahen das reelle (gegenständliche) Urbild [*proobraz*] der logischen Bestimmungen und Gesetze in den konkret-allgemeinen Formen und Gesetze der gegenständlichen Tätigkeit des gesellschaftlichen Menschen und machten damit jegliche subjektivistische Deutung der Tätigkeit selbst unmöglich [...] Marx und Engels bewiesen, dass die logischen Formen und Gesetze der Tätigkeit sind lediglich eine Folge (eine Widerspiegelung) von wirklichen, von keinem Denken abhängigen Gesetze der gegenständlich-menschlichen Tätigkeit (Iljenkow 1984, 186, 187).

Hier ist also der gesellschaftlichen Tätigkeit (der Praxis) selbst die Rolle des vermittelnden Dritten zwischen Denken und Sein gegeben. Die Tätigkeit ist, so kann man sagen, der "Kitt" der Iljenkowschen Identitätsphilosophie; sie bindet Subjektives und Objektives zusammen, so dass sie sich nicht gegenüberstehen – und sich auch nie gegenübergestanden haben. Denn die vermittelnde Praxis hat hier zugleich die Stelle des Prius eingenommen und so die gnoseologische Frage erübrigt, ob die Priorität dem Sein oder dem Denken zukomme. Im obigen Zitat benutzt Iljenkow die Terminologie des Leninschen *Materialismus und Empiriokritizismus,* indem er vom "Widerspiegelung" spricht, und scheint damit beim ersten Blick "jegliche subjektivistische Deutung der Tätigkeit" unmöglich gemacht zu haben. Tatsächlich steht aber mit dieser materialistischen Intention im Widerspruch, dass der individuelle Mensch die *logischen* Bestimmungen schon als ausserhalb ihn existierend vorfinden soll – das heisst, diese Bestimmungen sind doch nicht nur wiedergespiegelt, sondern haben ein "eigenes Sein".

Auch hier, in der Frage um den Ursprung der logischen Formen und Kategorien, zieht Iljenkow eine Demarkationslinie gegen Kants "Dualismus". In einem Text aus den 70er Jahren, betitelt *Dialektik des Ideellen,* schreibt er dazu:

> Alle die Schemata, die Kant als "transzendental-angeborene" Formen der Arbeit der Psyche des Einzelnen, als jeder Psyche apriorisch eigentümliche "innere Mechanismen" definierte, sind in der Tat vom Individuum von aussen her angeeignete (und ursprünglich ihm als "äussere" Bewegungsschemata einer von seinem Willen und Bewusstsein unabhängigen Kultur gegenüberstehende) Formen des Selbstbewusstseins des gesellschaftlichen Menschen, verstanden als eine historisch sich entwickelnde "Totalität aller gesellschaftlichen Verhältnisse" (Iljenkow 1991, 250).

Ganz wie Hegel, fügt Iljenkow hier zu den Kategorien und Ideen eine ontologische Funktion zu, und ganz wie bei Hegel ist die eigentliche Zielscheibe der "identitätsphilosophisch" motivierten Kritik eher ein "Dualismus" Kantischer Art denn der Idealismus.

Löst die Idee der "vermittelnden praktischen Tätigkeit" nun tatsächlich die Erwartungen ein, die man in sie investiert hat? Kann man die Kategorien gleichsam "ontologisieren", indem man sie zu Momenten der gesellschaftlichen Tätigkeit macht? Die von Iljenkow befürwortete Lösung wurde schon in den 60er Jahren unter einem Teil der sowjetischen Philosophen beliebt und man hat sie als eine bleibende Errungenschaft des Marxismus betrachtet. So schrieb Nelly Motroschilowa 1967 im Artikel "Ontologie" zur berühmten 5-bändigen *Filosofskaja enziklopedija,* dass der Marxismus – und nur er – habe das Problem endlich enträtseln können, das hinter den ontologischen Versuchen von Nicolai Hartmann, Husserl, Jaspers u. a. stehe – nämlich "das Problem der konkreten Identität (*toshdestwa*), des gegenseitigen Durchdringens des Subjektiven und Objektiven im gesellschaftlichen Sein, das von der menschlichen Tätigkeit gebildet worden ist". Vom Standpunkt dieses gesellschaftlichen Seins her müsse auch das Sein der Natur begriffen werden.[18]

Wie wir gesehen haben, sollte diese identitätsphilosophisch angelegte Theorie der Praxis Iljenkow zufolge das "Ding an sich" obsolet machen, denn in der praktisch-gegenständlichen Tätigkeit des Menschen würden "'Dinge an sich' sich dem Diktat des denkenden Menschen unterwerfen"; sie würden "sich bewegen und sich verändern gehorsam nach den Gezetzen

und Schemata, die das Denken ihnen diktiert", und nicht nur "der Geist [...],
sondern auch die Welt der 'Dinge an sich'" würden sich nach den logischen
Gesetzen bewegen (Iljenkow 1984, 200).

Dies lautet ja gut. Aber wie genaugenommen konnte man mit Berufung
auf die gegenständliche Praxis des Menschen von den "Dingen an sich" los
kommen? Auch hier würden wir weiter mit ein "Ding an sich" eben den Teil
der Aussenwelt bezeichnen müssen, auf den unsere Tätigkeit, unsere Praxis
noch nicht gereicht hat. Denn das liegt schon im Begriff des *gegenständlichen*
Praxis: sie muss – will man eben nun an einer materialistischen Deutung des
Praxisbegriffs festhalten – sich auf ein ausserhalb ihrer befindlichen
Gegenstand richten, und dann muss der Gegenstand wiederum, als eine
irreduzible Voraussetzung der Tätigkeit, vor seinem Eintreten in den Kreis
der menschlichen Praxis als ein Ding an sich bestimmbar sein.

In seiner identitätsphilosophischen Praxis-Theorie betrachtet Iljenkow
den Dualismus von Kant *nur* als etwas, was man überwinden muss. Es scheint,
dass hier ein Missverständnis hinsichtlich Kants Intentionen vorliegt, denn
der "Dualismus" war für Kant kein nur zu beseitigendes Problem, sondern
ein vernunftkritisches und erkenntnistheoretisches Postulat – es liesse sich in
Anspielung auf Occam sogar von einem "Kantischen Rasiermesser" zu
sprechen –, mit dessen Hilfe man subjektive und objektive Komponente der
Wirklichkeit genauer voneinander trennen und untersuchen kann. Auch das
"Ding an sich" muss im Zusammenhang dieser erkenntniskritischen Forderung
bewertet werden. Es ist schlicht falsch, im "Ding an sich" lediglich ein
Geständnis an Agnostizismus oder gar an Idealismus zu sehen. Bleibt dies
unberücksicht, rächt sich das Aufgeben der kritischen Intention von Kant
insofern, dass eine Restauration der Metaphysik dann wieder sich aufdrängt.

Noch eine abscliessende Bemerkung. Ich habe hier das Verhältnis von
Kant und Hegel vor allem *sensu scholastico* betrachtet, also vom Standpunkt
her, den Kant für "Schulbegriff" nannte. Aber die Verschiedenheit dieser
zwei Philosophen beschränkt sich natürlich nicht auf solche letztes Endes
doch "technische" philosophische Fragen wie die Bestimmung der
Erkennbarkeit der Dinge an sich. In "weltbürgerlicher Hinsicht" weisen diese
technischen Fragen auf andere, tiefere Spannungen hin. Vor allem markieren
die Namen Kants und Hegels zwei verschiendene Haltungen zur Moderne.
Während Hegel die "Entzweiungen" der modernen Welt beinahe um jeden
Preis aufheben und versöhnen wollte, nahm Kant die Sache gelassener. Ich
zitiere Herbert Schnädelbach:

> Für ihn [Kant – V.O.] waren die grossen Dichotomien, an denen sich sein Denken
> beständig abarbeitete, nichts Entsprungenes, sondern die wahre, durch Aufklärung
> endlich an den Tag getretene *condition humaine*; deswegen war für ihn die reale

Einheit der Gegensätze – sei es als vergangene, gegenwärtige oder zukünftig-utopische – kein möglicher Gedanke. So fasst Kant die Moderne im Hinblick auf ihre reale Unübersteigbarkeit ins Auge, ohne dem Denken die Hoffnung auf das, was anders wäre, zu verbieten. Hegel hingegen sagt: "Solche festgewordene Gegensätze aufzuheben, ist das einzige Interesse der Vernunft" [...] Mit Kant hat es keinen Sinn, eine Gesellschaft ins Auge zu fassen, in der Ding an sich und Erscheinung, Intelligibles und Empirisches, Sein und Sollen endlich zusammenfallen. Der Grund ist, dass Kant mit seinen grossen Dichotomien die Endlichkeit unserer Vernunft formuliert, während Hegel und die Hegelianer mit dem Topos "Entzweiung – Versöhnung" auch in der Theorie der Moderne in der Perspektive des Absoluten philosophieren (Schnädelbach 1996, 14, 17).

Auch Iljenkow bemühte sich, ähnlich Hegel, die Entzweiungen der sowjetischen Realität zu überwinden und zu versöhnen. Das führte tatsächlich zu einer Philosophie in der – wenigstens der Intention nach – absoluten Perspektiv, an der auch etwas Tragisches haftet.

Bemerkungen

[1] Vgl. dazu die interessante und materialreiche Analyse der sowjetischen "istoriko-filosofskaja nauka" bei van der Zweerde (1994), besonders Teil IV, Kap. 12 .

[2] Mamardaschwili geht so weit, dass er Kants Verbindung mit der späteren deutschen Transzendentalphilosophie überhaupt verneint – was wiederum eine zu extreme Position ist und der philosophiegeschichtlichen Wahrheit Abbruch tut: "Nach Kant fängt dann eine für mich widerwärtige Epoche an, die Epoche der eigentlichen deutschen Philosophie. In diesem Sinne ist Kant kein deutscher Philosoph..." (ebenda).

[3] Ich sage "eigentlich", denn Kant selbst ist nicht immer ganz konsequent und unterscheidet nicht überall deutlich zwischen Verstand und Vernunft; so z. B. spricht er in den einleitenden Betrachtungen zur transzendentalen Dialektik an einer Stelle vom "Blendwerke einer Erweiterung des *reinen Verstandes*" (*KdrV* B 352). Aber auch hier schärft er auf der nächsten Seite jedoch schon ein, dass die Grundsätze des reinen Verstandes "bloss von empirischem und nicht von transcendentalem, d. i. über die Erfahrungsgrenze hinausreichendem, Gebrauche sein" sollen.

[4] Auf die Bedeutung der Kantschen transzendentalen Logik und besonders der Antinomien für die Dialektik hatte W. F. Asmus schon in den 20er Jahren hingewiesen, doch scheint die Interesse an die genauere Erforschung dieses Themenkreises in der Sowjetzeit verhältnismässig lau gewesen zu sein. Eines der wenigen neueren Studien ist das von I. S. Narski verfasste 3. Kapitel "Kants Logik der Antinomien" im Sammelband *Filosofija Kanta i sowremennost* (1974, 72 –103), das auch eine Kritik der Ansichten von Asmus enthält.

[5] Ich kann hier unmöglich die Problematik des dialektischen Widerspruchs bei Hegel und in der Sowjetphilosophie umständlicher behandeln, da es zu weit vom heutigen Thema führen würde. Eine Diskussion zu derselben Problematik, die ich hier angestreift habe, findet man u. a. bei Arndt (1994, 216 ff.; Kapitel "Schwierigkeiten im Umgang mit Hegels Widerspruchsbegriff"). Arndt tadelt "die marxistisch-leninistische Tradition" darüber, dass sie "einer Substantiierung des Widerspruchsprinzips in der sich selbst bewegenden Materie nicht immer widerstehen konnte und so das Hegelsche Absolute unter anderem Namen wieder in Umlauf brachte". Diese Hegel-Interpretation lehnt vor allem an Lenins Äusserungen in den *Philosophischen Heften* an. Eine besonders typische Stelle bei Lenin lautet: "Spaltung des Einheitlichen und Erkenntnis seiner widersprechenden Bestandteile [...] ist das *Wesen* (eine der 'Wesenheiten', eine der grundlegenden, wenn nicht die grundlegende Besonderheit oder Seite) der Dialektik" (Lenin 1989, 338). Der Widerspruch ist zwar ein wichtiges Merkmal dialektischer Denkweise bei Hegel, wenn man jedoch sich darauf bechränkt und die ebenso grundlegende Rolle der Selbstbezüglichkeit und der Negation der Negation nicht genügend beachtet, wird der Unterschied zwischen formallogischem und dialektischem Widerspruch unklar. Tatsächlich weist schon die Triplizität der Kategorien deutlich darauf hin, dass die Dialektik bei Hegel etwas

mehr als eine blosse Widerspruchslogik ist – nämlich eine "Logik der Subjektivität". – Die vom Diamat vertretene Interpretation des Widerspruchs als eine ontologische Eigenschaft der objektiven Realität führt auch – darauf sei hier nur kurz hingewiesen – zum heiklen Problem des Verhältnisses einer so verstandenen "dialektischen Logik" zur formalen Logik. Bei Hegel entstand dieses Problem nicht, da für ihn die Tatsache, dass alle Dinge widersprüchlich seien, eben davon zeugte, dass das subjektive Prinzip (die Quelle der Antinomien und Widersprüche) nicht von der Aussenwelt separiert war, wie im "Dualismus" Kants, sondern innerhalb der Objektivität selbst wirkte – mit anderen Worten: der Widerspruch entspringt bei Hegel aus der Reflexion. Dialektisch war für Hegel nicht die Materie bzw. Substanz "an sich" (wie im Diamat), sondern erst die verschiedenen konkreten Gestalten, in der Substanz und Subjekt vermittelt sind.

6 Auch diese Behauptung ist nicht stichhaltig. Kant war eher der entgegengesetzten Ansicht. Für ihn war das Ich eine blosse Form des Bewusstseins, und er hob ausdrücklich hervor, dass wir keine Kenntnis vom "Subjekt an sich selbst" als Substrat aller Gedanken haben können (vgl. *KdrV* A 350). Ich erkenne als Subjekt mein eigenes Ich "gleich anderen Phänomen" nur wie ich mich *erscheine* (*KdrV* B 155). Die alte, auch von Descartes vertretene Vorstellung von der Dinghaftigkeit bzw. Substantialität des Ichs hielt Kant für einen blossen Paralogismus der rationalen Psychologie.

7 Von der neuesten einschlägigen Literatur kann ich hier als Beispiel das jüngst erschienene Buch des US-Amerikanischen Philosophen Arthur Collins nennen, in dem er die Diskussion der letzten Jahre zusammenfasst, und anstrebt, die meisten Argumente einer idealistischen Kant-Lektüre zu widerlegen (Collins 1999). Einige Thesen von Collins scheinen zwar problematisch zu sein (z. B. die Behauptung, dass ein richtiges Kant-Verständnis eine "anticartesianische" Optik verlangen würde). Eine ähnliche Tendenz zur "realistischen" Lektüre findet man im Peter Baumanns *KdrV*-Kommentar (Baumanns 1997).

8 Aus der Literatur dieser Periode wären u. a. die Sammelbände *Filosofija Kanta i sowremennost* (1974) und *Krititscheskie otscherki po filosofii Kanta* (1975) zu erwähnen. Die 250. Wiederkehr des Geburtstages von Kant in 1974 gab Regungen zu einer aktiven Kant-Forschung in der UdSSR, wie auch aus der von L. S. Dawydowa zusammengestellten Bibliographie ersichtlich ist (Dawydowa 1996).

9 Auch der Materialist Spinoza, auf den Iljenkow sich gern stützt, scheint ähnlich über die "Dinge an sich" zu denken: *"Idea cujuscunque affectionis Corporis humani adaequatam corporis externi cognitionem non involvit"* (*Eth.* II prop. 25), wo man sehr gut die *"Idea Corporis affectionis"* als "Erscheinung" und das *"Corpus externum"* als "Ding an sich" übersetzen konnte.

10 Die von Iljenkow zitierte Lenin-Stelle lautet: "...dass bei Hegel die Praxis als Kettenglied in der Analyse des Erkenntnisprozesses steht, und zwar als Übergang zur objektiven (nach Hegel 'absoluten') Wahrheit. Marx knüpft folglich unmittelbar an Hegel an, wenn er das Kriterium der Praxis in der Erhenntnistheorie einführt: siehe Thesen über Feuerbach" (Lenin 1989, 202).

[11] Der *locus classicus* dieser unter sowjetischen Philosophen oft diskutierten These lautet: "Im 'Kapital' [von Marx – V.O.] werden auf *eine* Wissenschaft Logik, Dialektik und Erkenntnistheorie {man braucht keine 3 Worte: das ist ein und dasselbe} des Materialismus angewendet, der alles Wertvolle von Hegel übernommen und dieses Wertvolle weiterentwickelt hat" (Lenin 1989, 316)

[12] Die entsprechende Lenin-Stelle auf deutsch in Lenin 1989, 84–85.

[13] Man dürfte auch sagen, dass Lenin im *Materialismus und Empiriokritizismus*, wo er gelegentlich auch Kant gegenüber der Kritik von Avenarius, Mach u.a. verteidigte, noch mehr "kantianisch" war als einige Jahre später in den *Philosophischen Heften*, wo er statt dessen Hegels Kant-Kritik mit Vergnügen aneignete – ohne Zweifel auch wegen ihrer politischen Anwendbarkeit gegen die kantianischen Neigungen der Revisionisten der II. Internationale.

[14] Es ist übrigens gerade so mit Spinoza, einen Lieblingsphilosoph Iljenkows – denn entgegen der weitverbreiteten Meinung über Spinoza als einen Monist sollte man nicht vergessen, dass er auf dem Niveau der Attribute den alten cartesianischen Dualismus von Denken und Ausdehnung beibehielt. Er hob sehr entschieden hervor, dass die Seele auf den Körper nicht wirken kann, ebenso wenig wie der Körper auf die Seele: *"Nec Corpus Mentem ad cogitandum, nec Mens Corpus ad motum, neque quietem, nec ad aliquid (si quid est) aliud determinare potest"* (*Eth.* III. prop. 2).

[15] Vgl. Oittinen 1992, Oittinen 1994

[16] Vgl. die Darstellung der Gnoseologie-Problematik in Iljenkow 1984, 190 ff.

[17] Ich habe diese eingehender in meiner früheren Arbeit kommentiert (Oittinen 1992, 145 ff.).

[18] Motroschilowa (1967, sub verbo *Ontologija*). Dass Motroschilowa hier eben die "iljenkowianische" Position vertritt, ist nicht zuletzt daraus ersichtlich, dass Iljenkow der einzige sowjetische – und überhaupt der einzige marxistische – Philosoph ist, auf den sie im Literaturverzeichnis zur ontologischen Problematik hinweist.

Literatur

Arndt, Andreas (1994), *Dialektik und Reflexion. Zur Rekonstruktion des Vernunftbegriffs,* Hamburg: F. Meiner Verlag

Baumanns, Peter (1997), *Kants Philosophie der Erkenntnis,* Würzburg: Königshausen + Neumann

Collins, Arthur (1999), *Possible Experience. Understanding Kant's Critique of Pure Reason,* Berkeley etc.:Univ. of California Press

Dawydowa, L. S. (1996), *Immanuil Kant – Bibliografitscheskij ukasatel,* Moskwa

Dietzsch, Steffen (1990), *Dimensionen der Transzendentalphilosophie 1780 – 1810,* Berlin: Akademie Verlag

Filosofija Kanta i sowremennost (pod obschtsch. red. T. I. Ojsermana), Moskwa: Mysl 1974

G. W. F. Hegel (1986), *Enzyklopädie der philosophischen Wissenschaften,* Bd. I, in: *Werke,* Bd. VIII, Frankfurt/Main: Suhrkamp

Horstmann, Rolf-Peter (1997), *Bausteine kritischer Theorie. Arbeiten zu Kant,* Frankfurt am Main: Philo

Iljenkow, E . W. (1984), *Dialektitscheskaja logika,* izd. 2-oe, M: Politizdat

Iljenkow, E. W. (1991), *Dialektika idealnogo,* in: derselbe, *Filosofija i kultura,* Moskwa: Izd. polit. literatury

Kant, Immanuel (1968), *Kritik der reinen Vernunft,* in: ders., *Werke (Akademie-Textausgabe),* Bd. III, Berlin: De Gruyter

Krititscheskie otscherki po filosofii Kanta, Kiew: Naukowa Dumka 1975

Lenin,W. I. (1989), *Philosophische Hefte,* in: ders., *Werke,* Bd. 38, Berlin: Dietz Verlag

Mamardaschwili, Merab (1997), *Kantianskie wariazii,* Moskwa: Agraf

Motroschilowa, N., *Ontologija,* in: *Filosofskaja enziklopedija,* tom 4, Moskwa: Is-wo "Sowetskaja enziklopedija" 1967

Oittinen, Vesa, *Aporien des Ideellen. Zur Dialektik-Konzeption Ewald Iljenkows,* in: DIALEKTIK 1/1992

Oittinen, Vesa (1994), *Ewald Iljenkows Spinoza-Deutung,* in: *Studia Slavica Finlandensia* t. XI, Helsinki

Sandkühler, H.-J. (1976), *Revolutionärer Materialismus als Erkenntnistheorie,* in: M. Buhr und T. I. Oiserman (Hrsgg.), *Revolution der Denkart oder Denkart der Revolution,* Berlin: Akademie Verlag

Schnädelbach, Herbert (1996), *Kant – Philosoph der Moderne,* in: Schönrich, G. und Kato, Yasushi (Hrsgg.), *Kant in der Diskussion der Moderne,* Frankfurt am Main: Suhrkamp (suhrkamp taschenbuch wissenschaft 1223)

Spinoza, B. de (1971), *Ethica,* in: ders., *Opera* (hrsg. von C. Gebhardt), Bd. II, Heidelberg

van der Zweerde, E. (1994), *Soviet Philosophy – The Ideology and the Handmaid,* Diss., Nijmegen

ПРИЛОЖЕНИЕ

"НАУКА ЛОГИКИ"

Э. В. ИЛЬЕНКОВ

The manuscript Nauka logiki *(Science of Logic) of Evald Ilyenkov was recently obtained by the Ilyenkov archive in Moscow. According to the curator of the archive, Dr. Alexei Novokhatko, the text was originally intended to serve as a foreword to the Russian translation of Hegel's* Science of Logic, *the first volume of which was published in 1970, the second and third subsequently in 1971 and 1972. This edition – the only separate Russian edition of Hegel's Logic – had a redaction collective to which even Ilyenkov belonged. However, for reasons unknown, his foreword was replaced by an another written by Mark M. Rozental. Ilyenkov used the materials of the foreword partly in some his later publications (for example, in* Dialekticheskaia logika *1974 and in such articles as* Gegel' i problema predmeta logiki *and* Gegel' i germenevtika). *In its original form the foreword is published here in the first time.*

Vesa Oittinen

20

"НАУКА ЛОГИКИ"

Э. В. Ильенков

Понять гегелевскую логику – значит не только уяснить прямой смысл ее положений, т.е. сделать для себя своего рода подстрочный перевод ее текста на более понятный язык современной жизни. Это лишь полдела. Важнее и труднее рассмотреть сквозь причудливые обороты гегелевской речи тот *реальный предмет,* о котором эта речь на самом деле ведется. Это и значит понять Гегеля критически – восстановить для себя образ оригинала по его характерно-искаженному изображению. Научиться читать Гегеля материалистически, так, как читал и советовал его читать В.И.Ленин, значит научиться критически сопоставлять гегелевское изображение предмета – с самим этим предметом, на каждом шагу прослеживая расхождения между копией и оригиналом.

Задача решалась бы просто, если бы читатель имел перед глазами два готовых объекта такого сопоставления – копию и оригинал. Но в таком случае изучение гегелевской логики было бы очевидно излишним, и представляло бы интерес разве что для историка философии. Оно не открывало бы читателю ничего нового в самом предмете, а в его гегелевском изображении обнаруживало бы, естественно, одни "искажения" – одни лишь несходства с изображаемым, одни лишь причуды идеалиста. В самом деле – глупо тратить время на изучение предмета по его заведомо искаженному изображению, если перед глазами находится сам предмет, или, по крайней мере – его точный, реалистически-выполненный и очищенный от всяких субъективных искажений портрет...

К сожалению, или по счастью для науки, дело обстоит не столь просто. Прежде всего возникает вопрос: с чем непосредственно придется сопоставлять и сравнивать теоретические конструкции "Науки логики", этой "искаженной копии"? С самим оригиналом, с подлинными формами и законами развития научно-теоретического мышления? С самим процессом мышления, протекающим в строгом согласии с требованиями подлинно-научной Логики?

Но это возможно лишь при том предположении, что читатель уже заранее им обладает, владея развитой культурой логического мышления в такой мере, что не нуждается ни в ее совершенствовании, ни в ее теоретическом изучении. Такой читатель и в самом деле имел бы право смотреть на Гегеля только сверху вниз, и мы не осмелились бы советовать ему тратить время на прочтение "Науки логики". Предположив такого читателя, мы могли бы лишь посетовать на то, что он до сих пор не осчастливил человечество своим руководством по логике, во всех отношениях более совершенным, нежели гегелевское, и тем самым не сделал изучение последнего для всех столь же ненужным, как и для себя лично.

Читатель с подобным самомнением не выдуман, нами. Он существует, и у него немало единомышленников. Из их рядов и рекрутируются ныне философы-неопозитивисты, всерьез полагающие, будто в их обладании находится "логика науки", "логика современного научного знания", точное и неискаженное описание логических схем научного мышления. Исходя из такого представления, неопозитивисты считают излишним и даже вредным уже простое знакомство с гегелевской логикой. Усомниться в основательности их претензий заставляет уже тот факт, что все вместе взятые неопозитивистские труды по логике не смогли и не могут воспрепятствовать тому могучему воздействию, которое оказала и продолжает оказывать на реальное научное мышление та традиция в логической науке, к которой принадлежит теоретическое наследие Гегеля. С другой стороны, анализ работ неопозитивистов показывает, что их претенциозная "логика науки" представляет собой всего-навсего педантически-некритическое описание тех рутинных логических схем, которыми давным-давно сознательно пользуется любой представитель математического естествознания. Именно поэтому "логика науки" ничему новому его научить и не может. Она просто показывает ему, как в зеркале, то, что он и без нее прекрасно знает – его собственные сознательные представления о логике собственного мышления, о схемах его собственной работы.

А вот в какой мере эти традиционные сознательно-применяемые в математическом естествознании логические схемы согласуются с действительной логикой развития современного научного знания – этим вопросом неопозитивистская логика попросту не задается. Она вполне некритически "описывает" то, что есть, и в этой некритичности по отношению к "современной науке" усматривает даже свою добродетель.

Между тем единственно-серьезный логический вопрос, то и дело вырастающий перед теоретиками конкретных областей научного познания, заключается именно в критическом анализе наличных логических форм с точки зрения их соответствия действительным потребностям развития науки, действительной логике развития современного научного знания. И в этом отношении гегелевская "Наука логики", несмотря на все ее связанные с идеализмом пороки, может дать современной науке бесконечно больше, чем претенциозная "логика науки". Именно для понимания действительных форм и законов развития современного научно-теоретического познания, которые властно управляют мышлением отдельных ученых зачастую вопреки их наличному логическому сознанию, вопреки их сознательно-принимаемым логическим установкам.

Приходится исходить из того, что подлинная Логика современной науки непосредственно нам не дана, ее еще нужно выявить, понять, а затем – превратить в сознательно-применяемый инструментарий работы с понятиями, в логический метод разрешения тех проблем современной науки, которые не поддаются рутинным логическим методам, выдаваемым неопозитивистами за единственно-законные, за единственно-научные.

Но если так, то критическое изучение "Науки логики" не может сводиться к простому сравнению ее положений – с той логикой, которой *сознательно* руководствуются современные естествоиспытатели, считая последнюю безупречной и не подлежащей сомнению; не следует думать, что Гегель прав только в тех пунктах, где его взгляды согласуются с логическими представлениями современных естествоиспытателей, а в случае их разногласия всегда неправ Гегель. При ближайшем рассмотрении ситуация может оказаться как раз обратной. Может статься, что именно в этих пунктах гегелевская логика находится ближе к истине, чем логические представления ныне здравствующих теоретиков, что как раз тут он и выступает от имени логики, которой современному естествознанию не хватает, той самой логики, потребность в которой назрела в организме современной науки и не может быть удовлетворена традиционными логическими методами.

Если всё это иметь в виду, то задача, перед которой оказывается читатель "Науки логики", рисуется по существу исследовательской. Трудность ее в том, что гегелевское изображение предмета, в данном случае мышления, придется критически сопоставлять не с готовым, заранее известным его прообразом, а с предметом, контуры которого только впервые и начинают прорисовываться в ходе самого критического преодоления гегелевских конструкций.

Читатель оказывается как бы в положении узника платоновской пещеры, он видит лишь тени, отбрасываемые невидимыми для него фигурами, и по контурам этих теней должен реконструировать для себя образы самих фигур, которые сами по себе так и остаются для него невидимыми... Ведь мышление и в самом деле невидимо...

Реконструировать для себя сам прообраз, представленный в гегелевской логике вереницей сменяющих друг друга "теней", каждая из которых своеобразно искажает отображаемый ею оригинал, читатель сможет в том случае, если ясно понимает устройство той оптики, сквозь которую Гегель рассматривает предмет своего исследования. Эта искажающая, но вместе с тем и увеличивающая, оптика (система фундаментальных принципов гегелевской логики) как раз и позволила Гегелю увидеть, хотя бы и в идеалистически-перевернутом виде, *диалектику* мышления. Ту самую логику, которая остается невидимой для философски-невооруженного взора, для простого "здравого смысла".

Прежде всего важно ясно понять, какой *реальный предмет* исследует и описывает Гегель в своей "Науке логики", чтобы сразу же обрести критическую дистанцию по отношению к его изображению. Предмет этот – *мышление*. "Что предмет логики есть *мышление* – с этим все согласны" – подчеркивает Гегель в своей "малой логике"/Гегель. Соч., т. I. М. – Л., 1929, стр.41/. Далее совершенно логично логика как наука получает определение "мышления о мышлении" или "мыслящего само себя мышления".

В этом определении и в выраженном им понимании нет еще ровно ничего ни специфически-гегелевского, ни специфически-идеалистического. Это просто-напросто традиционное представление о предмете логики как науки, доведенное до предельно-четкого и категорического выражения. В логике предметом научного осмысления оказывается само же мышление, в то время как любая другая наука есть мышление о чем-то другом, будь то звезды или минералы, исторические события или телесная организация самого человеческого существа с его мозгом, печенью, сердцем и прочими органами. Определяя логику как "мышление о мышлении", Гегель совершенно точно указывает ее единственное отличие от любой другой науки.

Однако эта дефиниция сразу же ставит нас перед следующим вопросом и обязывает к не менее ясному ответу: а *что такое мышление?*

Само собой разумеется, отвечает Гегель (и в этом с ним также приходится согласиться), что единственно-удовлетворительным ответом на *этот* вопрос может быть только самое изложение "сути дела", т.е. конкретно-развернутая теория, сама наука о мышлении, "наука логики", а не очередная "дефиниция".

/Сравни слова Ф.Энгельса: "Наша дефиниция жизни, разумеется, весьма недостаточна, поскольку она далека от того, чтобы охватить *все* явления жизни, а, напротив, ограничивается самыми общими и самыми простыми среди них. Все дефиниции имеют в научном отношении незначительную ценность. Чтобы получить действительно исчерпывающее представление о жизни, нам пришлось бы проследить все формы ее проявления, от самой низшей до наивысшей" – К.Маркс и Ф.Энгельс. Соч. т.20, стр. 84. И далее: "Дефиниции не имеют значения для науки, потому что они всегда оказываются недостаточными. Единственно реальной дефиницией оказывается развитие самого существа дела, а это уже не есть дефиниция" – там же, стр. 634–635/.

Однако в любой науке, а потому и в логике, приходится все же предварительно обозначить, контурно очертить хотя бы самые общие границы предмета предстоящего исследования – т.е. указать область фактов, которые в данной науке надлежит принимать во внимание. Иначе будет неясен критерий отбора фактов, а его роль станет исполнять произвол, считающийся только с теми фактами, которые "подтверждают" его обобщения, и игнорирует все прочие, неприятные для него факты, как не имеющие, якобы, отношений к делу, к компетенции данной науки, И Гегель такое *предварительное* разъяснение дает, не утаивая от читателя (как то делали и делают многие авторы книг по логике), что именно он понимает под словом "мышление".

Этот пункт особенно важен, от его верного понимания зависит все остальное. Не разобравшись до конца в этом пункте, не стоит даже приступать к чтению последующего текста "Науки логики", он будет понят заведомо неверно. Совсем неслучайно до сих пор основные возражения Гегелю, как справедливые, так и несправедливые, направляются как раз сюда. Неопозитивисты, например, единодушно упрекают Гегеля в том, что он, де, недопустимо "расширил" предмет логики своим пониманием "мышления", включив в его границы массу вещей, которые "мышлением" в обычном и строгом смысле назвать никак нельзя.

Прежде всего – всю сферу понятий, относившихся по традиции к "'метафизике", к "онтологии", то есть к науке "о самих вещах", всю систему *категорий* – всеобщих определений действительности вне сознания человека, вне "субъективного мышления", понимаемого как психическая способность человека, как лишь одна из психических его способностей.

Если под "мышлением" иметь в виду именно это, а именно психическую способность человека, психическую деятельность, протекающую в человеческой голове и известную всем как *сознательное рассуждение,* как "размышление", то неопозитивистский упрек Гегелю и в самом деле придется посчитать резонным.

Гегель действительно понимает под "мышлением" нечто иное, нечто более серьезное и, на первый взгляд, загадочное, даже мистическое, когда говорит о "мышлении", совершающемся где-то вне человека и помимо человека, независимо от его головы, о "мышлении как таковом", о "чистом мышлении", и предметом Логики считает именно это – "абсолютное", сверхчеловеческое мышление. Логику, согласно его определениям, следует понимать даже как "изображение бога, каков он есть в своей вечной сущности до сотворения природы и какого бы то ни было конечного духа" /Г.В.Ф. Гегель. Наука Логики. В трех томах, т. 1, М., 1970, стр. 103/.

Эти – и подобные им – определения способны сбить читателя с толку, с самого начала дезориентировать его. Конечно же, такого "мышления" – как некоей сверхъестественной силы, творящей из себя и природу, и историю, и самого человека с его сознанием нигде во вселенной нет. Но тогда гегелевская Логика есть изображение несуществующего предмета, выдуманного, чисто-фантастического объекта?

Как же быть в таком случае, как решать задачу критического переосмысления гегелевских построений? С чем, с каким реальным предметом, придется сравнивать и сопоставлять вереницы его теоретических определений, чтобы отличить в них истину от заблуждения?

С реальным мышлением человека? Но Гегель ответил бы, что в его "Науке логики" речь идет совсем не об этом, и что если эмпирически-очевидное человеческое мышление не таково, то это совсем не довод против его Логики, изображающей *другой* предмет. Зедь критика теории лишь в том случае имеет смысл, если эту теорию сравнивают с тем самым предметом, который в ней изображается, а не с чем то иным. В противном случае критика направляется мимо цели. Нельзя же, в самом деле, "опровергать", например, таблицу умножения указанием на тот очевидный факт, что в эмпирической действительности дело обстоит совсем не так, что там дважды две капли воды, например, дают при их "сложении" вовсе не четыре, а и одну, и семь, и двадцать пять, уж сколько получится в силу случайно складывающихся обстоятельств. То же самое и здесь. С фактически-протекающими в головах людей актами мышления сравнивать Логику нельзя уже потому, что люди сплошь и рядом мыслят весьма *нелогично*. Даже элементарно нелогично, не говоря уже о логике более высокого порядка, о той самой, которую имеет в виду Гегель.

Поэтому когда вы укажете логику, что реальное мышление человека протекает не так, как изображает его теория, он на это резонно ответит: тем хуже для этого мышления; и не теорию тут надлежит приспосабливать к эмпирии, а реальное мышление постараться сделать логичным, привести его в согласие с логическими принципами.

Однако для логики как науки отсюда происходит фундаментальная трудность. Если логические принципы допустимо сопоставлять только с "логичным" мышлением, то исчезает какая бы то ни была возможность проверить – а *правильны* ли они сами?

Само собой понятно, что они всегда будут согласовываться с тем мышлением, которое заранее согласовано с ними и совершается в полном соответствии с их предписаниями. Но ведь это и значит, что логические принципы согласуются лишь сами с собой, со своим собственным "воплощением" в эмпирических актах мышления.

Для теории в данном случае создается весьма щекотливое положение. Теория здесь соглашается считаться только с теми фактами, которые заведомо ее подтверждают, а все остальные факты приицпиально игнорирует как не имеющие отношения к делу. Любой "противоречащий", "опровергающий" ее положения, факт (факт "нелогичного", "не согласующегося с требованиями логики", мышления) она просто отметет на том основании, что он "не относится к предмету логики", и потому неправомочен в качестве критической инстанции для ее положений, для ее аксиом и постулатов... Логика имеет в виду только логически-безупречное мышление, а "логически-неправильное" мышление не довод против ее схем. Но "логически-безупречным" она соглашается считать только такое мышление, которое в точности подтверждает ее собственные представления о мышлении, рабски и некритически следуя их указаниям, а любое уклонение от ее правил расценивает как факт, находящийся за рамками ее предмета и потому рассматривает только как "ошибку", которую надо "исправить".

В любой другой науке подобная претензия вызвала бы недоумение. Что это за теория, которая заранее объявляет, что согласна принимать в расчет лишь такие факты, которые ее подтверждают, и не желает считаться с противоречащими фактами, хотя бы их были миллионы и

миллиарды? А ведь именно такова традиционная позиция логики, которая представляется ее адептам само собой разумеющейся… Но это
именно и делает эту логику абсолютно несамокритичной с одной стороны, и неспособной к какому бы то ни было развитию – с другой. Она,
как мифический Нарцисс, видит в реальном мышлении только себя,
только отражение своих собственных постулатов и рекомендаций, только
те ходы мысли, которые совершаются по ее правилам, а все остальное
богатство развивающегося мышления объявляет следствием вмешательства "посторонних", "внелогичных" и "алогичных" факторов,
интуиции, прагматического интереса, чисто-психологических случай-
ностей, эмоций, ассоциаций, политических страстей, эмпирических
обстоятельств, и т.д. и т.п.

С этой именно позицией связана и знаменитая иллюзия Канта,
согласно которой "логика" как теория давным-давно обрела вполне замк-
нутый, завершенный характер и не только не нуждается, а и не может
по самой ее природе нуждаться в развитии своих положений.

Эта иллюзия, как прекрасно понял Гегель, становится абсолютно
неизбежной, если предметом логики как науки считать исключительно
формы и правила *сознательного мышления,* или мышления, понимаемого как одна из психических способностей человека, стоящая в
одном ряду с другими психическими способностями, свойственными
человеческому индивиду. "Когда мы говорим о мышлении, оно нам
сначала представляется субъективной деятельностью, одной из тех
способностей, каких мы имеем много, как, например, память,
представление, воля и т.д." Но такой взгляд сразу же замыкает логику в
рамки исследования индивидуального сознания, тех правил, которые
мыслящий индивид обретает из своего собственного опыта, и которые
именно поэтому кажутся ему чем-то само собой разумеющимся и
самоочевидным, "своим".

"Мышление, рассматриваемое с этой стороны в его законах, есть
то, что обычно составляет содержание логики" /Гегель. Соч., т. I, стр.46.
Именно поэтому логика, исходящая из такого понимания мышления,
лишь проясняет, доводит до ясного сознания те самые правила, которыми любой индивид пользуется и без нее, и если мы изучаем такую
логику, то продолжаем мыслить как и до ее изучения, "может быть,
методичнее, но без особых перемен". Совершенно естественно, конс-
татирует Гегель, пока логика рассматривает мышление лишь как
психическую способность индивида и выясняет правила, которым эта
способность подчиняется в ходе индивидуально-совершаемого опыта,
она ничего большего дать и не может. В этом случае логика, "разумеется,
не дала бы ничего такого, что не могло бы быть сделано так же хорошо

и без нее. Прежняя логика и в самом деле ставила себе эту задачу" /Гегель. Соч., т. I, стр.42/.

С таким – оправданным, но ограниченным – взглядом на мышление как на предмет логики, связана и историческая судьба этой науки, тот отмеченный Кантом факт, что со времен Аристотеля она в общем и целом особых изменений не претерпела. Средневековые схоластики "ничего не прибавили к ее содержанию, а лишь развили ее в частностях", а "главный вклад нового времени в логику ограничивается преимущественно, с одной стороны, опусканием многих, созданных Аристотелем и схоластиками, логических определений и прибавлением значительного количества постороннего психологического материала – с другой" /Гегель. Соч., т. I, стр. 47/.

Это – почти дословное повторение слов Канта из "Критики чистого разума", констатация совершенно бесспорного исторического факта. Однако из этого факта Гегель делает вывод, прямо обратный по сравнению с выводом Канта:

"... если со времен Аристотеля логика не подверглась никаким изменениям, и в самом деле при рассмотрении новых учебников логики мы убеждаемся, что изменения сводятся часто больше всего к сокращениям, то мы отсюда должны сделать скорее тот вывод, что она тем больше нуждается в полной переработке" /Г.В.Ф. Гегель. Наука Логики, т. 1, стр. 105/.

Прежде всего Гегель подвергает "полной переработке" самое понятие *мышления*. В логике нельзя понимать мышление как одну из психических способностей человеческого индивида, как деятельность, протекающую под его черепной крышкой. Такое понимание оправдано и допустимо в психологии. Будучи без корректив перенесено в логику, оно становится ложным, слишком узким. Ближайшим следствием такого понимания оказывается тот предрассудок, согласно которому под "мышлением" сразу же понимается сознательно-совершаемое "рассуждение" – и только, и мышление поэтому предстаёт перед исследователем в образе "внутренней речи", которая, разумеется, может выражаться во вне и в виде устной, "внешней" речи, а также в виде графически-зафиксированной речи, в виде письма. Вся старая логика, начиная с Аристотеля, так именно дело и понимала. Для нее "мышление" – это что-то вроде "немой речи", а устная речь – это мышление так сказать "вслух".

Неслучайно поэтому логические исследования и производились в ходе анализа диалогов и монологов, процесса словесного выражения субъективной мысли, и мысль рассматривалась лишь в ее словесном "бытии", лишь в .форме предложений и цепочек предложений ("суждений"). В силу этого старая логика никогда не могла различить четко "субъект" (логического суждения) от "подлежащего" (как члена предложения), "предикат" – от "сказуемого", "понятие" – от "термина" и т.д. и т.п.

Заметим попутно, что все без исключения логические школы, прошедшие мимо гегелевской критики старой логики, этот древний предрассудок разделяют, как ни в чем ни бывало, и до сих пор. Наиболее откровенно его исповедуют неопозитивисты, прямо отождествляющие "мышление" – с "языковой деятельностью", а "логику" – с "анализом языка". Самое комичное во всем этом – то самомнение, с которым архаически-наивный предрассудок выдается ими за самоновейшее открытие логической мысли XX-го столетия, за наконец-то явленый миру принцип научной разработки логики, за аксиому "логики науки". Неопозитивистам кажется "непонятной мистикой" гегелевское представление о том, что предметом логики как науки является "чистое мышление", а не формы его словесного выражения. Как можно исследовать "мышление" помимо форм его проявления? Это недоумение на первый взгляд может показаться резонным,– недоумением трезвомыслящего теоретика, желающего изучать фактически-наблюдаемые явления "мышления", а не "мышление как таковое", как "чистую деятельность", ни в чем предметно себя не обнаруживающую...

Между тем как раз в этом пункте Гегель мыслит гораздо трезвее, чем все неопозитивисты, вместе взятые.

Кто сказал, что язык (речь) есть *единственная* фактически-эмпирически наблюдаемая форма, в которой проявляет себя человеческое мышление? Разве в поступках человека, в ходе реального формирования окружающего мира, в делании вещей человек не обнаруживает себя как *мыслящее* существо? Разве мыслящим существом он выступает только в акте говорения? Вопрос, пожалуй, чисто риторический.

Мышление, о котором говорит Гегель, обнаруживает себя в *делах* человеческих отнюдь не менее очевидно, чем в словах, в цепочках терминов, в кружевах словосочетаний, которые только и маячат перед взором логика-неопозитивиста. Более того, в реальных делах человек обнаруживает подлинный способ своего мышления гораздо более адекватно,чем в своих повествованиях об этих делах.

Кому неизвестно, что о человеке, об образе его мысли, можно гораздо вернее судить по тому, что и как он делает, нежели по тому, что и как он о себе говорит? Разве не ясно, что цепочки поступков обнаруживают подлинную логику его мышления полнее и правдивее, чем цепочки знаков-терминов? Разве не вошли в поговорку знаменитые сентенции: "язык дан человеку, чтобы скрывать свои мысли" и "мысль изреченная есть ложь"? При этом речь идет вовсе не о сознательном обмане другого человека, о сознательном сокрытии от него правды – "истинного.положения вещей", а о совершенно искреннем и "честном" самообмане.

Но если так, то *поступки* человека, а, стало быть, и результаты этих поступков, "вещи", которые ими создаются, не только можно, а и нужно рассматривать как акты обнаружения его мышления, как акты "опредмечивания" его мысли, его замыслов, его планов, его сознательных намерений, В логике, в науке о мышлении, не менее важно учитывать различие между словами и делами, сопоставлять дела и слова, чем в реальной жизни. Это простое соображение Гегель и выдвигает против всей прежней логики, которая, в духе схоластически-интерпретированного Аристотеля, понимала под "мышлением" почти исключительно устно или графически зафиксированную "немую речь", и именно потому судила о "мышлении" прежде всего по фактам его словесной "экспликации". Гегель же с самого начала требует исследовать "мышление" во всех формах его обнаружения, его "реализации", и прежде всего – в делах человеческих, в поступках, в делах, в актах созидания вещей и событий. Мышление обнаруживает себя, свою силу, свою деятельную энергию, вовсе не только в говорении, но и во всем грандиозном процессе созидания культуры, всего предметного тела человеческой цивилизации, всего "неорганического тела человека", включая сюда орудия труда и статуи, мастерские и храмы, фабрики и государственные канцелярии, политические организации и системы законодательства, всё.

Гегель тем самым прямо вводит *практику* – чувственно-предметную деятельность человека – в логику, в науку о мышлении, делая этим колоссальной шаг вперед в понимании мышления и науки о нем, "несомненно, практика стоит у Гегеля, как звено, в анализе процесса познания и именно как переход к объективной ("абсолютной", по Гегелю) истине. Маркс, следовательно, непосредственно к Гегелю примыкает, вводя критерий практики в теорию познания: см, тезисы о Фейербахе" /В.И.Ленин. Соч. 4-е изд., т. 38, стр.203/.

Именно на этом основании Гегель и обретает право рассматривать внутри Логики – внутри науки о мышлении – объективные определения вещей вне сознания, вне психики человеческого индивида, причем во всей их независимости от этой психики, от этого сознания. Ничего "мистического" или "идеалистического" в этом пока нет, в виду имеются непосредственно формы ("определения") вещей, созданных деятельностью мыслящего человека. Иными словами – формы его мышления, "воплощенные" в естественно-природном материале, "положенные" в него человеческой деятельностью. Так, дом выглядит с этой точки зрения как воплощенный в камне замысел архитектора, машина – как выполненная в металле мысль инженера, и т.д. и т.п., а все колоссальное предметное тело цивилизации – как "мышление в его инобытии", в его чувственно-предметном "воплощении". Соответственно и вся история человечества рассматривается как процесс "внешнего обнаружения" силы мысли, энергии мышления, как процесс реализации идей, понятий, представлений, планов, замыслов и целей человека, как процесс "опредмечивания логики", тех схем, которым подчиняется целенаправленная деятельность людей.

Понимание и тщательный анализ этого аспекта человеческой деятельности, ее "активной стороны", как называет его Маркс в "Тезисах о Фейербахе", также не есть еще "идеализм". Этот реальный аспект может быть понят и без всякой мистики. Более того, специально в логике его анализ как раз и составил решающий шаг этой науки в направлении к настоящему – "умному" – материализму, к пониманию того факта, что все без исключения "логические формы" суть отраженные в человеческом сознании и проверенные ходом тысячелетней практики всеобщие формы развития действительности вне мышления. Рассматривая "мышление" не только в его словесном обнаружении, но и в процессе его "опредмечивания", его "овеществления" в естественно-природном материале, в камне и бронзе, в дереве и железе, а далее – и в структурах социальной организации (в виде государственных и экономических систем взаимоотношений между индивидами), Гегель отнюдь не выходит за пределы рассмотрения *мышления,* за рамки предмета *логики* как особой наукм. Он просто вводит в поле зрения логики ту реальную фазу процесса развития мышления, без понимания которой логика не могла и не может стать действительной наукой, наукой *о мышлении* в точном и конкретном значении этого понятия.

Вводя в логику *практику,* а вместе с нею – и все те формы вещей, которые этой практикой "вносятся" в вещество.природы, и затем толкуя эти формы вещей вне сознания как "формы мышления в их инобытии", в их чувственно-предметном "воплощении", Гегель вовсе не перестает быть *логиком* в самом строгом и точном смысле слова.

Упрекать его приходится вовсе не за то, что он вводит в логику чуждый ей материал и выходит тем самым за законные границы науки о мышлении. С точки зрения последовательного материализма справедлив скорее как раз обратный упрек, в том, что он остается "чистым" логиком и там, где точка зрения логики уже недостаточна. Беда Гегеля в том, что "дело логики" поглощает его настолько, что он перестает видеть за ним "логику дела".

Эта своеобразная профессиональная слепота *логика* обнаруживает себя прежде всего в том, что практика, т.е. реальная чувственно-предметная деятельность человека,-рассматривается здесь *только* как "критерий истины", *только* как проверочная инстанция для "мышления", для свершившейся до нее и независимо от нее духовно-теоретической работы, а еще точнее – для результатов этой работы.

Практика поэтому и рассматривается здесь абстрактно, то есть освещается лишь с той стороны, лишь в тех ее характеристиках, которыми она и в самом деле обязана "мышлению", то есть представляет собой акт реализации некоторого замысла, плана, идеи, понятия, той или иной заранее разработанной цели, и совершенно не рассматривается "как таковая", в ее собственной, ни от какого мышления не зависящей, детерминации. Соответственно с этим и все результаты практической деятельности людей, вещи, созданные трудом человека, и исторические события с их последствиями, также принимаются в расчет лишь постольку, поскольку в них "опредмечены" те или иные "мысли". В понимании исторического процесса в целом такая точка зрения представляет собою, само собой понятно, чистейший ("абсолютный") идеализм. Однако по отношению к логике, к науке о мышлении, эта точка зрения представляется не только оправданной, но и единственно-резонной.

В самом деле – можно ли упрекать *логика* за то, что он строжайшим образом абстрагируется от всего того, что не имеет отношения к предмету его специального исследования, к мышлению, и любой факт принимает во внимание лишь постольку, поскольку тот может быть понят как следствие, как форма обнаружения *его предмета,* предмета *его науки* – мышления?

Упрекать логика-профессионала в том, что "дело логики" занимает его больше, чем *логика дела* (т.е. логика любой другой конкретной области человеческой деятельности) столь же нелепо, сколь нелепо корить химика за излишнее внимание к "делу химии"... Совсем не этот смысл кроется в известных словах Маркса, сказанных по адресу Гегеля.

Беда узкого профессионализма заключается вовсе не в строгом ограничении его мышления рамками предмета его науки. Беда его в неспособности ясно видеть связанные с этой абстрактной ограниченностью взгляда на вещи границы компетенции собственной науки. Пока химик занимается "делом химии", т.е. рассматривает все богатство мироздания исключительно под абстрактно-химическим аспектом, мыслит любой предмет во вселенной, будь то нефть или "Сикстинская мадонна" Рафаэля, только в понятиях своей науки – никому в голову, разумеется, не придет упрекать его в том, что его при этом мало интересует дело политэкономии или эстетики. Но как только он начинает мнить, будто в понятиях его специальной дисциплины как раз и выражается самая глубокая, самая интимная тайна предмета любой другой науки, его профессионализм сразу же оборачивается своими минусами. В этом случае ему начинает казаться, например, что биология – это лишь поверхностно-феноменологическое описание явлений, подлинную тайну которых раскрывает лишь он, химик, поскольку он занимается частным разделом своей науки – биохимией. В наказание за это самомнение он сразу же получает удар в спину от физика, для коего вся его химия – лишь поверхностное обнаружение глубинных "субатомных" структур. А над обоими посмеивается математик, для которого и биология, и химия и физика – всего-навсего "частные случаи" обнаружения универсальных схем соединения и разъединения "элементов вообще" внутри "структур вообще"...

Эта коварная иллюзия характерна и для Гегеля, для типичного профессионала-логика. В качестве *логика* он абсолютно прав, когда рассматривает и "высказывание" и "дело" исключительно с точки зрения обнаруживающихся в них абстрактных схем мышления, и только, когда логика любого дела интересует его лишь постольку, поскольку в нем обнаруживает себя деятельность мышления вообще. С этой точки зрения просматриваются лишь те формы, схемы, законы и правила, которые остаются инвариантными и в мышлении Ньютона, и в мышлении Робеспьера, и в мышлении Канта, и в мышлении Кая Юлия Цезаря. "Специфика" мышления всех этих персонажей его, как логика, интересовать, естественно, не может. Как раз от нее любой логик, и именно потому что он – логик, и обязан отвлекаться (абстрагироваться), чтобы разглядеть свой предмет, предмет своей специальной науки.

Мистицизм гегелевской логики, и одновременно та ее коварная особенность, которую Маркс назвал "некритическим позитивизмом", начинаются там, где специальная точка зрения логика принимается и выдается за ту единственно-научную точку зрения, с высоты которой только, якобы, и раскрывается "последняя", самая глубокая, самая интимная, самая сокровенная, самая важная истина, доступная вообще человеку и человечеству...

Как логик, Гегель вполне прав, рассматривая любое явление в развитии человеческой культуры как акт "обнаружения" силы мышления, и потому толкуя развитие и науки, и техники, и "нравственности" (в гегелевском ее понимании, включающем всю совокупность общественных отношений человека к человеку – от моральных до экономических) как процесс, в котором обнаруживает себя способность мыслить, т.е. как процесс *обнаружения* этой способности, и только.

Но стоит добавить к этому (в логике допустимому и естественному) взгляду немногое, а именно, что в специально-логических абстракциях как раз и выражена *суть самих по себе явлений,* из коих эти абстракции извлечены, как истина сразу же превращается в ложь. В такую же ложь, в какую тотчас же превратились бы совершенно точные результаты химического исследования состава красок, которыми написана "Сикстинская мадонна", как только в этих результатах химик усмотрел бы единственно-научное понимание этого уникального "синтеза" химических элементов...

Точно то же и тут. Абстракции, совершенно точно выражающие (описывающие) формы и схемы протекания логического процесса, мышления, во всех формах его "конкретного" осуществления – в физике и в политике, в технике и в теологии, в искусстве и в экономической жизнедеятельности, непосредственно и прямо выдаются за схемы процесса, *созидающего* все многообразие человеческой культуры, в составе которой они и были обнаружены.

Вся мистика гегелевской концепции мышления сосредоточивается в результате в одном единственном пункте. Рассматривая все многообразие форм человеческой культуры как результат "обнаружения" действующей в человеке способности мыслить, то есть как тот материал, в котором он – как логик – обнаруживает "предметно-явленные" схемы реализованного в них мышления, он утрачивает всякую возможность понять – а откуда же вообще взялась в человеке эта уникальная способность с ее схемами и правилами?

Возводя "мышление" в ранг божественной силы и энергии, изнутри побуждающей человека к историческому творчеству, Гегель просто-напросто выдает отсутствие ответа на этот резонный вопрос – за единственно-возможный на него ответ.

Мышление, по Гегелю, не *возникает* в человеке, а лишь *пробуждается* в нем, будучи до этого пробуждения некоторой дремлющей, лишенной сознания и самосознания, но все же вполне реальной активной силой. В человеке это "мышление" *просыпается,* обретает сознание самого себя, т.е. "самосознание", само себя делает предметом своей собственной деятельности, выступает уже как "мышление о мышлении", в чем и обнаруживается, де, его "подлинная природа", его "истинное лицо".

Но прямо и непосредственно это "мышление" рассмотреть себя не может, ибо оно невидимо, неслышимо и вообще неощутимо. Для того, чтобы рассмотреть самое себя, этому мышлению требуется некоторое зеркало, в котором оно могло бы увидеть себя как бы со стороны, как нечто "иное". Этим своеобразным "зеркалом" и становится для него создаваемый им предметный мир, совокупность его собственных "обнаружений" – в виде слова, в виде орудий труда, в виде государственно-политических образований, в виде статуй, книг и всех прочих созданий "мыслящего духа". Творя предметно-развернутое богатство человеческой культуры, "мыслящий дух", с самого начала обитающий в человеке, как раз и создает "вне себя" и "против себя" то зеркало, в котором он впервые сам себя и видит, правда, не понимая вначале, что в зеркале вещей и событий ему отражается его собственный образ и ничего более.

Во всей этой мистически-фантастической картине, превращающей реальное мышление реальных людей – в процесс "обнаружения" некоторой отличной от них самих, абсолютно не зависящей от их воли, от их желаний и потребностей, от их сознания и самосознания – вполне *объективной* – всемогущей схемы не так уж трудно разглядеть проступающие сквозь нее реальные черты вполне земного прообраза,-того мышления, с которого Гегель и срисовывает портрет "бога".

Это – не "мышление вообще", не "мышление как таковое", как представлялось самому Гегелю. Непосредственно – это мышление *профессионала-логика* со всеми его характернейшими чертами и особенностями, принятыми и выданными за универсальные особенности мышления вообще, за выражение "природы мышления как такового". Если это учитывать, то все загадочные определения, которые Гегель дает "мышлению", оказываются не только понятными, но подчас даже банально-самоочевидными.

Это он – логик – осуществляет ту работу, которая состоит исключительно в "мышлении о мышлении"; логика как наука это и есть "мыслящее само себя мышление". Осмысливать сам процесс мышления, доводить до сознания людей те схемы, законы и правила, в рамках которых совершается их собственное мышление, хотя они сами этих схем и правил ясно и не осознают, а подчиняются им под властным давлением всей совокупности обстоятельств, внутри которых они "мыслят" и действуют, поскольку они действуют именно *как мыслящие* существа. Это он – логик – рассматривает и описывает вовсе не свое собственное мышление, как индивидуально ему свойственную психическую способность, как психическую деятельность, протекающую в его индивидуальной голове, а те совершенно безличные схемы, которые отчетливо прорисовываются в ходе целенаправленной жизнедеятельности любого – каждого – человека, если ее рассмотреть "задним числом" и отвлекаясь при этом от всего того, что и как он сам при этом думал, что и как он в составе собственных действий осознавал (т.е. доводил до собственного сознания в ясной словесной форме).

Это он – логик EX PROFESSO (логик-профессионал) осуществляет в своем лице "самосознание" того "мышления", которое осуществляет не отдельный индивид наедине с самим собой, а только более или менее развитый коллектив индивидов, связанных в одно целое узами языка, обычаев, нравов и норм, регулирующих их отношения к "вещам"; в его лице и осуществляется "самопознание" того самого мышления, которое обнаруживает себя прежде всего не столько в немом монологе, сколько в драматически-напряженных диалогах и в результатах таких диалогов, в некоторых общих выводах из уроков столкновений между "мыслящими индивидами", в некоторых "правилах", которые они в итоге устанавливают в качестве общеобязательных, в нормах быта и работы, морали и права, в законах науки и заповедях религии, и т.д. и т.п.

Он, логик-профессионал, и олицетворяет собою процесс осознания тех форм, схем и законов, в рамках которых осуществляется *это* – коллективно-осуществляемое – мышление. Мышление, реализующее *себя* не только в монологах и диалогах, но и в сознательно-целенаправленных поступках, в формировании вещей и в протекании исторических событий, короче говоря, в процессе созидания предметного тела цивилизации, "неорганического тела человека". Мышление, которое – как предмет исследования – противостоит логику вовсе не в образе психофизиологического процесса, протекающего под черепной крышкой отдельного индивида, а как всемирно-исторический процесс развития науки, техники и нравственности. Формы и законы развертывания *этого* процесса (в ходе которого индивид с его психикой действительно играет подчиненную роль, роль исполнителя, а то и орудия исполнения, вне и независимо от него назревших задач, проблем, потребностей) – и составляют для логика-теоретика такой же *объективный* предмет исследования, каким для астронома выступают законы движения планет, звезд и галактик...

Формы и законы мышления, понимаемого таким образом, как естественно-исторический процесс, совершаемый не внутри одной-единственной головы, а только внутри миллионов голов, связанных сетью коммуникаций как бы в одну голову, в одно "мыслящее" существо, находящееся в непрестанном диалоге с "самим собой" – они то как раз и составляют объективный предмет Логики в ее гегелевском смысле. Этот вполне реальный предмет и является прообразом гегелевского "бога" – объективного Понятия, Абсолютной Идея.

За этими мистическими титулами везде кроется реальное *человеческое* мышление, каким оно выступает перед абстрактно-теоретическим взором логика-профессионала, т.е. исключительно в его всеобщих, очищенных от всего "частного", характеристиках. И та фразеология, в облачении которой этот реальный предмет выступает перед нами на страницах "Науки логики", поддается вполне рациональной расшифровке как в общем, так и в частностях. Но при одном условии – если эта расшифровка, эта перекодировка производится с точки зрения материалистического взгляда на *тот же самый* предмет, на мышление *в вышеобрисованном понимании,* а не в том понимании этого слова, которое предлагается психологией или, например, неопозитивистской "логикой науки".

Если под "мышлением" понимать что-то другое, скажем, субьективно-психическую способность и деятельность, протекающую в отдельной голове, и потому непосредственно фиксируемую в виде и образе "немой речи", "немого монолога", в виде и образе "высказывания" и цепочки таких "высказываний", и сопоставлять гегелевскую Логику *с так понимаемым* "мышлением", то она и в самом деле покажется чистым и абсолютным мистическим бредом, описанием "несуществующего предмета", выдуманного объекта – и только,

Если же сопоставлять гегелевское изображение с тем самым предметом, который в ней на самом деле и изображен – с мышлением, реализованным и реализуемым в виде Науки и Техники, в виде реальных поступков и действий человека ("мыслящего существа", "субьекта"), целенаправленно изменяющего как внешнюю природу, так и природу своего собственного тела, то в трудно-понимаемых оборотах гегелевской речи сразу же начинает просматриваться смысл куда более земной и глубокий, чем в псевдо-здраво мыслящей "логике науки".

Одновременно с этим становятся заметными и те "белые пятна", которые зияют в гегелевском изображении этого реального предмета, мышления, и которые Гегель вынужден маскировать вычурными оборотами речи, иногда даже просто с помощью лингвистической ловкости и непереводимой на русский язык игры немецкими словами, доставляющей массу мучений переводчикам его "Науки логики".

Дело в том, что идеализм, т.е. представление о "мышлении" как о всеобщей способности, которая лишь "пробуждается" в человеке к самосознанию, а не *возникает* в точном и строгом смысле на почве определенных – вне и независимо от него складывающихся условий, приводит к ряду абсолютно неразрешимых проблем и внутри самой логики. И эти то неразрешенные им, а на почве идеализма и принципиально неразрешимые, проблемы Гегель и вынужден "решать" чисто-лингвистическими средствами, т.е. просто увиливая от них с помощью иногда остроумных, иногда – просто невразумительных оборотов речи.

Всмотримся чуть пристальнее в его понимание мышления. Гегель безусловно делает колоссальной важности шаг вперед в его понимании, когда устанавливает, что это "мышление" осуществляется отнюдь не только в виде "слов" и "цепочек слов" ("высказываний" и "силлогизмов"), но и в виде "дел", в виде поступков человека и актов его труда, деятельности, непосредственно формирующей естественно-природный материал. В соответствии с этим "формы мышления" – как *логические* формы – и понимаются им как всеобщие формы всякой активно-целенаправленной деятельности человека, в каком бы материале в частности они ни "воплощались", будь то слова или вещи.

Логическая категория (логическое понятие) – это абстракция, одинаково охватывающая обе частные формы выражения "мышления вообще", и потому, естественно, равно игнорирующая "специфические особенности" каждой из обеих форм, взятых порознь. Именно поэтому в ней и выражена "суть речей и вещей" – а не только "вещей" и не только "речей", внутренняя форма движения и того и другого. В "логосе" – в "разуме" -выражены в логическом аспекте (в отличие от психологически-феноменологического) одинаково "/Sage und Sache" – "вещание и вещь", или, скорее, "былина и быль". (См. "Иенскую реальную философию" – Г.В.Ф.Гегель, "Работы разных лет". М.,1970, т. 1, стр. 292).

Кстати – весьма характерный для Гегеля (пример) игры словами, игры, высвечивающей однако генетическое родство выражаемых этими словами представлений. "Sage" – сказывание, сказание, вещание – откуда "Сага" – легенда о подвигах, *былина;* "Sache" – ёмкое слово, означающее не столько единичную чувственно-воспрнимаемуа вещь, сколько "суть дела", "положение вещей", "существо вопроса", фактическое положение дел (вещей), все то, что есть или было на самом деле, "быль". Русскому слову "вещь" буквально соответствует в немецком языке "Das Ding". Эта этимология используется и в "Науке логики" для выражения очень важного оттенка мысли, который в ленинском переводе и в ленинской – материалистической – интерпретации звучит так: "С этим введением содержания в логическое рассмотрение предметом становятся не "Dinge", а "die Sache, der Begriff der Dinge. – Не вещи, а законы их движения, материалистически"– см. В.И.Ленин, соч.т. 38, стр.82./

Однако же, делая колоссальнейшей важности шаг вперед в понимании "логических форм" мышления, Гегель останавливается на полпути и даже возвращается назад, как только перед ним встает вопрос о взаимоотношении указанных "внешних форм" мышления,– чувственно-воспринимаемых предметных форм "воплощения" деятельности духа (мышления), его "наличного бытия" или "существования", в которых он – мыслящий дух человека – становится *для самого себя* предметом рассмотрения.

Отказываясь считать *слово* (речь, язык, "сказывание") *единственной* формой "наличного бытия духа", Гегель, тем не менее, продолжает считать его преимущественной, наиболее адекватной своей сути, формой, в виде которой мышление противополагает себя самого – себе самому, чтобы рассмотреть само себя как нечто "иное", как некоторый отличный от самого себя предмет, чтобы на само себя взглянуть как бы со стороны.

"В начале было Слово", в применении к человеческому мышлению (мыслящему духу человека) Гегель сохраняет этот тезис Евангелия от Иоанна нетронутым, принимая его как нечто самоочевидное, и делая его основоположением (аксиомой) всей дальнейшей конструкции, точнее "реконструкции" развития мыслящего духа к самосознанию, к самопознанию.

Мыслящий дух человека пробуждается впервые (т.е. противополагает себя – "всему остальному") именно в Слове, через Слово – как способность "наименовывания", а потому и оформляется прежде всего как "царство Имён", названий. *Слово* и выступает как *первая*, и по существу и по времени – "предметная действительность мысли", как исходная и *непосредственная* форма "бытия духа для себя самого". Это – форма, в которой "мыслящий дух", противополагая самого себя – самому же себе, остается, тем не менее, "внутри себя самого".

Наглядно это выглядит так: один "конечный дух" ("мышление индивида") в Слове и через Слово делает себя предметом для другого такого же "конечного духа". Возникнув из "духа", как определенным образом артикулированный *звук* – Слово – будучи "услышанным" – опять превращается в "дух" – в состояние "мыслящего духа" другого человека. Колебания воздушной среды (слышимое слово) и оказываются в этой схеме чистым посредником между двумя состояниями духа,– способом отношения духа к духу, или, выражаясь гегелевским языком – духа к *самому себе.*

Слово (речь) и выступает здесь как первое орудие внешнего воплощения мышления, которое мыслящий дух создает "из себя", чтобы для самого себя (в образе другого мыслящего духа) стать предметом.

Реальное же орудие труда, каменный топор или зубило, скребок или соха, в составе этой конструкции начинает выглядеть как второе и вторичное – производное – орудие того же самого процесса "опредмечивания", процесса "опосредования" мышления с самим собой, как чувственно-предметная метаморфоза мышления.

Эта схема, яснее всего очерченная в "Иенской реальной философии", сохраняется далее и в "Феноменологии духа" и в "Науке логики". Состоит она в том, что "мыслящий дух" (или просто мышление) просыпается в человеке прежде всего как "наименовывающая сила" ("Namengebende Kraft"), а затем уже, достаточно осознав себя в слове, приступает к созиданию орудий труда, жилищ, городов, машин, храмов и прочих атрибутов материальной культуры.

Таким образом, в слове и речи Гегель видит ту форму "наличного бытия" мыслящего духа, в которой тот выявляет свою творчески-созидающую силу (способность) раньше всего — до и независимо от реального формирования природы трудом. Последний лишь реализует то, что "мыслящий дух" открыл в самом себе в ходе *проговаривания,* в ходе диалога самого себя с самим собой. Но при таком освещении и сам этот "диалог" оказывается лишь *монологом* мыслящего духа, лишь способом его "манифестации".

В "Феноменологии духа" вся история и начинается поэтому с анализа противоречия, возникающего между "мышлением", поскольку последнее выразило себя, то, что в нем содержится, в словах "здесь" и "теперь" — и всем остальным, еще не выраженным в этих словах, его же содержанием. "Наука логики" тоже предполагает эту схему, содержит в своем начале ту же самую, только неявно выраженную, предпосылку, мышление, осознавшее и осознающее себя прежде всего в слове и через слово. Неслучайно поэтому и завершение всей "феноменологической" и "логической" истории мыслящего духа, ее возвращение к своему исходному пункту: своего абсолютно-точного и незамутненного изображения "мыслящий дух" достигает, естественно, в печатном слове — в трактате по логике...

Вся эта грандиозная концепция истории "отчуждения" (опредмечивания) творческой энергии мышления и "обратного присвоения" ею плодов своего труда ("распредмечивания"), начинающаяся со слова и в слове же замыкающая свои циклы, как раз и есть та история, схема которой изображена в "Науке логики".

Разгадка этой концепции не так уж сложна, основанием всей сложной схемы служит старинное представление, согласно которому человек *сначала думает,* а затем уже — реально *действует* в мире. Отсюда и схема: слово — дело — вещь (созданная делом) — снова слово (на этот раз — словесно-фиксированный отчет о содеянном). А далее — новый цикл по той же самой схеме, но на новой основе, благодаря чему все движение имеет форму не "круга", а спирали, цикла циклов, "круга кругов", каждый из которых, однако, и начинается и заканчивается в одной и той же точке, в слове,

"Рациональное зерно" – и одновременно мистифицирующий момент этой схемы – легче всего рассмотреть сквозь аналогию (хотя это и больше, чем просто "аналогия") с теми метаморфозами, которые политэкономия выявила в анализе товарно-денежного обращения. Схема последнего выражается, как известно, в формуле: "Т – Д – Т". Товар (Т) выступает тут ж как "начало", и как "конец" цикла, а Деньги – как "посредующее звено" его, как "метаморфоза товара". Но в определенной точке бесконечно-замыкающегося на себя – циклического – движения Т – Д – Т – Д – Т– Д... деньги перестают быть просто "посредником" – *средством* обращения товарных масс – и обретают вдруг загадочную способность к "самовозрастанию". Схематически, в формуле, этот феномен точнейшим образом выражается так: "Д – Т – Д^1". Товару же, подлинному исходному пункту всего процесса в целом,-достается их прежняя роль – роль посредника и средства, мимолетной метаморфозы денег, в которую они "воплощаются", чтобы совершить акт "само-возрастания". Деньги, которые обрели это таинственное свойство, есть *Капитал,* и в образе капитала Стоимость получает "магическую способность творить стоимость в силу того, что сама она есть стоимость" – "она внезапно выступает как саморазвивающаяся, как само-движущаяся. субстанция, для которой товары и деньги суть только формы" /К.Маркс, "Капитал". – См. К.Маркс и Ф.Энгельс. Соч.т.23, стр. 1б5/. В формуле "Д – Т – Д^1" стоимость предстает как "автоматически действующий субъект" /там же, стр. 164/, как "субстанция-субъект" всего постоянно возвращающегося в свою исходную точку циклического движения; "...стоимость становится здесь субъектом некоторого про-цесса, в котором она, постоянно меняя денежную форму на товарную и обратно, сама изменяет свою величину, отталкивает себя как приба-вочную стоимость от себя самой как первоначальной стоимости, само-возрастает" /там же, стр.164/, и это происходит "на самом деле" /там же/.

В "Науке логики" Гегель зафиксировал абсолютно ту же самую ситуацию, только не в отношении "стоимости", а в отношении *знания* ("понятия", системы понятий, "истины"). Фактически он имеет дело с процессом накопления знания, ибо "понятие" – это и есть накопленное знание, так сказать, "постоянный капитал" мышления, который в науке всегда выступает как *терминологически-зафиксированное* "богатство знания", "понятие" *в форме слова.*

А отсюда и представление, совершенно аналогичное представ-лению о *стоимости* как о "самовозрастающей субстанции", как о "субстанции-субъекте", для которой товары и деньги — суть только метаморфозы, мимолетно-обретаемые и мимолетно-сбрасываемые ею "формы" ее "наличного бытия"...

Представим себе теперь экономиста, который пытается теоретически объяснить загадку "самовозрастания стоимости", взяв за исходный пункт своего объяснения Деньги, а не Товар,

В этом случае мы будем иметь абсолютно-точный эквивалент гегелевской концепции развития мышления. Гегель с самого начала фиксирует "мышление" (мыслящее познание, "понятие") в словесной форме его "воплощения", его "наличного бытия", как осмысленно-произносимое Слово. Реальные же вещи, созданные мыслящим человеком (орудия труда и потребления) в этой схеме неизбежно станут выглядеть как вторая и вторичная, производная, "форма воплощения" того же самого "мышления", которое сначала "оформилось" как Слово...

"Понятие", для которого слово и вещь (создаваемая человеком) оказываются лишь "формами" его "воплощения", мимолетно-пробегаемыми "метаморфозами", при таком объяснении и определяется как "автоматически действующий субъект", как "субъект-субстанция", как "саморазвивающаяся субстанция (= субьект всех своих изменений)"...

Эта схема, как легко понять, вовсе не является горячечным бредом и выдумкой идеалиста. Это просто такое же некритическое описание реального процесса производства и накопления знания ("понятия", "системы понятий"), каким является и политико-экономическая теория, бравшая за исходный пункт своего объяснения точно-зафиксированный, но теоретически не понятый ею факт. Тот факт, что Деньги, выступая как "форма движения капитала", как исходный пункт и цель всего циклически-возвращающегося к "самому себе" процесса, обнаруживают мистически-загадочную способность самовозрастания, "саморазвития".

В этом случае стоимости, уже "воплощенной" в деньгах, в известной денежной сумме, необходимо придется приписать "имманентно заключенную в ней" способность саморазвития...

Факт, оставленный тем самым без объяснения, и "превращается в мистически-загадочный факт. Ему приписывается — в качестве "имманентно-присущей" ему способности — свойство, которое на самом то деле принадлежит вовсе не этому факту, а совсем другому процессу, который *выражается* ("отражает себя") в его форме.

Маркс, раскрывая в "Капитале" тайну "самовозрастания стоимости" — тайну производства и накопления прибавочной стоимости — не по прихоти и не из кокетства, а намеренно и последовательносознательно использует всю приведенную выше терминологию гегелевской Логики, гегелевской концепции мышления, "понятия".

Дело в том, что идеалистическая иллюзия, создаваемая Гегелем-логиком, имеет ту же самую природу, что и практически-необходимые ("практически-истинные") иллюзии, в сфере которых вращается все сознание человека, насильно втянутого в непонятный для него, независимо от его сознания и воли совершающийся, процесс производства и накопления прибавочной стоимости, в процесс "самовозрастания стоимости". Логическая и социально-историческая схема возникновения этих иллюзий объективно и субъективно одна и та же,

Для капиталиста определенная сумма денег, определенная стоимость *в непременно-денежной форме,* является исходным пунктом всей его дальнейшей деятельности в качестве капиталиста (а потому предпосылкой и условием sine qua non этой деятельности), в качестве "персонифицированного капитала", а потому – и *формальной целью* этой его специфической деятельности, его жизнедеятельности как профессионала-капиталиста. Откуда и как возникает первоначально эта денежная сумма вместе с ее магическими свойствами, его специально интересовать не может. Это – "не его дело". Он, как "персонифицированный капитал", должен превратить эту денежную сумму в товары определенного рода, чтобы, переработав и продав эти товары, вернуть исходную денежную сумму *с приращением,* с "прибылью".

То же самое происходит и с профессионалом-теоретиком, с человеком, представляющим собою, своей личностью, "персонифицированное Знание", "персонифицированную Науку", "персонифицированное Понятие". Для него, для его профессии, Знание, накопленное человечеством, не им лично, и притом в строго зафиксированной словесно-знаковой форме, в виде "языка науки", выступает одновременно и как *исходный пункт,* и как *цель* его специальной работы. Его личное участие в процессе производства и накопления Знания ("определений Понятия") и заключается в том, чтобы приплюсовать к исходному Понятию (к полученному им в ходе образования знанию) *новые* определения.

Практика же, как вне и независимо от него совершающийся процесс созидания "вещей" и "вещи", созидаемые этой практикой, его интересует главным образом как процесс "овеществления" и проверки его теоретических выкладок, его рекомендаций, как процесс "воплощения Понятия", как "фаза логического процесса".

На "практику" теоретик неизбежно смотрит так, как смотрит драматург на спектакль, поставленный по его пьесе, его интересует, естественно, вопрос – насколько точно и полно "воплощен" его замысел, его идея, и какие уточнения он должен внести в свой текст, чтобы на сцене этот замысел получил еще более адекватное "воплощение"...

Поскльку Понятие (или система понятий с маленькой буквы) выступает для теоретика и как исходный пункт, и как цель его деятельности, он и на весь процесс в целом неизбежно смотрит со своей точки зрения – как на процесс, протекающий по схеме: Понятие – процесс "овеществления" Понятия – анализ результатов этого "воплощения" – выражение результатов этого анализа снова в Понятии. Понятие, совершив цикл своих превращений, снова "возвращается" к "самому себе", в исходную форму своего "наличного бытия" – в Слово, в формулу, в систему терминологически-отработанных определений.

Естественно, что с этой специальной точки зрения Понятие и начинает казаться "саморазвивающейся субстанцией", "автоматически действующим субъектом", "субъектом-субстанцией всех своих изменений", всех своих "метаморфоз".

Вопрос же о том, откуда вообще возникает самое Понятие, выступающее сначала в образе Слова, и уже затем – в виде Вещи, созидаемой Делом (сознательной и целесообразной деятельностью, опирающейся на Слово), становится с этой точки зрения, во-первых, неразрешимым, а, во-вторых – довольно безразличным. Столь же безразличным, сколь безразличен для капиталиста вопрос о том, откуда же вообще возникает Стоимость. Для него " для его жизнедеятельности – *наличие* стоимости является *предпосылкой,* такой же "естественной" и "необходимой", как наличие воздуха для живого существа. Его специально интересует уже не вопрос о том, откуда вообще берется "стоимость", а только вопрос о том, что и как он должен делать с этой "стоимостью", чтобы получить "прибыль", чтобы превратить ее в "самовозрастающую стоимость".

Происхождение *предпосылок,* при наличии которых вообще становится возможной его специфическая жизнедеятельность, ее специфические формы, правила и законы, предпосылок, созревающих вне, до и независимо от его собственной работы, его, естественно, специально интересовать не может. Он вынужден брать их как нечто готовое, как нечто данное, как нечто уже наличное, как *материал* собственной деятельности.

Аналогично смотрит на весь "внешний мир" и теоретик, профессионал умственного (духовного) труда, как на "сырье" или "полуфабрикат" производства и накопления Знания, "определений Понятия". "Понятие" с самого начала является той "стихией", которой он живет, которой он дышит, которую ои персонифицирует, тем "субъектом", от имени коего он выступает в качестве полномочного представителя.

Отсюда – из реальной формы жизнедеятельности профессионала-теоретика – и растут все те практически-необходимые иллюзии насчет "мышления" и "понятия", систематическое выражение которых и представляет собой гегелевская "Наука логики".

Поэтому понять гегелевскую логику легче всего, если смотреть на нее как на систематическое, и одновременно некритическое, описание тех "форм мышления", в рамках которых протекает весь процесс "производства Понятия", т.е. специальная деятельность профессионала-теоретика, профессионала умственного труда, человека, для которого Понятие (система понятий) является и исходным пунктом – *условием и предпосылкой* – и целью – *итоговым результатом* – работы, а "практика" играет роль "посредствующего звена" между началом и результатом, роль "метаморфозы Понятия", роль его "инобытия".

Если говорить еще точнее, то гегелевская Логика обрисовывает ту систему "объективных форм мысли", в рамках которых вращается процесс *расширенного воспроизводства* Понятия, процесс "накопления" определений понятий, процесс, который в его развитых формах никогда не начинается "с самого начала", а совершается как процесс "совершенствования" *уже наличных* понятий, как процесс преобразования *уже накопленного* теоретического знания, как процесс его "приращения". Понятие как таковое здесь всегда уже *предполагается* как своего рода плацдарм новых завоеваний, речь идет *о расширении* сферы познанного – а исходные понятия тут играют активнейшую роль. Чем больше капитал, тем большую он дает и прибыль, хотя бы *норма* этой прибыли и имела неуклонную тенденцию к понижению...

Всмотримся в аналогию процесса расширенного воспроизводства Понятия с процессом производства и накопления прибавочной стоимости, который на поверхности выглядит как процесс *"самовозрастания стоимости"*, взятой за исходный пункт. Здесь та же самая видимость – процесс в целом выглядит как процесс "саморазвития Понятия", как процесс "самовозрастания определений Понятия", и формы, в рамках которых протекает этот процесс, тоже кажутся "естественными" и "вечными" формами производства продукта труда вообще.

Если фиксировать отдельные формы проявлений, которые расширяющееся, "возрастающее" Знание попеременно принимает в своем жизненном кругообороте, то получаются такие определения: Наука (накопленное знание) есть слова ("язык науки"). Наука есть вещи (созданные на основе знания, "опредмеченная сила знания").

Знание ("понятие") становится здесь субъектом некоторого процесса, в котором оно, постоянно меняя словесную форму на предметно-вещественную, само изменяет свою величину, свои масштабы, отталкивает себя как прибавленное знание от себя самого, как исходного знания, *саморазвивается*. Ибо движение, в котором оно присо- единяет к себе новое знание, есть его собственное движение, следовательно, его возрастание есть самовозрастание, самоуглубление, саморазвитие. Оно получило магическую способность творить знание в силу того, что само оно есть знание...

Поэтому тут совершенно так же, как в процессе производства и накопления прибавочной стоимости реальные формы этого процесса выглядят как формы "само- возрастания стоимости", *логические формы* (реальные формы производства знания) начинают выглядеть как формы *саморазвития* этого знания. Тел самым они и *мистифицируются*.

И состоит эта мистификация "всего навсего" в том, что схема, совершенно точно выражающая моменты деятельности профессионала-теоретика, принимаются и выдаётся за схему развития знания вообще,

Абсолютно та же мистификация, что и в политэкономии, где "товар" и "деньги" оказываются "метаморфозами", которые попеременно принимает капитал, чтобы совершить акт "самовозрастания".

Формула капитала (= накопленного прибавочного труда): Д – Т – Д^1, в противоположность формуле простого товарного производства и обращения, где Деньги только "опосредствуют" обмен и "исчезают" в конечном пункте движения, в Товаре.

Но коварство этой формула (Д – Т – Д) заключается именно в том, что здесь"и товар и деньги функционируют лишь как различные способы существования самой стоимости: деньги *как всеобщий,* товар – как особенный и, так сказать, замаскированный способ ее существования" /"Капитал" – См. К.Маркс и Ф.Энгельс. Соч., т. 23, стр.164/.

И если движение "стоимости" рассматривается сразу в той форме, которую оно обретает в капитале, т.е. в форме "Д – Т – Д^1", где исходной точкой выступают деньги, а товар – играет роль посредника-средства акта "приращения" исходной денежной суммы, то "стоимость" уже неизбежно начинает представляться *субъектом* обеих "форм своего собственного проявления" – и денег , и товара, то есть некоторой таинственной "сущностью", которую мы уже вынуждены *предположить* существующей до своего "обнаружения" в деньгах и в товаре...

В этой формуле уже имплицитно (скрыто, неявно) заключено то представление, что и "товар" и "деньги" суть только мимолетные "метаморфозы стоимости", своего рода маски, в которых она выступает, поочередно их сбрасывая и надевая, чтобы совершить акт "самовозрастания". Мистификация заключена уже в том, что *товар* взят сразу как "форма проявления стоимости" – наряду с деньгами – в то время, как дело обстоит как раз наоборот, и сама "стоимость" первоначально *возникает, рождается* в качестве "формы товара", в качестве абстрактного момента этой "простейшей экономической конкретности". Разоблачая мистификации, связанные с категорией стоимости Маркс поэтому и подчеркивал, что его исследование начинается не с анализа "стоимости", а с анализа *товара.*

С логичесной точки зрения это принципиально важно, ибо именно анализ товара, товарной формы продукта труда, разоблачает тайну *рождения, возникновения* "стоимости", а затем – и тайну ее "проявления" в деньгах, в денежной форме.

Если же "товар" рассматривается сразу в той роли, которую он играет *в движении капитала,–* в процессе, точно выражаемом формулой "Д – Т – Д^1", в роли "опосредующего звена", замыкающего цикл, началом и концом коего выступают деньги, то тайна рождения стоимости становится принципиально неразрешимой, остается тайной.

Совершенно то же самое происходит с понятием "мышления", с "понятием понятия" в гегелевской схеме.

Гегель непосредственно исходит из рассмотрения мышления, уже развитого до степени *научного* мышления, *научного* познания,– мышления, уже превратившегося в Науку, и рассматривает не процесс *возникновения* знания, а процесс его *приращения,* в ходе которого ранее накопленное знание играет активнейшую роль.

Совершенно естественно, что реальные вещи, созидаемые реальной же деятельностью человека, рассматриваются здесь исключительно в той их роли, которую они играют в пределах этого процесса – процесса приращения уже накопленного знания – уже имеющихся "определений понятия", зафиксированных в слове, в "языке науки".

Гегель фиксирует те моменты, которые действительно пробегает процесс мышления в его развитой форме, в форме науки, как особой (обособившейся) сферы разделения общественного труда,– и формула, которая совершенно точно отражает тут поверхность процесса, выглядит так: С – Д – С^1, где С – словесно-зафиксированное знание, знание в его всеобщей форме, в форме "языка науки", в виде формул, схем, символов всякого рода, моделей, чертежей и т.д. и т.п.

Слово – язык в широком смысле – действительно и есть та всеобщая форма, в которой непосредственно выступает *накопленное* знание. Реальные же вещи (и события), создаваемые целенаправленной деятельностью человека, в пределах этой формулы действительно выступают как "опосредующее звено" процесса, началом и концом коего выступает Слово, знание в его всеобщей форме.

Слово и Вещь и выступают здесь как две формы "проявления", "осуществления" Знания, Понятия, которые это "понятие" проходит в своем жизненном кругообороте, постоянно "возвращаясь к себе".

Картина получается в точности такая же, как и на поверхности движения капитала, накопленного труда, выраженной формулой Д – Т – Д^1. В этой формуле выражено реальное свойство "стоимости", выступающей в образе и форме капитала. В пределах этой формулы (и реальности, ею выраженной) "стоимость постоянно переходит из одной формы в другую" никогда, однако, не утрачиваясь в этом движении, и превращается таким образом в автоматически действующий субъект" /см. "Капитал". – Соч., т. 23, стр.164/.

То же самое происходит и здесь. Гегелевское толкование "мышления" ("понятия") *как субъекта,* существующего вне, до и независимо от сознания человека, лишь на первый взгляд кажется диким, непонятным и несуразным.

На самом же деле это представление есть не что иное, как некритически-описанное реальное свойство человеческого мышления, развитого до степени научного мышления, мышления, как оно осуществляется в образе Науки. Ведь Наука – это и есть мышление, развившееся в особую сферу разделения общественного труда, обособившееся в особую сферу деятельности, *реально противостоящую* другим формам деятельности и, стало быть, осуществляющим их индивидам,

В виде Науки, в виде системы "определений понятия", мышление действительно, и вовсе не в фантазии идеалиста, противостоит индивиду с его сознанием и волей как *вне* его сознания существующая, как *до* его рождения сформировавшаяся, как абсолютно не*зависимо от* его индивидуального сознания и воли развивающаяся "реальность". Реальность, которая *непосредственно* "воплощена" в "языке науки", в ее терминологии, в ее формулах и символике, и которая затем "воплощается" также и вещах, создаваемых по ее предначертаниям, выступая *как производительная сила.* Как творческая сила, созревшая и осознавшая себя сначала в "слове", а затем уже выступившая из царства "теней Амента" в сферу вне ее существующей и ей противостоящей "грубо-материальной" действительности...

Вот это то Мышление, мышление в образе развивающейся науки и техники, как вполне объективный, т.е. не зависящий от воли и сознания индивида и даже *вне* сознания отдельного индивида совершающийся процесс, а вовсе не психический процесс, протекающий под черепной крышкой этого индивида, и есть тот *реальный предмет,* описанием форм и законов развития коего выступает "Наука логики". Это "мышление" осуществляется как совершенно безликий и безличный акт на протяжении всей истории человеческой культуры, и "субъектом", осуществляющим этот акт, оказывается только человечество в его развитии. Поэтому "логические формы" – это формы развития всеобщего, коллективно-осуществляемого, "дела", и в рамках *этого дела* они только и могут быть обнаружены.

Индивид с его "сознательным мышлением", "втянутый" в этот совершенно независимо от его воли и сознания совершающийся процесс, участвует в нем лишь постольку, поскольку его индивидуальное мышление вносит в общее дело, цели и формы которого заданы ему извне в ходе его образования, лишь такой "вклад", который *согласуется* с требованиями "всеобщего" развития и потому ассимилируется этим всеобщим развитием, *принимается* им, и таким образом превращается в штрих, в деталь – в "определение" – всеобщего "духа", всеобще-человеческого Мышления. В противном случае результат индивидуально-осуществляемого – "сознательного"- мышления отталкивается, не принимается, или же существенно *корректируется* "сознательным мышлением" других индивидов, иногда до неузнаваемости.

Этим путем "всеобщее мышление" и осуществляет себя через "индивидуальное", вызывая внутри этого индивидуального мышления – внутри "сознательного мышления" – совершенно неожиданные и непонятные для последнего коллизии, возмущения, противоречия, конфликты, антиномии, и тем самым заставляя индивида с его индивидуальным мышлением искать выход до тех пор, пока он этот выход не найдет или не будет отброшен в сторону как негодное орудие "всеобщего развития духа" – или "развития всеобщего Духа", что одно и то же.

Всеобщие – логические – формы и "правила",которым подчиняется это всеобщее развитие, хотя бы ни один из непосредственно-осуществляющих его индивидов того не осознавал, поэтому и не могут быть выявлены в "опыте" отдельного мыслящего индивида, в "опыте конечного мышления", как называет его Гегель. Они проступают только в масштабах того грандиозного жизненного кругооборота, который совершает "дух в целом", и в циклы которого вовлечены миллионы мыслящих индивидов, каждый из которых "мыслит" лишь отчасти в согласии с требованиями "всеобщего духа", а отчасти – в противоречии с ним.

Принципиальный недостаток всей прежней логики Гегель и видит прежде всего в том, что она пыталась нарисовать образ "мышления вообще", исходя из "опыта конечного мышления", по образцу (по "модели") индивидуально-осуществляемого мышления. Уже здесь был заключен принципиальный просчет, ибо Мышление вообще (которое

Гегель именует "бесконечным", "абсолютным" мышлением) представлялось просто как многократно-повторенное индивидуальное ("конечное") мышление. В ранг "логических" форм и законов мышления поэтому и возводились лишь формы и правила этого "конечного мышления", понимаемого *как вполне сознательно совершаемый акт,* т.е. те *общие* схемы, которые можно обнаружить в каждом сознательно осуществляемом процессе рассуждения, как схемы, *одинаковые* для всех и одинаково *признаваемые* каждым отдельно-мыслящим индивидом, как "правила", которые каждый такой индивид знает и признает как "свои", хотя и не всегда доводит их до ясной словесной формулировки.

Но поскольку индивид с его мышлением (понимаемым как сознательно-совершаемая деятельность) втянут в независимо от его воли и сознания совершающийся процесс развития Науки и Техники, постольку ход его мышления всегда существенно корректируется со стороны "всеобщего мышления", непосредственно выступающего против него как мышление "всех остальных индивидов", и в конце концов подчиняется его корректирующему воздействию.

Однако действия, которые индивидуальное мышление совершает тут как *свои собственные* действия, хотя и под давлением "извне", со стороны всеобщего (коллективного) мышления, будут осуществляться им без сознания того факта, что и в данном случае им управляют *логические* законы, законы Мышления. Эти законы и формы Мышления будут реализоваться через его индивидуальную психику *бессознательно.*

/Не вообще бессознательно, а без их *логического* осознания, т.е. без их выражения в логических категориях. Другим сознанием необходимости совершать такие действия индивид, конечно, будет. Только он всегда будет приписывать эти действия своего собственного мышления, не укладывающиеся в схематизм формальной логики, воздействию на мышление каких-либо иных, внелогичных и алогичных факторов – влиянию "созерцания" или "интуиции", "фантазии" или "воли","желаний" или "памяти", и т.д. и т.п., в то время как под маской всех этих "факторов" как раз и скрывается власть "мышления вообще" над его индивидуальным мышлением/.

Отсюда то и получается та нелепая ситуация, когда все действительные формы и законы, в рамках которых и в согласии с которыми всегда протекает реальное мышление в его реальном осуществлении, т.е. в виде Науки, Техники и Нравственности, воспринимаются и расцениваются не как формы и законы *Мышления,* а как совершенно "внешняя" по отношению к мышлению необходимость, и потому вообще не исследуются в логике как науке...

В связи с этим Гегель и вводит одно из своих важнейших различений, между "мышлением в себе" (an sich) – которое и составляет предмет, объект исследования в логике, и "мышлением для себя" (fuer sich selbst), т.е. мышлением, которое полностью осознает те схемы, принципы и законы, в рамках которых оно само всегда совершается, и совершается в вогласии с ними вполне сознательно, отдавая себе самому ясный отчет в том, что, как и почему оно делает.

Это и означало, что Мышление – благодаря Логике – должно стать "для себя" тем же самым, каким оно до Логики было лишь "в себе", в ходе стихийно-протекавшего акта созидания Науки, Техники и Нравственности.

Логика, толкуемая как "сознание", которое *это* мышление имеет о самом себе, "о своей чистой сущности", с одной стороны, и действительные "дела" этого мышления с другой – "являют столь огромное различие, что даже при самом поверхностном рассмотрении не может не бросаться тотчас же в глаза, что это последнее сознание совершенно не соответствует тем взлетам и недостойно их" /Г.В.Ф. Гегель. Наука Логики, т. 1, стр. 105)/.

Гегель ставит перед логикой задачу – сделать сознание мышления о самом себе – *тождественным* его предмету, то есть тем формам и законам, которым в действительности – вопреки своему наличному сознанию (имеющейся логике) – подчиняется в своем развитии "мышление в себе".

Ничего большего и не означает принцип *тождества субъективного и объективного,* как он понимается и формулируется Гегелем. Это означает всего навсего, что и "субъектом", и "объектом" в *Логике* является *одно и то же мышление.*Речь идет о согласовании схем "сознательного мышления" со схемами того "всеобщего мышления", которое сотворило весь мир науки, техники и нравственности,– об адекватном осознании последних, и ни о чем более.

Поэтому когда Гегель утверждает, что в Логике (именно и только в Логике! – чего нельзя упускать из виду) "противоположность между субъективным и объективным (в ее обычном значении) отпадает" /см. Г.В.Ф.Гегель. Соч., т.1, стр.53/, то это означает прямо и непосредственно лишь то обстоятельство, что в логике предметом (объектом) мышления выступает само же мышление, а не что-нибудь иное, что логика и есть "само себя мыслящее мышление", т.е. "субъект", сам себя сделавший *объектом* своей собственной деятельности, или же "объект", обретающий в логике сознание своих собственных действий, их схем и "правил", и тем самым становящийся "субъектом". Иными словами, здесь имеется в виду "субъект" и "объект" не в "обычном" значении этих терминов, а как чисто-логические понятия в гегелевском смысле этого слова, *как категории мышления,* причем мышления в разъясненном смысле, как способности, реализуемой в виде науки, техники и нравственности, а не только и не столько в виде *говорения,* в виде "немой речи".

Нетрудно заметить, что в этой схоластически-замаскированной форме Гегель совершенно точно выразил фундаментальную особенность человеческой жизнедеятельности, способность человека (как существа "мыслящего") смотреть на самого себя как бы "со стороны", как на "нечто другое", как на особый "предмет" ("объект"), или, иными словами, превращать *схемы своей собственной деятельности в объект ее же самой.*

(Это та самая особенность человека, которую молодой Маркс – и именно в ходе критики Гегеля – обозначил следующим образом:

"Животное непосредственно тождественно со своей жизнедеятельностью. Оно не отличает себя от своей жизнедеятельности. Оно *есть эта жизнедеятельность.* Человек же делает самоё свою жизнедеятельность предметом своей воли и своего сознания, его жизнедеятельность – сознательная. Это не есть такая определенность, с которой он непосредственно сливается воедино." /См. К.Маркс и Ф. Энгельс, "Из ранних произведений", М., 1956, стр. 565.

Поскольку Гегель рассматривает эту реальную особенность человеческой жизнедеятельности исключительно *глазами логика,* постольку он и фиксирует ее лишь в той форме, в какой она уже превратилась в схему мышления, в "логическую" схему, в правило, в согласии с которым человек уже более или менее сознательно строит свои частные действия (будь то в материале языка или в любом другом материале).

"Вещи" и "положение вещей (дел) вне сознания и воли индивида ("Dinge und Sache") и фиксируются им внутри этой схемы исключительно как ее "моменты", как "метаморфозы" мышления ("субъективной деятельности"), реализованного и реализуемого в естественно-природном материале, включая сюда и органическое тело самого человека. Поэтому особенность человеческой жизнедеятельности, описанная выше словами Маркса, и выглядит в гегелевском изображении как "осуществляемая" человеком *схема мышления.*

Реальная картина человеческой жизнедеятельности в ее реальных особенностях и получает здесь перевернутое, с ног на голову поставленное, изображение.

В действительности человек "мыслит" в согласии с этой схемой потому, что такова его реальная жизнедеятельность. Гегель же говорит наоборот: реальная человеческая жизнедеятельность такова потому, что человек *мыслит* в согласии с определенной схемой. Естественно, что все реальные определения человеческой жизнедеятельности – а через нее – и "положения вещей" вне головы человека, фиксируются здесь лишь постольку, поскольку они "положены мышлением", выступают *как результат* мышления.

Естественно – ибо логика, специально исследующего мышление, интересует уже не "вещь" (или "положение вещей") как таковая, как до, вне и независимо от человека с его деятельностью существующая реальность (последнюю рассматривает вовсе не он, логик, а физик или биолог, экономист или астроном), а "вещь", как и какой она выглядит в глазах науки – т.е. в результате деятельности мыслящего существа, "субъекта", в качестве *продукта* мышления, понимаемого как деятельность, специфическим продуктом которой и является *понятие* – понимание существа дела.

В понимании "сути дела" деятельность мышления и резюмируется, "объективируется", и потому "определения понятия", непосредственно выступающие как определения "вещей", для логика суть снятые в продукте определения деятельности, этот продукт создавшей.

Поэтому тезис Гегеля, согласно которому различение между "субъективным" и "объективным" в обычном значении этих слов не касается логики с ее своеобразным углом зрения, вовсе не есть проявление наивной слепоты идеалиста по отношению к этому очевиднейшему различению, а есть сознательно-принятая установка на выявление тех, и именно тех форм и законов деятельности мыслящего существа, которые имеют вполне объективный характер, т.е. не зависят от воли и сознания самих мыслящих индивидов, хотя и реализуются именно и только через сознательно-волевые акты (действия) этих индивидов, через их "субъективность".

Это – объективные формы и законы самой субъективности, те схемы ее развития, которым она безусловно подчиняется даже в том случае, если субъект их не сознает. В этом случае они реализуются помомо и даже вопреки его воле, его сознательно-осуществляемым действиям, вопреки тем "логическим схемам", в согласии с которыми он *сознательно* строит схемы своих действий.

Гегель, иными словами, прослеживает диалектику "субъективного" и "объективного" в том ее виде, в каком она уже успела выразиться (отразиться) внутри "субъекта", внутри самого процесса мышления, процесса развития понятий.

Под "объективным" тут имеется в виду объект не сам по себе, а объект, как он представлен в понятии, как понятие ("понимание" объекта, предоставленное логику-профессионалу современной ему наукой, современным ему Мышлением с больший буквы.

Это-то "мышление", представленное в его результатах, для логика и есть тот единственный "объект", который он исследует, И в этом объекте он обнаруживает явные ножницы, явное расхождение, между тем, что мыслящий человек делает *вполне сознательно* – т.е. отдавая себе отчет в том, что и как он делает, в понятиях известной ему "логики" – и тем, что он делает *на самом деле*. не отдавая себе в том такого отчета, а приписывая необходимость такого рода действий, не укладывающихся в схемы известной ему логики, "внелогическим" факторам и обстоятельствам, заставляющим его систематически "нарушать" сознательно-исповедуемые им логические правила и императивы...

Его собственное мышление, таким образом, опровергает те самые "правила", которые он считает "законами мышления", т.е. "впадает в диалектику", в ту самую диалектику, которая безусловно запрещается этими правилами.

Поэтому-то явное расхождение между "логикой", понимаемой как совокупность сознательно-применяемых "правил" сознательного рассуждения – и Логикой, как подлинным – объективным законом развития мышления, до сих по не осознанным, и трактуется Гегелем как противоречие *внутри мышления,* выражающееся также и внутри сознательного мышления, мышления в согласии с "правилами". Здесь оно выступает как постоянное, систематически (т.е. закономерно) осуществляемое "нарушение правил", продиктованное невозможностью их соблюсти *в реальном* мышлении.

Гегель демонстрирует это обстоятельство на мышлении, которое продуцирует понятия о самом себе, т.е. на мышлении, как оно выступает в самой логике, реализуется как "логика", он фиксирует тот факт, что "правила", устанавливаемые этой логикой, нарушаются уже в самом ходе установления этих самых правил... Претендуя на роль законодательницы всего царства мышления, традиционная логика ведет себя как своенравный удельный князек, считающий "законы", издаваемые им для подданных, обязательными для всех – но только не для себя самого.

Все так называемые "логические законы", долженствующие играть роль правил доказательства, условий доказательности мышления, эта логика, однако, не доказывает, а просто постулирует, утверждает как догмы, в которые надлежит слепо веровать, не задаваясь вопросом – почему? Она их не обосновывает, не "опосредует", а просто заверяет, ссылаясь на то, что наша "способность мышления" так уж устроена...

Особенно отчетливо это видно там, где традиционная логика формулирует так называемый "закон достаточного основания".

"Формальная логика дает установлением этого закона мышления дурной пример другим наукам, поскольку она требует, чтобы они не признавали своего содержания непосредственно, между тем как она сама устанавливает этот закон, не выводя его и не доказывая его опосредствования. С таким же правом, с каким логик утверждает что наша способность мышления так уж устроена, что мы относительно всего принуждены спрашивать об основании, с таким же правом мог бы медик на вопрос, почему утопает человек, упавший в воду, ответить: человек так уж устроен, что он не может жить под водой"/Г.В.Ф.Гегель, Соч.т.1,стр.208/.

Конечно же, ирония Гегеля абсолютно справедлива – "закон", который провозглашается "логическим законом", т.е. правилом, которому обязано подчиняться мышление вообще, мышление в любом его частном применении, утверждается как раз через вопиющее его нарушение.

Гегель же требует от логики, чтобы она была прежде всего сама логичной, ведь если логика – тоже наука, тоже мышление, то в развитии собственных положений и понятий она и обязана первой соблюдать все те требования, которые она формулирует как всеобщие, как "логические". Поскольку она сама их не соблюдает, она и доказывает, помимо своей воли и своих сознательных намерений, что формулируемые ей правила всеобщими, т.е. логическими, не являются.

Далее. Эта логика требует от мышления "последовательности". Но – "основной ее недостаток обнаруживается в ее непоследовательности, в том, что она соединяет то, что за минуту до этого она объявила самостоятельным и, следовательно, несоединимым..." /Гегель. Соч., т. I, стр.110/.

Поэтому то и внутри самой этой "логики", и внутри мышления, руководствующегося диктуемыми ею правилами, царит безвыходный плюрализм, отсутствие какой бы то ни было необходимой связи между отдельными утверждениями. Она кишит формальными противоречиями, только предпочитает этого обстоятельства не замечать.

Так, провозглашая "закон тождества" и "запрет противоречия в определениях", "закон противоречия", высшими и абсолютными законами мышления вообще, эта логика позволяет себе в первых же строках своих изложений заявлять, что *логика есть наука*. Но ведь логической формулой такого рода заявлений (Иван есть человек", "Жучка есть собака", "логика есть наука" и т.д. и т.п.) является прямое отождествление непосредственно различных, нетождественных определений (Особенное есть всеобщее, единичное есть общее).

Мышлению, которое "осознает себя" в виде традиционной формальной логики, *"недостает простого сознания* того, что, постоянно возвращаясь от одного к другому, оно объявляет неудовлетворительным каждое из этих отдельных определений, и недостаток его состоит просто в неспособности свести воедино две мысли (по форме имеются налицо лишь *две* мысли" /там же, стр.111.

Эта манера рассуждать ("мыслить"), согласно которой все вещи на свете надлежит рассматривать "как со стороны тождества их друг другу", "так и со стороны их отличий друг от друга", "с одной стороны – так, а с другой стороны – эдак", т.е. прямо наоборот – "в одном отношении как одно и то же, а в другом отношении – как не одно и то же" – как раз и составляет подлинную логику этой "логики".

В силу этого прежняя логика и соответствует, в качестве теории, той самой практике мышления, которая "логична" лишь по видимости, а на деле никакой необходимости в себе не содержит.

Эта логика (как теория, так и практика ее "применения") на самом деле ("в себе") *насквозь диалектична* в ее собственном, укоризненном, смысле этого слова; она кишит неразрешенными противоречиями, делая при этом вид, будто никаких противоречий нет. Она постоянно совершает действия, запретные с точки зрения ее же собственных постулатов, ее "законов" и "правил", только не доводит этого факта до ясного осознания, до выражения через свои собственные принципы...

Внутри самой теории логики эта диалектика выражается уже в том, что так называемые "абсолютные законы мышления" – точнее "те несколько предложений, которые устанавливаются как *абсолютные законы мышления"* – оказываются "при ближайшем рассмотрении *противоположными друг другу;* они противоречат друг другу и взаимно упраздняют одно другое" /Г.В.Ф.Гегель. Соч., т. V, стр. 481/.

Гегель, как нетрудно заметить, ведет критику традиционной логики – и мышления, этой логике соответствующего – тем самым "имманентным" способом, который и составляет одно из главных завоеваний его собственной Логики. А именно – он противопоставляет утверждениям ("правилам" и "законам") этой логики не какие то другие *утверждения,* а процесс практической реализации ее же собственных положений в реальном мышлении. Он показывает ей ее собственное изображение в зеркале ее же собственного "сознания", ее же собственных основоположений.

Он не оспаривает ее представления, ее "понятия мышления", т.е. соглашается с нею в том, что *"сознательное мышление"* (.которое она только и исследует) действительно таково, что оно действует в согласии с теми самыми "правилами", которые оно само себе задает и потому признает как "кодекс", по которому его можно и нужно судить. Он показывает, однако, что именно неукоснительное следование принципам "сознательного мышления" необходимо, с неумолимой силой, приводит к отрицанию этих самых принципов, в чем и обнаруживается *их собственная абстрактность* – т.е. неполнота и односторонность.

Это – та самая критика рассудка с точки зрения самого же рассудка, которую начал уже Кант в своей "Критике чистого разума". Это та самая критика, которая приводит к выводу, что "диалектика составляет природу самого мышления, что в качестве рассудка оно должно впадать в отрицание самого себя, в противоречие..." /Г.В.Ф.Гегель. Соч.,т. I,стр.28/.

К этому выводу пришел уже сам Кант, и если до Канта "логика" могла быть несамокритичной *по неведению,* то теперь она может сохранять свои позиции лишь а том случае, если будет уже вполне сознательно отворачивать свой нос от неприятных для нее фактов,-если она сделается уже *сознательно несамокритичной.*

Главную слабость старой – чисто-формальной – логики Гегель и видит в том, что она, на самом деле нагромождая противоречия на противоречия, старается этого своего собственного "продукта" не замечать, старается вновь и вновь делать вид, будто никаких "противоречий" в ее составе нет, что это – лишь "мнимые противоречия", "противоречия в разных отношениях" или "в разное время" (т.е. на разных страницах ее собственных изложений), и тем самым оставляет их в мышлении *неразрешенными.*

Гегель видит главную и самую острую проблему, вставшую перед логикой как наукой в результате трудов Канта, Фихте и Шеллинга именно в том, чтобы найти, выявить и указать реальному мышлению логический метод разрешения противоречий, в которые оно впадает именно потому и постольку, поскольку и в силу того, что оно сознательно и неукоснительно руководствуется традиционной логикой, т.е. обладает лишь относительно верным, но крайне абстрактным, сознанием относительно самого себя, абстрактно-неполноценным "самосознанием".

В этом именно и заключается действительное отличие гегелевской логики от всех предшествующих ей логических концепций. А вовсе не в том, как до сих пор утверждают адепты архаически-до-гегелезского состояния логической мысли, что прежняя логика, якобы, заботилась об "освобождении" мышления от "противоречий в определениях", а Гегель задался злокозненной целью эти противоречия в мышлении узаконить, придать им статус "правильной формы" любой логической конструкции и реконструкции действительности. Такое объяснение гегелевского отношения к "противоречию" и до сих пор вдохновляется желанием во что бы то ни стало дискредитировать идею диалектической логики при неспособности справиться с нею на теоретической почве.

Дело между тем обстоит как раз наоборот. Гегель совершенно согласен с прежней логикой в том отношении, что "логических" про-тиворечий, в смысле *неразрешенных,* "неопосредованных" противоре-чий, в смысле антиномий, в составе логически-разработанной теории (в том числе в составе самой логики) быть "не должно".

В этом он видит "рациональное зерно" пресловутого "запрета противоречия". Согласно Гегелю "противоречие" должно быть не только выявлено мышлением, не только остро зафиксировано им, но и должно найти свое логически-теоретическое *разрешение.* Более того, это разрешение противоречие должно быть достигнуто тем же самым логическим процессом, который его и выявил, на пути дальнейшего развития определений понятия, *понимания сути дела,* в которой оно обнаружилось.

А не на пути софистического жульничества, не на пути жалкого самообмана и самовнушения, диктуемого желанием во что бы то ни стало "доказать", что никакого противоречия в мышлении нет и быть не может, если это мышление было "правильным" (т.е. в точности соблюдало все "правила" формальной логики), а есть лишь "видимость противоречия", получающаяся от смешения "разных смыслов термина", "разных отношений" и т.п. Короче говоря, прежняя логика всегда пытается истолковать выявившееся в мышлении противоречие как результат и показатель *ошибки,* допущенной этим мышлением где то "раньше", т. е- как результат *отступления* от "правил", совершенного где-то в ходе предшествующих "рассуждений".

Такое толкование *происхождения* противоречий в определениях понятия развенчал до конца уже Кант, и после Канта настаивать на нем просто стыдно. Гегель утверждает в полном согласии с Кантом, что "противоречие" в мышлении (в составе определений понятия) возникает вовсе не в силу неряшливости, недобросовестности или "недосмотра", а именно как неумолимо-неизбежный результат самого что ни на есть "правильного" мышления (т.е. мышления, сознательно руко-водствующегося т.н. "абсолютными законами мышления" – законом тождества и запретом противоречия).

Однако – в отличие от Канта – Гегель понимает и утверждает, что эти противоречия могут и должны быть разрешены на пути дальнейшего *логического* развития определений понятия, что они не могут сохраняться навеки-вечные в форме антиномий.

Но – и все дело именно в этом – именно для того, чтобы мышление могло их разрешить, оно обязано предварительно их четко и резко зафиксировать, именно как антиномии, именно как *неразрешенные* противоречия, как логические, как действительные, а вовсе не как "мнимые".

Такому отношению к противоречиям традиционная логика как раз и не учит. И не только не учит, а и прямо мешает научиться, поскольку упрямо толкует эти противоречия как результат ранее допущенного "нарушения" правил "сознательного рассуждения". На основе такого – докантовского, "докритического" представления – она и разрабатывает хитроумнейшую технику *избавления* от противоречий, технику их *упрятывания* от сознания, технику их "шунтирования", то бишь их *замаскировывания,* проявляя при этом изощреннейшую лингвистическую ловкость, словесную изворотливость.

Этим она делает мышление, доверившееся ее рецептам, слепо-несамокритичным, приучая его упорствовать в догмах, в абстрактно-непротиворечивых утверждениях и избегать реальных проблем, подлежащих научному разрешению, ибо реальная проблема, неразрешенная еще мышлением, всегда "логически" выражается в виде антиномии, в виде неразрешенного противоречия в определениях понятия, в составе теоретической конструкции.

Поэтому то Гегель с полным правом и определяет традиционную формальную логику как логику *догматизма.*

Чисто-формальная логика отличается от гегелевской вовсе не тем, что первая "запрещает", а вторая – "разрешает" противоречия в определениях понятий, как это до сих пор стараются изобразить представители формально-логической традиции. Отличие их в том, что они дают мышлению, столкнувшемуся с противоречием, прямо противоположные, исключающие друг друга, рекомендации относительно путей, на которых должно достигаться разрешение противоречия.

Старая – догегелевская – логика, столкнувшись с противоречием, получившимся именно как неизбежный результат неукоснительного следования ее собственным "правилам", всегда "пятится" перед ним, отступает *назад* – в предшествующий этому неприятному факту ход "рассуждения" (т.е. реально оборачивается педантически-лингвистическим анализом *терминов,* из коих были сплетены цепочки этого предшествующего "рассуждения") и не успокаивается до тех пор, пока не обнаружит *там* "ошибку", "смешение разных смыслов слов", употребление термина "в разных отношениях" и т.д. – "неточность", которая и привела, де, к "противоречию"...

Тем самым *противоречие* становится неодолимой преградой на пути такого мышления *вперед,* по пути дальнейшего *развития* определений понятия, на пути дальнейшего теоретического исследования "сути дела". Двигаться по этому пути вперед она безусловно запрещает до тех пор, пока "ошибка" не будет обнаружена в ходе предшествующего появлению противоречия движения "рассуждения".

Отсюда то и получается, что в конце концов такое мышление (и такая "логика") вынуждена спасаться от противоречий бегством все дальше и дальше "назад", в низшие формы своего собственного развития: "мышление, потеряв надежду своими собственными силами разрешить противоречие, в которое оно само себя поставило, возвращается к тем разрешениям и успокоениям, которые дух получил в других своих формах..." /Г.В.Ф.Гегель. Соч., т. I, стр.28-29/.

Это абсолютно неизбежно, поскольку противоречие получилось на самом то деле вовсе не в результате "ошибки", и никакой ошибки в предшествующем "рассуждении" обнаружить ему в конце концов, после долгих попыток, так и не удается (все было "правильно") – приходится отступать еще дальше "назад", спасаясь в "непротиворечивый покой" предшествующих "сознательному рассуждению" форм мышления – в область *низших* (по сравнению с логическим мышлением) форм сознания – в область "созерцания", в область "интуиции", в сферу "представления", в те области духа, где "противоречия" действительно нет, но только по той причине, что оно еще не выявлено и не выражено в предельно-строгом "языке науки"...

(Разумеется, Гегель никогда не думал отрицать известной пользы *проверки* предшествующего появлению противоречия хода "рассуждения" с целью выяснить – не было ли в нем допущено формальной неточности или терминологической погрешности. Часто бывает и так, и "противоречие" оказывается чисто-словесным – мнимым. Беда формальной логики не в том, что она вообще имеет в виду такие противоречия и рекомендует соответствующий путь избавления от них. Беда ее в том, что она только такие противоречия и знает, считая, что других не бывает. Поэтому чисто-формальная логика исключает гегелевскую, в то время как гегелевская включает ее на правах относительной истины, лишь ограничивая пределы истинности ее соображений, и лишая ее тем самым того *абсолютного* значения, которое та сама себе – своим правилам – придает...)

Диалектика, сознательно используемая как метод развития определений понятия, и есть Логика, включающая в себя как процесс *выявления* (ясного осознания и строгого выражения в языке науки) *логических противоречий* (бессознательно и помимо своей воли продуцируемых "рассудком" – т.е. мышлением в согласии с правилами формальной логики), так и процесс *их конкретного разрешения* путем логического же развития определений понятия, т.е. в составе более конкретного и глубокого понимания того самого предмета, в выражении коего обнаружилось "противоречие", на пути более высокого развития науки, техники и "нравственности" (под коей Гегель понимает всю совокупность общественных отношений человека к человеку), то есть всей той действительности, которую он именует "объективным духом". Это движение, в котором должно активно участвовать "субъективное мышление", и оказывается в его "Науке логике" единственно-рациональным путем разрешения возникающих внутри него (внутри "сознательного рассуждения") логических противоречий.

Этой своей особенностью гегелевская Логика и оказывается на голову выше любой другой логической концепции, а ее изучение – поучительным и по сей день.

12. XI .70 Э. Ильенков

KIKIMORA PUBLICATIONS

Series A

Temkina, Anna (1997): Russia in Transition: The Case of New Collective Actors and New Collective Actions. ISBN 951-45-7843-0

Мустонен, Петер (1998): Собственная его императорского величества канцелярия в механизме властвования института самодержца 1812–1858: К типологии основ имперского управления. ISBN 951-45-8074-5

3 Rosenholm, Arja (1999): Gendering Awakening : Femininity and the Russian Woman Question of the 1860s. ISBN 951-45-8892-4

4 Lonkila, Markku (1999): Social Networks in Post-Soviet Russia: Continuity and Change in the Everyday Life of St. Petersburg Teachers. ISBN 951-45-8911-4

Series B

Vihavainen, Timo ja Takala, Irina (red.) (1998): В семье единой: Национальная политика партии большевиков и ее осуществление на Северо-Западе России в 1920–1950-е годы. ISBN 5-230

Granberg, Leo (ed.) (1998): The Snowbelt: Studies on the European North in Transition. ISBN 951-45-8253-5

Sutela, Pekka (1998): The Road to the Russian Market Economy: Selected Essays 1993–1998. ISBN 951-45-8409-0

4 Törnroos, Jan-Åke & Nieminen, Jarmo (eds.) (1999): Business Entry in Eastern Europe: A Network and Learning Approach with Case Studies. ISBN 951-45-8860-6

5 Miklóssy, Katalin (toim.) (1999): Syitä ja seurauksia: Jugoslavian hajoaminen ja seuraajavaltioiden nykytilanne: seminaari 8.4.1999, Helsinki. ISBN 951-45-8861-4

Винников, Александр (1998): Цена свободы. ISBN 5-89739-002-9

Лебина, Н. Б. (1999): Повседневная жизнь советского города : нормы и аномалии : 1920 и 1930 годы. ISBN 5-87516-133-7, 5-87940-004-0

8 Lejins, Atis (ed.) (1999): Baltic Security Prospects at the Turn of the 21st Century. ISBN 951-45-9067-8

9 Komulainen, Tuomas & Korhonen, Iikka (ed.) (2000): Russian Crisis and Its Effects. ISBN 951-45-9100-3

10 Salminen, Ari & Temmes, Markku (2000): Transitioteoriaa etsimässä. ISBN 951-45-9238-7

11 Yanitsky, Oleg (2000): Russian Greens in a Risk Society: A Structural Analysis. ISBN 951-45-9226-3

13 Oittinen, Vesa (ed.) (2000): Evald Ilyenkov's Philosophy Revisited. ISBN 951-45-9263-8

Orders:
Aleksanteri Institute
P.O.Box 4
00014 University of Helsinki
Telephone +358-9-191 24175
Telefax +358-9-191 23822
E-mail: kikimora-publications@helsinki.fi